THE CANON OF

THOMAS MIDDLETON'S PLAYS

To Rita

for a second pair of eyes

The Canon of
Thomas Middleton's Plays

INTERNAL EVIDENCE FOR
THE MAJOR PROBLEMS OF AUTHORSHIP

DAVID J.LAKE
Senior Lecturer in English
University of Queensland

CAMBRIDGE UNIVERSITY PRESS

Published by the Syndics of the Cambridge University Press
Bentley House, 200 Euston Road, London NW1 2DB
American Branch: 32 East 57th Street, New York, N.Y.10022

© Cambridge University Press 1975

Library of Congress Catalogue Card Number: 74-25661

ISBN: 0 521 20741 X

First published 1975

Printed in Great Britain by Redwood Burn Limited
Trowbridge and Esher

and bound by Tinlings (1973) Limited
Prescott, Lancs.

Contents   Page

vi

Appendices

Preface

"Only numbers can annihilate," said Admiral Nelson: a maxim true enough when it comes to dealing not only with hostile ships of the line, but also with Jacobean plays of doubtful authorship. The origin of this study was my appreciation of the effective ways--two scholarly versions of the Nelson touch--in which numbers had been handled by Cyrus Hoy and Alvar Ellegård in their successful onslaughts on the problems, respectively, of the Beaumont and Fletcher canon and the Junius Letters. In my attack on the major authorship questions of the Middleton plays, which include some of the most vexed controversies of Jacobean attribution, I have tried to combine the massed statistical force of Ellegård with the textual caution of Hoy. To what extent I have succeeded will appear below.

To carry out this work in Australia has at times been difficult, and would have been impossible but for the persevering help of the Queensland University Library Reference and Acquisitions staff; in particular, of Mr. Spencer Routh, Reference Librarian, and Mr. Val Prescott, Acquisitions Librarian. I am also deeply indebted to many people, most of whom I have not met, in libraries and universities in Australia, Britain, and America, who have sent materials and/or answered queries; in particular, the staff of the Bodleian Library and the British Museum, and the following scholars: Charles Barber, Thomas Berger, Fredson Bowers, A. C. Cawley, Standish Henning, Cyrus Hoy, J. C. Maxwell, James McManaway, Peter B. Murray, Harold J. Oliver, George R. Price, and Samuel Schoenbaum.

Nearer home, I am grateful to Professor Kenneth G. Hamilton, Head of the Department of English, University of Queensland, for early encouragement and advice; to Professor Peter D. Edwards, who for some time supervised a thesis rather remote from his own special field of Victorian prose, and yet assisted with useful criticism; to Dr. Robert J. Jordan, who took over the supervision from Professor Edwards and aided me with his deep knowledge of seventeenth century drama; and to my statistical advisers in the Queensland University Department of Mathematics, Mr. Brian L. Adkins and Mr. Henry M. Finucan. My debt to Mr. Finucan is especially deep, since he has taught me, over the years preceding and including this study, almost everything I know about the application of statistics to the problems of Jacobean authorship. However, any errors that I may have made here are my own responsibility alone.

I am also indebted in another (quasi-literal) sense to the University of Queensland's Department of English research funds, without which this study would have been impossible.

Last, but very far from least, I am indebted to my wife, Marguerite Ivy Lake, for constant encouragement and for help in checking all sorts of text, old and new. Thanks to her second pair of eyes, I can give the same assurance as Alvar Ellegård--every page of my corpus has been read at least twice.

January 1975   D.J. Lake

Sources: a statement

Every work which appears in the bibliography has been seen by
me, if only in microfilm or photofacsimile, and quotations have been
taken directly from these sources unless otherwise stated in the
appropriate place. Quotations in original old spelling, when cited
as linguistic evidence, are placed in italics (represented by under-
lining in typescript); quotations in modernized spelling are placed
in quotation marks.

Where I use the results of previous scholarship, I make due
acknowledgments. Where no acknowledgment is made, the findings are
my own, and, to the best of my knowledge, have not been anticipated by
others.

Symbolization

Symbol   Significance

r.f.   Relative frequency.

v   Verso. In references to texts, verso pages are indicated
by "v", but recto pages are specified by the absence of "v";
thus "Bl" = signature Bl recto.

x   In table cells, " x " means "not counted".

+   In table cells, " + " means "occurs" (number of
instances not specified)

[ ]   In table cells, square brackets enclose numbers quoted
from the counts of Cyrus H. Hoy ("The Shares of Fletcher and
his Collaborators in the Beaumont and Fletcher Canon," SB,
1956-62).

,   In tables, to save space in assembling data, two feature-
columns are often combined, the numbers of instances being
separated by a comma. In the heading the two feature-names
are also separated by a comma. The number in the column
before the comma refers to the item in the heading before the
comma; the number in the column after the comma refers to the
item in the heading after the comma. (Thus in Table I.1 the
numbers "7,3" under the heading 'slife, life mean "7 instances
of 'slife, 3 of life".)

:   In tables, a colon is used instead of a comma in a
combined column (see immediately above) when the ratio of the
two features juxtaposed is significant. Thus in Table 2.3(1)
the total "24:8" under the heading ay:yes indicates 24 instances of ay beside 8 instances of yes, a significant ratio.

.   In most tables a single period is used instead of a zero,
to aid rapid inspection of significant absences.

..   Two unspaced periods between words in collocations (e.g.
hair..an end) indicate non-specification of contiguity but
specification of sequence; thus, hair..an end includes hair
an end and hair stand an end, but not an end of hair.

/   A single oblique between words in collocations (e.g.
Adam/Eve) indicates non-specification of contiguity or
sequence, i.e. the parts of the collocation separated by the
oblique may appear with or without separation by other words
in the same sentence, and in either order.

/ /   Phonemic symbols (enclosed between obliques) have phonetic
        values as in Helge Kökeritz, Shakespeare's Pronunciation
        (New Haven: Yale Univ. Press, 1953), p.xi.

/ /   Exact spellings (such as /vppot'h/) are enclosed between
        obliques where there is danger of confusion with generalized
        spellings (such as upo'th').

*   Numbers of words (for play lengths) followed by an asterisk
        have been fully counted; numbers of words not asterisked have
        been estimated (see I.1.4.2).

>   Before dates, ">" means "up to and including'.

<   After dates, "<" means "commencing from and including".

Abbreviations of Series and Periodical Titles

Materialien	Materialien zur Kunde des älteren Englischen Dramas[1]
MLR	Modern Language Review
NQ	Notes and Queries
PBSA	Papers of the Bibliographical Society of America
RES	Review of English Studies
SAB	Shakespeare Association Bulletin
SB	Studies in Bibliography
SP	Studies in Philology
TLS	The Times Literary Supplement

---

[1] I use this German form of the title to refer to the series edited
by W. Bang; the continuation edited by Henry De Vocht is cited
hereinafter as Materials for the Study of the Old English Drama.

1. Preliminaries

1.1. Introduction

1.1.1. Aims and scope

This study is an attempt to deal with, and to offer solutions for, the major problems of the canon of Thomas Middleton's plays. Thirteen plays will be subjected to detailed examination; five of these are included in the traditional canon of The Works of Thomas Middleton edited by A. H. Bullen,[1] while the remaining eight have all been attributed wholly or in part to Middleton during the nineteenth and twentieth centuries.

One of the plays in Bullen, The Widow, is only barely a doubtful case, since it is accepted by nearly all students of Middleton today as a work of his sole authorship; I have, nevertheless, decided to treat it initially as a questionable work because in the first edition (Q 1652) it is attributed, on the title-page and in a preface "To the Reader", to Jonson and Fletcher as well as Middleton, and by one of our early authorities, Francis Kirkman (1661), to Middleton and Rowley.

The remaining twelve plays of doubtful authorship I shall call "the problem plays". They comprise the following:

In Bullen: Anything for a Quiet Life; Blurt, Master Constable;
The Family of Love; The Spanish Gipsy.

Not in Bullen: The Bloody Banquet; 1 Honest Whore; The Nice Valour;
The Puritan; The Revenger's Tragedy; The Second Maiden's Tragedy;
Wit at Several Weapons; A Yorkshire Tragedy.

The crucial issues differ through this range of plays. Middleton's presence is not doubted in Anything for a Quiet Life: the question to be settled is whether the play is his unassisted work or a collaboration with Webster. 1 Honest Whore is known by impeccable external evidence, namely, Henslowe's diary,[2] to be a Dekker-Middleton collaboration; but some critics have doubted whether Middleton's hand can be detected in the

---

[1] 8 vols. (London, 1885-86; rpt. New York: AMS Press, 1964). Cited hereinafter as "Bullen". All line references to plays of the traditional Middleton canon are to this edition unless otherwise specified: quotations, however, are from the texts studied, which are specified in Appendix I.1.6 ("List of abbreviations").

[2] Philip Henslowe, Diary, ed. R. A. Foakes and R. T. Rickert (Cambridge, Eng.: Cambridge Univ. Press, 1961), p.209.

play as we have it. For the rest, in every case the issue is whether Middleton is concerned at all, and if so, then to what extent.

The Middleton canon has long been controversial, and at least one of the problem plays, The Revenger's Tragedy, has been the subject of detailed (but not, as I shall show, exhaustive) examination and polemic since Middleton's claim was first urged by E.H.C. Oliphant in 1926.[1] The question of the authorship of Blurt, Master Constable was first raised in the same article by Oliphant, but the internal evidence for this problem has never yet received satisfactory detailed treatment. The same is true of A Yorkshire Tragedy, another attribution to Middleton by Oliphant;[2] also of The Puritan, though Middleton's authorship has been suspected or confidently maintained since the time of Bullen[3] and Fleay.[4] The Family of Love has been a problem since 1948, when Gerald J. Eberle claimed to find Dekker's hand in it, in a rather unsatisfactory article.[5] Going further than Eberle, George R. Price has stated, "After several attempts to discover evidence for either Dekker or Middleton . . . I conclude that it belongs to neither of them."[6] But the negative evidence for this conclusion has not been itemized. Nor has any detailed work been done on The Spanish Gipsy since it was attributed to Ford by H. Dugdale Sykes.[7] The Second Maiden's Tragedy has been well treated already by Richard H. Barker[8] and Samuel Schoenbaum,[9] and The Nice Valour and Wit at Several Weapons

---

[1] "The Authorship of The Revenger's Tragedy," SP, 23 (1926), 157-168.

[2] The Plays of Beaumont and Fletcher (1927; rpt. New York: AMS Press, 1970), p.457.

[3] Bullen, I, lxxxix-xc.

[4] Frederick G. Fleay, A Biographical Chronicle of the English Drama, 1559-1642, 2 vols. (1891; rpt. New York: Burt Franklin, n.d.), II, 93.

[5] "Dekker's Part in The Familie of Love," Joseph Quincy Adams Memorial Studies, ed. J. G. McManaway et al. (Washington, D. C.: Folger Library, 1948), pp. 723-38.

[6] Thomas Dekker (New York: Twayne, 1969), pp. 177-78

[7] "John Ford, the author of The Spanish Gipsy," MLR, 19 (1924), 11-24; rpt. in Sykes, Sidelights on Elizabethan Drama (London: Oxford Univ. Press. 1924), pp. 183-199.

[8] "The Authorship of The Second Maiden's Tragedy and The Revenger's Tragedy," SAB, 20 (1945), 51-62, 121-133.

[9] Middleton's Tragedies (1955; rpt. New York: Gordian Press, 1970), pp. 183-202.

by Cyrus Hoy;[1] but I shall be able to present further evidence in
support of their conclusions.

These questions of the Middleton canon, long debated but seldom
if ever settled, will have to be faced whenever a new complete edition
of the dramatist is undertaken. A new edition is urgently required,
since Bullen's text, which is little more than a reprint of that of
Dyce,[2] is both modernised and highly inaccurate. Meanwhile, satisfactory old-spelling editions are available for only about half of
Middleton's undoubtedly unassisted plays, and also for only about
half of the problem plays. It is to be hoped that any new standard
edition will contain those plays not in Bullen which, I shall show,
are substantially or wholly Middleton's work. A truly complete and
accurate Dramatic Works would be a great help for the study of a
major Jacobean dramatist who has, perhaps, been relatively under-valued
in the past.

The main concern of this study will not be to allot scenes in
collaborate plays, but to establish the presence or absence of Middleton's hand in the text in question. Scenes will be allotted, but only
as a means to this end. I would suggest that the division of scenes
in a play where the identities of the collaborators are not in doubt--
as in Middleton's and Dekker's The Roaring Girl--though interesting
as an exercise, is of somewhat limited critical importance. A
collaboration is essentially a work for which each of the authors
concerned is jointly responsible, and not merely in the scenes which
he has written himself. The actual writing out of a play is the last
stage in its composition; much of the value of the work will depend
on the previous stages of plotting and arrangement of scenes; and
presumably each collaborator will be involved here, in a relationship
which we cannot now determine.

This consideration points to an unavoidable limitation of all
studies of authorship based, as this one will be, on analyses of
internal linguistic evidence. If two writers have worked on a play

---

1 "The Shares of Fletcher and his Collaborators in the Beaumont and
   Fletcher Canon (V)," SB, 13 (1960), 77-108. This is one of a series
   of papers in SB, 1956-1962, which will hereinafter be cited as
   "Shares". The complete series, Parts I-VII: SB, 8 (1956), 129-46; 9
   (1957), 143-62; 11 (1958), 85-106; 12 (1959), 91-116; 13 (1960),
   77-108; 14 (1961), 45-67; 15 (1962), 71-90.

2 Thomas Middleton, Works, ed. Alexander Dyce, 5 vols. (London:
   E. Lumley, 1840).

not simultaneously but successively, it may well happen that only the hand of the second writer is detectable, the final draft being essentially his alone. However, in such a case I would suggest that it is reasonable to regard the play as being "by" the second author only. It is not likely that this situation can have arisen very often; and one would want very strong grounds, including external evidence, to postulate the presence of the dramatist thus completely "revised out". Nevertheless, the possibility remains as a potential solution in the case of those plays where the internal evidence flatly contradicts the seventeenth century ascription.

1.1.2. External and internal evidence

The relationship between and relative values of external and internal evidence have been discussed at length, notably by Sir Edmund K. Chambers,[1] the contributors to the volume edited by David V. Erdman and Ephraim G. Fogel, Evidence for Authorship,[2] and recently by Samuel Schoenbaum in his very useful Internal Evidence and Elizabethan Dramatic Authorship.[3] According to Schoenbaum, "external evidence may and often does provide incontestable proof; internal evidence can only support hypotheses or corroborate external evidence", (p. 150). It is difficult to object to this formulation; but perhaps it places the emphasis a little one-sidedly. One of the hypotheses that internal evidence may support is, after all, the theory that the external evidence in some particular case is wrong.

The method of using internal evidence is essentially comparative and contrastive. Let us suppose, for example, that we have three plays, V, W, and X, given by external evidence to Author One, and two other plays, Y and Z, given by external evidence to Author Two. Let us further suppose that internal evidence shows unambiguously that V and W are almost identical in linguistic style and in such bibliographical peculiarities as spelling; that Y and Z are also very similar in all

---

[1] William Shakespeare: A Study of Facts and Problems, 2 vols. (Oxford: Clarendon Press, 1930), I, 208-225; and The Disintegration of Shakespeare (London: British Academy, 1924).

[2] Ithaca, N.Y.: Cornell Univ. Press, 1966.

[3] London: Edward Arnold, 1966. Hereinafter cited as Internal Evidence.

such respects, but differ greatly from V and W; and that X agrees in
every respect with the $Y+Z$ group, and disagrees in every respect with
the $V+W$ group. The natural conclusion to be drawn will be that X is
mis-attributed, and was written, at least in its final form, not by
One but by Two. It must be emphasized, however, that this conclusion
is not reached by merely preferring internal to external evidence,
since the argument for the re-attribution of X depends wholly on the
external evidence for the authorship of $V,W,Y,$ and Z, which must be
assumed to be correct. In fact, canonical studies by means of
internal evidence cannot reasonably be undertaken by any one who
wantonly mistrusts external evidence: for without some unquestioned
attributions no other attributions can be questioned.

I would suggest that in this matter there are three possible
attitudes, two of which are unreasonable. The first of the faulty
attitudes is that which I have just mentioned: wanton mistrust of
external evidence, usually coupled with easy belief in the value of
any internal clue which makes against the external evidence and the
received opinion. This is disintegrationism, and it has had a sad
history, well surveyed by Schoenbaum (Internal Evidence, passim).
The opposite attitude—staunch belief in all external evidence, no
matter how late nor how unreliable the authority from which it springs—
is equally a fault, though it has no established name. Schoenbaum
would call it "traditionalism" (ibid.,p.122); but traditions may
be good as well as bad, and respect for good tradition is not a fault
at all. I would prefer to label the error "doxolatry", a coinage
which might be defined as 'unreasonable veneration for assertions
that lack credentials". For example, it is doxolatry to attribute to
Dekker the pamphlet The Batchelars Banquet: the ascription was first
made, according to F. P. Wilson,[1] in a sale catalogue of the year 1800
by some unknown person without reasons stated; and internal evidence
shows that the pamphlet's literary and linguistic style is unlike
Dekker's.[2]

---

[1] The Batchelars Banquet, ed. F.P. Wilson (Oxford: Clarendon Press,
1929), xxiii.

[2] Ibid., xxv-xxvii. I shall offer further evidence in support of
Wilson's conclusion in Appendix IV.1.

The reasonable attitude, which I hope is my own, is the mean between these opposite faults. Schoenbaum (_Internal_ _Evidence_, p. 122) calls it "conservatism": it is the attitude taken by Sir Edmund Chambers towards the problems of the Shakespeare canon, and towards Elizabethan-Jacobean authorship in general. On this view, external evidence is to be treated with that degree of respect which it seems to deserve, and its deficiencies supplied by internal evidence. The external evidence for the authorship of some of Middleton's plays, as I shall show in Section 1.2, amounts to historical certainty, since it dates from within the author's own lifetime in circumstances where fraud or ignorance can be ruled out; but for every one of the problem plays (with the exception of _1_ _Honest_ _Whore_) the external evidence is late and/or suspect. Hence the need for studies like this one.

1.1.3. Desiderata for internal evidence

External and internal evidence have opposite advantages and disadvantages. As a rule external evidence is perfectly valid, that is, unambiguous evidence for authorship; but its reliability varies, and seldom in a way that can be quantified. Internal evidence may achieve high reliability if it is of the right kind; but its validity is always open to challenge, at least in principle. Thus in the imaginary example of 1.1.2 above, it might be objected that play _X_, though resembling the work of author Two, is in fact a work of One imitating the style of Two, the first edition having been printed from a transcript of One's work made by Two. Of course, such a theory is highly improbable; indeed, it borders on fantasy. Nevertheless, it may suggest some precautions to be taken in the use of internal evidence. Schoenbaum has recommended eight principles for canonical investigators (_Internal_ _Evidence_, pp. 162-83); I shall now propose four desiderata for internal evidence.

Reliability may be achieved by using only items that are
(1) objective: unambiguously defined features, recognition of which is not a matter of opinion;
(2) quantifiable (since differences between authors are in most features matters of greater or lesser frequency, not of invariable use or non-use).

Validity may be achieved by using only items that are

(3) likely (a priori) to correlate with authorship rather than
with other factors (the other factors including transcription,
compositorial practices, influences of genre or theatrical fash-
on, imitation, censorship, or common use in the period);

(4) shown (a posteriori) to correlate with authorship rather than
with such other factors, by means of comparisons which will
tend to eliminate these factors.

The last of these desiderata is one that has often been neglected
in the past; but it is essential. It is especially important that
all evidence claimed to reveal authorship should be shown to be truly
distinctive. This can only be done by what has been called "the
negative check":[1] that is, not only must resemblance(s) be pointed
out, but the non-occurrence of the feature(s) in question must be
demonstrated in many other texts of the same period.

1.1.4. Types of unsatisfactory internal evidence

The four desiderata above rule out or severely restrict the use of
some types of internal evidence which have been popular in the past,
including all of the following, which I shall list in descending order
of hopelessness.

1.1.4.1. Literary value

This evidence--if one can call it that--is usually employed
against common authorship of works which, in modern opinion, differ
greatly in value. But the difference is not an objective feature,
and may be due to a historical change of taste. The argument is in-
validated by many notorious instances of variable quality within a
single author's oeuvre. Shakespeare certainly wrote Titus Andronicus
as well as Hamlet. Wordsworth wrote the complete works of Wordsworth.

1.1.4.2. Authorial attitude

Attitudes on religious, moral, or political matters have sometimes
been used as evidence for authorship. In some favorable cases the
argument may be plausible: for example, a clearly anti-Catholic play

---

[1] By M. St. Clare Byrne, in "Bibliographical Clues in Collaborate
Plays," The Library, 4th ser., 13 (1932), 24.

can hardly be attributed to a known Catholic. But too often the attitude in question is a matter of critical conjecture. Arguments from Middleton's supposed morality or amorality are all of this kind.

1.1.4.3. Genre

Generic classification, whether broad or fine, of the play as a whole has often been used as an authorship argument. Thus it has been suggested that Middleton did not write The Revenger's Tragedy because this is a tragedy, whereas his extant early works are all comedies;[1] that he did write it, because it is 'like The Phoenix in its bitterness, like A Mad World and A Trick in its irony";[2] and that he did not write The Phoenix unassisted because this is not a London comedy.[3] Such arguments lack several or all of the desiderata listed in 1.1.3. Reliability is weak, since even when the generic classification is objectively verifiable it is scarcely quantifiable, as the whole play has to serve as a single item of evidence. And validity is radically suspect, since play-type is strongly influenced by fashion and imitation.

1.1.4.4. Plot-varieties and stage devices

Elements of plot and staging can be satisfactory evidence as regards objectivity, but they are mostly open to all the other objections. In general, the more striking the device or motif, the more easily it is imitated. Minor devices which occur with sufficient frequency are not so vulnerable, and can be perfectly legitimate evidence if quantified and subjected to the negative check. The most useful of these, probably, is the "group speech" described below (1.1.5.1.3).

1.1.4.5. Imagery

The evidence of imagery has not been well handled in the past, although in principle it might be if some inherent difficulties could be overcome. One would have to define "image", and adopt some

---

[1] R. A. Foakes, "On the Authorship of The Revenger's Tragedy," MLR, 48 (1953), 136.

[2] Richard H. Barker, Thomas Middleton (New York: Columbia Univ. Press, 1958), p.64.

[3] Daniel B. Dodson, "Thomas Middleton's City Comedies," Diss. Columbia, 1954, p.86.

objective linguistic or semantic classification of image-types.

Some previous investigators have made the mistake of arguing from prevailing images directly to the background of the author. Una Ellis-Fermor, examining The Atheist's Tragedy and The Revenger's Tragedy[1], found in them both imagery relating to the operations of life in a manor house in more or less well watered country. In The Atheist's Tragedy she noted "the imagery of a man who at some time in his life (I should think at an early and impressionable period) lived in a district where rivers and their tributaries were the main features of the landscape. More than this, I should say it was the imagery of a man who had handled small sail-boats on these same waters" (p.292). In support she quotes:

> I prithee let this current of my teares,
> Direct thy inclination from the warre   (I.ii.2-3)

and a few other lines of similar nature. In The Revenger's Tragedy she also found images of streams, and "one very notable image that suggests the experience of a county subject to frequent droughts" (p. 297). On the strength of these resemblances, she decided that the author of both plays was the same man, Tourneur; incidentally, her article contains no negative check, since the imagery of Middleton is never examined for suggestions of streams or small sail-boats. Not long after Ellis-Fermor's work, there appeared another study, by Marco Mincoff, who found that the imagery of The Revenger's Tragedy suggested a townsman author, hence Middleton.[2]   The method of imagery has lain in some disfavour ever since.

1.1.4.6. Parallel passages

This type of evidence has been grievously abused in the past. The average "parallel passage" cited in argument has been (1) undefined as to objective points of similarity, (2) hence uncountable for statistical purposes, (3) striking in thought or diction and hence open to imitation, (4) not subjected to the negative check. Thus the

---

[1] "The Imagery of The Revenger's Tragedie and The Atheist's Tragedie," MLR, 30 (1935), 289-301.

[2] See Schoenbaum, Internal Evidence, p. 186. I base my remarks on Schoenbaum's report: I have been unable to obtain a copy of Mincoff's rather inaccessible article (the reference to which, given by Schoenbaum, seems to be wrong).

evidence has been lacking in all four of my desiderata.   But all these
faults are avoidable.   If the parallel is defined, counted, fairly
unobtrusive, and searched for through a whole corpus of comparison
plays, it becomes usable as a parallel collocation, the "parallel"
consisting in a recurrence of identical elements (see below, 1.1.5.1.1.7).

1.1.5.   Types of satisfactory internal evidence

The various forms of unsatisfactory evidence just listed are not
wholly useless: they may serve, in a particular problem, to arouse
suspicion or to confirm a judgment arrived at by other methods.   But in
isolation they cannot provide convincing proof.

Such proof is obtainable only from formally defined and countable
linguistic or bibliographical items which satisfy the criteria of
validity.   Validation is achieved mainly by checking the same items
through an extensive corpus which should include the suspected authors
of the play(s) investigated and as much other contemporary material
as can reasonably be handled.   To this end I have chosen a corpus of 132
plays (inclusive of undoubted Middleton and problem plays; all listed
in Table I.1) drawn mainly from the period of Middleton's literary
career (1597-1627), and through this corpus I have counted the occurrences
of 201 items (178 in Table I.1, 23 in Table I.2).   The results of this
count, being the main data on which this study is based, are given in
Appendix I.

I can claim no originality for the general methods or particular
tests which I employ.   They have, with insignificant exceptions, all
been used over the past fifty years in authorship investigations,
though not systematically on most of the Middleton or problem plays.
For methods I am mainly indebted to the exemplary studies of eighteenth
century problems by Alvar Ellegård[1] and by Frederick Mosteller and David
L. Wallace,[2] and to previous investigations in Jacobean drama by Cyrus
Hoy ("Shares") and Peter B. Murray.[3]   My debt is especially large

---

[1]
A Statistical Method for Determining Authorship: the Junius Letters,
1769-1772 (Göteborg; Göteborg Univ., 1962). Hereinafter cited as A
Statistical Method.

[2]
Inference and Disputed Authorship: The Federalist (Reading, Mass.:
Addison-Wesley, 1964).

[3]
A Study of Cyril Tourneur (Philadelphia: Pennsylvania Univ. Press,
1964), pp. 159-189.   Hereinafter cited as Cyril Tourneur.

to Professor Hoy, from whose counts I quote, and whose work in several respects I am supplementing and extending.

The evidence used in this study falls into two main categories, stylistic and sub-stylistic, the latter being confined to spelling. There is also another independent dichotomy, into items which are members of synonymous groups (usually pairs) and those which are not. For example, it's: 'tis and 'em: e'm are synonymous pairs, the first pair stylistic, the second sub-stylistic; whereas the contraction ha' and the spelling of verbal forms in -cst are unpaired items, the first stylistic, the second sub-stylistic. The importance of the distinction between paired and unpaired items lies in the different methods of statistical handling: the paired items yield ratios which are often significant as representing an authorial preference; unpaired items of course yield no ratio, and so have to be used to produce a relative frequency--which I have expressed usually as so many instances per standard play-length of 20000 words.

1.1.5.1. Stylistic evidence

Under this heading I include all items which belong to the linguistic substance of the play as a written text. Such items may be divided into three main sub-classes: speech-prefixes, items of versi-fication, and all other textual items, which I shall refer to collect-ively as "items of diction", and survey immediately below.

1.1.5.1.1. Diction

1.1.5.1.1.1. Exclamations

The main advantage of exclamations as criteria of authorship is that they are relatively unpredictable from the context of dramatic situation; nor are the trivial exclamations, mere noises of impatience or disgust such as pish or tush, normally used to create characters. Moreover, authorial preferences are striking. Middleton's fondness for the fairly rare push (first noted, it seems, by Pauline G. Wiggin[1]), has long been famous. I have noticed that he also uses tut quite frequently in his early plays, whereas Dekker uses tush. Middleton's high frequency of the interjection why was noted by Mark Eccles.[2]

---

[1] An Inquiry into the Authorship of the Middleton-Rowley Plays (Cambridge, Mass.: Radcliffe College, 1897), p.38.

[2] "Middleton's Birth and Education," RES, 7 (1931), 438.

1.1.5.1.1.2. Oaths

The same advantages, on the whole, apply to oaths, but here some disturbing factors have to be allowed for--censorship, characterization, and settings in times or places which may inhibit some oaths and favour others. In spite of all such factors, there are clear patterns of authorial preference. Schoenbaum has recorded Middleton's liking, in his early work, for faith, troth, and 'sfoot,[1] and his occasional use of cuds me.[2] In this study I have investigated all the oaths in the 132 corpus plays; Table I.1 accounts for all oaths formed from the name of God in any guise, and for whatever others seemed significant for authorship.

1.1.5.1.1.3. Affirmative particles

The ratio between the affirmative particles ay and yes was used as a test of authorship in Henry VIII and The Revenger's Tragedy by MacDonald P. Jackson.[3] I have extended this test to all the corpus plays.

1.1.5.1.1.4. Connectives

The choices observed in a text between such exact synonyms as among: amongst; beside: besides; between: betwixt; toward: towards; and while: whilst: whiles can provide extremely useful criteria of authorship, since during the Elizabethan-Jacobean period each member of these sets of alternatives was current, and, I have found, was not differentially favoured in different contexts, genres, or stylistic registers. Moreover, some authors exhibit very strong preferences for one alternative out of each pair or triad: for example, I have found not a single whilst in Chapman's original poems, nor a single while in Marston's (see Appendix IV), and the same preferences appear in all the plays of each dramatist (see Table I.1). Middleton shows a clear (and unusual) preference for beside over the commoner form besides. It is not usually necessary to distinguish between the prepositional and adverbial uses of beside and besides:[4] authors who prefer one form or the other seem to prefer it for both uses, as

---

1 Middleton's Tragedies, pp. 175-76.

2 Ibid., p. 196.

3 "Affirmative Particles in Henry VIII," NQ, 206 (1962), 372-74.

4 Moreover, the primary spatial meaning of these words occurs very rarely in plays, so that synonymy is nearly perfect. Even besides himself ("distracted") occurs, as in Blurt, sig. B1 (Bullen, I, 14; I.i.215).

may be seen from Table I.1, where each use is recorded separately.

A disadvantage of these synonymous connectives as criteria of authorship is that, with the exception of between: betwixt, they would seem to be very vulnerable to textual corruption; yet the very strength and consistency of the preferences found in many authors' works, emanating as they do from many different printing-shops, show that corruption did not often occur.

Tests of connectives have not previously been applied to problems of Elizabethan-Jacobean authorship, but have been used by Ellegard and by Mosteller and Wallace.

1.1.5.1.1.5. Colloquialisms and contractions

Here are included most of the tests applied by Hoy and Murray, except that I have not counted contractions of pronouns + will, since these are very numerous in all the authors studied, and therefore would not provide easy discriminators of authorship, but merely a mass of unmanageable data. The categories of "colloquialisms" and "contractions" overlap considerably, since probably all contractions are also colloquialisms, but has and does (as opposed to hath and doth), and perhaps ye (in place of you), are colloquialisms without being contractions.

One contraction-pair which may require special mention is it's: 'tis. The usual contraction of it is in our period was 'tis, but it's also occurs; sporadically in most writers (including Middleton), but, I have noticed, frequently in a few, such as Dekker and Jonson. Since it is appears in contracted form very frequently in Elizabethan-Jacobean drama, the occurrence or non-occurrence of it's provides a useful test of authorship. (To the best of my knowledge, this test has not previously been used in any authorship investigation.)

1.1.5.1.1.6. Selected single words

Almost every student of Middleton must have felt that this author's vocabulary, at least in his mature work, is characteristic. I have tested all the words proposed by Schoenbaum,[1] and a few others as well, but

---

[1] Middleton's Tragedies, p. 196.

of the commoner words I have selected only one for registration through
the corpus plays--Middleton's favorite comfort. His relative frequency
for this word is certainly much higher than average, and, moreover,
contrasts strongly with Dekker's very low frequency. Middleton seems to
have a liking for abstract nouns in general--blessing, goodness, joy,
and others--but this is not a very powerful test of authorship, especially
as the trait is less striking in his early and comic work (see below,
1.2.4).

1.1.5.1.1.7. Collocations

Under this heading I include all combinations of more than one
word (other than oaths) co-occurring in the same sentence. Some of
these items have been used in the past as "parallels". I hope that
I have rescued them for legitimate use by defining the collocation
and recording the number of instances of it through the entire corpus.
The definition consists of the words which appear in the column-headings
of Table I.1 (or under "Collocation" in Table I.2), either in the order
specified, or, when words are separated by an oblique line (/), in any
order. Near approaches to the formally defined collocation are given
in footnotes to Table I.1. Thus under Adam/Eve are recorded all
instances of the co-occurrence of the words "Adam" and "Eve", in either
order, in the same sentence; a footnote records an instance in Jonson
where "Eve" appears in the possessive form.

Some of the collocations are counted only when they occur in some
particular grammatical or semantic pattern. Single words in special
senses may also be regarded as collocations, since the special sense
is always established by the context.

Collocations have the advantage, quite often, of high distinctiveness,
but usually the disadvantage of low frequency. They are best used in
combination with colloquialisms and contractions to show that such items
do not signify a mere transcript or superficial revision, but true
authorship.

1.1.5.1.2. Versification

"Verse tests" are relatively unpopular at present among canonical
investigators, partly because they have been abused in the past. They
must certainly be handled with caution, especially when there is any
reason to suspect mislineation. However, in favorable cases they

can deliver an unambiguous verdict. I shall use a verse test for the
problem of The Revenger's Tragedy; this will be given in Appendix II.

1.1.5.1.3. Speech prefixes

Barker has noticed that in Blurt, Master Constable "there are a good
many chorus speeches . . . far more than in any play known to have been
written by Middleton" (Thomas Middleton, p. 199). By a "chorus speech"
Barker presumably means a speech given to a whole group speaking in
unison. I use the term "group speech" in a perhaps slightly wider sense,
to refer to any speech given to more than one character on stage speaking
simultaneously; by "chorus speech" I mean exclusively a speech prefixed
All or Omnes.

The two significant features here, I would claim, are the relative
frequency of all group speeches, and the preference for the form All
or the form Omnes to indicate a chorus speech. Of course the frequency
of group speeches is affected by genre: political plays tend to have
higher frequencies, as is shown by the extreme contrast between Coriolanus
(52) and The Tempest (1). Nevertheless, authorial tendencies are also
obvious from Table I.1, and Dekker's frequencies are clearly outstanding.
His preference for Omnes, and Middleton's preference for All, are
equally striking (see 2.1, 2.2).

In addition, the form of the prefix used to label a numbered character may be significant for authorship. Middleton is much given to
using the "number only" form (for example, 1. instead of 1 Gent. or
whatever), but this is too common a habit to provide useful evidence.
Much less common is the form Gent. 1 (etc.): most authors put the
numeral before the word or abbreviation. This feature may be of some
significance in the problem of The Bloody Banquet (see 5.1.4.2.1.2).

1.1.5.2. Sub-stylistic evidence: spelling

The only sub-stylistic evidence which I have examined systematically
is spelling; punctuation, hyphenation, and other orthographic habits,
though sometimes furnishing valid evidence, would, if explored thoroughly,
involve work far beyond the scope of this study.

During Middleton's lifetime (1580-1627) the spelling of English was
still far from standardization, even in such common words as "has" and
"does", and while compositors would generally eliminate the more eccentric
spellings found in copy, the preferences of the writer of the manuscript,

whether author or scribe, would usually penetrate to the printed text to a greater or lesser extent. It is noticeable, for example, that the printed works of Chapman and Dekker almost invariably give "does" its modern spelling, whereas those of Marston and Jonson, and the early quartos of Middleton, very frequently have <u>dos</u> or <u>do's</u>. Since several different printing houses are involved for each writer, and in the case of Middleton <u>dos</u> and <u>do's</u>, not <u>does</u>, appear in the autograph Trinity manuscript of <u>A Game at Chess</u> (see 1.2.1), it is clear that these preferences are authorial, and may be significant for canonical problems.

However, spelling evidence must be used with caution. It is hardly available for texts printed after the closing of the theatres (1642), since by that time modernization had set in. For earlier texts, the appearance of an author's more peculiar spellings may provide valid evidence of his presence; but the absence of these spellings does not prove the contrary, since they may well have been eliminated by scribal or compositorial intervention. Finally, positive spelling evidence is not, strictly speaking, proof of authorship as such; especially in collaborate plays, it may happen that one author has copied out a text composed by another.

In spite of these drawbacks, however, spelling evidence is often suggestive, and I shall offer it wherever it is relevant.

The choice between certain synonymous contractions lies in the uncertain area between spelling and diction. I follow the principle that forms which are pronounced differently are not mere matters of spelling: thus, I regard <u>i'th</u>: <u>i'the</u>; <u>a'th'</u>: <u>a'the</u>; <u>o'th'</u>: <u>o'the</u>; <u>'tas</u>:<u>'t has</u>, and <u>'tad</u>:<u>'t had</u> as substantively differing pairs, since each difference seems to imply the omission or retention of a phoneme, the vowel of <u>the</u> or /h/. On the other hand, I regard <u>a'th'</u>:<u>o'th'</u> and <u>a'the</u>: <u>o'the</u> as merely spelling variants. The series <u>thou'rt</u>: <u>th'art</u>; <u>we're</u>: <u>w'are</u>; <u>you're</u>: <u>y'are</u> and <u>they're</u>: <u>th'are</u>[1] is more troublesome: <u>you're</u>: <u>y'are</u> at least would seem to represent a phonemic difference, but variations recorded in Table

---

[1] These are generalized spellings: the first member of each pair represents any spelling which clearly retains the vowel of the pronoun (e.g. <u>weere</u>, <u>your</u>, <u>the're</u>, <u>there</u>, <u>their</u>); the second any spelling which clearly preserves the vowel of the verb (e.g. <u>yar</u>, <u>thare</u>). I owe this distinction and the device for representing it to Murray, <u>Cyril Tourneur</u>, p.166.

I.1 between printed works of the same author show that printing houses
treated the whole series with as much freedom as spelling variants.
Thus, Rowley's A Shoemaker a Gentleman has only you're, but his other
plays only y'are (each of his plays had a different printer). A very
striking instance occurs within the text of Joshua Cooke's Greene's
Tu Quoque. This play, as Greg remarks,[1] is shown by variations in
running titles to have been printed in two sections (perhaps by different
shops), sheets G, H, I, K, having quoque on 1r and 2r, the rest (B-F,
L-M) always Quoque. There are 8 instances of you're, but none of y'are,
in G-K, and 8 instances of y'are, but none of you're, in the rest of the
play. I conclude that you're: y'are, though probably not a mere spelling
variant, had better be treated with all the precautions needful for
spelling evidence.

1.1.6. Structure and methods of this study

The arrangement of sections in this study is based partly on
chronology, but essentially on logical necessity. Section 1.2 reviews
the undoubted work of Middleton, with emphasis on the corroboration of
external by internal evidence: the limits of the undoubted canon are
reached when this corroboration seems to be lacking. Section 1.3 adds
The Widow to the canon of Middleton's unassisted plays. Thereafter
within the two main chronological divisions of Middleton's work, before
and after 1610, I have sought first to purify the traditional unassisted
canon, then to add it; and, other things being equal, I have moved from
works whose authorship is relatively certain to those which are more
doubtful. Section 2 deals with early problem plays traditionally ascribed
wholly or in part to Middleton; Section 3 with early problem plays
outside the traditional canon; Section 4 with all problem plays later
than 1610; and Section 5 with The Bloody Banquet, of which both the
authorship and the date are doubtful.

The arguments through all sections are sequential, in the sense that
if a doubtful play is shown to be probably an unassisted work of
Middleton, later arguments will have to be compatible with this assumed

---

[1] W. W. Greg, A Bibliography of the English Printed Drama to the
Restoration, 4 vols. (London: The Bibliographical Society 1939-59),
I (1939), 464.

fact. But every case will be argued primarily on the basis of comparisons with Middleton's undoubted plays (including The Widow).

I must acknowledge a substantial methodological debt to Schoenbaum (Internal Evidence, passim) for many salutary warnings. I have noted his principle that "parallels from plays of uncertain or contested authorship prove nothing" (p. 192); but I do not think this principle should be pressed too far.[1] I attach some weight to parallels (including linguistic evidence) from collaborate play scenes whose authorship can be proved by other good evidence; especially when the item in question does not occur in the undoubted works of the other collaborator(s)--as, for instance, the i' contractions which occur (see 1.3) in Middleton scenes in the Middleton-Rowley plays, but in no Rowley scene or Rowley play. Similarly, parallels from problem plays whose authorship has been previously proved on other grounds may be allowed some evidential value.

The arguments offered in this study are all basically statistical, since no single feature in isolation can provide certainty: it is the combination of several rare features, or a great many less rare ones, which can yield a probability so high as to constitute a proof "beyond reasonable doubt". For most problems the calculation of these probabilities will have to be left to intuition; but in some favorable cases an explicit calculation can be attempted. The two most favorable cases, because of the abundance of the linguistic evidence available, are those of The Puritan and The Revenger's Tragedy; for each of these plays there will be offered (3.1.6., 3.2.7) an explicit statistical argument based on the methods of Ellegård, resulting in a statement of odds in favour of the authorship solution proposed.

1.1.7. The Table I.1 corpus

The 132 plays in the Table I.1 corpus comprise samples of the work of some dramatists (e.g. Jonson and Massinger), and all the undoubted plays of many others (justifications of inclusions and exclusions of

---

[1] Schoenbaum's methodological purism is attractive at first sight: at the outset of this study I followed it rigorously. But I found that it gave a seriously misleading impression of Dekker's typical usages c.1604-05 of why and 'em (see 2.1.1.3.1 and 2.1.3), which can best be studied in the Ho collaborations. Thereafter, I abandoned purism for a more flexible but still cautious approach.

particular plays are given in Appendix I.1.2). I have included in the
corpus all the major dramatists writing during Middleton's career except
Shirley and Davenant, who in any case began writing only at the end of
Middleton's lifetime, and whose styles (especially verse styles) are
easily distinguished from those of Middleton and the later problem plays.
Some minor dramatists have been included to provide enough comparative
material within the appropriate genres for the Puritan and Revenger's
Tragedy statistical arguments. To make the selection of the corpus plays
I have read every play written for the London commercial stages by
known authors within the period 1600-1627: the authors excluded are
those whose linguistic styles are very different from those of the problem
plays.

I believe that Table I.1 contains within itself a summary proof
of many of my contentions; for instance, that certain features, including
exclamations, oaths, contractions, and (in some cases) spellings,
correlate with authorship rather than with other factors such as censorship
or printing house practices. However, more explicit proofs of these
contentions will be given in the appropriate places.

1.2. The undoubted canon and its limits

1.2.1. Thomas Middleton: basic certainties
1.2.1.1. The 12-play canon

It is usually agreed that Middleton wrote at least twelve plays unassisted. In roughly the order of composition, as far as this is known or can be reasonably surmised, they comprise the following:

Play title	Probable date of composition [1]	Substant-ive text	Date of surname attribution
The Phoenix	1603-04	Q 1607	1661
Michaelmas Term	1605	Q 1607	1656
A Mad World, my Masters	1605-06	Q 1608	1656
A Trick to Catch the Old One	1605-06	Q 1608	1616
Your Five Gallants	1606-07	Q n.d.	1608 (?)
No Wit, No Help like a Woman's	1612	O 1657	1653
A Chaste Maid in Cheapside	1613	Q 1630	1630
More Dissemblers Besides Women	c.1615	O 1657	1653
The Witch	c.1616	MS	> 1627
Hengist, King of Kent	c.1616-20	MSS	1661
Women Beware Women	c.1612-27	O 1657	1653
A Game at Chess	1624	MSS	1624

Though there has long been a scholarly consensus on this 12-play canon, that has not precluded the doubts of a few disintegrators as to Middleton's sole authorship of some of these plays. Indeed, there is not a sharp division between absolutely undoubted and utterly doubtful attributions. The Widow is a fringe item, sometimes included in the "undoubted" unassisted canon; and the evidence for Middleton's author-ship of the other twelve plays varies in certainty. In all cases but one, internal evidence is involved, and must be heavily relied on when the external evidence is relatively late.

---

[1] In this study it is assumed that dates of composition differ from dates of first production by not more than a few months.

The dates in this list represent my own opinions arrived at after consulting a great many authorities and considering their arguments. But nothing material is at stake in the placing of a play a few years earlier or later. What is certain is that the first five plays are pre-1608, and the last seven post-1610. My dates do not differ great-ly from those of R. C. Bald, "The Chronology of Middleton's Plays," MLR, 32 (1937), 33-43.

The best broad category of external evidence--attribution to the
author by Christian name and surname within his own lifetime--exists
in respect of only two of these twelve plays; and, of course, not even
this category of evidence need be undoubted. Fraud can be ruled out,
since in his time Middleton, unlike Shakespeare, was not famous enough
to attract apocryphal attributions. But ambiguous reference is a
distinct possibility.

1.2.1.2. Middleton's identity and career

Thomas Middleton the dramatic poet is best defined as "the author of
A Game at Chess". One must adopt some such formulation if one is to
pursue disintegration, even in a spirit of Cartesian doubt, as far as
it will go; and, moreover, there certainly were at least two Thomas
Middletons in Jacobean London; most likely there were several. In 1613
one Thomas Middleton, who was certainly our dramatist,[1] wrote the pageant The Triumphs of Truth in honour of the Lord Mayor of that year,
Sir Thomas Middleton. And three Thomas Middletons, none of them the
dramatist, entered Gray's Inn in 1594-96.[2] It is therefore not absurd
to maintain, like Swinburne, that a work printed in the lifetime of the
dramatist (1580-1627) with a dedication subscribed "Thomas Middleton"
could have been written by another man of the same name.[3] But disintegration of a canon can begin to deny authorship only when one work is
accepted as quite undoubted. In Middleton's case, that work must be
A Game at Chess.

For A Game at Chess the contemporary external evidence is unanimous,
trustworthy, and copious, for the play caused a national sensation: it
was the greatest box-office success in the annals of Tudor-Stuart drama,
and it impinged on the international affairs of Europe.[4] The author was
referred to as "Middleton" (and once "Midleton the Poet") in official
records both before and after the scandal broke.[5] We know that he was
a Thomas Middleton because "Tho. Middleton" appears on the title pages

---

[1] Internal evidence for this conclusion will be offered in Appendix III.

[2] Eccles, 'Middleton's Birth and Education," 434-35.

[3] Introduction to the Mermaid series Thomas Middleton, ed. H. Ellis, 2 vols.,
I (London: Vizetelly, 1887), xxxii-xxxiii. Swinburne doubted the
dramatist's authorship of The Wisdom of Solomon Paraphrased (Q 1597), for
which see Appendix III.

[4] See A Game at Chess, ed. R. C. Bald (Cambridge, Eng.: Cambridge Univ.
Press, 1929), pp. 1-25.

[5] Ibid., pp. 159, 161-62, 166.

of four out of the six manuscripts in which the play has come down to us.[1] One of these four fully-ascribed manuscripts (the Malone MS.), a presentation copy for a patron, contains a dedicatory stanza in a hand not that of the scribe of the manuscript; this stanza is signed "T.M." in the same hand as that of the stanza itself. Here, clearly, we have the poet's autograph. A fifth manuscript, now in the library of Trinity College, Cambridge (Trinity MS. 0.2.66), bears these same initials "T.M." on the title-page, and is written throughout in the hand of the Malone dedicatory stanza: presumably, therefore, it is holograph.

The same hand occurs as the signature of a Thomas Middleton of London who entered Queen's College, Oxford in 1598, aged 18.[2] Of Middleton the Oxford student and his family the records are fairly copious: I will here give only a brief summary of the life of this Thomas Middleton, who must be the same person as the author of A Game at Chess, touching merely on those points that may be relevant to questions of authorship.

He was born in April 1580, the son of a successful London bricklayer who was also a gentleman possessed of a coat of arms. As we have seen, he entered Oxford in 1598; but he left without taking a degree some time between 28 June 1600 and 8 February 1600/1, on which latter date he was described, in the course of legal proceedings, as remaining "here in London daylie accompaninge the players".[3] He first appears as a playwright working in collaboration for Henslowe on 22 May 1602.[4] By October-November 1602 he was completing unassisted a tragedy, Randal Earl of Chester (now lost), for the Admiral's Men.[5]

From 1602 onwards Middleton seems to have pursued uninterruptedly a literary career, and from 1613 onwards increasingly in connection

---

[1] Bald, in the textual introduction to his edition of A Game at Chess, pp. 26-29; also, "A New Manuscript of Middleton's Game at Chesse," MLR, 25 (1930), 474-78; and "An Early Version of Middleton's Game at Chesse," MLR, 38 (1943), 177-80.

[2] Eccles, "Middleton's Birth and Education," 436-37. The account given here of Middleton's life is mainly indebted to Eccles' articles.

[3] Eccles, "Thomas Middleton a Poett," SP, 54 (1957), 525; Peter G. Phialas, "Middleton's Early Contact with the Law," SP, 52 (1955), 192.

[4] Henslowe, Diary, p. 201. The play, Caesar's Fall, is lost.

[5] Ibid., pp. 205-06.

with the City of London, for which he wrote many pageants. From
1620 onwards he held the post of City Chronologer. But in spite of
all these honorable employments, he seems never to have been finan-
cially secure. After writing his last pageant, The Triumphs of
Health and Prosperity (1626), he died (1627; buried 4 July), leaving
a widow who had to petition the City for charity.

1.2.2. Middleton's style and spelling in A Game at Chess

From the Trinity manuscript of A Game at Chess we can gain a clear
view of Middleton's linguistic style and spelling habits, which will
enable us to check the authenticity of other plays.[1]

1.2.2.1. Linguistic style

Middleton's linguistic style in drama, as revealed by A Game at
Chess, tends to be colloquial. He uses a wide range of contracted
forms, including some pronoun-verb contractions which were relatively
rare in the Jacobean period: I'm, I've, sh'as (for "she has"), 'tas,
'tad (for "it has, it had"), we're, you're, y'ave, they're, and they've,
beside the commoner contractions I'd, thou'rt, thou'st, he's, she's,
she'd, 'tis, y'are, you'd, they'd, and many others.[2] He prefers 'em
(38 instances) to them (5 instances), has to hath (41 to 3), and does
to doth (8 to 0). He is notably given to the weakest form of on or
of, spelt a (7 instances: e.g. a purpose, II.i.177). Speeches begin
with the colloquial interjection why in twelve instances (there are
also four non-initial instances). There is one instance of the
exclamation puh (III.ii.25), and three of the unusual push (Induction,
76; II.ii.271; IV. i.169), a variant of "pish" which occurs in the
Table I.1 corpus outside the Middleton and problem plays only six

---

[1] The text on which this study is based, and to which line references
are given, is the edition of R. C. Bald, which takes the Trinity MS.
as the basic copy text except for IV.iv.51-119 and a few shorter passages,
which are missing in the Trinity MS. and supplied from the Bridge-
water-Huntington MS. However, Bald's edition is unreliable as to the
placing of apostrophes, and is substantially in error in IV.ii.17,
where Bald's first word is T'as, whereas the Trinity MS. very clearly
reads ha's. My statistics for substantive forms are based on Bald's
text with this one word corrected; but for spellings of 'em, has and
does I follow the Trinity MS., which I have consulted in microfilm.

[2] Spellings of contractions in this study are normalized, as here,
except in quotations of particular instances or when exact spellings
are in question. Where there is danger of confusion, exact spellings
are enclosed between pairs of oblique lines, e.g. /facst/.

times (once each in plays by Chapman, Cooke, Dekker, Field, Haughton, and Sharpham).

1.2.2.2. Spelling

The characteristics of Middleton's spelling have been well described already, notably by Price,[1] and Murray;[2] I will mention here only a few significant characteristics. A Game at Chess reveals a highly unusual habit of spelling the preterite and past participle inflection of verbs ending in -ce as -cst:/dispencst, facst/(twice),/inducst, placst/(twice),/prauncst, seducst, silencst/(twice),/spicst, unpennancst/. Has occurs in 30 out of 40 instances as /ha's/ or /h'as/; and only 5 times in the Trinity manuscript do these forms stand for the contraction of "he has".[3] Middleton's preferred spelling of has would seem to be /ha's/(20 instances, excluding those standing for "he has"). Does appears invariably as /do's/ (6 times) or /dos/ (twice), not /does/. The contraction of "them" is only twice spelt /'em/--both times in cramped situations on the right margin of the manuscript.[4] There are 4 instances of /em/, but overwhelmingly the spelling is /e'm/ (27 instances or even /em'/ (4 instances;[5] presumably the latter would have been interpreted by a Jacobean compositor as /e'm/.

In several pronoun-verb contractions in A Game at Chess Middleton prefers to elide the vowel of the verb rather than that of the pronoun: thou'rt, not th'art; weere or wee're, not w'are; they're or theire, not th'are. As noted in 1.1.5.2, it is not certain whether this is a matter of spelling only or was reflected in pronunciation.

---

[1] "The Authorship and Bibliography of The Revenger's Tragedy," The Library, 5th ser., 15 (1960), 262-77, especially 267-68.

[2] Cyril Tourneur, pp. 161-189.

[3] Trinity MS.fols. 14v (twice), 18v, 31r, 41r. I read as /h'as/ any case where the apostrophe comes before the middle of the a; as/ha's/ when it comes after. One cannot always distinguish very certainly.

[4] Fols. 33v, 48v.

[5] I read as /e'm/ all cases where the apostrophe is over the middle area of the m (Middleton's usual position for it); /em'/ where the apostrophe is on or beyond the imaginary upward extension of the last downstroke of the m, namely, in fols. 4r, 10v, 15r, 20v. The distinction between Middleton's /'em/ and his /e'm/ is perfectly clear.

1.2.3. The rest of the unassisted canon

1.2.3.1. Other plays attributed to Middleton up to 1627.

1.2.3.1.1. A Trick and Your Five Gallants

Only two plays were printed in Middleton's lifetime bearing the full name "Thomas Middleton", and both were collaborations.[1] But the second edition of A Trick to Catch the Old One (1616) has the title-page ascription "By T. Midleton". The first edition of Your Five Gallants (Q n.d.; probably 1608[2]) has "Written by T. Middleton". Both Trick (first edition, Q 1608) and Your Five Gallants share the salient peculiarities of style and spelling found in A Game at Chess--the preference for the colloquial forms 'em, has, does over them, hath, doth; the exclamation push (4 instances in Trick, 6 in Your Five Gallants); preterite/past participle forms in -cst; the spellings /e'm, h'as/ or /ha's/, and /do(')s/; and so forth, through a whole range of features. It is true that the first quartos of the two plays were both printed in the same shop, that of George Eld; but other dramatic works printed by Eld in 1607-08, a period in which, apparently, there was no known change in his work force,[3] do not show any compositorial favoring of these colloquialisms and spellings, which correlate rather with authorship.[4] Evidently, both Trick and Your Five Gallants are not only by the author of A Game at Chess, but also printed from his autograph.[5]

1.2.3.1.2. A Mad World, my Masters

The same spelling and linguistic features are evident in A Mad World, my Masters, a play whose first edition (Q 1608) bears the title-page

---

[1] The Roaring Girl (Q 1611) and A Fair Quarrel (Q 1617), both discussed below (1.2.5).

[2] Presumably publication followed without delay on the entry in the Stationers' Register, 22 March 1608; for which see Edward Arber, A Transcript of the Registers of the Worshipful Company of Stationers, 1554-1640, 5 vols. (1875-94; rpt. New York: Peter Smith, 1950), III, 372. This work is hereinafter cited as "Arber".

[3] Murray, Cyril Tourneur, p. 162; D. F. McKenzie, "A List of Printers' Apprentices, 1605-1640," SB, 13 (1960), 120.

[4] Murray, Cyril Tourneur, Table I. pp. 174-77; see also my Tables I.1 and 3.1(1) for Eld's printings of Barnes' Devil's Charter, Tomkis' Lingua, Jonson's Volpone, and Marston's What You Will, all in 1607. That Eld printed Volpone has been established by J. A. Lavin, "Printers for Seven Jonson Quartos," The Library, 25 (1970), 331-38.

[5] As has often been pointed out by bibliographers; e.g. Price, "The Early Editions of A trick to catch the old one," The Library, 5th ser., 22 (1967), 207-13; Bald, "The Foul Papers of a Revision," The Library, 4th ser., 26 (1945), 37-50.

formula "Composed by T.M." This formula is in any case almost a Middleton signature: it appears as "Composde by T.M." on the title page of the first edition (second issue) of Trick (Q 1608); and the Folger manuscript (Folger shelf-mark v.a.342) of A Game at Chess has an autograph title-page inscribed with the words "Compos'de by Tho: Middleton".[1] A Mad World was printed in two parts, sheets A-E by Henry Ballard, and sheets F-I by Nicholas Okes;[2] it is interesting that Middleton's /e'm, ha's, do(')s/ appear in the portions of both printers, indicating that their copy was a holograph. The style of Mad World, with 6 instances of push, 10 of puh, 60 of why, and 9 of I've, is completely Middletonian.

Thus the three printed plays, Trick, Your Five Gallants, and Mad World, together with the manuscript Game at Chess, provide a solid core of certainty for Middleton's dramatic work: clearly his style did not alter in its basic features between 1608 (or a little earlier) and 1624. We may expect that other genuine unassisted plays datable within this period will manifest similar characteristics.

1.2.3.1.3. The Witch

This expectation is satisfied as regards style, if not spelling, by The Witch, a play never printed in the seventeenth century, but extant in a manuscript written by the King's Men's scribe Ralph Crane, who also produced three of the Game at Chess manuscripts.[3] The Witch is inscribed with the name "Tho. Middleton" both on the title page and below the author's dedicatory epistle to Thomas Holmes; the likeliest date of composition is about 1616 (Bald, "Chronology", 41,43). There are not many oaths or exclamations in the play (for example, no push), but there is the usual prevalence of 'em, has, and does over them, hath, and doth, and many Middletonian contractions appear: I'd, I'm, I've, thou'rt, sh'as, we're, you're, they're. Other forms are not typical

---

[1] Bald, "A New Manuscript, " 474.

[2] Okes' hand in the printing was discovered by Standish Henning, and briefly announced in his edition of A Mad World (London: Edward Arnold, 1965), p. xx. The simplest proof of Okes' presence is that the tail ornament matches Ornament No. 31 in C. William Miller, "A London Ornament Stock: 1598-1683," SB, 7 (1955), 125-51. (Henning: private communication.)

[3] See F. P. Wilson, "Ralph Crane, Scrivener to the King's Players," The Library, 4th ser., 7 (1926), 194-215; and Bald, "An Early Version." My study of The Witch is based on the edition of W. W. Greg and F.P. Wilson (Oxford: The Malone Society, 1948), and line numbers refer to this text.

of Middleton, but are paralleled in other Crane manuscripts, for instance the "Jonsonian" elisions /I'am, I'haue, we'are/, which probably
represent original Middletonian /I'me, I'ue, weere/.

1.2.3.2. A Chaste Maid in Cheapside

The Crane manuscript of The Witch provides the last attribution of
a play to Middleton alone before the dramatist's death in 1627. A
Chaste Maid in Cheapside (Q 1630) has a full title-page ascription:
"By Thomas Midelton Gent." The style of the play is clearly Middletonian
throughout, though somewhat diluted as to certain features; for instance,
there are only 17 'em beside 27 them. Middleton's more distinctive
spellings, such as /e'm/ and words ending in -cst, are absent, so that
we may suppose that a scribal copy underlies the printed text.[1]
Nevertheless, several distinctive contractions occur, namely I've, you're
and they're, and there is one push.

1.2.3.3. The Moseley attributions, 1653-57

After A Chaste Maid, there is no recorded attribution of a play to
Middleton alone until 9 September 1653. On that date Humphrey Moseley
entered in the Stationers' Register More Dissemblers Besides Women,
Women Beware Women, and No Wit, No Help like a Woman's, ascribing them
all to "Mr. Tho. Midleton". Four years later he published all three
as "by Tho. Middleton"--More Dissemblers and Women Beware Women in one
octavo volume, Two New Playes (O 1657), and No Wit separately (O 1657).
Middleton's authorship of these plays is not doubtful: though spelling
evidence is lacking, the pattern in all of 'em, has, does rather than
them, hath, doth, and the appearance of sh'as, you're and they're, are
quite Middletonian; in addition, No Wit has five instances of push,
while the other plays have pish--which may represent push as modified
by scribal transmission.[3]

---

[1] See the introduction by Charles L. Barber to his edition of A
Chaste Maid (Edinburgh: Oliver and Boyd, 1969), p.10.

[2] G. E. Briscoe Eyre, A Transcript of the Registers of the Worshipful
Company of Stationers, 1640-1708, 3 vols. (1913-14; rpt. New York:
Peter Smith, 1950), I, 428-29. This work is hereinafter cited as
"Eyre".

[3] For the scribal nature of the copy for Two New Playes, see the
introduction by Charles L. Barber to his edition of Women Beware
Women (Edinburgh: Oliver and Boyd, 1969), p.13.

A minor problem arises in the case of No Wit: the text has certainly suffered interpolation or alteration after Middleton's death,
since there is a reference in III.i.288-89 (O 1657, sig. E7) to the
year 1638. Moreover, James Shirley's Poems (1646) contain "A Prologue
to a play in Ireland ; call'd No wit to a Woman's".[1] The date 1638
certainly fits Shirley's known residence in Ireland, so that it has
sometimes been assumed that our text of No Wit represents a revision
by Shirley for an Irish production. But apart from the single passage
mentioned above, there is no trace of a non-authorial hand, certainly
not of Shirley's, which would probably be noticeable.

In a parallel case, Cyrus Hoy was easily able to detect Shirley's
revision of Fletcher's The Night Walker by the appearance of the typical
contractions shat (for "shalt"), shannot, wot, wonnot, and d'ee.[2] None
of these appears in No Wit; moreover, Middletonian contractions rare
in Shirley's plays (such as I'm and I've) are if anything rather more
abundant than is usual in late Middleton, whereas we might expect a
revision to have diluted these features. We may conclude that beyond
the single passage noted there is no evidence for any late tampering,
and we may therefore admit No Wit to the unassisted Middleton canon.[3]

1.2.3.4. The 1656 attributions: "Rogers and Ley" and "Archer"

In 1656 there appeared two soi-disant "exact and perfect" catalogues
of printed plays. The first of these was prefixed to Thomas Goffe's
play The Careless Shepherdess, published by Richard Rogers and William
Ley; the second was appended to The Old Law (by Massinger [?], Middleton,
and Rowley; see below, 1.2.5.5, 4.4), published by Edward Archer.[4]
The Rogers and Ley catalogue[5] is a wretched performance. As Greg

---

[1] The interpolation and the link with Shirley are noted by Bullen
(I,xl). My quotation of the Shirley prologue title is from Greg,
Bibliography, II, 886, the first edition of Shirley's Poems not
being available on microfilm.

[2] "Shares," SB, 12 (1959), 109; see also 13 (1960), 78.

[3] The date of composition of No Wit was most probably 1612, as has
been convincingly shown by Lowell E. Johnson, in "A Critical Edition
of Thomas Middleton's No Wit, No Help like a Woman's," Diss.
Wisconsin, 1964, pp. lxxiv-lxxvii.

[4] Both catalogues are reprinted in Greg, Bibliography, III, 1320-38.

[5] I refer to the catalogues of 1656 hereinafter as "Rogers and Ley"
and "Archer" purely for convenience: it is not known who (if any one)
edited them.

remarks, "the titles seem to have been jotted down, perhaps from
dictation, and sent to press with little or no revision".[1] Only a
minority of plays are attributed to authors, and many of these attributions are obviously wrong or ludicrously garbled. For example, "Bondman'
gets two entries: the first time it is ascribed to "Messenger", the
second time to "Fletcher". The latter entry is doubtless due to the
entry "Bonduca, Fletcher" in the line below. Elsewhere, "Marstone" is
credited with "Fanne" (a turned-letter error for "Faune"). Even more
ridiculous mistakes are discussed by Greg in his excellent article
on all the early play-lists.[2] Yet interestingly, "Rogers and Ley" contains
one entry which seems to correct by omission an earlier title-page ascription. The Widow had been published in 1652 with a title-page and address
"To the Reader" both of which gave the authors of the play as Jonson,
Fletcher and Middleton, in that order. "Rogers and Ley" lists the play
as "Widdow, by Midleton" (see below, 1.3).

The Archer catalogue is a better piece of work, but it is still
very far from being truly "exact and perfect". It is, in the first
place, not an authority entirely independent of Rogers and Ley, for
it repeats some of the earlier list's more elementary errors, including
the attribution to Marston of "Fanne". Thus the Archer attribution of
The Widow again to Middleton alone may have no significance. Much
more interesting are three other entries:

Family of love	$\left	c^3 \right	$	Thomas Middlton [sic]	[Item 207] [4]
Michaelmas tearm	$\left	c \right	$	Thomas Middleton	[Item 360]
Mad world my masters	$\left	c \right	$	Thomas Middleton	[Item 364]

---

[1] Bibliography, III, 1321.

[2] "Authorship Attributions in the Early Play-Lists," Edinburgh
Bibliographical Society Transactions, 2 (1946), 305-29.

[3] The "C" in the central column of the Archer list is a classifier
meaning "Comedy".

[4] Item numbers for the early play-lists are quoted from Greg's
reprints.

The last of these entries confirms our belief in Middleton's authorship of A Mad World by expanding the initials "T. M." to the full name. The other two attributions are of totally anonymous plays.

1.2.3.4.1. Michaelmas Term

Michaelmas Term, as it happens, is given by Rogers and Ley to Chapman. But this may have been due to a mechanical error, since the line above the entry reads "Monsier D'Oliva. Chap." And internal evidence sustains the Archer list against its predecessor, for the play (Q 1607) has the full range of Middletonian features, both of style and spelling-- the exclamations push and puh, the contractions I've, sh'as, 'tas, we're, you're, they're; overwhelming preferences for 'em, has, does over them, hath, doth; and plentiful instances of the spellings /e'm, ha's/ and /do's/. Middleton's authorship of Michaelmas Term has never been questioned: the play was clearly printed from his autograph.[1]

1.2.3.4.2. The Family of Love

The situation is very different as regards The Family of Love (Q 1608). This play contains neither push nor puh; no I'm, I've, sh'as, 'tas, we're, you're, they're; more hath than has, nearly as many doth as does, and them more than twice as often as its contracted. form--which is spelt in every case (21 times) /'hem/ or /hem/, spellings never used by Middleton. In short, on a superficial examination The Family of Love reveals hardly any Middletonian features, and several positively non-Middletonian ones. Thus it certainly cannot be accepted as a member of the undoubted canon; it will be examined in detail in 2.3.

1.2.3.5. The Kirkman attributions, 1661

The next attributions to Middleton appear shortly after the Restoration. In 1661 Francis Kirkman, a bookseller, publisher, and collector

---

[1] See Richard Levin's edition of Michaelmas Term (London: Edward Arnold, 1967), xxii-xxiii. Interestingly, like Mad World, Michaelmas Term (Q 1607) had two printers, Thomas Purfoot jnr. for sheets A-B, and Edward Allde for the rest of the play (see George Price, "The First Editions of Your Five Gallants and of Michaelmas Term," The Library, 5th ser., 8 [1953] , 26-28). The Middletonian /ha's, do's/ are frequent, and /e'm/ predominant, in both printers' portions. Contrast Allde's 1607 quarto of Sharpham's The Fleer (Table I.1), where the spellings are consistently /a(')m, has, does/.

of old plays, appended his own drama catalogue to a reprint of the inter-
lude Tom Tyler and his Wife.[1] Kirkman's list is a great improvement on
Archer, but it is still not an entirely independent authority, since it
repeats some of Archer's obvious mistakes.[2] Among Kirkman's original
attributions are two anonymous plays which he gives to Middleton: Blurt,
Master Constable (Q 1602) and The Phoenix (Q 1607), both printed by
Edward Allde.

1.2.3.5.1. The Phoenix

The Phoenix is certainly Middleton's, as it exhibits nearly the full
range of features that we have noted in A Game at Chess. There is a
great preponderance of the colloquial forms 'em, has, and does, which
are very frequently spelt /e'm, ha's, do's/, thus suggesting autograph
copy;[3] contractions include I've, sh'as, 'tas, we're, you're, and
they're; and though there is no push there are two instances of puh.

Daniel B. Dodson has claimed[4] that Dekker's hand is to be found in
the play, mainly in the first and last scenes. But his arguments are
nearly all of the types discussed in 1.1.4: he relies heavily on rather
commonplace parallels of image and idea. And the passages which he
claims most confidently for Dekker are full of Middletonisms. Thus,
for example, the Duke's very first speech contains two Middleton contractions which never occur in Dekker's undoubted work, wee're and I'ue
(I.i.6,7; sig. A2). The rest of this "Dekker" scene contains /ha's/
twice (A2, A2v) and /e'm/ (A3). Similarly, the last scene from Tangle's
entrance (V.i.267; Klv) to the end, a section claimed by Dodson as due
to Dekker imitating Jonson's Poetaster, contains /ha's/ (Klv, twice),
/do's/ (K2v), and two instances of I'ue (K2, K2v).

It would seem reasonable, therefore, to include The Phoenix in the
undoubtedly unassisted Middleton canon.

---

[1] Kirkman's catalogue is reprinted in Greg, Bibliography, III, 1338-52.
Kirkman produced a revised catalogue in 1671, but his revisions do not
affect the problems of the Middleton canon.

[2] For example, the ascription of The Duchess of Suffolk to Heywood, and
of The Arraignment of Paris to Shakespeare. (Greg, "Authorship Attributions," 321-22).

[3] Price, "Setting by Formes in the First Edition of The Phoenix,"
PBSA, 56 (1962), 426-27.

[4] "Thomas Middleton's City Comedies," pp. 74-98.

1.2.3.5.2. Blurt, Master Constable

The same cannot be said of Blurt, Master Constable. Here we find neither push nor puh, but a range of oaths quite foreign to Middleton's practice--Ho God, by Jesu, God's lid, gods me, Gods my life, and O Lord. Has and does predominate, but they are spelt invariably /has/ and /does/; nor is there a single instance of 'em (in any spelling), I"m, I've, sh'as, 'tas, we're, or you're, and only one instance of they're. Moreover, a few contractions appear which Middleton rarely or never uses: it's, wod, and wut.[1]   Thus the usage of Blurt is both positively and negatively unlike that of Middleton, and so the play must be excluded from the undoubted canon and reserved for detailed examination later (2.2).

1.2.3.6. Hengist, King of Kent (The Mayor of Quinborough)

On 13 February 1661 Henry Herringman entered in the Stationers' Register "A Comedie called the Maior of Quinborough, By Tho: Middleton",[2] and the same year published the work in quarto with the same ascription. This is the play which I shall refer to by its more suitable alternative title, Hengist, King of Kent--not a comedy, indeed, but a tragedy with a comic sub-plot. Hengist exists in three early texts: Herringman's Q 1661, and two manuscripts closely related to each other. The quarto represents an inferior and shortened version of the play, with an altered ending; the better of the two manuscripts (the Lambarde) is the basis of the edition used for this study.[3] The style of Hengist is clearly Middletonian, though some of the features found in A Game at Chess are missing, probably through repeated scribal copying. Thus there are five instances of pish, but no push; no I've, sh'as, 'tas, we're, or you're, but I'm and they're occur, and there is a very great preponderance of the colloquial forms 'em, has, and does.

---

[1] In this study I treat wut as a contraction of woult, but wod, wud, etc. as merely spelling variants of would. However, it is possible that wod, wud, etc. were also true contractions, and that l was sounded in would; see Helge Kokeritz, Shakespeare's Pronunciation (New Haven: Yale Univ. Press, 1953), pp. 311-12.

[2] Eyre, II, 288.

[3] Hengist, King of Kent, ed. R. C. Bald (New York: Scribner's, 1938). All my line references are to this edition. Bald describes the early texts (pp. xxiv-xxxvi), showing that the manuscripts are scribal copies of a prompt-book.

Middleton's presence in Hengist has never been denied; but Swinburne[1] and Charles W. Stork[2] have suggested William Rowley as the author of the comic scenes. The linguistic evidence is not very strong, but what there is of it tends to disprove Rowley's presence. Rowley uses the contractions i'th', o'th', and on't much more sparingly than Middleton: thus in his nearly contemporary All's Lost by Lust (Q 1633; first performance, c.1619-20)[3] the instances of i'th', o'th', o'the, and on't total only 6 in combination over the whole play, nearly 2000 lines (Table I.1); whereas in the main comic scenes of Hengist (III.iii.1-259; IV.i; V.i), over 680 lines of text we find 8 i'th', 5 o'th', and 11 on't, totalling 24--which represents an average relative frequency for the whole group of contractions about twelve times as high as Rowley's. Moreover, V.i contains two instances of the contraction y'ad (lines 252, 256) and one of the exclamation pish (line 284), neither of which occurs in Rowley's plays.[4] We may fairly conclude that there is no substantial case against Middleton's sole authorship, and add Hengist to the unassisted canon.

1.2.3.7. Anything for a Quiet Life

The list of seventeenth century attributions of plays to Middleton alone ends in 1662 with the publication by Kirkman of the comedy Anything for a Quiet Life. The title page of Q 1662 declares it to be written by "Tho. Middleton, Gent." However, examination of the play's textual features reveals anomalies. The linguistic pattern resembles that of Hengist, but there are fewer instances of 'em than of them, and very few of I'm; moreover, Middleton's style seems to be altogether missing from certain sections of the play, notably the whole of Act I. This pattern has suggested the theory that Anything for a Quiet Life is a collaboration: H. Dugdale Sykes was the first to propose Webster as

---

[1] Mermaid series Thomas Middleton, I, xxii.

[2] William Rowley, his All's Lost by Lust and A Shoemaker a Gentleman, ed. C. W. Stork (Philadelphia: Univ. Pennsylvania, 1910), introduction pp. 46-47.

[3] For the dates of Hengist and All's Lost, see Gerald E. Bentley, The Jacobean and Caroline Stage, 7 vols. (Oxford: Clarendon Press, 1941-68), IV (1956), 884-85; V (1956), 1018-20. This work is hereinafter cited as "Bentley".

[4] Middleton has y'had elsewhere in Hengist (I.ii.37), in No Wit (Clv), and twice in More Dissemblers (E7, F8).

the author of about half the play.[1]   It is certainly true that the
linguistic pattern of <u>Anything</u> <u>for</u> <u>a</u> <u>Quiet</u> <u>Life</u> cannot be matched in
any play of the unassisted canon;   for which reason it must be excluded
and reserved for investigation later (4.1).

1.2.4.   <u>Development of Middleton's style</u>

Up to this point I have been delimiting the canon of relatively
undoubted plays on the basis of comparison with <u>A</u> <u>Game</u> <u>at</u> <u>Chess</u>.   But
before going on to review the collaborate plays attributed to Middleton,
it will be useful to consider his stylistic development.   <u>A</u> <u>Game</u> <u>at</u>
<u>Chess</u>, after all, dates from near the end of Middleton's life; and in
fact it is not in all respects an adequate representative of his earlier
manner.

The dates of composition of Middleton's plays have been well treated,
on the whole, by Bald ("Chronology"); his table of dates (p.43) has been
only slightly refined upon by later scholars.   Bald emphasizes the most
important chronological fact about Middleton's oeuvre: that it falls into
two very distinct halves, with a lacuna of perhaps four or five years
between the early (pre-1608) comedies and the later (post-1612) comedies,
tragi-comedies and tragedies.   Between the last of the early plays
(probably <u>Your</u> <u>Five</u> <u>Gallants</u>) and the first of the later plays (probably
<u>No</u> <u>Wit</u>) Middleton's style changed considerably.

Reference to Table I.1 will show that the early plays are marked by
the frequent use of oaths which tend later to disappear ('<u>sfoot</u>, '<u>slid</u>),
or to be used much more sparingly (<u>faith</u>, <u>troth</u>, <u>mass</u>).   Exclamations
also dwindle: <u>puh</u>, <u>pup</u>, and <u>tut</u> are frequent in the early plays but
rare or absent in the later, and there is also a decline in the frequency
of the interjection <u>why</u>.   On the other hand, <u>heyday</u> or <u>h(o)yday</u> appears
more frequently later.

There are also changes in versification and vocabulary which in
combination produce a marked "later manner".   Middleton's verse, from
his earliest undoubted play (<u>Phoenix</u>, 1603-04) onwards, is largely

---

[1] "A Webster-Middleton Play: <u>Anything</u> <u>for</u> <u>a</u> <u>Quiet</u> <u>Life</u>," in <u>Sidelights</u> <u>on</u>
<u>Elizabethan</u> <u>Drama</u>, pp. 159-172.

end-stopped, with considerable use of feminine endings and rhyme; between the earlier and the later plays the percentage of feminine endings increases from about 25% to about 45%,[1] while the frequency of rhyme decreases. At the same time, the use of a number of abstract words increases. Glory, joy, precious, sin, strange, and some others, are cited by Schoenbaum[2] as a proof of Middleton's authorship of The Second Maiden's Tragedy, but they are not very reliable for this purpose, since they mark Middleton's later style only, and especially his serious passages; however, if Second Maiden is proved to be Middleton's on other grounds, then the high frequency of these words in the play may show that the "late manner" was already fully developed by 1611, the date of the problem play.

In general, dating is an essential factor in authorship arguments: a doubtful play must be compared with plays of known authorship of a similar date. This poses a difficulty, certainly in the case of Blurt (Q 1602), and probably in that of The Family of Love,[3] since we have no reliable information on Middleton's dramatic style before 1603.

I.2.5. Collaborations traditionally ascribed to Middleton

In one sense, all collaborations must be regarded as "doubtful plays", for it is seldom possible to be certain that any section of text represents the unassisted and unrevised work of a single author. Four of the collaborations attributed to Middleton in the seventeenth century are also problematic as to authorial presence. Of the seven plays so attributed, two belong to Middleton's early period, and five to the later.

1.2.5.1. The Honest Whore

The First Part of The Honest Whore was published in 1604, presumably about November,[4] with Thomas Dekker's name alone on the title page.

---

[1] Contrast the figures given by Barker, "The Authorship of the Second Maiden's Tragedy and The Revenger's Tragedy," p. 127, and those on p.56: Phoenix, 26.8%, Michaelmas Term, 24% but No Wit, 45.2%, Chaste Maid 46.3%.

[2] Middleton's Tragedies, p. 196.

[3] Dated 1602 by Bald ("Chronology," 36, 43); see also 2.3.2.

[4] The Stationers' Register entry (which names no author) is dated 9 November 1604 (Arber, III, 275).

But Henslowe's _Diary_ records a payment of £5 by 14 March 1604 to
"Thomas deckers & midelton in earneste of ther playe Called the pasyent
man & the onest hore" (p. 209). Henslowe can hardly have been mistaken
about this; yet Middleton's hand in the play is nowhere very obvious at
first glance. This authorship problem will be dealt with in 2.1.

A Second Part is first mentioned, without author's name, in the
Stationers' Register entry of 29 April 1608 (Arber, III, 376). No
edition followed upon this entry, but 2 _Honest_ _Whore_ was published in
1630 with the title-page ascription to Thomas Dekker alone; the same
ascription occurs in the S. R. entry of 29 June 1630 (Arber, IV, 238).
Thus there is no external evidence to associate Middleton with the Second
Part of The _Honest_ _Whore_; nor is there any evidence that a two-part play
was even contemplated in 1604,[1] since the titles of the two quartos of
1 _Honest_ _Whore_ published in that year read as follows:

Q1: The Honest Whore, With, The Humours of the Patient Man, and the
Longing Wife.

Q2: The Converted Curtezan With, The Humours of the Patient Man,
and the Longing Wife.[2]

Since there is not the slightest trace of Middleton's style in 2 _Honest_
Whore (as the features recorded in Table I.1 testify), I shall treat
that play as undoubtedly a work of Dekker alone.

1.2.5.2. The Roaring Girl

The _Roaring_ _Girl_ was published in 1611 as "Written by T. Middleton
and T. Dekker". The date of composition, according to Bald ("Chronology",
37-39), may have been 1605, but was more probably 1607-08 (see also
2.1.1.4). The authorship of this play is not controversial, since the
styles of Middleton and Dekker appear clearly in separate scenes. Further
evidence supporting the usual scene-ascriptions will be offered in 2.1.1.4.

---

[1] I believe that 2 _Honest_ _Whore_ was not written immediately after Part I,
but most likely c. 1607. This is suggested by the much lower 'em:them
ratio and much lower frequency of oaths containing the name of God in
the second play. These features contrast not only with 1 _Honest_ _Whore_
but also with the Dekker sections of _Westward_ _Ho_ and _Northward_ _Ho_.
See below, 2.1.1.

[2] In this study title-pages or parts of title-pages are transcribed
according to the system used by Bentley in The _Jacobean_ and _Caroline_
Stage (and described by him, III, viii-ix), except that I ignore italics.

1.2.5.3. A Fair Quarrel

A Fair Quarrel, first published in 1617 as by "Thomas Midleton and William Rowley," was probably composed in 1615 or 1616 (Bald, "Chronology," 40,43), and is thus the first of the "later" collaborations traditionally ascribed to Middleton. There is no major controversy about the authorship, as the play falls fairly clearly into "Rowley" and "late Middleton" scenes. However, some fresh evidence for the authorship of particular sections will be offered in 4.4, which deals with the general "Middleton-Rowley" problem, in Wit at Several Weapons and elsewhere.

1.2.5.4. The Changeling

The Changeling was published in 1653 by Moseley as by "Thomas Middleton and William Rowley". It was licensed for performance by the Master of the Revels, Sir Henry Herbert, on 7 May, 1622.[1] Again, there is no major authorship controversy involved. I shall give evidence for the authorship of particular scenes in 4.4.2.5.

1.2.5.5. The Old Law

The Old Law (Q 1656) is given by its publisher, Edward Archer, to "Phil. Massinger. Tho. Middleton. William Rowley." Bald dates the composition of the play about 1616 ("Chronology," 41-43), but Baldwin Maxwell prefers 1618.[2] Probably all critics agree that Middleton and Rowley can be found in the text, but Massinger's share is dubious. This problem will be treated in 4.4.3.

1.2.5.6. The Spanish Gipsy

The Spanish Gipsy (Q 1653)[3] was attributed by its publisher, Richard Marriott, to "Thomas Midleton and William Rowley". This ascription was generally accepted till Sykes claimed the whole play for John Ford in 1924. Middleton's hand is not easily detectable in the text, and neither is Rowley's. This problem will be dealt with in 4.5.

1.2.5.7. The Widow

Finally, there is The Widow, a comedy ascribed in the 1652 quarto to Jonson, Fletcher, and Middleton. This will be the subject of investigation in the next section.

---

[1] Bentley, IV, 862.

[2] Studies in Beaumont, Fletcher and Massinger (1939; rpt. London: Frank Cass, 1966), pp. 138-146.

[3] The play was licensed by Herbert on 9 July 1623 (Bentley, IV, 893).

1.3. The Widow

The problem of The Widow[1] provides an encouraging precedent to
canonical investigators who make use of internal evidence, for in this
case, in the opinion of the great majority of scholars, the internal
evidence has refuted the original ascription, and that in spite of
repeated attempts to vindicate it. One of the most recent of these
attempts was made by myself, as will be described below (1.3.3): the
collapse of my theory in the face of negative checks has confirmed my
earlier belief that the present consensus in justified.

1.3.1. Early attributions and later opinion

The title-page attribution of Q 1652 is probably the responsibility
not so much of the publisher, Humphrey Moseley, as of the actor
Alexander Gough, the author of the preface "To the Reader". Moseley,
after all, was not averse to publishing plays as by Middleton alone: the
examples of No Wit, More Dissemblers, and Women Beware Women should
acquit him of any suspicion of fraud in this case, if fraud there was.
On the other hand Gough seems to go out of his way to repeat the attribution, referring to "this lively piece, drawn by the art of Johnson,
Fletcher, and Middleton".

Those scholars who in recent times have made the most thorough
studies of Jonson and Fletcher are unable to find either Jonson or
Fletcher in the play. Percy and Evelyn Simpson declare: "In our opinion
the play shows no sign of Jonson's hand. If he had collaborated, we
could hardly have failed to trace him in one scene, which travels over
ground familiar to him. In IV.ii Latrocinio and Occulto . . . pick
the pockets of their patients. The style is unmistakeably Middleton's,
in spite of the resemblances to The Alchemist, the mountebank scene in
Volpone, and the picking of Cokes' pocket in Bartholomew Fair."[2]
Cyrus Hoy finds the language pattern of The Widow entirely uncharacteristic
of Fletcher.[3]   These modern opinions derive support from the testimony
of Dyce, who records that in his copy of the quarto the names of Jonson
and Fletcher on the title page had been crossed out and the word "alone"

---

[1] See Bentley, IV, 900-03. My account of early attributions and later
opinions is heavily indebted to Bentley's useful summary.

[2] Ben Jonson, Works, ed. C. H. Herford and P. and E. Simpson, 11 vols.
(Oxford: Clarendon Press, 1925-52), X (1950), 339.

[3] "Shares," SB, 13 (1960), 78.

written, in an "old hand", after "Tho: Middleton".[1] "Old hands" are not
necessarily good authorities: in the case of The Second Maiden's Tragedy
successive "old hands" attribute the play to Thomas Goffe, Chapman, and
Shakespeare--wrongly in each case, as will be shown in 4.2. However,
this particular old hand seems to be supported by other seventeenth
century opinions. Bentley (IV, 901) notes that The Widow was included
in no early folio of Jonson or of Beaumont and Fletcher. I have already
noticed (1.2.3.4) the entries in the Rogers and Ley and Archer catalogues
which print only Middleton's name. Kirkman's catalogue gives the play
to "Midleton & Rowly", but Rowley's hand is not traceable in the text
(see below, 1.3.3), and no recent scholar has taken this ascription
seriously. It does, however, again suggest early dissatisfaction with
the "Jonson and Fletcher" of the 1652 edition. It is significant, too,
that the one constant factor in all the early attributions is the name
of Middleton.

1.3.2. Date of composition; comparison plays

The date of The Widow, established by parallels and a topical reference to the execution of Mrs. Turner in November 1615, is generally
agreed to be about 1616 (Bentley, IV, 902). Hence the appropriate comparison texts for the purpose of authorship investigations might be the
seven later Middleton plays, Jonson's Bartholomew Fair (1614) and The
Devil is an Ass (1616), and of Fletcher's unassisted plays especially
Monsieur Thomas, The Mad Lover, The Chances, The Loyal Subject, and The
Humorous Lieutenant, which probably date from between 1610 and 1619.[2]
Rowley has left so little undoubted unassisted work--only three plays[3]--
that for comparison purposes it had better all be taken into account.

1.3.3. Internal Evidence for authorship

The clearest proof of Middleton's sole authorship of The Widow is

---

[1] Thomas Middleton, Works, ed. Dyce, III, 339. The copy with these title-
page alterations is in the Dyce Collection of the Victoria and Albert Museum
(press mark 25.A.99).

[2] I follow Hoy's determination of Fletcher's unassisted plays, excluding therefore Wit Without Money ("Shares," SB, 8 [1956], 134). For the
dates of these five plays see Chambers, The Elizabethan Stage, 4 vols.
(1923; rpt. Oxford: Clarendon Press, 1951), III, 228; Bentley, III,
373-75, 318-23, 370-72, 343-46.

[3] All's Lost by Lust (c.1619-20), and the earlier rather doubtfully dated
A Shoemaker A Gentleman (c.1608?) and A Woman Never Vexed (c. 1610?).
For the exclusion of A Match at Midnight see App. I.1.2.1.

provided by the pattern of contractions. Hoy has noted the negligible use of ye (which eliminates Fletcher) and the great use of y'are, y'ave, and y'have (which eliminates Jonson). These points are valid, and there are others which Hoy has not cited: above all, the very frequent use in the play of I'm, I've, and they're. The table below displays this evidence (excerpted for convenience from Table I.1).

Table 1.3(1). The Widow: some significant feature-totals

	pish	tush	ha'	I'd	I'm	I've	thou'rt	you're, they're	le'me	i'
Middleton										
NWNH	3	.	.	17	31	17	5	6,15	.	.
CMC	3	1	14	1	11	1	.	4,6	.	.
MDBW	2	.	.	7	26	2	2	6,5	.	.
Witch	.	.	4	3	14	3	8	7,10	.	.
Heng.	5	.	.	6	28	.	.	,6	.	.
WBW	5	.	.	6	34	.	.	2,9	.	.
GC	.	.	2	8	27	2	3	5,5	.	.
Widow	9	.	26	12	62	23	7	9,25	4	7
Jonson										
BF	.	.	[137]	5	.	.	.	.	2	58
DA	.	.	[100]	4	2	.	.	.	.	30
Fletcher										
M.Thom.	.	.	1	.	1	.	.	1,	.	1
ML	1	.	2	.	.	.	.	1,	.	.
Chan.	.	.	.	.	6	.	.	,1	.	.
L.Sub.	.	.	2	.	2	.	.	,2	.	.
HL	.	.	.	.	.	.	.	,1	.	.
Rowley										
Sh.G.	.	3	.	7	7	.	1[a]	5,	.	.
WNV	.	2	.	15	13	.	.	.	.	.
ALL	.	13	4	2	8	.	.	.	.	.

Notes   For abbreviations of play titles in this and all subsequent tables, see the list of abbreviations in App. I.1.6.2.
   The figures for ha' in square brackets are quoted from Hoy's table in "Shares," SB, 14 (1961), 64. All other figures are based on my own counts. I'm, I've do not include I'am, I'ave; thou'rt, you're, they're do not include th'art, y'are, th'are. The contraction i' includes all elisions of in except those followed by the definite article or the noun faith.   [a]Occurs as thor't

It will be clear that all but two of the features tabulated for The Widow support the theory of Middleton's sole authorship. The exceptions are the contractions i'[1] and le'me ("let me"). These are without parallel in the 12-play Middleton canon, and seem to

[1]Comprising i'thee, E4v; i'my, F3v, G2; i'thy, F4, Glv; i'moon light, G3v; i'your, Hl.

suggest touches from the hand of Jonson.[1] Once the suspicion of
Jonson's presence is aroused, it can be supported by other scraps of
evidence, such as the elision of "you" in V.i.278, sig. I2v--

> Are yo' he' faith, my chain of gold? I'm glad on't

--and two instances of I'ave (Flv, Hlv). Both these features approximate
Jonsonian practices.[2] Also, the 26 instances of ha' (for "have") seem
rather a high figure for late Middleton, but easily explicable if due
to the presence of Jonson.

That, indeed, is what I thought these features indicated when I
first examined the text of The Widow. I did not believe that any portion
of the play was unadulterated Jonson, because the "Jonsonian" features
occur imbedded in Middletonian passages. Thus, the yo' in in V.i.278
is in the same line as the Middletonian contraction I'm. This situation
could easily be explained if Middleton had revised a Jonsonian text, or
vice versa.

However, the theory is defeated if we take into account the Middleton-Rowley collaborations. Neither i' nor le'me occurs in Rowley's
unassisted work, whereas i' is fairly frequent in sections of A Fair
Quarrel, The Old Law, and the masque The World Tossed at Tennis which
are attributable for other reasons to Middleton.[3] Le'me occurs in a
clearly Middletonian scene in Wit at Several Weapons (IV.i; Beaumont
and Fletcher 1647 Folio, page 82, column a), and appears there in the
same phrase in which it occurs in The Widow: le'me see.[4] As for the
other contractions, yo' for "you" occurs in Your Five Gallants, sig.
D2 (yo'ue, for "you have"), and I'have (though probably not authorial)
does occur in The Witch (e.g. line 519) and in More Dissemblers (e.g.
B3v); so that these contractions in The Widow may easily be due to
Middleton, a scribe, or a compositor. Of course, they may for all that
be due to Jonson; but the theory of his presence is clearly an unnecessary one, since there is nothing in The Widow that cannot be accounted
for otherwise.

---

[1] Le'me in The Widow (II.i.175, sig. D2, twice; III.i.17, Elv; IV.ii.10,
G2) was noticed by Oliphant, in The Plays of Beaumont and Fletcher, p.
495.

[2] For example, Jonson in the 1607 quarto of Volpone has yo'are twice
(Clv, Glv) and I'have four times (G4, H1, I2, M2v).

[3] See 4.4. Middleton's authorship of sections containing i' is proved
mainly from the occurrence of I've and we're.

[4] See 4.4.4. Middleton's authorship of IV.i. is proved by the occurrence of I've and we're, as well as five instances of i'.

There is even less evidence for Fletcher or Rowley--in fact, none at all. Oliphant (The Plays of Beaumont and Fletcher, p. 494) suggests rather hesitantly that "the first nine speeches of V.i" could be Fletcher's. But this passage contains no instance of any of Fletcher's very individual patterns of repetition, and V.i.2 (H2v) has they'r which is rare in Fletcher's usage. Probably Oliphant was influenced by the cadence of the verse, which has a high proportion of feminine endings. But Middleton's later verse is not always distinguishable from Fletcher's in this respect.

Assuming, then, that the text of The Widow as we have it is due to Middleton alone, we are left with two problems. The first is that of the strange distribution of Middletonian i', which appears in plays only (if we exclude the doubtful Family of Love) in The Widow and in the Middleton scenes of the collaborations with Rowley. There are two possible explanations: either i' has been suppressed by scribes or compositors in some of Middleton's later plays, or the feature in Middleton's usage was truly sporadic, and by sheer chance happens to occur only in texts of somewhat doubtful authorship. I think the latter explanation is more likely to be the true one, since i' does not occur (except in the combination i'th') in the holograph Game at Chess.[1] It is noticeable that the distribution of late Middletonian ha' is also somewhat sporadic, and this feature too appears regularly in the Middleton scenes of the collaborations with Rowley; but in Middleton's usage ha' is much more frequent than i', and therefore the problematic distribution does not quite occur. It also follows from the laws of chance that if an author has left a very considerable body of work in texts whose authorship happens to be disputed, odd distributions like that of Middletonian i' are almost certain to occur in some low-frequency features. A possibly similar case--that of woult--will be examined in 3.1, 3.2 and 3.3.

The second problem is that of Alexander Gough's attribution. This need not necessarily have been fraudulent: the plot of the play is rather more in Fletcher's manner than in Middleton's, and the Jonsonian parallel in IV.ii (noticed by the Simpsons: see 1.3.1) is obvious. Jonson and Fletcher could have helped to plot the play, or even have done some writing in it which Middleton later "revised out". The

---

[1] There are two instances of i' in Middleton's undoubted Inner Temple Masque, i'these (A3v) and i'me [=in me] (B2). Spelling evidence shows this masque to be printed from a Middleton autograph: see Appendix III, Table III(2).

important point, for the purposes of this study, is that in its present
form the text may be regarded as pure Middleton, and therefore may be
used as a basis of comparison in further authorship arguments. Henceforth, then, I shall treat The Widow as a member of Middleton's
undoubtedly unassisted 13-play canon.

The table below gives the distribution of significant features
through the text of the play.

Table 1.3(2). The Widow: distribution of significant features

Scene	Length (lines)	pish	ha'	I'd	I'm	I've	thou'rt	you're they're	le'me	i'
1.1	226	.	.	.	4	1	1	,1	.	.
1.2	252	.	2	.	3	.	1	3,	.	.
2.1	205	3	3	1	11	2	1	1,3	2	.
2.2	182	3	2	2	9	5	1	1,5	.	.
3.1	117	1	1	.	4	2	.	2,2	1	.
3.2	130	.	2	1	2	.	.	.	.	1
3.3	142	1	4	2	3	1	1	,2	.	.
4.1	153	.	4	.	4	1	.	,2	.	3
4.2	294	.	4	1	7	2	1	,2	1	3
5.1	457	1	4	5	16	9	1	2,8	.	.
Totals:	2158	9	26	12	63	23	7	9,25	4	7

Notes   In this and subsequent scene tables (not text), arabic
numerals are used under the column heading Scene or Section to
signify Act and Scene. The line-count here is that of Bullen.

2. Earliest Middleton

2.1. 1 Honest Whore

2.1.1. Middleton and Dekker, 1600-1608

The three problem plays of the earliest years of Middleton's career,
1600-04--Blurt, Master Constable, The Family of Love, and 1 Honest Whore--
all involve the possible or certain authorship of Thomas Dekker.
Middleton's collaborations with Dekker began at least as early as May
1602, as we know from Henslowe's Diary (p. 202), and continued till at
least the date of The Roaring Girl (probably 1607-08). The three
problem plays are best approached by moving gradually from certainty
to uncertainty: this will necessitate a preliminary comparison of the
unaided work of Middleton and Dekker, 1600-08, followed by an examination
of their collaboration in The Roaring Girl, followed in turn by an
attempt to ascertain their shares in the least problematic of the
problem plays, 1 Honest Whore. Experience gained in this problem may
then prove useful for the more difficult problems of Blurt and The Family
of Love.

2.1.1.1. Collaborations in 1604: the argument of Schoenbaum

In 1604 there were at least two Middleton-Dekker co-operative vent-
ures, for Dekker acknowledges Middleton's authorship of Zeal's speech
in his Magnificent Entertainment for James I given on 15 March;[1] while,
as noted in 1.2.5.1, Henslowe paid £5 to Dekker and Middleton in earnest
for the Prince's Men's play [1] Honest Whore before 14 March, and the
first and second editions of the play were printed before the end of
the year.

Henslowe could hardly have been mistaken about the double authorship,
but so little of Middleton's style is apparent in 1 Honest Whore that
a problem of authorial presence does arise. Schoenbaum, attacking the
meagre items of internal evidence previously presented, went so far as
to suggest that Middleton "possibly . . . withdrew altogether from the
collaboration".[2] He argued that Middleton's contribution must in any
case have been minimal, or else Dekker, who was so scrupulous about one
speech in his pageant, would certainly have acknowledged it. The point

---

[1] Thomas Dekker, Dramatic Works, ed. Fredson Bowers, 4 vols. (1953-61;
rpt. with corrections, Cambridge, Eng.: Cambridge Univ. Press, 1964-70),
II (1964), 299. This edition is hereinafter cited as Dram. Works.

[2] "Middleton's Share in The Honest Whore, Parts I and II," NQ, 197
(1952), 3-4.

is well taken, though perhaps the absence of an authorial preface to
1 Honest Whore somewhat diminishes its force: the title-page attribution was presumably the work of the publisher, Thomas Man. But
certainly it is necessary to examine the text of 1 Honest Whore to
determine whether Middleton withdrew (or was revised out) or did
actually contribute to the final version of the play.

2.1.1.2. Bases for comparison: the unassisted Dekker corpus

    To distinguish Middleton's work from Dekker's in 1 Honest Whore
it is necessary to compare the unassisted plays of the two authors,
especially those not too distant in time from 1604. For Middleton
the five early comedies are suitable, The Phoenix being almost exactly
contemporary.

    As regards Dekker, the situation is not quite so favorable. I
would suggest that there are seven plays, ranging over about twenty years,
which may be taken to constitute an undoubtedly unassisted Dekker
corpus; as follows:

Play title	Probable date of composition[1]	First edition[2]	Printer
The Shoemaker's Holiday	1599	Q 1600	V. Simmes
Old Fortunatus [revised version]	1599	Q 1600	S. Stafford
Satiromastix	1601	Q 1602	Edw. Allde
2 Honest Whore	c.1605-07	Q 1630	Eliz. Allde
The Whore of Babylon	c.1605-07	Q 1607	?
If This Be Not a Good Play the Devil is in it	1611-12	Q 1612	T. Creede
Match Me in London	c.1611-20	Q 1631	{ B. Alsop & T. Fawcett

    I believe it likely that The Noble Spanish Soldier (c. 1622-31;
Q 1634) and The Wonder of a Kingdom (c. 1623-31; Q 1636)are also

[1] The dates of the first three Dekker plays are non-controversial; the
dates given for the rest represent my own opinions based on the evidence
summarized in Chambers' The Elizabethan Stage, III, 290-98 and Price's
Thomas Dekker, pp. 172-75.

[2] My study of Dekker's plays is based on the edition of Fredson Bowers,
but I have also consulted the first editions, especially to check the
exact form of speech prefixes such as Omnes. I have used Bowers' edition
also for all the Dekker collaborations and plays of doubtful authorship
contained in it, except 1 Honest Whore.

unassisted Dekker plays, but because of the title-page attribution of
the former to "S.R.", and the obvious relationship of both to John Day's
Parliament of Bees,[1] they can hardly be called "undoubted". Several
also of the seven plays which I have called "undoubtedly unassisted"
have been called in question in the past, but on very flimsy grounds.
I have already dealt with the authorship of 2 Honest Whore (1.2.5.1);
two other cases are perhaps worth mentioning.

Marston's hand has been suspected in Satiromastix, because the play
is the avowed "untrussing" of Jonson by "the Poetasters" (Satiromastix,
preface "To the World, " Dram. Works, I, 309, Line 12), i.e. Marston
and Dekker. Yet the title-page names Dekker alone, and the preface,
which is certainly Dekker's,[2] continually uses the first person singular; for example, "in untrussing Horace, I did onely whip his fortunes"
(lines 23-24); "the limmes of my naked lines" (line 43); "I dedicate
my booke" (lines 48-49); and several other similar phrases. These
points are noted by Price (Thomas Dekker, p. 54), who concludes very
reasonably that the reference to "the Poetasters" is not to Marston and
Dekker as authors, but as characters in Satiromastix, i.e. Crispinus
and Demetrius, who untruss Horace-Jonson in V.ii. Moreover, there is
not a trace of Marston's style in the text of the play, as the features
totalled in Table I.1 make clear, but plentiful signs of Dekker.
Marston in his contemporary What You Will (1601; Q 1607) decidedly
prefers hath and doth; Satiromastix decidedly prefers has and does.
Marston hardly ever uses it's or between, and never I'd or wou't;[3]
Satiromastix has all these forms in abundance. Bowers finds (Dram. Works,
I, 301-02) that the copy for Satiromastix was a Dekker autograph, as is
shown by typical spellings. Thus the external evidence and every
category of internal evidence points to Dekker as sole author. Marston
doubtless assisted Dekker with advice and encouragement, but that does
not affect the authenticity of the text for purposes of comparison.
Advice is not authorship.

---

[1] See Bentley, III, 257-60, 273-75.

[2] This is confirmed by Dekker's betweene (line 8) and It's (line 16),
and the typically very high frequency of parentheses.

[3] I use the generalized form wou't for all l-less spellings of "woult":
Dekker's normal spelling of wou't is /wut/, as in all instances in
Satiromastix. Similarly, I use wou'd for any l-less spelling of
"would".

Daborne's presence has sometimes been suspected in If This Be Not because of a remark in the preface to his tragedy A Christian Turned Turk (Q 1612), where he claims that if he had wished to see his name in print he "had prevented others shame in subscribing some of [his] former labors, or let them gone out in the diuels name alone". But the inference from this dark saying is by no means certain, and in any case Daborne's hand is not traceable in If This Be Not; for an obvious example, the play's does:doth ratio of 25:1 contrasts strongly with Daborne's overall ratio of does, 4 :doth, 50 in his two plays (see Table I.1). Many features of If This Be Not (most strikingly the high rate of Omnes; for which, see below) make it clear that the play is very pure Dekker throughout.

2.1.1.3. Dekker and Middleton: differences

Granted, then, that we have seven unassisted plays of Dekker, we may examine their features (totalled in Table I.1) and contrast the usages of Dekker and Middleton. Only three of the Dekker plays--Satiromastix, 2 Honest Whore, and The Whore of Babylon--are near enough in time to 1 Honest Whore to provide a valid comparison,[1] but all the plays must be taken into account if we are to gain an adequate picture of Dekker's stylistic development.

2.1.1.3.1. Dekker's stylistic development, 1599-1608; the Ho plays

In some respects Dekker's style was evolving rapidly over the period 1600-05; unfortunately we have no unassisted play from 1602-04 to trace the progress of the changes, and only two--2 Honest Whore and The Whore of Babylon--to illustrate their outcome. Moreover, the genre of The Whore of Babylon (political allegory) may render it a little suspect as a source of evidence for Dekker's use of colloquialisms. In the circumstances, it will be prudent to take into account also the Dekker scenes in Westward Ho and Northward Ho, which have been distinguished from those of Webster on the basis of linguistic evidence by Peter B. Murray.[2] The two Ho plays, both published in 1607, are dated by Chambers at late 1604 and late 1605 respectively;[3] hence Westward Ho is especially close

---

[1] As regards the use of linguistic features such as colloquialisms and contractions; but the other plays can be used as a source of parallel collocations.

[2] "The Collaboration of Dekker and Webster in Northward Ho and Westward Ho," PBSA, 56 (1962), 482-86. My study of the Ho plays is, like Murray's, based on Dram. Works.

[3] Elizabethan Stage, III, 295.

in date to 1 Honest Whore. According to Murray, in Westward Ho Dekker
wrote Act II and IV.ii-V, and in Northward Ho I.ii-II.i, IV, and
V.i. 360-517; Webster wrote the rest of both plays except Northward Ho,
V.i.263-359 (of uncertain authorship). Murray's assignments are based
exclusively on the distributions of ha', has:hath, does:doth, 'em,
and I'm; I have checked them with additional evidence. It will be
convenient to summarize this evidence in the table below, where "Dekker"
and "Webster" refer to Murray's assignments (the "uncertain" portion
of Northward Ho being left out of account).

Table 2.1(1). Westward Ho and Northward Ho

	Westward Ho		Northward Ho	
	"Dekker"	"Webster"	"Dekker"	"Webster"
it's	4	.	4	.
Total gp. sp.	36	2	23	3
Omnes	15	1	20	1
wou'd	12	2	18	1
wou't	3	.	.	1

The distributions of it's and of group speeches--both features
favoured by Dekker, but not Webster, as can be seen from Table I.1--
clearly support Murray's divisions (for wou'd and wou't, see 2.1.1.3.2).
I shall therefore regard them as at least largely correct, and draw
upon the Dekker sections where necessary in the following account of
Dekker's stylistic development.

Like several other Jacobean dramatists, Dekker made progressively
more use of colloquial forms, changing first from hath and doth, which
predominate in the plays of 1599, to has and does in Satiromastix
(1601); then, between 1601 and the date of 2 Honest Whore, he adopted
the contractions 'em and I'm.[1] These developments made Dekker's hand
more difficult to distinguish from Middleton's: indeed, as regards the
use of 'em and I'm, by late 1604 Middleton and Dekker are identical
twins, since in Westward Ho Dekker has 63 'em to 19 them, and 20 I'm to
22 I am; in Northward Ho, 19 'em to 9 them, and 23 I'm to 7 I am.[2]

---

[1] This series of changes is noted by Murray in "The Collaboration of
Dekker and Webster," 484.

[2] Dekker's use of 'em seems to have fallen off again before he wrote
2 Honest Whore ('em, 9:them, 74). The same decline is perhaps reflected
in The Whore of Babylon (7:116), but the genre difference may also be
involved here.

Luckily, another development serves to differentiate the two authors.
Before 1601 Dekker used the English form All to indicate a chorus-
speech; then, in Satiromastix, both All and Omnes; thereafter,
consistently, only Omnes[1]--whereas Middleton uses exclusively All in his
early comedies (and still in the vast majority of cases in his later
work). These prefix-forms are certainly authorial, since spelling
agreements with A Game at Chess indicate autograph copy for all five
early Middleton comedies (see 1.2.3), and Fredson Bowers finds
indications of autograph copy also for each of Dekker's unassisted plays;[2]
it is, of course, highly improbable that compositors would ever have
translated prefixes from English to Latin or vice versa.

2.1.1.3.2. Stable differences between Dekker and Middleton

As far as the evidence goes (and with the proviso that we have none
for Middleton's drama before 1603-04), it seems that certain differences
between the usages of Dekker and Middleton remained stable over the
period up to 1608. These are summarized in Table I.1. It may be useful
now to review the more important ones.

2.1.1.3.2.1. Exclamations

Dekker uses umh (as well as hum), and tush but never tut.
Middleton uses hum but never um or umh, and in his early plays tut but
never tush. Middleton's frequencies of push and puh are much higher than
Dekker's. His frequency of why is also somewhat higher (but see 2.1.3).

2.1.1.3.2.2. Oaths

Dekker regularly writes the name of God undisguised in such
expressions as God's lid (Old Fortunatus, IV.i.26; Satiromastix,
I.ii.385, IV.i.173), God's me (Shoemaker's Holiday, I.iv.31, IV.i.49),
God's so (Satiromastix, I.ii.276, II.ii.52; 2 Honest Whore, I.ii.1,
II.i.140), a Gods name (Shoemaker's Holiday, I.ii.60), and several others.
Middleton never uses the form God's undisguised, or even (in his undoubted
plays) the word God in a phrase which can be classified as an oath; he
also totally avoids the common expression of thanks, godamercy. In place
of God's he sometimes uses the euphemistic forms Cud's or Coad's, which
I have not found elsewhere in the Table I.1 corpus. This difference

---

[1] All does not include prefixes containing more than one word, such as All
three or All women: Dekker does continue to use these.

[2] Dram. Works, I, 9, 108-09, 301-02; II, 133, 493; II, 115, 253.

cannot be due to censorship, for at least two Middleton plays--Phoenix
and Michaelmas Term-- were acted before the 1606 Act of Abuses, which in
any case applied only to words spoken on stage, not to words in print.[1]
Nor did censorship suppress God's so in the 1630 quarto of 2 Honest Whore
nor the very mouth-filling oaths of Jonson's plays up to and including
Bartholomew Fair (acted 1614; published 1631), which has God's lid, God's
my life, God's so, O God, fore God, and a God's name.[2] Tables I.1 and I.2
show that the general disappearance of oaths including the undisguised
name of God is a phenomenon only of the period after 1615--and Lord
can still be found in the Caroline drama (e.g. in Brome's Northern Lass)
in spite of Sir Henry Herbert's notorious strictness; but Middleton
(unlike Dekker) avoids even Lord from his earliest undoubted work onwards.
Indeed, Phoenix contains the revealing euphemism "Jove" in a context where
its use sounds very odd: the disguised prince, in reply to the Jeweller's
Wife's remark My husband's newly brought a bed, makes the quip And
what ha's Ioue sent him? (IV.ii.24;H3) --where God would be normal in
real speech, and probably unobjectionable on stage. This squeamishness
clearly contrasts with Dekker's robustness. Middleton also avoids the
"strong" oaths 'sheart and 'sdeath, which Dekker uses.

On the other hand, Middleton uses the common oath byrlady, which
Dekker does not; and Middleton makes greater use of mass.

2.1.1.3.2.3. Affirmative particles

Both authors make increasing use of yes in their later work, but
Middleton's ay:yes ratio is always higher than Dekker's.

2.1.1.3.2.4. Connectives

Middleton clearly prefers beside (adverb or preposition) to besides;
Dekker even more clearly prefers besides. Middleton's use of while
and whilst is variable, but Dekker nearly always writes whilst.

2.1.1.3.2.5. Contractions

Middleton is outstanding among Jacobean dramatists in his considerable use of I've, t'as, and we're, which Dekker does not use at all.

---

[1] Chambers, William Shakespeare, I, 238-39.

[2] See App. I.3 for corpus plays first performed June 1606-December 1615
and containing Jesu(s), Lord('s), or God('s) in oaths.

Middleton's frequencies of y'ave, they're, and on't are all much higher than Dekker's. On the other hand, Dekker's frequency of it's[1] is equalled only by Jonson among the major dramatists, whereas Middleton in his early period uses it's only three times in five plays, and never more than once per play.

2.1.1.3.2.6 Comfort

We have already seen (1.1.5.1.1.6) that Middleton's frequency of the word comfort is remarkably high, and that of Dekker remarkably low.

2.1.1.3.2.7. 'Has

The ellipsis of "he" before "has" is another feature for which Middleton's frequency is much higher than Dekker's. There are never less than 4 instances of 'Has[2] in any early Middleton play, and no less than 12 in Phoenix; there are never more than 3 instances in any Dekker play, and four of his seven plays have no instance at all.

2.1.1.3.2.8. Wou't; wou'd and other spellings.

Middleton never uses the l-less contraction of woult, nor even the form woult in any of his undoubted plays; Dekker uses wou't (spelt /wut/) fairly frequently in Satiromastix, 2 Honest Whore, and If This Be Not. Similarly for l-less spellings of would: Middleton never uses them, but Dekker does so frequently in all his plays (except The Whore of Babylon)from Satiromastix onwards. Whatever the phonologic status of wou'd: would, Dekker clearly uses the l-less spelling as a colloquialism, since it does not occur in his prose, nor in the serious Whore of Babylon, nor in the less colloquial plays of 1599 (neither does wou't). Both wou'd and wou't also appear in texts which we can confidently attribute to Dekker. The distribution in the Ho plays has been given in Table 2.1(1): nearly all the l-less forms occur in Murray's "Dekker" scenes,[3] as we might expect, since Webster has only one l-less form in his three plays-- woo'd in The Devil's Law Case, sig. B2. There are 15 instances of wou'd and 1 of wou't (/wo't/) in The Wonder of a Kingdom; 18 wou'd, 1 wou't (/woo't/) in The Noble Spanish Soldier. The late Dekker-

---

[1] It's occurs once in Dekker's autograph addition to Sir Thomas More.

[2] 'Has is capitalized to indicate its occurrence in clause-initial position.

[3] The exceptions in Westward Ho probably indicate Dekker's presence in a "Webster" scene: wud twice in IV.i.112 three lines after em. Similarly in Northward Ho, wut in III.i.101 and wud in III.i.110 are followed a few lines later by Omnes, so that the suggestion of Dekker is strong.

Massinger collaboration The Virgin Martyr shows a similar pattern to
that of the Ho plays. Massinger in his unassisted plays never uses
wou'd; in the collaboration there are 12 instances of wou'd (/wud/) in
II.i, II.iii, III.iii, and IV.ii, all scenes given by scholarly consensus
to Dekker.[1] There is no considerable possibility that all these l-less
forms are due to compositors, since the nine different Dekker texts
involved had nine different printers.[2] In the case of Northward Ho, we
can establish fairly conclusively that the l-less spellings are not
compositorial, since George Eld in 1607 printed six other plays of the
Table I.1 corpus--Devil's Charter, Lingua, Puritan, Revenger's Tragedy,
Volpone, and What You Will, and, as we have seen (1.2.3.1.1), did not
take on new workmen during this period. There is no instance of wou't
in any of these six plays, and only one of wou'd (/wood/, in What You
Will, D2).

Dekker also differs from Middleton in his spellings of the common
words has and does. Middleton, as we have seen, wrote /ha's/ and
/do(')s/, but it is apparent from the almost invariable spellings of
Dekker's works, dramatic and non-dramatic, that he wrote /has/ and
/does/. The authenticity of /does/ is confirmed by its appearance in
Dekker's addition to Sir Thomas More (Dram. Works, I, 4, line 4).

2.1.1.4. The Roaring Girl

Before we attempt to distinguish the shares of Middleton and Dekker
in 1 Honest Whore on the basis of the features discussed above, it will
be useful to test these, and others which may be suggested by Table I.1,
on the various scenes of The Roaring Girl, since for this play there is a
fair degree of critical agreement as to the shares of the two authors.

The views of various scholars are summarized by Barker (Thomas
Middleton, p. 170); the most painstaking division, based partly on
linguistic features, is that of Price.[3] Barker's division (op. cit.,

---

[1] See Bowers, in Dram. Works, III, 369.

[2] For the undoubted plays, Edward Allde, Elizabeth Allde, Thomas Creede,
and Bernard Alsop and Thomas Fawcett (see 2.1.1.2); for Westward Ho (Q 1607)
William Jaggard; for Northward Ho (Q 1607), George Eld; for Wonder of a
Kingdom, Robert Raworth; for Noble Spanish Soldier, probably John Beale;
for Virgin Martyr (Q 1622), Bernard Alsop. See Bowers' textual introductions in Dram. Works.

[3] "The Shares of Middleton and Dekker in a Collaborated Play," Papers of
the Michigan Academy of Science, Arts, and Letters, 30 (1944), 601-15.

pp. 171-76) does not differ much from Price's, except in Act I, which Price treats as mixed, but Barker ascribes wholly to Dekker.

2.1.1.4.1. Text

Bowers argues convincingly (Dram. Works, III, 5-8) that the copy for the quarto (printed by Nicholas Okes, 1611) was a transcript made by Dekker. It follows from this textual situation that contractions and spellings typical of Dekker will carry less weight as evidence of authorship than contractions and spellings typical of Middleton.

2.1.1.4.2. Date of composition

The date of composition of The Roaring Girl is controversial, estimates ranging from 1604 to 1610. I believe that Bald's dating, 1607-08 ("Chronology," 37-39), is correct, as will be shown below (2.1.1.4.5).

2.1.1.4.3. Authorship division

In testing authorial discriminators, it is important to avoid circularity of argument. For collaborate plays, the principle to be observed is that features to be tested must not themselves be used to prove authorship. I shall therefore use the more reliable Middleton-Dekker discriminators[1] first to check the ascriptions of Price and Barker, and then use the checked ascriptions to test features which in the textual circumstances may be less reliable. Into the category of the "less reliable" must go the Dekker contraction it's and the spelling wou'd (wou't does not occur). Among the "more reliable" I will include as D markers the exclamation hump and the oath ud's so, neither of which occurs in Middleton.[2] Table 2.1(2) checks authorship, on the assumption (probably not far from the truth) that each author wrote whole scenes.

---

[1] For the sake of brevity, I shall refer to such "reliable discriminators" as "markers". Thus "M markers" will be features which reliably indicate the presence of Middleton, "D markers" that of Dekker. Less reliable features, when they are used to suggest authorship, will be called "pointers".

[2] Hump occurs three times in The Shoemaker's Holiday (V.v.15, 26, 33); ud's so once in 2 Honest Whore (IV.ii.27)--cf. also God's so in Satiromastix, 2 Honest Whore, and Dekker sections of the Ho plays.

Table 2.1(2). The Roaring Girl: authorship

Scene:	1.1	1.2	2.1	2.2	3.1	3.2	3.3	4.1	4.2	5.1	5.2	Totals
Length: (lines)	114	252	379	194	201	249	214	213	324	329	266	2735
M markers												
life	.	.	5	1	2	.	.	1	.	.	1	10
I've	.	.	.	1	1	.	.	3	.	.	1	6
we're	.	.	1	.	.	.	.	1	.	.	.	2
y'ave	.	.	.	.	.	.	.	.	.	.	1	1
push	.	.	3	.	.	.	.	1	1	.	.	5
puh	.	.	6	.	.	.	.	.	.	.	.	6
mass	.	.	4	.	1	.	.	.	.	.	.	5
ALL	.	.	1	.	.	.	.	.	.	.	.	1
while	.	.	.	1	.	.	.	.	.	.	1	2
/ha's/	.	.	.	.	.	.	.	.	.	.	3	3
'thas,'thad	.	.	1	.	3	.	.	.	.	.	.	4
D markers												
tush	.	.	.	.	.	2	.	.	2	.	.	4
umh	1	.	.	.	.	4	.	.	.	.	.	5
hump	.	.	.	.	.	.	1	.	.	.	.	1
ud's so(ul)	.	.	.	.	.	.	.	1	1	.	.	2
'sdeath	.	.	.	.	.	.	.	1	.	.	.	1
'sheart	.	.	.	.	.	.	.	1	.	.	.	1
OMNES	.	7	.	.	.	1	.	.	4	14	1	27
Lord	.	.	.	.	.	1	.	.	1	.	.	2
God('s)	.	.	.	.	.	1	.	.	2	.	.	3
godamercy	.	1	.	.	.	.	.	.	.	.	.	1
M-D score:	-1	-8	+21	+3	+7	-9	-1	+6	-11	-15	+6	-2

Notes   Life is the oath "[God's] life". Words in capitals are speech-prefixes. 'Thas, 'thad are presumed to be Dekker's rewriting of Middleton's 'tas, 'tad. The order of features is roughly that of reliability, the most reliable being placed furthest from the middle of the table.

From this table one can decide the authorship of any scene simply by subtracting the number of D markers from the number of M markers: a positive score will indicate Middleton, a negative score Dekker. This mechanical procedure works quite well for most scenes, because there is not much subtracting to do: the separation of features by scenes is nearly perfect, as we should expect with such markers if each author did write whole scenes. The results for I.i and III.iii do not seem very reliable, but at least the signs are probably right: both scenes display the verse and other characteristics of Dekker. The single push in IV.ii is compatible with Dekker's authorship, since Dekker uses push in Satiromastix (I.ii.48); the single Omnes in V.ii may be due to Dekker's transcribing hand.

It is reasonable to assume, therefore, that The Roaring Girl can be divided as follows:

    Middleton: II, III.i, IV.i, V.ii.   Total: 5 scenes, 1253 lines.

    Dekker: I, III.ii-iii, IV.ii, V.i.   Total: 6 scenes, 1482 lines.

This division agrees on the whole with that of Barker.

2.1.1.4.4. Test of Middleton-Dekker discriminators

We can now examine how the "less reliable" Middleton-Dekker discriminators are distributed between the two authors' shares. This information is tabulated below.

Table 2.1(3). The Roaring Girl: M/D discriminators, etc.

	M features						D features			M-D	Daters	
	'heart	com-fort	'Has	on't	why	ay	yes	it's	wou'd		'foot	'sfoot
Middleton Scenes 2.1	1	.	2	5	6	4	2	.	.	+16	.	.
2.2	.	.	.	1	8	.	.	.	.	+9	.	.
3.1	3	.	1	.	4	1	1	1	.	+7	.	.
4.1	.	.	1	2	1	8	.	1	.	+11	1	.
5.2	1	4	.	.	3	3	.	.	.	+11	.	.
Totals:	5	4	4	8	22	16	3	2	.	+54	1	.
Dekker Scenes 1.1	.	.	.	.	.	.	4	.	.	-4	.	.
1.2	.	.	1	.	1	1	3	.	1	-1	.	.
3.2	.	1	.	.	4	.	7	.	.	-2	.	.
3.3	.	.	.	.	2	3	2	.	.	+3	.	.
4.2	.	.	.	.	3	.	5	1	.	-3	1	2
5.1	1	.	.	.	.	2	1	.	3	-1	1	.
Totals:	1	1	1	.	10	6	22	1	4	-8	2	2
Whole play totals:	6	5	5	8	32	22	25	3	4	+46	3	2

This table is not designed to test authorship, but it may be interpreted as confirming in general the scene assignments made above. Since the whole-play total of M-D is far from zero, the score of +3 for III.iii does not mean that the scene is likely to be by Middleton: in fact the evidential value of why twice, ay three times and yes twice over 214 lines is very low. The two instances of it's in the Middleton scenes are probably traces of Dekker's transcription. Otherwise, it is notable that all the discriminators perform much as might have been expected from comparisons of the Middleton and Dekker unassisted plays, if not rather better: <u>on't</u>, <u>wou'd</u>, and the <u>ay</u>:<u>yes</u> ratio in particular function surprisingly well, and we are thereby encouraged to use them as authorship criteria in <u>1</u> <u>Honest</u> <u>Whore</u>.

2.1.1.4.5. Applications to 1 Honest Whore

A little caution may be needed, however, in applying some of these results to our main problem, because the two tables above contain clear indications of a later date of composition for <u>The</u> <u>Roaring</u> <u>Girl</u>. In that play Middleton uses the oath <u>life</u> 10 times, <u>heart</u> 5 times, and <u>foot</u> once; he does not use the exclamation <u>tut</u> or the oaths '<u>sfoot</u> or '<u>slid</u>. This pattern of oaths and exclamations is very similar to that of <u>No</u> <u>Wit</u> and <u>Chaste</u> <u>Maid</u>; it bears some resemblance to the pattern of <u>Your</u> <u>Five</u> <u>Gallants</u>, which was probably Middleton's last "early" comedy,[1] but it is fairly remote from the pattern of <u>Phoenix</u>, <u>Michaelmas</u> <u>Term</u>, <u>Mad</u> <u>World</u>, and <u>Trick</u>. Since <u>puh</u> does occur, however, and the <u>ay</u>:<u>yes</u> ratio is high, the likely date for <u>The</u> <u>Roaring</u> <u>Girl</u> is 1607-10. The evidence from Dekker's share points in exactly the same direction: with only one instance of <u>Gods</u> <u>so</u> (III.ii.148) and two instances of <u>Oh</u> <u>God</u> (IV.ii.138), Dekker's relative frequency of oaths containing the name of God is clearly much lower here than in the <u>Ho</u> plays of 1604-05,[2] and presumably reflects the decline which led to the disappearance of such oaths by the date of <u>If</u> <u>This</u> <u>Be</u> <u>Not</u>. The low rate of <u>it's</u> also suggests a late date. In several other features--the <u>ay</u>:<u>yes</u> ratio, the co-occurrence of <u>foot</u>, '<u>sfoot</u>, '<u>sdeath</u>, and <u>ud's</u> <u>so</u>--the Dekker scenes of <u>The</u> <u>Roaring</u> <u>Girl</u> resemble <u>2</u> <u>Honest</u> <u>Whore</u>, which, as we have seen, dates probably from about 1607, or at least later than the <u>Ho</u> plays. All things considered, 1608 seems to be the likeliest date for <u>The</u> <u>Roaring</u> <u>Girl</u>, which would thus be four years later than <u>1</u> <u>Honest</u> <u>Whore</u>. Hence conclusions as to the distinctiveness of features derived from their performance in the later collaboration may need some modifications as we turn now to apply them in the problem of <u>1</u> <u>Honest</u> <u>Whore</u>.

---

[1] It must be later than 5 November 1605 because of the allusion to the Gunpowder Plot in II.ii.14. Chambers (<u>Elizabethan</u> <u>Stage</u>, III,440) gives several reasons for the date 1607. The high frequencies of <u>heart</u> and <u>life</u> suggest relative proximity to <u>No</u> <u>Wit</u> and <u>Chaste</u> <u>Maid</u>.

[2] In the Dekker sections of <u>Westward</u> <u>Ho</u> the absolute frequency figures for such oaths are <u>God's</u>, 5; <u>God</u>, 5. For <u>Northward</u> <u>Ho</u> they are <u>God's</u>, 6; <u>God</u>, 6. (These figures exclude <u>gotz</u> Sacrament.)

2.1.2. 1 Honest Whore: text

There were two editions of 1 Honest Whore in 1604, presumably in rapid succession about November-December; the second edition, which has the altered title The Converted Curtezan, embodies revisions which seem to have been carried out by Dekker alone.[1]   Since Middleton's contribution will be contained, least tampered with, in the first edition, I have taken this (Q1) as the basis of my study. (Line references will be given to Dram. Works.)

Q1 was printed, according to Bowers (Dram. Works, II, 3), in three sections, comprising sheets A-B, C-D, and E-K; Valentine Simmes printed A-B, but the printers of the other sections are unknown. Hence spelling evidence will have to be used with caution.

2.1.3. 1 Honest Whore: whole-play totals

It is always possible to make a preliminary test of any argument that a play is a collaboration by comparing the whole-play feature-totals of the play in question with the corresponding totals of unassisted plays by the authors claimed to be involved. If we compare the totals for 1 Honest Whore in Table I.1 with those of nearly contemporary Dekker and Middleton plays, it becomes clear at once that Dekker was the major, but probably not the only, contributor. 1 Honest Whore agrees with Dekker's practices as regards all of the following features:

Exclamations: umh, tush.

Oaths: Lord, God's, God, 'sblood, 'sheart, ('s)nails.

Connectives: besides, whilst.

Contractions: it's, wou't; absence of I've, y'ave; low frequency of on't.

Prefixes: abundance of Omnes.

Comfort: only one instance.

Spellings: wou'd, does.

In several other respects, the figures for 1 Honest Whore are compatible with the authorship of either Dekker or Middleton, and are therefore useless as criteria at this stage. In this category I would place the frequency of why (47; relative frequency, 36.8[2]), which is obviously higher

---

[1] This is the likeliest conclusion from the evidence presented by Bowers, Dram. Works, II, 10-14.

[2] Relative frequency (abbreviated 'r.f.") in this study is estimated at so many instances per 20000 words (unless otherwise specified), usually to one decimal place.

than that in Satiromastix (24; r.f., 21.4) or in 2 Honest Whore (16; r.f., 12.9). But there are 25 why in the 1518 lines of Dekker's share of Westward Ho, which yields roughly the same relative frequency as the 47 why in the 2821 lines of 1 Honest Whore (lines being counted from Dram. Works). The lower rate in Northward Ho (10 why in Dekker's 1246 lines) suggests that Dekker's use of why rose to a brief maximum in 1604, and then declined; but the maximum was high enough to render why in 1 Honest Whore as useless for our purposes as 'em or I'm.

There are, however, several features whose whole-play totals do suggest the hand of an author other than Dekker, who could be Middleton. One notices the preponderance of ay over yes (not paralleled in the Ho plays), and the occurrence of byrlady, of certain spellings, and of the contraction exlent (which will be discussed in 2.1.4, s.v. I.v.a). Even if we were unable to allot specific scenes, we could say from these features that Middleton has probably contributed to the final text.

We may now proceed to look for traces of Middleton in the various sections of the play.

2.1.4. 1 Honest Whore: authorship divisions

It seems to be impossible to make authorship divisions in 1 Honest Whore with any great assurance; what one finds in the text are sections of apparently pure Dekker interspersed with sections of mixed authorship, and probably nowhere a scene which can be claimed for Middleton alone. I have assigned to "Middleton and Dekker" those sections where I think Middleton's presence is more probable than his absence; for the rest I am not at all confident, and Middleton may be present in some of the sections I have allotted to Dekker alone. Table 2.1(4), below, will summarize the linguistic evidence exclusive of parallel collocations, but there are so few certain Middleton markers in the text that the argument will often have to rely on such collocations. Mathematical methods, such as served for The Roaring Girl, will not be useful for assigning sections.

2.1.4.1. Summary of attributions

Middleton and Dekker: I.i, iii-v.a (to George's first exit, line 132); III.i.a (to line 50).

Dekker with minor assistance from Middleton: II.i; III.i.b, iii; IV.iii.

Dekker alone: I.ii, v.b; III.ii; IV.i-ii, iv; V.

2.1.4.2. Survey of scenes

I.i. (M. and D.) The first feature that suggests Middleton is the prefix All repeated twice on sig. A2; but in Gods name (line 5) points to Dekker. So does the spelling woud on A3 (I.i.72), which can hardly be due to the compositor if Bowers is right in identifying him with Compositor A of Shoemaker's Holiday, Q1 (Dram. Works, II, 4). Sbloud (A3, I.i.61) does not occur in Middleton's undoubted plays, but is found in The Puritan. The Middletonian birlady (A3v, I.i.102),[1] and the ratio ay, 3:yes, 1 for the whole scene, faintly suggest Middleton.

I.ii. (D.) Dekker's presence is signalled as early as line 3 by godamercy (A4), and is confirmed again and again by god sa me, O God sir, Gods so, gods lid, Gods my life (twice), woud (A4, I.ii.20), and its (A4v, I.ii.26). There is an interesting parallel to Dekker's unassisted plays in the collocation new Moone . . . horne mad . . . cuckold (B1, I.ii.90-93). This is a favorite witticism which occurs once in If This Be Not (III.ii.42-44) and three times in Match Me (I.iv.89, II.ii.22, II.iv.90), as well as twice in Dekker's IV.ii of Westward Ho (lines 140, 207-08); there is no instance in Middleton's undoubted plays.

I.iii. (M. and D.) The verse of the first part of this scene (up to the waking of Infelice) sounds more like Dekker's than Middleton's. Infelice's exclamation Oh God, what fearefull dreames? (B2v, I.iii.36) is perhaps more likely to be Dekker's. But Middleton's presence is strongly suggested by the three instances of the phrase la you now, which Dekker never uses. The third instance, in the Duke's Why la you now, you'le not beleeue mee (B3, I.iii.61) closely parallels Quomodo's Why la you now, you would not beleeue this (Michaelmas Term, I2, V.iii.33); the locutions are surely too colourless for one to be an imitation of the other. The ratio ay, 2: yes, O for the scene also suggests Middleton.

I.iv. (M. and D.) There are no good indicators of authorship in this short scene, but the rapid succession of ay (three times) and on't (twice) suggest Middleton. Sbloud (B4, I.iv.46) is more likely to be Dekker's.

---

[1] Be Lady occurs in a Dekker scene of The Roaring Girl (III.ii.232).

I.v.a. (M. and D.) Middleton's presence in the first 132 lines of
I.v is suggested by the ratio ay, 5: yes, 1, by the exclamations puh (twice)
and pah, by on't (twice), and by the phrase sonnes and heires (B4v, I.v.
26-27). Son(s) and heir(s) is a favorite Middleton expression which is
never used in Dekker's undoubted plays (though it does occur in Dekker's
Westward Ho, II.i.211). Again, /Ha's/ in line 50 (C1) is at once a
Middleton spelling and the elliptic 'Has for "he has".

Best evidence of all is the form exlent on C1v (I.v.86). This is not
a mere matter of spelling, but a contraction of "excellent" to a dissyll-
able, as is shown by the spelling ex'lent in Michaelmas Term (B4; I.ii.21),
and the spellings of all four instances in More Dissemblers--exc'lent
(C7; II.iii.81), exc'llent (D6v, III.ii.73; F4, V.i.168), and ex'lent
(D8v; IV.i.61). The spelling exlent, which occurs in Trick (H1; IV.v.168),
seems to be the one favored by George Eld's compositors of 1607-08, for
it also occurs in a Webster scene of Northward Ho (III.i.24). But apart
from the instances in Middleton's plays the contraction is extremely rare--
there is only one other instance in the undoubted plays of Table I.1,
/exc'lent/ in Ford's The Fancies Chaste and Noble (C4). Thus its occurrence in this scene of 1 Honest Whore is a very good proof of Middleton's
participation.[1]

On the other hand, this section of I.v does not sound like pure Middleton. 'Sblood, twice (C1, C1v), suggests Dekker. And George's sales-talk
epithet for his "taffataes"--affable (B4v, I.v.19)--occurs also in the
similar speech by Bilbo in Match Me (II.i.153).

I.v.b. (D) Dekker's presence becomes obvious at line 134 in the
oath Gods my life (C2), and is confirmed by Sheart (C3), to which, as
we have seen, Middleton always prefers the milder heart. The spelling
they're in the first line of C3 (I.v.184) might suggest Middleton if we
knew more about the printing of this section.

II.i. (D., with M.) The signs of Dekker are superabundant: Gods my
pittikins, Gods my pitty, Gods so, byth' Lord (twice), Godamercy, vmh
(four times), wut, wou'd (four times), it's (four times) and Omni. [sic]
(three times). There are also two instances of Marry muff, an expression

---

[1]Middleton's use of ex'lent was first pointed out by myself in "Middleton's Hand in The Puritan: the Evidence of Vocabulary and Spelling,"
NQ, 217 (December, 1972), 456-60.

never used in Middleton's plays, but occurring in Satiromastix (I.ii.347) and 2 Honest Whore (V.ii.278, 415). If confirmation is needed, it is provided by the ratio ay, 4: yes, 10, which should be fairly reliable over so long a scene. But strangely enough, the best spelling evidence for Middleton's presence also occurs here: e'm on C4 (II.i.16), facst on D1 (II.i.106) and fac'st on D1v (II.i.129). The contraction T'has (D3v, II.i.265) and possibly the exclamation Pah (D2v, II.i.211) also suggest Middleton.

III.i.a. (M. and D.) This is the only section of 1 Honest Whore where an early Middletonian manner becomes almost unmistakeable, and even here the pure effect lasts only for a few speeches--perhaps only for the first by Fustigo. The second of these (E2, III.i.10-11) contains the Middletonism Spoke like, a form of speech-opening used when one character comments on the preceding utterance of another. The most amusing instance is perhaps Andrugio's Spoke like the sister of a Puritan Midwife (More Dissemblers, C7; II.iii.68). The collocation is quite rare outside the Middleton canon, and never occurs in Dekker's undoubted plays (see Table I.1).[1]

Other pointers to Middleton are the co-occurrence, within 50 lines, of faith (three times), troth (three times), mass, puh, sh'as, and ay but no yes. But even here I think traces of Dekker are perceptible: the playfulness of language (Lacedemonian, mallicolly), and besides (E2, III.i.16), not beside.

III.i.b. (D., with M.) Dekker's presence is signalled at line 52 (E2v) by the oath Sneales (i.e. "God's nails"), followed at line 56 by Nailes. One or other form of this oath occurs in Shoemaker's Holiday, If This Be Not, and Dekker's Addition to Sir Thomas More; Middleton never uses it. Other Dekkerisms here include: as God judge me, O Lord, Tush, it's, Omn[es] (three times). The ratio ay, 5:yes, 2 suggests that Middleton may also have done some writing in this section, and he was very likely responsible for George's last speech (Flv, III.i.251-53), which contains two Middletonisms:

Well, if youle saue me harmlesse, and put me vnder couert barne . . .

---

[1]   But in The Roaring Girl there are three instances of Spoke like (I.ii.236, III.i.124, III.iii.139), two of them in scenes assigned above to Dekker.

The collocation save .. harmless occurs three times in Middleton's undoubted plays (Michaelmas Term, F4, III.iv.112; Trick, D4, III.i 137-38; No Wit, Flv, IV.i.85); vnder Couert Barne occurs in Phoenix (F4, III.i.75). Neither collocation occurs in Dekker's unassisted plays (though saue him harmles occurs in Westward Ho, V.iv.200-01).

III.ii. (D.)   Dekker's authorship is indicated by the oaths Gods my life, God dam me . . . if, and by Mary gup (which occurs in Shoemaker's Holiday, I.ii.31, but never in Middleton). Bellafront's speech attacking the Bawd (F2, III.ii.30-42) sounds like a Middleton cliche, and its verse is somewhat Middletonian, but there is nothing in it that Dekker could not have written.

III.iii. (D., with M.) There are not many reliable marks of authorship here. Omn[es], Sbloud, and the spellings th'art (three times) and th'are suggest Dekker; but ay, 3:yes, O; subaudi (F3, III.iii.20); and sonne & heire (F3v, III.iii.60) point to Middleton. Schoenbaum ("Middleton's Share," p.3) discounts subaudi, but he has noticed only the instance in The Family of Love, whereas the word occurs also, in the same context of illicit sexuality (subaudi lechery), in Your Five Gallants (E3v, III.iv.11); there is no other instance in Table I.1. I suspect this scene is Middleton revised by Dekker.

IV.i. (D.) The only definite suggestions of Middleton here are the phrase by their Copy (F4v, IV.i.3) and the two instances of /they're/ on Gl (IV.i.62,63), and these are flimsy evidence. It is possible, of course, that Dekker is here revising Middleton: the collocation by .. copy occurs four times in Middleton (Phoenix, Kl, V.i. 237; Trick, C4, II.i.322-23; No Wit, E3, III.i.65; Women Beware Women, K4v, III.i.59), never in Dekker. But Dekker is notably fond of parentheses, and there are ten pairs of parentheses in the first two quarto pages of the scene, including two pairs round single words--(then), (now)--on F4v.

IV.ii. (D.) This short scene contains one god sa me. There is a possible parallel to Middleton in Fustigo's Cods life I was neere so thrumbd since I was a gentleman (G3v, IV.ii.17), which faintly resembles Sam Freedom's Coades-Nigs, I was never so disgrac'st, since the houre my mother whipt me (Trick, C4, II.i.329-30). Both utterances contain the word "God's" disguised by a change of G- to C-, but the vowel phoneme of Cods is presumably short and that of Coades is certainly long.

The resemblances between the two speeches are in fact of that general kind which often occurs in borrowings; whereas repetitions of favorite locutions by the same author usually present us with items identical in minute particulars.

IV.iii. (D., with M.) Dekker's authorship is indicated by gods my life, A Gods name, and vmh (twice). The sequence of ten instances of ay to only one of yes from line 56 to the end of the scene probably indicates some contribution from Middleton.

IV.iv. (D.) There are few good indicators of authorship here. W'are (H2v, IV.iv.27), and possibly Thei'r (H3, IV.iv.33), might suggest Middleton, but /W'are/ is at least an un-Middletonian spelling. Vmh (H3v, IV.iv.74) more clearly points to Dekker.

V.i. (D.) Dekker's authorship is indicated by Its (I1, V.i.70) and Omn[es] (I1v, V.i.98). There is no reason to suspect Middleton's presence.

V.ii. (D.) The final scene is very full of indications of Dekker's authorship, but even here I am not quite sure that Middleton did not have a hand in at least one passage. The Sweeper's speech on I3v (V.ii. 125-29) contains the sentence:

> Citizens sons and heires are free of the house by their
> fathers copy . . .

As we have seen, both son(s) and heir(s) and by .. copy are Middletonisms. But apart from this single passage, the evidence is all for Dekker, comprising O God (twice), gods so (twice), bith Lord (twice), gods santy, Tush, Omnes (13 times), wut (twice), it's (three times), and the ratio ay, 8:yes, 10. The ratio 'em, 14: them, 8 is, as we have seen, perfectly compatible with Dekker's colloquial style of 1604-05 as revealed in the Ho plays.

2.1.5. Conclusion

In conclusion, I think it may be said that all the evidence points to very close collaboration by Middleton and Dekker in 1 Honest Whore. Certainly Dekker is the main author, but equally certainly Middleton did not withdraw from the joint venture. It is likely that he was mainly employed to furnish first drafts which Dekker revised. The very different relationship between the two authors a few years later in The Roaring Girl is perhaps an indication of Middleton's higher reputation as a dramatist after the production of his plays of 1605-07.

The totals of markers in Table 2.1(4), below, furnish a method of expressing numerically (but roughly) the size of Middleton's contribution to 1 Honest Whore. 8 Middleton markers out of 65 total (M+D) markers = 8/65 = 12.3 per cent. Alternatively, the "Middleton and Dekker" sections total 478 lines, or 16.9 per cent of the whole play; and Dekker's share in these sections probably at least balances Middleton's share elsewhere. Unless Middleton did much writing which was revised out of the final text, one hopes in the interests of justice that Henslowe's £5 was not divided equally.

Table 2.1(4). 1 Honest Whore: M/D discriminators

Section	Length (lines)	M markers					D markers				
		pah	byr-lady	sub-audi	ex-lent	/e'm/, /facst/	wou't wou'd	'sbl-ood	'sheart, ('s)nails	Lord God(s)	Umh
1.1	143	.	1	.	.	.	,1	1	.	,1	.
1.2	136	.	.	.	.	.	,1	.	.	,7	.
1.3	100	.	.	.	.	.	.	.	.	,1	.
1.4	53	.	.	.	.	.	.	1	.	.	.
1.5.a	132	1	.	.	1	.	.	2	.	.	.
1.5.b	106	.	.	.	.	.	.	2	1,	,1	.
2.1	456	1	.	.	.	1,2	1,4	.	.	2,4	4
3.1.a	50	.	.	.	.	.	.	.	.	.	.
3.1.b	255	.	.	.	.	.	.	.	,2	1,1	.
3.2	84	.	.	.	.	.	.	.	.	,2	.
3.3	129	.	.	1	.	.	.	1	.	.	.
4.1	199	.	.	.	.	.	.	.	.	.	.
4.2	43	.	.	.	.	.	.	.	.	,1	.
4.3	177	.	.	.	.	.	.	.	1	,2	2
4.4	120	.	.	.	.	.	.	.	.	.	1
5.1	116	.	.	.	.	.	.	.	.	.	.
5.2	522	.	.	.	.	.	2,	.	.	2,5	.
Total:	2821	2	1	1	1	1,2	3,6	8	1,2	5,25	7

Total of markers: M = 8; D = 57

Section	Length (lines)	M pointers							D pointers			
		puh, mass	ALL	on't	't has	com-fort	'Has, /ha's	ay	yes	it's	OMNES	tush
1.1	143	.	2	.	.	.	.	3	1	.	.	.
1.2	136	1,	.	.	.	.	1,	.	1	1	.	.
1.3	100	.	.	.	.	.	.	2	2	.	.	.
1.4	53	.	.	2	.	.	.	3	.	.	.	.
1.5.a	132	2,	.	2	.	.	1,1	6	1	.	.	.
1.5.b	106	.	.	.	.	.	.	.	1	.	.	.
2.1	456	.	.	.	1	.	.	4	10	4	3	.
3.1.a	50	1.1	.	.	.	.	.	1	.	.	.	.
3.1.b	255	,2	.	1	.	.	.	5	2	1	3	1
3.2	84	.	.	.	.	.	.	1	.	.	.	.
3.3	129	.	.	.	.	.	.	3	.	.	1	.
4.1	199	.	.	.	.	.	1,	1	2	.	.	.
4.2	43	.	.	.	.	.	.	.	.	.	.	.
4.3	177	.	.	.	.	.	.	10	2	.	.	.
4.4	120	.	.	.	.	.	1,	2	1	.	.	.
5.1	116	.	.	.	.	.	.	3	1	1	1	.
5.2	522	,2	.	1	.	1	.	8	10	3	13	1
Total:	2821	4,5	2	6	1	1	4,1	52	34	10	21	2

Notes "Markers" here include only Middleton features which do not appear in Dekker's undoubted plays, and Dekker features which do not appear in Middleton's undoubted plays. God('s) here includes godamercy. More reliable discriminators are placed at the extremities of the table.

2.2. Blurt, Master Constable

2.2.1. Text

Blurt, Master Constable was entered in the Stationers' Register
for the copy of Edward Allde on 7 June 1602 (Arber, III, 207). In the
same year appeared the only early quarto (Q 1602), published by Henry
Rockytt, a close associate of Allde, and printed by Allde himself, as
has been proved by Thomas Berger, in his useful critical edition of
the play.[1]

Allde in the same year printed two other plays, the anonymous
Alarum for London and Dekker's Satiromastix. Berger shows (pp. 16-19, 21)
that all three plays were set by the same single compositor.

From an inspection of the text I conclude that the copy for the
play was an authorial draft annotated for performance; and this finding
is confirmed by Berger (pp. 19-21). The hand of the annotator is most
clearly shown by the "early warning" on sig. F2v, A song presently within;
also by the frequent mention of properties in stage-directions. The
hand of the author is shown by indecision in specifying characters --
the "Boy" who is to exit on A3v, and the women who are to take the two
parts of the song on C3-C3v (Berger, loc. cit.). (There is also abundant
evidence to suggest autograph copy once the authorship question has been
decided.)

Berger (p.61) finds no variants in the surviving copies of the
quarto; but there is one rather different text of a part of Blurt to
be considered. The Folger Library copy of Q 1602 lacks the last four
pages, H2-H3v, and these have been supplied in manuscript by the same
person (scribe or author) who wrote or transcribed the manuscript play
Dick of Devonshire (Anon.; composed c. 1626), as has been shown by
James G. McManaway.[2] The four-page Blurt manuscript contains some
significant variants, one a certainly correct emendation of the quarto
text (MS. signe for Q's figure, H2v, the rhyme-word being mine), and the
others including three instances of I'm where the quarto reads I am
(Q, H2=MS. first page, twice; Q, H3 = MS. third page, once). McManaway
decides (p.30) that the scribe of Blurt had access to a manuscript

---

[1] "A Critical Old-Spelling Edition of Thomas Dekker's Blurt, Master
Constable (1602)," Diss. Duke, 1969.

[2] "Latin Title-Page Mottoes as a Clue to Dramatic Authorship," The
Library, 4th ser., 26 (1946), 28-36.

source, probably prompt copy; but even if this conclusion is accepted,
we are not bound to assume that the three I'm are authorial, since
I'm does not appear at all in the quarto, whereas I am occurs 70 times.
Most probably, in each case the scribe contracted I am to I'm without
authority, in order to "improve" the metre--just as Dyce and Bullen
did more then two hundred years later.[1] I shall show (5.1.4.2) that the
scribe of Blurt interfered considerably not only with the text of Dick
of Devonshire (if he did not compose it) but also with those of The
Bloody Banquet and of Robert Davenport's A New Trick to Cheat the Devil.
By all indications, he was not a person to follow copy closely. I shall
therefore treat Q 1602 as the only reliable authority for the text of
Blurt.

2.2.2. Date of composition

The date of composition of Blurt is fixed accurately by the reference
in the last scene (H3v, V.iii.179) to Spaniards in Ireland. The Spanish
raid in Ireland began in September 1601,[2] so that composition must have
been completed after this date, and before the Stationers' Register entry,
7 June 1602.

Since the date 1601-02 is two years earlier than that of Middleton's
earliest undoubted play, Phoenix, a question arises as to the validity
of the comparative method. But the lack of exactly contemporary Middletonian drama is not fatal: it is possible to rely on usages which are
not likely to vary appreciably in two years, such as preferences for
certain connectives, and (to some extent) spellings.

2.2.3. Authorship controversy

The title page of Q 1602 contains no mention of authorship. It
reads as follows:

Blvrt Master-Constable. Or The Spaniards Night-walke. As
it hath bin sundry times priuately acted by the Children of Paules.
---Patresq; securi. Fronde comas vincti canant, et carmina dictant.
[Device] London, Printed for Henry Rockytt [etc.]

---

[1] Bullen's text of Blurt is liberally sprinkled throughout with silent
alterations to I'm wherever this gives a smoother verse line than Q's
I am.

[2] Chambers, Elizabethan Stage, III, 439.

The first explicit recorded attribution is that of Francis Kirkman, 1661, to Middleton (see above, 1.2.3.5). Kirkman's attribution became the settled tradition, unquestioned till 1926, when Oliphant remarked in the course of his Revenger's Tragedy article that Blurt seemed to be falsely attributed to Middleton and to be "in reality the work of Thomas Dekker" ("The Authorship of The Revenger's Tragedy," p. 166). Oliphant's suggestion was supported by Eccles in "Middleton's Birth and Education," (1931; pp. 432-34). Eccles used his discovery that Middleton was born in 1580 (not "c. 1570") to cast doubt on Middleton's authorship of Blurt; certainly, the assured and sophisticated manner of the play does not seem like the work of a tyro barely 22 years old. The Phoenix is a very different and much clumsier performance. However, Eccles' negative argument, "there is no real evidence that Middleton turned professional playwright before 1602" (p. 432) has been pressed too far by later critics, who have been corrected by Phialas and by Eccles himself (see above, 1.2.1.2; Eccles, "Thomas Middleton, a Poett," p. 525). Middleton left Oxford between 28 June 1600 and 8 February 1600/1, and by the latter date he was "daylie accompaninge the players" in London, so that it is not quite impossible for him to have written Blurt in 1601-02.

Since 1931 many scholars have come to accept the arguments for Dekker's authorship of Blurt, but there have been no major studies relying on accurately cited linguistic evidence. Probably the best work of this kind is the brief summary by Barker (Thomas Middleton, pp. 197-200), which notes some oaths, the high frequency of chorus speeches, and a few not very impressive parallels. On the other hand, two items of external evidence have been found which point, more or less uncertainly, to Dekker's authorship.

The first is a passage in the anonymous play Wily Beguiled (Q 1606), cited by Schoenbaum:[1]

And then there wil be Robin Goodfellow, as good a drunken
rogue as liues: and Tom Shoemaker; and I hope you wil not deny
that hees an honest man, for hee was Constable oth Towne.
(Lines 1661-64.)

---

[1] "Blurt, Master Constable: A possible Authorship Clue," Renaissance News, 13 (1960), 7-9. My quotations from Wily Beguiled are from the edition by W. W. Greg (Oxford: Malone Society, 1912).

As Schoenbaum remarks, "the entire passage is irrelevant to the action
and transparently topical". A reference a few lines earlier to "an
honest Dutch Cobbler" (lines 1642-43) certainly reinforces the suggestion
that "Tom Shoemaker" means "Tom Dekker, author of The Shoemaker's
Holiday"; after which it seems likely that "to be 'Constable oth Towne'"
means "to be the author of Blurt, Master Constable".

The second item is reported by Juliet Gowan.[1] She notes that in
Edward Pudsey's commonplace book[2] extracts from Blurt occur in close
proximity to quotations from Dekker, whereas Pudsey "nowhere shows signs
of having read Middleton" (p.47).

At present, the controversy over the authorship of Blurt remains
unresolved. Most responsible scholars are aware that there is at least
strong suspicion of Dekker's authorship; yet David M. Holmes, in a
recent full-length study, is so confident of Middleton's authorship that
he erects a considerable critical argument for Middleton's art and
morality upon the evidence of this play.[3]

2.2.4. Authorship

2.2.4.1. Evaluation of external evidence

It may be well to begin the investigation into the authorship of
Blurt by evaluating the external evidence. The only evidence for
Middleton is Kirkman's attribution: now, Kirkman's accuracy in ascribing
anonymous dramatic works has been well analysed by Greg, on whose showing
(if we exclude Blurt) Kirkman is wrong at least as many times as he is
right.[4] Thus in the doubtful case of Blurt, even when the evidence of
Kirkman is considered in isolation, the chance a priori that Middleton
is the author is only about 50 per cent. This is not negligible, but
it is not enough for a confident attribution. Since, as we have seen, the
other external evidence all tends to cast doubt on Middleton's authorship, it is probably best to regard Blurt as a wholly anonymous play, and
to make a fresh start in an unprejudiced attempt to find the author.

---

[1] "Edward Pudsey's Booke and the Authorship of Blurt, Master Constable,"
Research Opportunities in Renaissance Drama, 8 (1965), 46-48.

[2] MS, Bodleian Library, Eng. poet. d.3.

[3] The Art of Thomas Middleton: A Critical Study (Oxford: Clarendon Press,
1970). See also "Thomas Middleton's Blurt, Master Constable or The
Spaniard's Night Walk," MLR, 64 (1969), 1-10.

[4] "Authorship Attributions," 328-29. Kirkman's correct attributions are:
1 and 2 If You Know Not Me, Imperiale, Queen of Aragon, Bloody Banquet,
Tamburlaine, Phoenix. Incorrect: Country Girl, Downfall and Death of
Robert Earl of Huntingdon, Two Wise Men, Apollo Shroving, Lord Hay's
Masque, Misfortunes of Arthur, Cynthia's Revenge.

2.2.4.2. Possibilities of authorship

The field of possible authors is necessarily unlimited, but the likeliest candidates might be among those dramatists known to have been active in 1601-02, and to have written for the boys' companies-- Middleton, Chapman, Day, Dekker, Jonson, Marston, and Webster (Daniel, also in this category, is so unlikely on literary grounds that he can safely be eliminated; I have in fact tested him by the methods to be described below, and find him unlikely also linguistically). I will therefore confine the inquiry to these seven authors in the first instance, and then later consider others who were writing for the theatre in 1601-02.

Should we be looking for a single author, or for more than one? Many partisans of Dekker have hesitated to claim Blurt for him exclusively. For example, Fredson Bowers excluded Blurt from his edition of Dekker, explaining: "Whether or not Dekker collaborated in Blurt . . . it is most improbable that he was the major contributor" (Dram. Works, IV, vii). George Price also suggests "an unknown collaborator" (Thomas Dekker, p.173). But these are unargued opinions, perhaps motivated by a desire to re-concile internal evidence with Kirkman's attribution. In fact there are no obvious signs of heterogeneity in Blurt--the same marked manner and distinctive usages appear (as I shall show below, 2.2.4.6) in all scenes. This is not an infallible proof of single authorship,[1] but at least it does not suggest collaboration. It is also perhaps relevant to note that the great majority of boys' companies' plays which have survived are by single authors: in the years 1600-10 inclusive there are thirty-three single-author plays to only eight collaborations.[2] In any case, a single author for an anonymous play is the simpler hypothesis. It is always difficult, if not impossible, to prove beyond question that there

---

[1] Schoenbaum (Internal Evidence, p. 168) notes the "consistency of texture" of the collaboration Eastward Ho.

[2] This estimate is based on the plays listed in A. Harbage, Annals of English Drama, revised S. Schoenbaum (London: Methuen, 1964). The collaborations are: Westward, Northward, and Eastward Ho, The Woman Hater, Cupid's Revenge, The Dumb Knight, The Coxcomb, and The Insatiate Countess.

is no second hand in a play; but it is surely best to assume that Blurt had only one author , unless and until evidence is found to suggest the contrary. I will proceed on the assumption of single authorship to identify the principal author of Blurt, and then consider whether a collaborator needs to be postulated.

2.2.4.3. Identification of the best candidate

We may first attempt to eliminate some of our seven "likely" candidates by comparing their linguistic habits with features of the Blurt quarto. In this way we may find a good candidate, whose authorship can then be verified or falsified by a more searching investigation.[1]

2.2.4.3.1. A synonyms test

As a preliminary test, let us examine the usage of our seven candidates and Blurt in the synonymous connectives and the synonym pair it's: 'tis. As usual, we must first select reasonable comparative samples of the work of each author. For Middleton, the only possible sample comprises the five early comedies. For Chapman and Day, I suggest all the comedies in Table I.1. For Dekker, the first five plays (Shoemaker through Whore of Babylon) are not too distant in date as regards these features; Satiromastix is especially suitable, since it was composed only a few months earlier than Blurt, and we have seen (2.1.1.2) that doubts about its single authorship are quite unfounded. For Jonson, the comedies in Table I.1 from Every Man In through Volpone are suitable in date. For Marston and Webster, all the plays[2] in Table I.1 can be used: though several are tragedies, this will not affect the argument, since the features to be examined do not seem to vary by genre among the plays of these authors. Webster's plays, unfortunately, are all much later in date than Blurt, so that in his case we must make allowances for possible changes in usage.

---

[1] It is my purpose here to make explicit and formal, for once, and as an example, what usually remains implicit and informal: a discovery procedure for an excellent authorial candidate. There will be no need (or space) to repeat this procedure for other problem plays, but it is similar processes of elimination that have led me to identifications of authors concerned (e.g.) in Ram Alley, A Yorkshire Tragedy, and The Spanish Gipsy.

[2] Jack Drum, long believed to be Marston's on internal evidence, has recently been confirmed as his by the evidence of Pudsey's commonplace book: see David L. Frost, The School of Shakespeare (Cambridge, Eng.: Cambridge Univ. Press, 1968), p.277. Pudsey's note (fol. 40^v) reads: Jack Drum marston.

Table 2.2(1) sets out the data for this test. In the first row, for comparison purposes, I have given the figures for Alarum for London (printed by Allde, like Blurt, in 1602), which is almost certainly by none of the authors who appear in the table. For each author I have given the figures for (1) the play nearest in date to Blurt,(2) the total of the select corpus described above, (3) the play in this corpus, other than that "nearest in date", which shows the extreme variation in a sense unfavorable to the arguments I shall employ below--the "worst" case. (The eliminations to be described below would follow no matter which play were chosen as "worst", as may be seen from the full data given in Table I.1.)

Table 2.2(1). The Blurt candidates: a synonyms test

| | amo- | | besid- | | betw- | | whil- | | it's | 'tis |
	-ng	-ngst	-e	-es	-een	-ixt	-e	-st		
Alarum for London	1	3	2	.	.	2	1	7	.	11
Blurt	3	.	.	8	4	.	1	3	7	27
Middleton Phoen.	3	4	2	1	7	.	2	.	.	66
5 comedies	24	32	26	5	24	6	13	5	3	309
MWM	1	5	6	1	2	2	3	3	1	56
Chapman GU	1	2	2	4	.	12	4	.	.	58
6 comedies	2	36	2	35	4	46	41	1	14	247
HDM	.	3	.	3	4	2	4	.	.	34
Day IG	1	7	.	.	.	11	1	11	.	51
3 comedies	1	21	1	3	1	19	1	21	.	129
Law Tr.	.	6	1	1	1	3	.	5	.	34
Dekker Sat.	6	6	1	5	3	.	1	8	10	83
5 plays	21	27	3	27	14	2	1	53	55	311
Wh.B.	1	5	.	3	3	.	.	18	3	41
Jonson Poet.	3	3	1	7	4	3	9	11	8	65
5 comedies	19	27	10	40	28	17	38	24	61	301
EMO	7	11	.	10	14	3	8	3	25	72
Marston WYW	4	.	.	.	.	6	.	9	.	52
8 plays	19	6	2	4	.	26	5	87	1	377
Malc.	3	5	1	2	.	3	1	16	.	52
Webster WD	.	7	.	3	10	.	9	3	.	55
3 plays	5	11	2	8	28	.	19	6	1	174
DLC	4	.	1	5	10	.	5	1	.	65

Note: figures for beside and besides are totals combining the adverbial and prepositional forms.

In employing the table, it may be reasonable to adopt the following rules: that an author is eliminated from consideration as a <u>Blurt</u> candidate only if his usage in the select corpus, as established by the concurrence of his "nearest" play, his total, and his "worst" play, clearly disagrees with that of <u>Blurt</u> in the high-frequency feature <u>it's</u>: '<u>tis</u> plus any one other feature. "Disagreement" would imply negligible use of <u>it's</u> (say, less than 5% of <u>it's</u>/(<u>it's</u> + '<u>tis</u>)), and opposite preference in the other features. These rules embody a large safety factor, which can be tested by examining Table I.1 to see whether they would eliminate any of our playwrights as a candidate for the authorship of any of his own undoubted plays. They certainly would not: the "worst" cases here are probably Middleton's <u>No Wit</u> and <u>The Widow</u>, with about 5 per cent. of <u>it's</u> but no other feature disagreement with the select corpus, and <u>A Game at Chess</u>, written twenty years later than <u>The Phoenix</u>, having clear preferences for <u>betwixt</u> and <u>whilst</u>, but no instance of <u>it's</u>.[1]

Applying these rules, then, to the problem of <u>Blurt</u>, we see that Middleton is eliminated, since he strongly prefers <u>beside</u>, and makes negligible use of <u>it's</u>, whereas the author of <u>Blurt</u> strongly prefers <u>besides</u> and chooses the form <u>it's</u> for the contraction of "it is" in 7 cases out of 34 (i.e. 21%). Middleton also slightly prefers <u>amongst</u> to <u>among</u>, and in most of his early plays <u>while</u> to <u>whilst</u>, so that his usage disagrees more or less with that of <u>Blurt</u> in four out of the five features in the table. It is noteworthy that this elimination of Middleton is effected by evidence never previously cited in this controversy, nor, to the best of my knowledge, in any other authorship argument in the field of Elizabethan drama. (However, since Middleton is the traditional author, I will continue to compare his usage with that of <u>Blurt</u>.)

Day is eliminated by negligible use of <u>it's</u>, <u>among</u>, and <u>between</u>; Marston by negligible use of <u>it's</u> and <u>between</u>. Moreover, Marston's very low frequency of either <u>beside</u> or <u>besides</u> (only 2 <u>beside</u> and 4 <u>besides</u> in his entire works, dramatic and non-dramatic[2]) renders him an unlikely

---

[1] I do not mean the <u>it's</u> test to be employed negatively: an author who often uses <u>it's</u> may well have a play with no instance of <u>it's</u> at all, e.g. Jonson's <u>Cynthia's Revels</u>. But an author who in several contemporary plays makes negligible use of <u>it's</u> is not likely to be the author of a play like <u>Blurt</u> where <u>it's</u> is plentiful.

[2] See Appendix IV.3.

author for Blurt.

Chapman barely survives, if we agree that his use of it's is not always negligible, though his preferences for amongst and while are the opposites of those found in Blurt, and he usually prefers betwixt.

If we can trust the evidence of Webster's three plays, he does not seem a very likely candidate, since his preference for while is opposite to that of Blurt, and he makes almost no use of it's.

The only clear survivors of the synonyms test are Dekker and Jonson. Of the two, Dekker fits the usage of Blurt rather better, since he shows strong preferences for besides, between, and whilst, whereas Jonson shows weaker preferences for besides and between, and no consistent preference for whilst. There is especially close resemblance between the usages of Blurt and of the nearly contemporary Satiromastix.

There is, of course, the possibility, which can never be completely eliminated, that the differences between Blurt and Middleton, and the agreements with Dekker, are due to scribal or compositorial intervention. Scribal interference is, however, very unlikely, since, as we have seen, all the early Middleton plays, all the unassisted Dekker plays, and Blurt itself, seem to have been printed from autograph copy.[1] The intervention of compositors is a possibility, and may to some slight extent account for resemblances between Blurt and the Allde quarto of Satiromastix; but there is no reason to believe that the Blurt compositor would have systematically introduced such forms as it's and besides into the text, since neither besides nor it's occurs in his text of Alarum for London. It is notable that the preferences in Alarum are opposite to those in Blurt for every one of the tabulated features except while: whilst. Hence the very close resemblance between the preferences of Blurt and Satiromastix cannot be attributed to the common compositor.

It is also relevant to remember that none of Middleton's undoubted plays, even of those transmitted by scribes (such as Ralph Crane's text of The Witch) and/or in editions of the 1650s, is so deviant as Blurt from the Middleton norms for connectives and it's.

---

[1] See above, 1.2.3, 2.1.1.3.1, 2.2.1.

2.2.4.3.2. Group speeches

Assuming, then, that we have not been misled by transmission accidents, we have succeeded in narrowing the field of likely Blurt candidates among extant dramatists to Dekker, Jonson, Chapman, and Webster. We can narrow it still further by comparing speech-prefixes. Barker (Thomas Middleton, p.199) has noted the high frequency of chorus-speeches in Blurt. In fact, not only the frequency but also the form of the Blurt chorus-speeches is significant. The table below gives the essential data for the surviving Blurt candidates and for Alarum, Blurt, and Middleton. This time the five Dekker plays are listed separately, since a change of usage (All to Omnes) must be recorded; for the other authors the play in the third row is that with the highest rate of group speeches.

Table 2.2(2). The Blurt candidates: group speeches

		Length (words)	Total group sp.	Group speeches per 20000 wds	Chorus speeches: ALL	OMNES
	Alarum	13126	1	1.5	1	.
	Blurt	18037*	20	22.2	.	17
Dekker	Sh.H.	19276	20	20.8	16	.
	OF	25636	25	19.5	8	.
	Sat.	22397*	22	19.6	4	10
	2HW	24832*	47	37.9	.	43
	Wh.B.	21807	53	48.6	.	36
Middleton	Phoen.	20840*	5	4.8	3	.
	5 comedies	101654*	24	4.6[a]	18	.
	YFG	21878*	10	9.1	9	.
Jonson	Poet.	28727	12	8.4	1	.
	5 comedies	154574	30	4.1[a]	10	.
	Poet.	---------------------- as above --------------------
Chapman	GU	21995	3	2.7	.	1
	6 comedies	121696	27	4.8[a]	3	9
	Mons.	16636	10	12.0	.	1
Webster	WD	26285*	5	3.8	.	2
	3 plays	75081	15	4.0[a]	.	2
	DM	24790	8	6.5	.	.

Notes *Fully counted. [a]This relative frequency is obtained by averaging the relative frequencies of all plays in the select corpus, not by pooling instances in the whole select corpus and then dividing by the total corpus length, i.e. each play is given equal weight in determining the average relative frequency.

Obviously, Dekker's fondness for group speeches is quite remarkable: his average relative frequency over the period 1598-1608, as represented by the five plays in the table, is 29.3 per 20000 words. The relative frequency in Blurt, 22.2, is a little lower than this, but higher than the relative frequencies of the earlier Dekker plays. No other "likely" candidate comes anywhere near the rate of Blurt: the highest rate among them is that of Chapman's Monsieur D'Olive, which still has only a little more than half the rate of Blurt. Moreover, this highest rate is produced by nine instances of a pair of characters speaking together: Chapman's rate of chorus-speeches is unremarkable in all his comedies. Middleton's highest rate of group speeches in his later plays is 10.8 per 20000 in both Chaste Maid and No Wit, so that he never attains even half the rate of Blurt.

It is also highly significant that the author of Blurt uses the Latin form Omnes for all his chorus speeches. As we have seen (2.1.1. 3.1), Omnes is the form Dekker adopted when he was writing Satiromastix in 1601, and used invariably thereafter.[1] Middleton uses Omnes only twice--once in Hengist (V.ii.290) and once in Women Beware Women (L6, III.ii.240), both late plays whose texts have been transmitted by scribes (see 1.2.3.3, 1.2.3.6). But All occurs 42 times in his 13-play canon. It is highly unlikely that if he had written the chorus-speeches in Blurt, he would have preferred Omnes to All in every one of 17 instances.[2] The same consideration applies to Jonson, who almost invariably prefers All to Omnes (see Table I.1).

It would seem, therefore, that the group-speech test eliminates all the "likely" candidates except Dekker. In frequency and in form of prefix, the group speeches in Blurt are just what we could expect of a Dekker play of 1601-02. In combination with the synonyms test, this evidence therefore enables us to choose Dekker as, prima facie, an excellent candidate for the authorship of Blurt.

2.2.4.3.3. The first sentence

Before seeking further evidence which may put Dekker's authorship of Blurt beyond reasonable doubt, it may be well to assure ourselves

---

[1] It occurs 188 times in his seven undoubted plays, with 84 instances in If This Be Not.

[2] It is possible to express this unlikeliness mathematically if we assume (1) that 2 Omnes out of 44 chorus speeches, i.e. 1/22, represents Middleton's probability of using Omnes on any one occasion, (2) that the 17 occurrences of Omnes in Blurt are independent of each other. Then the probability of Middleton writing a run of 17 Omnes in Blurt is the reciprocal of 22^{17}, i.e. one chance in 66190,000,000,000,000,000,000 (by 4-figure logarithms).

that the linguistic evidence examined above has not led us to a super-
ficially attractive but erroneous guess. For this purpose, we may seek
the confirmation of collocations in the text. We need not go very far
for these, since the first sentence of the play furnishes what we need:

Hipol [ito]. I Mary Sir, the onely rising vp in Armes, is
in the armes of a woman: peace (I say still) is your onely
Paradice, when euerie Adam may haue his Christmas Eue . . . (A2)

This contains two parallels to Dekker, the one probable, the second
certain.

(1) The pun on "rising up in arms" is echoed in the theatre-masque
The Sun's Darling, II.i, a scene usually ascribed to Dekker:[1]

Humor. Com then, let thou and I rise up in arms,
    The field embraces, kisses our alarms. (II.i.208-09)

(2) The collocation Adam/Eve is used twice in Dekker's undoubted
plays, both times in sexual contexts: Satiromastix, III.i.148; Match Me,
IV.i.95. This collocation is surprisingly rare in other dramatists,
as Table I.1 shows. It does not occur at all in Middleton. The only
instance among the "likely" candidates, in Jonson's Every Man In, I.iv.15,
has no reference to sexuality.

There are many more good collocational parallels in Blurt to Dekker's
works, as will be shown below (2.2.4.6); but those in the first sentence
of the play will suffice at this stage to show that our objective
linguistic tests have not led us astray.[2]

2.2.4.4. Confirmation of Dekker's authorship

2.2.4.4.1. Spelling evidence; wou'd; wou't; hyphens

The spellings of several common words in Blurt--for example, has
and does--agree with those found in Dekker's works, not with those (for
example, h'as or ha's and do(')s) found in Middleton's early comedies
and his holograph Game at Chess (see Table I.1). However, since Dekker's
spelling is unremarkable, that is not a strong argument in favour of

---

[1] E.g. by Price, Thomas Dekker, p. 110.

[2] This, I believe, is the basic usefulness of parallel collocations:
they should never be relied on to prove a case alone; but the lack of
parallels is a suspicious circumstance in any authorship case, and
therefore parallels should be cited as "defensive" evidence.

his authorship rather than that of (for example) Webster. It is true, but trivial, that there is remarkable agreement in the spelling of contractions--/Ile, you'll, we'll/ (etc.) and they're--between Blurt and Satiromastix; but since /Ile/ and the ‸ll spellings are those also used in Alarum for London, these resemblances must be due to the common compositor. (That Alarum is not by Dekker is shown by its preferences for beside and betwixt, and considerable use of ye--35 instances--as well as its lack of group speeches.) As Alarum also contains has but not h'as or ha's, it could be argued that the compositor of Alarum and Blurt would not have reproduced Middleton's spellings even if he had met them in copy.

The case is different when we come to the forms in Blurt of wou'd (3 times) and wou't (once), spelt /wod/ (D2v; F3, twice) and /wut/ (C4v). As we have seen, (2.1.1.3.2.8) there is no such l-less spelling in Middleton, but these forms are very frequent in Dekker's plays from Satiromastix onwards. The spelling /wut/ is precisely that used for every instance of wou't in his unassisted plays; /wod/ occurs in 12 instances out of 14 wou'd in Satiromastix, once in 2 Honest Whore (I.ii.113), and once in If This Be Not (I.ii.221)[1]: presumably it is a compositorial spelling for Dekker's /wud/.[2] But the forms wou'd and wou't were almost certainly not introduced into Blurt by the compositor, since in Alarum /would/ occurs, but neither wou'd nor wou't. The l-less forms are fairly distinctive: Table I.1 shows that the only one of the "likely" Blurt candidates who uses both wou'd and wou't is Dekker.

This evidence, then, strongly confirms Dekker's authorship of Blurt, and suggests, moreover, that the copy for the play was Dekker's auto-graph. This suggestion is reinforced by the fairly high frequency of hyphens in Blurt, which has been noted and contrasted with the lower rates of Middleton by Berger (pp. 44-45). The high rate of hyphenation in Blurt can hardly be due to the compositor, since the rate in Alarum is quite low (by my count, excluding line-end hyphens, only 48 in 49 quarto pages, less than half the rate of 140 hyphens in 60 pages of Blurt). Dekker's liking for hyphens is noted both by Berger and by Bowers (Dram. Works, III, 373, fn.).

---

[1] As wo'd.

[2] /wud/ is by far the commonest spelling of wou'd in Westward and Northward Ho, 2 Honest Whore, If This Be Not, and Match Me.

2.2.4.4.2. Exclamations

There are two instances in Blurt of the exclamation umh, both spelt /vmh/ (F2, twice). Middleton never uses umh, but always hum; Dekker uses both, and his spelling of umh almost invariably includes the final h.[1] There is no instance of umh or hum in Alarum or Satiromastix.

The two instances of tush in Blurt (A4v, twice) also accord with Dekker's habits, not with Middleton's. The 17 why (r.f. 18.9 per 20000 words) represent a relative frequency less than half that of Middleton's lowest in his early plays (r.f. 39.3 in Phoenix); compare Shoemaker (23.8), Old Fortunatus (18.7), Satiromastix (21.4), 2 Honest Whore (12.9), Whore of Babylon (6.4); average for early Dekker, 16.6. The most distinctive exclamation in Blurt is ptrooh, the "shooing" noise used on sig.G2 (IV.iii.159); this occurs with the same spelling in Satiromastix (IV.iii. 194; cf. also Tprooth, Satiromastix, V.ii.281), but is elsewhere paralleled in the Table I.1 plays only in Chapman's May Day by phtroh and ptrough (IV.iv.63).

It is perhaps significant that none of Middleton's typical exclama- tions--push, puh, tut--occur in Blurt.[2]

2.2.4.4.3. Oaths

Barker has noted (Thomas Middleton, p.199) the occurrence in Blurt of several oaths used by Dekker but not by Middleton: God's lid (C2; cf. Old Fortunatus, IV.i.126; Satiromastix, I.ii.385, IV.i.173); God's me (C2v, E3, Flv; Shoemaker, I.iv.31, IV.i.49); ud's foot (G3v; Satiromastix Epilogue; 2 Honest Whore, IV.i.163); and Ho God (Dlv, twice; Old Fortunatus, I.i.331). This list can be extended with the oath-colloc- ations marry muff (twice in Blurt; once in Satiromastix, twice in 2 Hon- est Whore); byth' Lord (once in Blurt; once in Shoemaker; once in the Satiromastix Epilogue; twice in 2 Honest Whore); and by Jesu (once in Blurt; twice in Satiromastix). The whole pattern of oaths in Blurt is similar to that of Dekker's early plays, and unlike that of Middleton's, as Table I.1 shows. As we have seen (2.1.1.3.2.2), Middleton does not use the name of God undisguised in an oath in any undoubted play, and certainly never the form God's or Jesu(s).

---

[1] There is only one exception in the unassisted plays, vm in 2 Honest Whore, V.ii.408. There is a significant press-variant in Match Me, Flv, where Vm was corrected to Vmh (noted by Bowers; see Dram. Works, III, 260, 299, 351).

[2] Middleton uses push and tut already in his verse satire Micro-Cynicon, published 1599; see Appendix III, Table III(2).

The oaths 'sfoot, 'slid, and 'slight, which are found in Blurt, might suggest the presence of Middleton; but in fact 'sfoot is frequent in Dekker's scenes in the Ho plays, and both 'sfoot and 'slid occur in Satiromastix. 'Slight, admittedly, is not one of Dekker's usual oaths, but then it is not found in Middleton either before Your Five Gallants (1606-07; see 2.1.1.4.5). The low frequencies of faith and troth in Blurt are much more compatible with Dekker's authorship than with Middleton's.

2.2.4.4.4. Ay : yes

The ay:yes ratio in Blurt (8:7) approximates to the ratios in Dekker's Satiromastix (19:16) and earlier plays; Middleton's early plays show a decided preference for ay.

2.2.4.4.5. Colloquialisms and contractions

As we have seen (2.1.1.3.1), Dekker adopted the colloquial forms has, does, 'em and I'm during the period 1600-05, but has and does appeared in his usage before 'em and I'm. In Satiromastix there is no instance of 'em, and only 1 I'm beside 40 I am, but has and does are clearly predominant. Exactly the same pattern appears in Blurt, as Table I.1 shows. As regards has and does, this hardly makes against the claim of Middleton, since his usage differs little as to has and not at all as to does from post-1600 Dekker's. But the non-appearance of Middleton's favorite 'em and I'm in Blurt is very striking. Not only do the preferences for them and I am suggest Dekker's authorship: if the date of the play had been doubtful, they, in combination with the has and does, would have enabled us to date Blurt to a position in Dekker's oeuvre adjoining Satiromastix--where the external evidence shows that it does belong.

Let us now consider some features in which Dekker's usage remained relatively stable. Unfortunately, the evidence here is essentially negative. In Blurt there is no t'as, we're, y'ave, or on't, every one of which appears in every one of Middleton's early comedies, and none of which is favored by Dekker. The non-appearance of on't is especially striking, since this is one of Middleton's favorite contractions, never occurring less than 13 times in any one of his plays. Moreover, the total of some other contractions is low, in accordance with Dekker's habits: you're, y'are, they're and th'are have a combined total of 5 in Blurt; with this we may compare the totals 7, 9, 11 for Shoemaker,

Old Fortunatus, and Satiromastix respectively, and contrast the much higher totals for Phoenix (28) and the other early Middleton plays (lowest
total, 17 in Trick). The one contraction (apart from wou't) which Dekker
favors but Middleton does not--it's--has been noticed already; the 7:27
ratio of it's:'tis in Blurt is much higher than the highest ratio in
Middleton, but well within the Dekker range.

2.2.4.4.6. Collocations and vocabulary

Not only are Middleton's contractions absent from Blurt: his typical
vocabulary is largely absent, too. For example, there are never fewer
than 7 instances of the word comfort in any undoubted early Middleton
comedy, or fewer than 4 instances of the phrase I (do) protest. But in
Blurt comfort occurs only once (D3v; III.i.10), and I (do) protest not
at all: which compares well with Dekker's low frequency for both items
(only 4 comfort and 3 I (do) protest in the five early plays; no instance
of either in Satiromastix). The lack of comfort in Blurt (as in 1 Honest
Whore) really must count for something, since Dekker's rate for this word
is so extraordinarily low, well below the average for the period. Another
interesting lack in Blurt is that of the ellipsis 'Has for "he has":
there is only one instance in Blurt (B3; I.ii.150), whereas there are never
less than 4 in any early Middleton play, never less than 3 in any Middleton
play, early or late, and no less than 12 instances in the play nearest
in date to Blurt, the 1603-04 Phoenix. Dekker, with 5 instances of 'Has
in his five early plays, or 7 in seven plays, averages about 1 per play--
the exact frequency of Blurt.

The positive evidence of I love alife and numerous Dekkerisms will
be considered below (2.2.4.6).

2.2.4.5. Possible collaborators

So far the argument has been confined to authors known to have
written for boys' companies, and from these Dekker has emerged, through
objective tests, as so good a candidate that it is reasonable to assert
that Blurt is substantially his. If the play is by a single author, that
author is Dekker or some writer whose style is indistinguishable from
Dekker's style of 1601-02. If Dekker had any collaborator (which so
far there is no reason to suspect), we should look for one among those
authors known to have collaborated with him about this time, and who
have left unassisted plays from which their usage may be determined.
Obviously any collaborator in Blurt would have to share several usages

with Dekker; a substantial contributor would have to share a great many,
to have escaped detection in all our tests.

The authors to be considered here are Heywood, Munday, Haughton,
and Chettle. The first two can be quickly dismissed. Heywood strongly
favors amongst rather than among, and makes negligible use of it's;
moreover, in his earlier works, roughly contemporary with Blurt, he
hardly ever uses has or does, preferring hath and doth, and the same
preferences are visible in his holograph The Captives (see Table I.1),
which has no instance of among, it's, has, or does. It is also, of
course, extremely unlikely that Heywood would have collaborated in a
play for a boys' company. Munday can also be ruled out: he prefers
beside, hath, and doth, and uses ye with very great frequency--165
times in his short holograph John a Kent, and 122 times in Sir Thomas
More (Hand S),[1] whereas ye occurs only once in Blurt.

There remain William Haughton and Henry Chettle, who collaborated
with Dekker in Patient Grissil (Q 1603) in 1599; they have left only
one unassisted play each, Haughton's Englishmen for my Money (Q 1616;
written early 1598) and Chettle's Hoffman (Q 1631; written 1602).[2] Both
writers share many usages with Dekker; the table below sets out only
the more significant differences.

Table 2.2(3). Haughton and Chettle

		why	faith, marry	between: betwixt	while: whilst	I've	Total gp.sp.	OMNES
	tut							
Blurt	.	17	6,11	4:0	1:3	.	20	17
Dekker Sat.	.	24	9,6	3:0	1:8	.	22	10
Haughton Eng.	5	67	28,26	2:5	1:6	.	5	.
Chettle Hoff.	1	15	2,3	3:0	17:2	2	6	5
Patient Grissil	2	17	16,5	2:1	1:8	.	14	.

Unfortunately, with regard to these authors we are hampered by the
paucity and unsuitability of the comparative material. Not very much

---

[1] There are quite enough similarities between the features recorded for
John a Kent and Sir Thomas More in Table I.1 to disprove the theory that
Munday was only the scribe of the latter: the very high frequency of ye
in both plays constitutes the most striking item.

[2] See Chambers, Elizabethan Stage, III, 334-36 for Haughton and III,
263-67 for Chettle.

can be learnt from Patient Grissil: the shares of the contributors cannot
be distinguished with much confidence; the play was written two years
earlier than Blurt, about the time of Dekker's re-making of Old Fortunatus,
and was printed from non-autograph copy (Bowers, Dram. Works, I, 210).
Haughton's play is four years earlier than Blurt, and Chettle's is a
tragedy. In the circumstances it is only fair to ignore the fact that
both Haughton and Chettle seem to prefer hath and doth to has and does.
In other respects, Haughton's usage is not grossly unlike that of Blurt:
he makes use of it's and wou'd (though he does not use wou't), prefers
betwixt, and is very fond of marry and why. Chettle is an even better
candidate. In addition to the features shown in the table above, he
uses besides, wou'd, and it's (6 it's in Hoffman beside 32 'tis). He
seems to prefer the Latin prefix-form Omnes, though he is not as fond
as Dekker of group speeches, nor does he use wou't. It is true that he
strongly prefers while to whilst (a preference which appears consistently
also in his prose works), but this does not affect the totals in Patient
Grissil. Probably his most important difference from Dekker is his use
in 1602 of I've; if this feature occurs twice in a tragedy, it would be
likely to occur with even greater frequency in a contemporary comedy. But
all this is not much to go upon: we really do not have enough material from
Chettle or Haughton to be sure of many features of their dramatic usages.

However, I do not think that Chettle or Haughton or any one other
than Dekker had a major hand in Blurt: basically for negative reasons.
Major collaboration is usually detectable by the disturbance of an author's
predictable features. Thus, Middleton's presence in 1 Honest Whore is
clearly revealed by that play's ay:yes ratio, and the occurrence of
birlady and exlent (see 2.1.3). Even Patient Grissil shows some
contamination of Dekker's style: most clearly in the low relative frequency of its group speeches (decidedly lower than that of any unassisted
Dekker play, little more than half that of Blurt[1]); perhaps also in the
appearance of tut, which Dekker never uses. But Blurt, once we accept it
as a Dekker play, shows no significant contamination at all: the match with
the features of Dekker's nearly contemporary work, and especially with
Satiromastix, is nearly perfect.

---

[1] This is a rough estimate based on the number of quarto pages in
Patient Grissil (82; cf. Blurt's 60 pp.).

2.2.4.6. Survey of scenes

I attribute every scene of Blurt to Dekker: the evidence does not
render any more complex hypothesis necessary. To support this propos-
ition I shall now survey the text scene by scene, stressing the collocational parallels to Dekker's plays. The distribution of features more
easily tabulated will be displayed in Table 2.4(4), at the end of this
section.

Some preliminary remarks on the general literary style of the play
may be useful. I would lay not too much stress on the striking manner-
isms--the plentiful vocative phrases such as my little Mer-maides, my
little lecherous Baboone, thou little morsel of Iustice, and the general
running to death of the word "little"--though these features have abundant parallels in Shoemaker, Old Fortunatus, and Satiromastix. After all,
because these tricks are striking, they could have been imitated. It is
the more particular parallels, often of apparently insignificant phrases,
which are more useful for purposes of attribution.

I.i.

The parallels in the first sentence (lines 1-4) have been noted above
(2.2.4.3.3).

I.i.69 (A3): hayre stand vp an end. Cf. haire stands vp an end, in
Satiromastix, V.ii.286, and other hair .. an end collocations,
Satiromastix, II.ii.32, IV.i.93, IV.iii.89; also times siluer foretop
stands/An end, in Match Me, III.i.97. The collocation "hair .. an end"
occurs nowhere in the Table I.1 plays except in Dekker; Tourneur and the
author of Dick of Devonshire use hair .. on end (Atheist's Tragedy, H4v;
Dick, line 1329).

I.i.72-73 (A3): most terrible Tamberlaine. Cf. the reference to Tamburlaine in Shoemaker, V.iv.53, and the vocative phrase mad Tamberlaine
in Satiromastix, IV.iii.169-70. The value of such allusions has often
been attacked by critics of the comparative method on the ground that
"any one could have made them". The fact is that they did not: Table I.1
shows that allusions to Tamburlaine are surprisingly rare. W.J. Lawrence
has noted[1] other theatrical allusions in Blurt and in Dekker--Thamar
Cham and Mephostophiles--but he has not noticed Dekker's typical method

---

[1] "Dekker's Theatrical Allusiveness and What it Reveals," in Lawrence's
Speeding up Shakespeare (1937; rpt. New York: Blom, 1968), pp. 114-19.

of employing these names, that is, as aliases, and usually in vocative phrases. This trick is used a few times in Shoemaker and Old Fortunatus, rather more often by Sir Gosling in Westward Ho (V.iii), but enormously (almost in every possible speech) by Tucca in Satiromastix: there it is an amplification and modernization of Tucca's classical and mythological vocatives in Poetaster. There is a reference to Tamburlaine in Middleton's pamphlet The Black Book (Dl; Bullen, VIII,25), but the literary (often theatrical) allusion used as a vocative is a Dekker habit quite foreign to Middleton's style.

I.i.207 (A4v): my French prisoner. Cf. my French prisoner is in loue, Old Fortunatus, III.i.161; the whole situation and atmosphere is parallel here. There is no parallel in Middleton.

I.i.213-14 (Bl): because Ile be sure he shall not start [i.e. "escape"]. Cf. because you shal be sure ile not start [i.e. "escape"], Old Fortunatus, V.ii.35. I have found no parallel elsewhere (see Table I.2). The likeness between these collocations is very striking, but the collocations themselves are so unremarkable that imitation is very unlikely.

I.i.214-15 (Bl): Ile locke him in a little low roome besides himselfe. Cf. hee's besides himselfe, in Northward Ho, IV.iii.44 (a Dekker section; there is no parallel in Webster). There is, of course, no instance of besides himself in Middleton; the usage shows the perfect synonymity of beside and besides in the period.

I.ii.

I.ii.58 (B2): Most cleare Mirrour of Magistrates. Another vocative embodying a literary allusion--this time to a non-theatrical work, the collection of poetry entitled Mirror for Magistrates (1563). Non-theatrical literary allusions are also fairly common in vocatives in Satiromastix, though most refer to characters in romance or ballads.

I.ii.58-59 (B2): I am a seruitor to God Mars. Cf. a follower of god Mars, in Northward Ho, IV.i.86 (a Dekker section), in reply to a similar question, "what are you?"

I.ii.90 (B2), 175, 177, 178 (B3-B3v): Signior no. A pun on the sense "Mr. Nobody". Cf. Match Me, IV.iv.49; also the character "Signior No" in The Noble Spanish Soldier. The collocation is fairly rare (see Table I.1); there is no instance in Middleton.

I.ii.97 (B2v): rowlie, powlie. Cf. rowly-powlies, in Satiromastix, I.ii.331. The phrase is rare (see Table I.1); there is no instance in Middleton.

II.i.

II.i.72-73 (C1): by the Crosse of this, Dandyprat. "This" probably refers to Hippolito's sword (as well, punningly, to the coin "dandiprat"). Cf. by the crosse of his pure Toledo, in Old Fortunatus, III.i.292. There is nothing similar in Middleton.

II.i.127 (C1v): snipsnap [a rapid pistol-shot]. Cf. Snip snap, in Old Fortunatus, I.i.49. The phrase is rare (see Table I.1), though it does occur twice in Anything for a Quiet Life (D2, E2) in scenes by Middleton.

II.i.130 (C2): Signior no. See above (I.ii).

II.i.132 (C2): No point. Dekker is fond of this French negative (see Table I.1), and does not always use it in a French context. Cf. Shoemaker, IV.iv.96; Old Fortunatus, V.i.128, 138; Match Me, II.i.15. There is no instance in Middleton.

II.ii.

II.ii.193 (D1): mary muffe. Cf. Satiromastix, I.ii.347; 2 Honest Whore, V.ii.278, 415. There is no instance in Middleton's plays (see Table I.1).

II.ii.214 (D1v): Ho God, Ho God. Cf. ho God in Old Fortunatus, I.i.331. This parallel was noted by Barker (Thomas Middleton, p. 199). I have noticed no other instance of this curious collocation, with "ho" replacing "O".

II.ii.287-88 (D2v): giue sharpnes to my Toledo. Cf. Toledo for "sword" in Old Fortunatus, III.i.292. There is no instance in Middleton.

III.i.

III.i.62 (D4v): bi'th Lord. Cf. By the lord in Shoemaker, V.ii.185; by'th Lord, in 2 Honest Whore, III.ii.40, IV.i.174 and the Satiromastix Epilogue; bith or byth' Lord in Westward Ho, II.iii.118, V.iii.23; Northward Ho, IV.iii.175 (all Dekker scenes; Webster does not use this oath). The collocation of the contraction by'th+Lord is uniquely Dekker's in the Table I.1 corpus (Marston, Chapman, and Munday use by the Lord).

III.i.123-36 (E1-E1v). Song with four repeats of the refrain Pitty, pitty, pitty. Cf. the song in Old Fortunatus with three repeats of pittie, pittie, one of pittie, pittie, pittie (I.ii.20-35). A unique parallel (see Table 1.2).

III.i.153 (Elv): by Iesu. Cf. Satiromastix, I.ii.288, IV.iii.177.
(Haughton has Oh Iesus in Englishmen, Hlv.)

III.i.164 (E2): I loue alife. This is the one phrase in the play
which suggests the presence of Middleton, since it is not found in Dekker,
but occurs eight times in Middleton's plays, beginning with three
instances in Trick (C3v, twice, II.i.267, 270; F3, IV.iii.12). The phrase
is fairly rare (see Table I.1).

III.ii.

This short scene contains two instances of oh God (lines 23-24; E2v),
which at least point rather to Dekker than to Middleton.

III.iii.

See Appendix IV.1 for the authorship of The Batchelars Banquet,
which is neither by Dekker nor by Middleton, nor, probably, is the source
for this scene.

III.iii.107 (E4v): your lilly sweating hands. Cf. lillie hands in
Shoemaker, I.i.226. The phrase is surprisingly rare (no instance in
Middleton). Cf. also sweating hands, in Old Fortunatus, III.i.355, a
unique parallel (see Table I.2).

III.iii.152 (F1): Lillie hand. See above.

III.iii.171-72 (F1): get a fore-game . . . win a rubbers. Cf.
fore-game . . . play out a rubbers, in Satiromastix, V.ii.351-52 (another
unique parallel: see Table I.2).

IV.i.

IV.i.42 (F2v): Mary Muff. See above (II.ii.193).

IV.i.47 (F2v): god-amercie. The expression of thanks used by Dekker
(and others) but never by Middleton.

IV.i.51 (F2v): marie snicke vp. Cf. goe snicke-vp, in Shoemaker,
I.ii.50. See Table I.1 for the rarity of "snick up": there is no instance
in Middleton. The whole volley of contemptuous phrases beginning with
"marry--" in this passage is exactly in Dekker's manner, as in Shoemaker,
I.ii.31-32, and 2 Honest Whore, V.ii.278.

IV.i.55 (F2v): goe by olde Ieronimo. This tag from Kyd's Spanish
Tragedy is not uncommon, but Middleton never uses it, whereas Dekker
does, in the same fashion as a vocative, in Satiromastix, I.ii.372; also,
in reported speech, in Shoemaker, I.ii.41.

IV.ii.

    IV.ii.22 (F3): <u>pusse-cattes</u>. Cf. <u>Pusse-cat</u>, in <u>Satiromastix</u>, V.ii.
325. I have found only one instance outside Dekker, in Sampson's <u>The</u>
<u>Vow-Breaker</u>, I.iii.90.

IV.iii.

    IV.iii.113 (G1): <u>Pusse-Cattes</u>. See above.

    IV.iii.159 (G2): <u>ptrooh</u>. See 2.2.4.4.2, above.

V.i.

    This short scene is marked as Dekker's by three instances of <u>Omnes</u>
(G2-G2v).

V.ii.

    This scene is marked as Dekker's by the oaths <u>vds</u> <u>foote</u> (G3v, V.ii.78),
and <u>O God</u> (G4, V.ii.86), as well as by group speeches, and parallels
noted by Barker (<u>Thomas Middleton</u>, p.200).

V.iii.

    V.iii.47 (H1v): <u>Garlicke</u> . . . <u>follow stronglie</u>. Cf. the colloc-
ations of "garlick" with "strong": <u>strong garlicke Comedies</u>, <u>Satiromastix</u>,
I.ii.334; <u>Garlike</u> . . . <u>strong</u> reason, <u>If This Be Not</u>, IV.ii.10. For the
rarity of this collocation, see Table I.1. There is no instance in
Middleton.

    V.iii.167 (H3): <u>Signior no</u>. See above, I.ii and II.i.

    V.iii.186 (H3v): <u>And Tragicke shapes meete Comicall euent</u>. There
is an almost exact anticipation of this formula in <u>Satiromastix</u>: <u>to wed</u>
<u>a Comicall</u> euent / <u>To presupposed tragicke Argument</u> (V.ii.113). I have
found no other instance of the collocation <u>tragic/comical event</u>. This
parallel is especially convincing, since it is not a particularly
striking locution, and suggests that a single dramatist is using the same
set of words to deal with the problem of ending two comedies written
in close succession.

2.2.4.7. <u>Conclusion</u>

    The survey of scenes in <u>Blurt</u> has shown that Dekker's hand in visible
literally from the first to the last sentence of the play, and with no
obvious gaps. Every scene is marked by Dekker parallels and/or linguistic
practices; probably the only suggestion of any collaborator is the phrase
<u>I love alife</u>, which may point to Middleton. It is, of course, impossible

to exclude the possibility that Middleton did contribute in a minor way to Blurt (especially as we have no data on his dramatic manner in 1601-02), and that this accounts for Kirkman's attribution; but an authorship case should never be erected upon one instance of one feature. I conclude, therefore, that the evidence for Middleton is too weak to be relied on, and, unless and until more is discovered, we should assume that Blurt is an unaided play by Dekker.

Table 2.2(4), below, gives the distribution of linguistic evidence.

Table 2.2(4). Blurt: significant features. Segment 1

Scene	sigs.	tush	umh	why	Lord	God's, God	'sfoot, ud's foot	'slid	'slight	faith, troth	ay: yes
1.1	A2-B1	2	.	2	.	.	1,	.	1	1,2	2:2
1.2	B1-B4	.	.	1	.	.	1,	1	.	.	1:1
2.1	B4-C2v	.	.	1	1	1,	1,	.	.	.	.
2.2	C2v-D3v	.	.	6	.	1,2	1,	1	.	2,2	:1
3.1	D3v-E2	.	.	.	1	.	1,	.	1	2,1	1:2
3.2	E2v-E3	.	.	1	.	,2	.	.	.	.	.
3.3	E3-F1v	.	.	1	1	2,	.	.	.	,1	.
4.1	F1v-F2v	.	2	2	.	1,	.	.	.	.	1:
4.2	F2v-F3v	.	.	.	.	.	.	.	.	.	.
4.3	F3v-G2	.	.	3	.	.	.	.	.	.	3:1
5.1	G2-G2v	.	.	.	.	.	.	.	.	.	.
5.2	G2v-G4v	.	.	.	.	,1	,1	.	.	1,3	.
5.3	G4v-H3v	.	.	.	.	.	.	.	.	,1	.
Totals:		2	2	17	3	5,5	5,1	2	2	6,10	8:7

Table 2.2(4). Blurt: significant features. Segment 2

Scene	sigs.	amo-ng	bes-ides	betw-een	while:whilst	them	has:hath	does:doth	I am	it's:'tis
1.1	A2-B1	1	2	.	:2	6	5:2	5:	4	:1
1.2	B1-B4	.	2	.	.	1	7:1	2:	17	2:4
2.1	B4-C2v	.	1	3	.	2	.	2:	1	:1
2.2	C2v-D3v	2	1	.	.	14	5:	5:	14	2:10
3.1	D3v-E2	.	.	.	:1	1	2:4	:2	3	:2
3.2	E2v-E3	.	.	.	.	.	.	1:	.	.
3.3	E3-F1v	.	1	.	1:	7	1:	.	3	:6
4.1	F1v-F2v	.	.	.	.	.	.	.	8	:1
4.2	F2v-F3v	.	.	.	.	.	.	1:	2	1:1
4.3	F3v-G2	.	.	.	.	.	.	1:	11	2:
5.1	G2-G2v	.	.	1	.	.	1:2	1:	.	.
5.2	G2v-G4v	.	.	.	.	3	:2	1:	3	.
5.3	G4v-H3v	.	1	.	.	1	.	.	4	:1
Totals:		3	8	4	1:3	35	21:11	19:2	70	7:27

Segment 3

Scene	sigs.	th'art, y'are	they're	wut	wod	OMNES	Other gp.sp.	com-fort	'Has
1.1	A2-B1	.	.	.	.	.	.	.	.
1.2	B1-B4	1,	.	.	.	.	.	.	1
2.1	B4-C2v	,1	.	.	.	.	.	.	.
2.2	C2v-D3v	.	.	1	1	1	.	.	.
3.1	D3v-E2	.	.	.	.	1	.	1	.
3.2	E2v-E3	.	.	.	.	.	.	.	.
3.3	E3-F1v	.	1	.	.	2	.	.	.
4.1	F1v-F2v	,2	.	.	.	.	.	.	.
4.2	F2v-F3v	.	.	.	2	.	.	.	.
4.3	F3v-G2	,1	.	.	.	3	.	.	.
5.1	G2-G2v	.	.	.	.	3	.	.	.
5.2	G2v-G4v	.	.	.	.	1	2	.	.
5.3	G4v-H3v	.	.	.	.	6	1	.	.
Totals:		1,4	1	1	3	17	3	1	1

2.3. The Family of Love

2.3.1. Text

The Family of Love was entered in the Stationers' Register on 12
October 1607 for the copy of the publishers, John Browne and John Helme
(Arber, III, 360). The entry mentions no author, but specifies the acting
company: "as yt hath bene Lately acted by the Children of his Maiesties
Reuelles". The title page of the quarto, which appeared in 1608, contains
a similar formula and a motto:

> The Familie of Love. Acted by the Children of his Maiesties
> Reuells. Lectori. Sydera iungamus, facito mihi Iuppiter adsit,
> Et tibi Mercurius noster dabit omnia faxo.

There are also an unsigned authorial "To the Reader," a list of
characters, a prologue, and an epilogue, which will be examined below.
Q 1608 was printed by Richard Braddock,[1] who in the same year printed
two other plays, A Yorkshire Tragedy and John Day's Humour out of Breath.
Since A Yorkshire Tragedy is itself a problem play, only Humour Out can
serve as a comparison text to provide indications of compositorial habits.
The authorship of Humour Out has sometimes been questioned because of the
description in Day's preface of the play as "sufficiently featur'd too,
had it been all of one man's getting", and George Wilkins has been suggested
as a collaborator,[2] but the case has never been proven and is probably
baseless.[3] The question, besides, is unimportant for our purposes, since
neither Day nor Wilkins is suspected of having had a hand in The Family
of Love.

Andrew Dillon, in his unpublished edition of The Family,[4] decides
(pp. xvii-xx), from the full marking of entrances and exits of all main
characters, and from the frequency of anticipated entrances, that the copy
for the quarto was probably a prompt-book.

2.3.2. Date of Composition

The date of composition of The Family has been much disputed, estimates
ranging from about 1601 to 1607, the earlier dates being

---

[1] Greg, Bibliography, I, 336. Braddock's device is on the title page.

[2] The collaboration theories are summarized by Robin Jeffs in his
introduction to the reprint of Bullen's edition of The Works of John
Day (London: Holland Press, 1963), p. xx.

[3] The features of Humour out of Breath recorded in Table I.1 match quite
well the features of Day's other two plays.

[4] "Thomas Middleton, The Family of Love: a critical old-spelling edition,"
Diss. New York, 1968.

combined usually with theories of major or minor subsequent revision.
Some of the motivation for choosing an early date has sprung from a
desire to confirm the Archer attribution of the play to Middleton alone:
since Middleton's style as we know it from the early undoubted comedies
is not obvious in The Family, one can postulate that several years
earlier still that style had not yet been developed. But to obtain
an unbiased verdict on the authorship we must avoid such reasoning, and
attempt to determine the date without making any authorship assumptions
at all.

The natural inference from the Stationers' Register entry and the
title-page statement would be that the play was fairly recent, since
the Children of the King's Revels, as Chambers remarks, "can hardly
have existed before 1607" (Elizabethan Stage, III, 440). But this
inference is contradicted by the authorial "To the Reader," which begins:

> Too soone and too late, this work is published: Too soone,
> in that it was in the Presse, before I had notice of it, by
> which meanes some faults may escape in the Printing. Too
> late, for that it was not published when the general voice
> of the people had seald it for good, and the newnesse of it
> made it much more desired, then at this time: For Plaies
> in this Citie are like wenches new falne to the trade, onelie
> desired of your neatest gallants, whiles the'are fresh . . .
>
> (Alv)

These remarks would seem to require some considerable time between
the date of first performance and that of publication; but there is no
way of telling how much time would have to elapse to provide an
explanation, satisfactory to the author, of a slump in the play's
popularity. Luckily, we do not have to decide, for there are definite
indications in the text of a date earlier than 1607.

Baldwin Maxwell, in "A Note on the Date of Middleton's The Family
of Love,"[1] points to allusions in I.iii.109[2] (B2v) and IV.iii.45-46 (F3)
to "the whole new liuery of Porters" and "the spick & span new set vp Company
of Porters", and connects these references with a ballad on the Porters'
new organization, entered in the Stationers' Register on 15 June 1605

---

[1] Elizabethan Studies and Other Essays in Honor of George F. Reynolds
(Boulder, Colorado: Univ. of Colorado, 1945), 195-200.

[2] Scene division and lineation in this study follow Bullen's edition,
in spite of some odd scene-divisions noted below (2.3.3.6.2).

(Arber, III, 292). It is very reasonable to conclude, as Maxwell does, that these references taken with the ballad fix a date in mid-1605. Maxwell is probably wrong, however, in thinking that this is the date of the first version of the play, for there are certainly allusions to earlier events: the lost play of Samson mentioned by Henslowe on 29 July 1602 (Diary, p.204) and witnessed by the Duke of Stettin-Pomerania on 14 September 1602,[1] and the siege of Geneva by Charles Emmanuel of Savoy from 22 December 1602 till July 1603.[2] It is possible, as Maxwell says, that the reference to the Samson play is not to the first performance, but the allusion to the siege would presumably not have been topical after mid-1603. Mistress Purge, trying to explain away the disappearance of her ring, says "I gaue it to the reliefe of the distressed Geneua" (Il, V.iii.278). Collections were being taken for "the distressed Geneva" in England in early 1603. It must be admitted, however, that it is not therefore quite certain that The Family must date from early 1603, since, as I shall show below (2.3.3.4), the same Geneva reference occurs in a play which cannot be earlier than 1608;[3] and, after all, the fictitious date of the action of a play is not always the same as the actual date of performance.

Possibly more conclusive evidence of different strata in the text are the changing names of certain characters: the page Shrimp is called Smelt in the list of Actorum Nomina (Alv); Glister's servant Vial is called Viall by his master on A2v, but on his later entries he is not addressed by name, and his speeches are headed Nun.[4]; lastly, the name which Dryfat assumes as a fake Proctor is given within the text five times as Poppin (Glv; H2v; H3v, twice; H4v) and five times as Exigent (H2v; H3; Ilv, twice; I2v).[5] Maxwell ("A Note," p. 196) has tried to rebut this evidence, but his account is textually inaccurate: Vial, as we have seen, is addressed once by name, and Poppin appears more often than "once", and not merely in "some copies". Since the manuscript copy

[1] Barker, Thomas Middleton, p. 159.

[2] Dillon, p. xiii.

[3] Ram Alley, sig. I4: but there the reference is clearly to a time anterior to the play's action, i.e. the past career of Throat.

[4] Presumably for "Nuntius". The S.D. on C2 is Enter Wall, which must be an error for Viall.

[5] So in the copy of Q on which I have based this study--the Huntington Library copy called "II" by Dillon. Where Huntington II reads Poppin on H2v (V.iii.41), some other copies read Exigent. The other alternations occur in all copies, so that Poppin appears at least four times, and Exigent at least five times.

for the quarto was most likely a prompt-book, the vacillations between
Poppin and Exigent must represent revision during the play's stage
career--and revision which there is no reason to attribute to the original
author: any such inconsistencies in the author's fair copy would surely
have been removed when the prompt-book was prepared. Dillon (p.xxiv)
shows that the revision was from Poppin to Exigent, and conjectures
plausibly that the alteration may have been written in the margin, so
that it was sometimes overlooked by the compositor. Of course, revisions
of names do not prove any major revisions of the substance of the play;
but when they are found co-occurring with two sets of topical allusions
appropriate for dates two or three years apart, they do suggest that at
least minor revisions have taken place. The likely history of The
Family, therefore, as indicated by the allusions, is as follows: original
version, 1602-03; revision, mid-1605. Of course, there may well have been
more than one revision. Since there is no trace of the King's Revels
company before 1607, the implication of the conjectural history outlined
above would be that the play was written for another company--perhaps the
Paul's Boys, who ceased playing in 1606.

For the purposes of the authorship problem, it is noteworthy that
topical allusions indicate no date earlier than September 1602. This
is a little more than a year before the first performance of The Phoenix
(20 February 1604, according to Chambers[1]), which presumably was written
by Middleton during the latter months of 1603.[2]

2.3.3. Authorship

2.3.3.1. Linguistic evidence and possible theories

The authorship controversy on The Family began as recently as 1948[3],
which is surprising when one compares the feature-totals in Table I.1
for that play with those of Middleton's plays from Phoenix onwards, for
there are gross discrepancies of linguistic style between The Family and
the undoubted canon. Various normal features of Middleton's early
period are missing. There are no instances of push, puh, 'sfoot, 'slid,

---

[1] Elizabethan Stage, III, 439.

[2] Baldwin Maxwell, in "Middleton's The Phoenix," Joseph Quincy Adams
Memorial Studies, ed. James G. McManaway (Washington: Folger Library,
1948), pp. 743-53, argues for a date of composition, indicated by topical
references, between June and December 1603.

[3] With Eberle's article, "Dekker's Part in The Familie of love."

only one of troth, and one of mass only where it is quoted for discussion
(Blv; I.iii.32); Middleton's preferences for beside and toward are
reversed (beside, 1: besides, 11; toward, 0: towards, 2), and so is
his early preference for between over betwixt--apparently trivial but
really highly significant features, since they correlate with authorial
preferences and nothing else, and, as we have seen (2.2.4.3.1), they are
not usually radically disguised even by scribal copying. Moreover,
Middleton's invariable habits of colloquialism--preference for 'em over
them, has over hath, and negligible use of doth--are all absent from The
Family; and so are his distinctive contractions, I'm, I've, sh'as, t'as,
we're, y'ave, they're, his favorite ellipsis 'Has, and the phrase I (do)
protest, while features he uses with great frequency, such as on't and
comfort, are down to non-distinctive figures. Spellings also are quite
unlike Middleton's practices, some startlingly so, such as 'hem instead
of 'em or e'm, though since the quarto copy was presumably scribal, this
is hardly significant.

Most interesting of all are the features relatively invulnerable to
transmission factors in which The Family is positively unlike Middleton:
the frequent use of 'a for he (41 instances), and the occurrence of oaths
which Middleton never uses--Lord, four times (D2v; D4v, twice; G4v),
gogs nownes, Gogs blude (both on E2v), the quoted oath God refuse them
(Blv, twice), and the phrase before God (D4v; III.iii.14), which Mistress
Purge interprets as an oath. In view of the likely date of the play,
little more than one year earlier than The Phoenix, Middleton's sole
authorship becomes quite incredible. Some of these oddities, no doubt,
could be explained away as due to the unusually rapid development of a
precocious author feeling his way towards a stable style; but surely not
all of them at once. In particular, the very frequent 'a is a striking
mannerism; it is hard to believe that if Middleton had used the colloquial
pronoun so often in The Family he would never again, in his thirteen
undoubted plays and several collaborations, have used it more than five
times in a single play, and not at all in ten plays out of thirteen (see
Table I.1).

The various anomalies of style in The Family have been explained by
several theories:

(1) The play is pure Middleton, but very early.

(2) The play is a collaboration. (Eberle suggests Middleton and Dekker.)

(3) The play is probably by a single author, but whether the authorship is single or not, Middleton is not concerned at all. (Price's theory: Thomas Dekker, p. 177-78.)

2.3.3.2. The presence of Middleton

As I have stated above, I find the first of these theories impossible to accept unless the date of the play is pushed back much earlier than 1602. Middleton may have written like this when he was first "accompanying the players" in 1600, but there is no allusion in the text to support so early a date; a date in 1600 would imply at least two, or possibly three, later revisions to insert the 1603 and 1605 allusions and the Exigent alterations; and it is not altogether probable that every one of these revisions would have been carried out by the original author, a member of the acting troupe being just as likely a candidate for the task of revision, so that the theory of single authorship would be imperilled in any case.

Of the remaining theories, the last is the more immediately attractive, since the text does not at first sight divide into sections of markedly different style, if one excepts the alternations between the romantic verse of Gerardine and Maria and the "realistic" prose comedy, alternations which are clearly intended for contrast and not therefore requiring to be explained by dual authorship. I have a certain sympathy with the Price theory, since it has the virtue of simplicity, and at the beginning of this investigation I held it myself; but it is wrong. For Middleton's presence in the text can be demonstrated beyond reasonable doubt.

The decisive evidence is that of collocations and vocabulary. In my Table I.1 corpus I have found one author alone who uses the Latin word subaudi (invariably in contexts of lechery); who uses suspectless (for "without suspicion"); and who refers to the poet Chaucer (invariably with reference to Chaucer's "broad" or sexually frank manner). That author is Middleton, and all of these unique features appear in The Family of Love. In such matters, there is safety in numbers; one uncommon parallel may be due to imitation, two possibly to imitation coupled with a rare coincidence, but three is really too much. And these three are hardly very striking, so that imitation can probably be ruled out. I will list the instances below.

(1) Shr. [imp] Loue (subbandy lust) a Punke in this place subintell-
igitur. (D3; III.ii.28-29) Obviously subbandy is a turned-letter error
for subbaudy. Cf. Your Five Gallants, E3v, III.iv.11 (and 1 Honest Whore;
see above, 2.1.4.2, s.v. III.iii).

(2) suspectless (D3; III.ii.55). Cf. Your Five Gallants, B3,
I.ii.82; Glv, IV.v.86; I3v, V.ii.53.

(3) Ger. [ardine] . . . in re stands all my rest, / which I in Chaucer
stile do tearm a iest (D2v; III.i.54-55). Cf. (i) No Wit: Wid. [ow] . . .
how many honest words have suffered corruption, since Chaucers days?
A Virgin would speak those words then, that a very Midwife would blush
to hear now . . . (C2v, II.i.81-84). (ii) More Dissemblers: Dond. [olo]
'Tis not good to jest, as old Chaucer was wont to say, that broad famous
English Poet (Cl; I.iv.36-37).

There are other Middletonisms, too; among the collocations, fetch it
againe (Blv; I.iii.27) and three instances of tut, man (A3v, I.ii.68;
A4v, I.ii.148; E4, IV.i.14); ten other instances of tut; one of hum; three
of byrlady; and about the right proportion of ay to yes (24:8). We may
note also the euphemisms for "God": the undisguised name hardly occurs in
an unequivocal oath except in quotation, and we have Gudgeon's with the
name of Ioue I coniure thee (E2v; III.vi.36-37); also before Ioue (E4;
IV.i.44). Moreover, the "conjuring" scene (E2v; III.vi) contains the
pseudo-Greek gibberish of which Middleton is so fond: very similar passages occur in More Dissemblers, I.ii (B5v) and IV.i (Elv-E2), where, as
here in The Family, the gibberish ends by approaching more or less closely
to intelligible English. Savorwit plays similar games with pseudo-Dutch
in No Wit (B7-B7v; I.iii).

2.3.3.3. The presence of Dekker

Dekker's hand in The Family of Love was first postulated by Eberle in
the article that opened the authorship controversy, and he has been
supported by Dodson. Neither argument need be examined in great detail,
since both are thoroughly faulty in method, assuming as fact the most
speculative attributions (including Dekker's authorship of The Batchelars Banquet and Canaan's Calamity) and drawing freely without supporting argument on disputed and collaborate plays for Dekker "touchstones".

Nevertheless, I am inclined to think that there is a little fire behind all this smoke. I cannot agree with Eberle that Dekker wrote about half the play, since there are few traces of his linguistic habits in the text, indeed perhaps none that might not be as well accounted for by the presence of another collaborator. Thus, there is no it's, but 48 instances of 'tis; admittedly, the wo't (twice, A4v), wod on B1v, and wud on B2 could be Dekker's, but in isolation these forms are not decisive. Dekker might account for towards and besides, but probably not for the majority of betwixt; nor has he left much impression on the play's oaths and exclamations. There is obviously an enormous linguistic contrast between The Family and Blurt or 1 Honest Whore. If Dekker is to be confidently identified in The Family, it will have to be on collocations alone; and his share cannot be very large. Like Eberle, I find Dekker in the play because of one or two passages which seem to be full of Dekkerisms and empty or almost empty of Middleton; unlike Eberle, I am inclined to go little further. I am, indeed, fairly confident of Dekker's presence only in one short scene, II.i, which is no more than a single speech of 23 lines (B3v-B4), a soliloquy by Purge.

Here it is true, as Eberle says (p.729), that doings is a word much used by Dekker but seldom by Middleton. Much more distinctive is the collocation of Moone . . . hornes in a context of cuckoldry; as we saw in 2.1.4.2 (s.v. 1 Honest Whore, I.ii), this is a favorite Dekker witticism, occurring four times in his undoubted plays and twice in Westward Ho, but never in Middleton. Dog cheape (B4; II.i.20) is also not found in Middleton, but occurs in If This Be Not (II.ii.85), and the very last phrase, wink at small faults (B4; II.i.23), occurs word for word in Match Me (IV.i.40); once more, never in Middleton. If the main author of this speech is really Middleton, we have here an uncomfortable number of coincidences with Dekker's habits of phrasing; and these three parallels are in addition to the ones cited by Eberle to justify his attribution of the passage. However, even here we are surely not faced with Dekker alone, since the last sentence begins with Tut, which Dekker never uses.

If it is granted that II.i is mainly Dekker's, we are encouraged to look for him elsewhere in the play. On the balance of probabilities, I would give him the main authorship of the following sections:

I.ii. 1-52 (prose and song). In addition to the points made by
Eberle (pp. 726-28) I have noticed Grammercies Lipsalue my neate Courtier
(A3; I.ii.31); cf. Shoemaker, I.i.151: gramercy my fine foreman. "Gramercy"
or"gramercies" does not occur at all in Middleton's unassisted plays.

II.i and II.ii. For the nine lines of II.ii I have nothing to add
to Eberle's account (p. 729). Dekker is indeed fond of Greek-and-Trojan
references, Middleton not.

IV.ii.89-100. As Eberle points out, repercussiue, used of the Sun,
and Tartarian are favorite Dekker expressions. But this same passage of
rapturous verse contains the pronoun 'a: A mounts in triumph (F2v); whereas
'a is even rarer in Dekker than in Middleton, with only two instances in
the undoubted plays, both in colloquial prose (Shoemaker, I.ii.25;
Satiromastix, III.i.26). The only instance in Middleton's verse is in
Allwit's decidedly colloquial speech in Chaste Maid (B4v; I.ii.16):
Not onely keepes my Wife, but a keepes me. The 'a used here in The Family
without scruple as to its tonal effect is one of the signs of a third hand
in the play, as will be shown below.

IV.iii.1-95 (to the reading of the letter). I am inclined to think
that Eberle is right in associating Dekker with the most important of the
"porter' passages; if so, the implication would be that Dekker's part in
the play belongs to 1605, and hence that he was a reviser rather than an
original collaborator with Middleton; but he may have been both. Eberle
has given no evidence to attribute the rest of IV.iii to Dekker; in fact,
it sounds much more like Middleton.

Thus Dekker's share, in my opinion, amounts to two very short scenes
and three sections of other scenes where his presence is more probable than
his absence--a total of 191 lines; and it is doubtful that any of these
sections represents his work untouched by others. It may be that Eberle
is right in thinking that Dekker is present in several other scenes, such
as III.iii, IV.iv, and all three scenes of Act V, but these scenes are
also marked by Middletonisms, and the linguistic evidence is unfavorable
to the Dekker claim. Moreover, several of the phrases untypical of Middleton which Eberle claims as Dekkerisms may in fact be due to a third
hand. For Dekker's participation in the play is totally inadequate
to explain all the divergencies from Middleton's likely style of
1602: by 1605 Dekker's usages of 'em, I'm, has, and does were

indistinguishable from Middleton's early-period usages and very different from those of The Family, and even as early as Satiromastix in
1601 Dekker had largely rejected hath and doth.

We must look elsewhere for an author who uses 'a abundantly; who
prefers betwixt to between; who disfavors 'em and has but makes substantial use of doth; and rejects or uses very sparingly the Middletonian contractions I'm, I've, sh'as, we're, y'ave, they're, on't, the
word comfort, and the ellipsis 'Has--or as many of these features as
possible, so that we can explain the deficiencies of The Family by the
diluting hand of such an author acting as a reviser. If Middleton was
the original author of 1602, and Dekker the reviser of 1605, then the
required third man might well be a later reviser who caused the Poppin/
Exigent alternations.

2.3.3.4.   The presence of Barry

The required author is, I believe, Lording Barry,[1] the author of
the comedy Ram Alley (composed 1608; Q 1611, printed by George Eld),
and impresario of the King's Revels' children in 1607-08. Nearly
everything about Barry's linguistic style fits our requirements: most
obviously the abundant 'a in Ram Alley, which is nearly all verse--'a
occurring even in the Prologue and Epilogue:

> A vowes by Paper, Pen and Inke,
>
> And by the learned Sisters drinke . . . (Prologue, A2)

> A dares not glory nor mistrust . . . (Epilogue, I4v)

This way of beginning a verse line with 'A followed by a present-tense
verb seems to be a Barry mannerism, paralleled by A mounts in The Family
(F2v; IV.ii.94). Other features in which Barry's usages in Ram Alley
meet our requirements include woud (B3v), wo't (D2) and woot (F3v),[2]
the exclusive use of betwixt, the substantial use of doth, the very low
frequency of 'em and comfort, and the non-use of I'm, I've, sh'as, we're
and on't. But we need something highly distinctive in the way of a
parallel to reassure us that we have got the right man--and the parallel

---

[1] For an account of the life and colorful career of Barry, see the
monograph by C. L'Estrange Ewen, Lording Barry, Poet and Pirate (London:
printed for the author, 1938), and Claude E. Jones' introduction to
his edition of Ram Alley in Materials for the Study of the Old English
Drama, 23 (1952). I accept Jones' dating of the composition and first
performance of Ram Alley (p. x).

[2] The spelling /wo't/ is precisely that of The Family (A4v, twice), whereas
Dekker's spelling of wou't is /wut/ (see 2.2.4.4.1), and that of
Humour Out is /woot/ (three times, C3). It is interesting also that,
as in Ram Alley, in The Family there are at least as many wou't as wou'd,
whereas Dekker always has more wou'd than wou't.

exists; in fact, more than one. There can be no doubt about releefe
for the distressed Geneua (Ram Alley, I4), which is nearly identical in
wording with the reliefe of the distressed Geneua in The Family, V.iii.278.
No such reference to "distressed Geneva" occurs in any other play of
the 132-play Table I.1 corpus. Since the reference in The Family, which
belongs to early 1603, must have been the original one, it is likely
that Barry lifted the phrase from Middleton's play, which had obviously
passed through his hands just before he wrote Ram Alley; hence the
parallel indicates contact rather than common authorship. Rather clearer
evidence of Barry's editing (at least) of The Family is the list of
personae on Alv. This is entitled Actorum Nomina, and it is divided into
two sections, a main one for male characters, and a following short
one entitled Weomen. The character-list of Ram Alley (A2v) is headed
Actorum nomina and has a second section entitled Women. These features
do not occur in other King's Revels plays of this period--Day's Humour
Out, Sharpham's Cupid's Whirligig, Mason's The Turk, Armin's Two Maids
of Moreclacke, or Markham and Machin's The Dumb Knight--nor in any of
Middleton's or Dekker's plays,[1] so that the link is clearly between
The Family and Ram Alley alone. Moreover, there are unambiguous signs
of Barry's hand in the text of The Family. We have the oath blud (for
"God's blood") in A4 (I.ii.81), a form never used by Middleton or Dekker,
or indeed by any other author in the corpus except Barry, who has bloud
three times (Ram Alley, F3v, G4, I3v). We have noticed already the use
of "Jove" (2.3.3.2); Barry has a great many instances of "Jove" instead
of "God"--eleven in all--so that if Middleton had not censored his own
text, Barry was quite capable of doing so for the King's Revels'
performances of 1607. But Barry does not avoid the divine names so
consistently as Middleton, and has four instances of Lord in Ram Alley,
which exactly match the four in The Family. Interestingly enough, both
The Family and Ram Alley have characters swearing by Pluto: in the name
of Pluto (Family, G2; IV.iv.108); by Pluto (Ram Alley, G2v and G3).

---

[1] Dekker's lists are undivided and headed Dram(m)atis Personae; Middleton
probably never provided his own lists, since there are none attached to
his early comedies or his holograph Game at Chess. Several of his
later plays have character-lists segregated by sex, but none has the title
Actorum Nomina or any sub-title.

Indeed, the agreement between Barry's play and The Family in the matter
of oaths and exclamations is quite considerable: we notice in particular
mass (once only, each play) and tut (Family, 13; Ram Alley, 10). All
of this suggests that Barry's hand on The Family of Love was not a light
one, and that his contribution to the general effect of the final text
may have been more important than Dekker's. Since the list of Actorum
Nomina is presumably his work, he must have written Smelt for Shrimp;
which may have been a slip, but more probably represents a last-minute
change to a more amusing and expressive name; I would credit Barry also
with the changes from Nuntius to Vial and from Poppin to Exigent.

2.3.3.5. Evolution of the present text: summary

The general history of the play was probably as follows: first
version by Middleton (perhaps with minor aid from Dekker), 1602-03;
revision and/or additions by Dekker, mid-1605; transfer to King's Revels'
company, 1606-07; revision by Barry, 1607. At some point in this series
of changes at least one scribal transcript intervened to produce the
spelling 'hem, which is probably not Barry's, since the three instances
of the contraction of them in Ram Alley are spelt em or 'em, and
probably not compositorial.[1] The revisions by Barry probably com-
prised: (1) a major revision of the text, during which Barry "improved"
the style of the play to his own satisfaction for the first production
by the King's Revels company; (2) alterations of characters' names, some
of them probably during the play's run in 1607. I do not think that
Barry added passages of any length to the Middleton-Dekker text; if he
had done so, these would very likely have included some allusion belonging to 1607.

2.3.3.6. Authorship divisions

I must emphasize that the authorship divisions given below are
merely those which seem to me likely on the balance of available evidence.
When a play has been revised and transcribed as often as The Family

---

[1] Dillon finds (xxvi-xxvii) that two compositors set The Family, the
better workman producing only the nine pages A2v, B2v, C1v, D1v, E3v,
F3v, H1, H2, I2v. The spelling 'hem occurs four times in this portion
(H1, twice; H2, twice), and 'hem or hem seventeen times elsewhere. No
contraction of them occurs in Humour Out; in A Yorkshire Tragedy the
spelling is /em/.

appears to have been, it becomes very difficult to disentangle the authorship of the various sections with any confidence. If I am in error, I have at least tried to err on the side of simplicity. I have therefore not tried to limit Barry's revision by sections, though it is more obvious in some sections than in others.

2.3.3.6.1. Summary of attributions

Middleton: "To the Reader", Prologue, Epilogue.

Barry: "Actorum Nomina".

Middleton, revised by Barry: I.i, ii.b (53-169), iii; II.iii-iv; III; IV.i-ii.a (1-88), iii.b (96-139), iv;V.

Dekker, revised by Barry: I.ii.a (1-52); II.i-ii; IV.ii.b (89-100), iii.a (1-95).

2.3.3.6.2. Survey of scenes

"To the Reader" (M.). If I am right in identifying the principal original author as Middleton, then this preface, clearly dating from 1608, is probably his. On the whole, internal evidence may be said to support the attribution, for there are similarities here to Middleton's only undoubted dramatic preface, that prefixed to The Roaring Girl. Both prefaces stress the changeableness of playgoers' tastes; both contain the words vent and Termers. It must be admitted, though, that there are also pointers to Dekker: seald it for good is paralleled by if you set your hands and Seales to this [i.e. applaud the play] in the Epilogue to Satiromastix; more importantly, the ending, with Farewell but no signature, is in line with Dekker's normal practice in a great many works: Shoemaker, Satiromastix, and the prose works Wonderful Year, News from Hell, Four Birds of Noah's Ark, Dekker his Dream, Strange Horserace, and Penny-wise, Pound-foolish. Middleton's prefaces, on the contrary, are normally signed and lack the word Farewell: thus, in Roaring Girl, Wisdom of Solomon, Black Book, and Father Hubbard's Tales. But there is one Middleton work, written just about this time, which does have nearly the right end-formula: the pamphlet Sir Robert Sherley (Q 1609), in which the preface is headed "To the Reader" (A4), and the ending is simply Vale, Latin for "Farewell" (B1; Bullen, VIII , 304). Also against Dekker's authorship of the Family preface is the contraction the'are (line 8), since Dekker contracts they+are much less frequently

than Middleton. The preceding word <u>whiles</u> must represent an exceptional
usage, no matter who wrote the preface (see Table I.1). I think the
attribution to Middleton is justified by the balance of probabilities,
but I am not confident about it.

"Actorum Nomina" (B.). See above, 2.3.3.4.

Prologue (M.). This, presumably, is the original prologue for the
first version of 1602-03, since it admits that "opinion hath not blazd
his fame," which may have been true of Middleton in 1602-03, but hardly
much later. It is noticeable that the prologue clearly implies single
authorship for the version it refers to; hence if Dekker had any share in
the original version, it could not have been a large one. Moreover, the
original principal author could not have been Dekker, who was famous long
before 1602; indeed, before 1600, since he is named in 1598 by Francis
Meres as among those eminent "for Tragedie" (<u>Palladis</u> <u>Tamia</u>, Oo3).
There is just a faint possibility that the prologue is Barry's for the
1607 production, since the reference to <u>the</u> <u>fruit</u> <u>of</u> <u>many</u> <u>an</u> <u>hower</u> (line
6) matches references in the <u>Ram</u> <u>Alley</u> Prologue and Epilogue to the long
time spent in composition. Probably the resemblances are merely due to
plagiarism by Barry. (See below, for a similar problem as regards the
Epilogue.)

I.i. (M., rev. B.) Barry's hand is suggested by '<u>a</u> twice in the
first speech, and three more times on the same page (A2), including one
instance in verse (<u>why</u> <u>a</u> <u>loues</u>, <u>or</u> <u>hates</u>). The same piece of verse
contains the verb <u>axe</u> (for "ask"), which has no parallel elsewhere in
Middleton. On A2v there are three more instances of '<u>a</u>.

Maria's verse speeches in this scene are a fair sample of the verse
of the lovers' raptures scattered through the play. Such passages are
decidedly different in versification from the norm of Middleton's early
period, being much more masculine-ended and regular in metre and line-
length than one finds in the comedies from <u>Phoenix</u> onwards. However, this
cannot be used as an argument against Middleton's authorship, or in favour
of a very early date for the play, since these verse raptures contain a
strong element of parody, in particular of the early Shakespearean style
of <u>Romeo</u> <u>and</u> <u>Juliet</u>.

I.ii.a(D., rev. B.) Barry's presence is suggested by '<u>a</u> on A3 (I.ii.
9). For Dekker, see above (2.3.3.3).

I.ii.b. (M., rev. B.) Barry is presumably responsible for blud
(A4) and wo't (A4v, twice; I.ii.125, 133).

I.iii. (M., rev. B.) Signs of Barry are the thickly crowded
instances of 'a: eight on B1 in the first twelve lines of the scene,
and eight more in B1v-B3v; also perhaps wod (B1v; I.iii.28) and wud
(B2; I.iii.61). The mention of Bocardo (B1; I.iii.8) indicates local
knowledge of Oxford, hence the hand of Middleton. Possibly ten words
on B2v--(vnlesse the whole new liuery of Porters set their shoulders)
⌈I.iii.108-09⌉ -- are an insertion by Dekker; they must date from 1605,
whoever wrote them.

II.i-ii. (D., rev. B.) See above, 2.3.3.3.   There is no way of
telling whether these soliloquies were part of the original version of
the play; they could well be additions of 1605. The Tut in II.i.21
could be a trace of Barry's revision or inaccurate copying of Dekker's Tush.

II.iii. (M., rev. B.)   The only (very doubtful) sign of Barry's
revision is the absence of I'm as against three instances of I am on C1.

II.iv. (M., rev. B.) Barry is somewhat more evident here, with
betwixt, them, I am, and doth, but only one 'hem, and no I'm or between
(see Table 2.3, below). There is also the adjectival phrase Inne of Court
⌈dyning Tables⌉ on C1v; Barry has Inne a Court man in Ram Alley (B2),
whereas Middleton has Innes a Court-man in Mad World (F1; III.iii. 148)
and Ins-a-Court man in Widow (B4; I.i.216), though of course the s-less
form could have arisen in transcription or type-setting.

III.i-ii. (M., rev. B.) This is the quarto's III.i, divided by
Dyce and Bullen into two scenes. In Bullen's III.i the only suggestions
of Barry are doth in line 7, and the lack of contractions; in III.ii,
Lord (D2v; III.ii.19) and the lack of I'm beside five instances of I am.
Signs of Middleton in III.i-ii are certain and plentiful: the Chaucer
reference, "subaudi" and suspectless (see above, 2.3.3.2).

III.iii. (M., rev. B.) Possible signs of Barry include O Lord
(line 21) and Lord (line 35), both on D4v. It is interesting to note
i'theyr ⌈kinde⌉ (line 10, D4), which, if due to Middleton, exemplifies
the usage of i' + possessive employed by him only in plays of doubtful
or collaborate authorship, The Widow, and The Inner Temple Masque

(see 1.3.3). This distribution, as we have seen, must be due to sheer chance.

III.iv-vi. (M., rev. B.) This is the quarto's III.iii, divided by Dyce and Bullen into three scenes. III.iv--one speech of ten lines-- contains another instance of i' in the phrase deuills turd i'thy teeth; also one instance of comfort, so that the impression of Middleton's manner is fairly strong. Barry's presence in III.vi, the pseudo-conjuring scene, may be indicated by 'a twice on E2v and perhaps by the strange oaths gogs nownes, Gogs blude (E2v, III.vi.28).

III.vii. (M., rev. B.) I give this attribution for the sake of simplicity, the scene being contiguous to preceding and following Middleton scenes: there are no clear indications of authorship.

IV.i. (M., rev. B.) Two instances of 'a may signify Barry's presence (E4v, F1). The four hath (three in prose) but no has in this scene may be due to the immaturity of Middleton's style of 1602-03, or just possibly to scribal intervention; Barry prefers has.

IV.ii.a (M., rev. B.) There are few indicators of authorship, but the prose lacks Middleton's usual contractions.

IV.ii.b. (D., rev. B.) See above, 2.3.3.3.

IV.iii.a. (D., rev. B.) See above, 2.3.3.3. The first part of this section, lines 1-37, belong to the main action of the Gerardine-Maria plot, but could be a replacement by Dekker of original work by Middleton. Lines 38-95 belong almost entirely to 1605. The seven instances of I am but no I'm in this section may suggest that Barry expanded Dekker's contractions as well as Middleton's.

IV.iii.b. (M., rev. B.) See above, 2.3.3.3.

IV.iv (M., rev. B.) Signs of Barry include eleven instances of 'a (seven on G1v), and betwixt twice (F4v, G1). The revision is further indicated by besides twice (G1, G2v) and towards (G2), but no instance of Middleton's preferred between, beside, or toward.

V.i-iii. (M., rev. B.) The authorship of the first two scenes of Act V is rather doubtful, but I'm, O: I am, 5 in V.i suggests Barry; the short V.ii, with two instances of comfort (V.ii.6, 26) is more likely to be Middleton's than Dekker's. In V.iii the ratio ay, 7: yes, 1 is against Dekker's authorship, and the lack of I'm suggests the revision.

Epilogue. (M.) The authorship of the Epilogue is probably the
same as that of the Prologue, presumably Middleton's. Both Prologue
and Epilogue use the rhyme fauor(s)-labor(s); but, interestingly, the
Ram Alley epilogue has labour-fauour. If the Family Epilogue is not
by Barry, then this may be another case of plagiarism by the impresario
and future pirate, who apparently did not enjoy the creative aspects
of composition, to judge from his remarks about his working hours--
tedious houres, according to the Ram Alley epilogue, line 2.

2.3.3.7. Conclusion

I must confess that the theory outlined above is one about which
I am not confident in detail. I think it is correct in essentials,
and it "saves the appearances"; but it is not a simple theory, and therefore not very attractive. Perhaps there is more Middleton and less
Barry in the text than I have supposed; but in that case the date of
the original play will have to be pushed back earlier than 1602, and at
least three revisions (1602-03, 1605, and 1607) will have to be
postulated. A theory of that kind is no simpler than the one I have
proposed. At least we can be sure that The Family of Love is not an
unmodified play by Middleton alone.

Table 2.3, below, gives the distribution of linguistic evidence.

Table 2.3.   The Family of Love: significant features

Sect-ion	Lines	tut	Lord	blood, Pluto	byr-lady	ay: yes	betw-een: -ixt	'a	(')hem: them	has: hath	does: doth	I am	wou' wou'
1.1	61	1	.	.	.	.	.	8	.	:1	.	1	.
1.2.a	52	.	.	.	.	.	.	1	.	1:1	.	.	.
1.2.b	117	3	.	1,	.	1:	.	.	:3	.	:1	1	,2
1.3	184	2	.	.	.	3:	.	16	:5	1:	2:1	3	2,
2.1	23	1	.	.	.	.	.	.	:2	:2	.	.	.
2.2	9	.	.	.	.	.	.	.	.	.	.	.	.
2.3	103	.	.	.	.	2:	.	.	3:3	2:2	1:	3	.
2.4	286	.	.	.	.	3:1	:2	.	1:8	1:4	3:2	4	.
3.1-2	180	1	1	.	.	1:	.	.	1:	3:	1:1	6	.
3.3	137	.	2	.	1	4:1	1:	.	2:5	1:	1:	4	.
3.4-6	92	.	.	.	.	.	.	2	1:	2:2	.	3	.
3.7	38	.	.	.	.	.	.	.	.	.	.	.	.
4.1	128	1	.	.	.	:1	.	2	:2	:4	.	.	.
4.2.a	88	.	.	.	.	.	.	.	:1	.	.	.	.
4.2.b	12	.	.	.	.	.	.	1	:1	.	.	.	.
4.3.a	95	.	.	.	.	1:1	1:	.	1:	1:1	.	7	.
4.3.b	44	.	.	.	.	.	.	.	.	1:	.	1	.
4.4	181	1	.	,1	.	:1	:2	11	:1	.	1:	4	.
5.1	142	.	1	.	.	2:2	.	.	4:4	3:2	1:	5	.
5.2	52	.	.	.	.	.	.	.	:1	.	:2	.	.
5.3	455	3	.	.	2	7:1	1:	.	8:11	3:10	2:1	6	.
Tot-als:	2479	13	4	1,1	3	24:8	3:4	41	21:47	19:29	12:8	48	2,2

Note   Scenes are numbered as in Bullen, but grouped in Act III to restore the original scene-divisions of Q 1608.

3. Additions to the early canon

3.1. The Puritan

With the problem of The Puritan, this study for the first time passes from the traditional canon of Middleton to the speculative ground of plays attributed in the seventeenth century to other authors, but more recently claimed as Middleton's. However, in the case of The Puritan the step is not a bold one: probably the majority of scholars today accept Middleton's authorship, at least as a collaborator, and there is no other serious candidate in sight. Much extremely cogent evidence has been published already, notably by Mark Eccles.[1] My task here shall be to list such evidence with accurate figures for the various features, to adduce further evidence, and to show what conclusion can be drawn from a statistical argument modelled on the methods of Ellegård. It will be demonstrated that Middleton is indeed the author, and probably the sole author, of The Puritan in its present form.

3.1.1. Text

In the Stationers' Register for 6 August, 1607 (Arber, III, 358) there was entered for the copy of George Eld "A book called the comedie of the Puritan Widowe," and the edition followed at once, Eld printing it in his own shop. The title page of Q 1607 bears the words:

> The Pvritaine Or The Widdow of Watling-streete. Acted by
> the Children of Paules. Written by W.S. [Eld's device and imprint.]

Archer's play-list in 1656 expanded the initials "W.S." to "Will. Shakespeare", and thereafter The Puritan[2] entered the Shakespeare Apocrypha via the Third Folio.

Luckily for textual studies, Eld printed no less than ten other plays in 1607-08, a period during which the staff of his shop is not known to have altered.[3] Seven of these plays are in the Table I.1 corpus-- The Devil's Charter, Lingua, Volpone, What You Will, Trick, Your Five Gallants, and The Revenger's Tragedy. Apart from the last, all these

---

[1] "Middleton's Birth and Education," pp. 437-39. My study of The Puritan incorporates material which I have published in "Middleton's Hand in The Puritan" (1972).

[2] The conventional title for this play is a poor one: it would be far better re-named as "The Puritan Widow", following the S.R. entry, the head title and running titles.

[3] As Murray pointed out in Cyril Tourneur, p. 162. No apprentices were freed by or bound to Eld between 7 October 1605 and 15 December 1608: see D.F. McKenzie, "A List of Printers' Apprentices, 1605-1640," p.120.

are of known authorship.[1]

Donald F. Kaiser, in his unpublished edition of The Puritan,[2] finds that the copy for Q 1607 was probably the author's manuscript, since stage-directions are inadequate, some exits in particular being confusing.

3.1.2. Date of composition

The date of composition and of first performance was almost certainly 1606. The central character of the play, George Pyeboard, is clearly meant (with a pun on peel, "baker's shovel") to stand for George Peele; the Merrie Conceited Jests of George Peele was entered in the Stationers' Regist on 14 December 1605 (Arber, III, 308). The extant pamphlet is dated 1607, but there may have been an earlier issue or edition: some of the Jests are certainly used in The Puritan. What especially helps to fix the date is that Sunday 13 July, referred to on sig. F4, III.v.290,[3] fits the calendar of 1606. The play can hardly be later than 1606, because the Children of Paul's ceased acting before the end of that year.[4]

3.1.3. Authorship controversy

All considerable English-speaking critics from Malone onwards have rejected Shakespeare's authorship; Middleton seems to have been first proposed by Fleay (Biographical Chronicle, II, 92-93), who was supported by Bullen (I, lxxxix-xc) and very many others. A prominent early dissenter was C. F. Tucker Brooke, who objected that the author must have been an Oxford man, because of the knowledge of that university displayed in I.ii, and hence not Middleton but probably Marston (Shakespeare Apocrypha, xxxi-xxxii). Brooke's objection was turned into an argument in favour of Middleton by Eccles when he discovered the facts of Middleton's early life

---

[1] The other plays printed by Eld in 1607-08 are: Northward Ho, The Travails of Three English Brothers (by Day, Rowley, and Wilkins), and The Conspiracy and Tragedy of Charles Duke of Byron (Chapman). The two latter are of little use for comparison purposes, since they lack colloquialisms.

[2] "The Puritan, or, the Widow of Watling Street: a critical edition," Diss. Wisconsin, 1966, pp. lxxiv-lxxvii.

[3] Line references to The Puritan are to the edition by C. F. Tucker Brooke, in The Shakespeare Apocrypha (1908; rpt. Oxford: Clarendon Press, 1967).

[4] These facts are summarized by Chambers, Elizabethan Stage, IV,42.

and Oxford career ("Middleton's Birth and Education"). Eccles also briefly
mentioned some of the overwhelming stylistic evidence for Middleton--
"inconspicuous turns of phrase" such as give him his due, troth you say true;
the frequent use of comfort, the interjections push, puh, why, and the oaths
'sfoot and mass; and the occurrence of the contractions h'as, sh'as, t'as,
t'ad and uppo'th'.[1] Since this article of 1931, little further work has
been done on The Puritan: Eccles' case has rested, with Middleton triumphant.
That Eccles was right is easily seen from a brief examination of Table I.1:
the features of The Puritan correlate extremely well with those of the early
Middleton plays, and differ sharply from those of Marston's.

The date of composition, 1606, implies that The Puritan is contemporary
with Trick and Mad World, probably the most successful of Middleton's early
comedies. This synchronism has deterred some critics, notably Barker,
from accepting Middleton's authorship of what is admittedly a rather crude
play. However, the argument from relative literary values is, as usual, a
weak one. Since The Puritan was concocted to serve up "merry jests"--i.e.
broad farce--some crudity might perhaps be expected.

3.1.4. Spelling evidence

The one major category of evidence not cited by Eccles is that of
spelling. It would take a very elaborate study to show in how many respects
the spellings in The Puritan agree with Middleton's practices and disagree
with the spellings of plays by other authors printed by Eld in 1607-08;
I have therefore confined this investigation to a few of the more distinctive
spellings--those of 'em, has, does, some pronoun + verb contractions, and
the preterite/past participle forms of verbs ending in -ce.

---

[1] I must acknowledge a deep debt to Professor Eccles. His epoch-
making article not only revolutionized the study of Middleton by revealing crucial external evidence; it also suggested the most useful
categories of linguistic evidence which form the basis of my own work.

Table 3.1(1), below, displays this evidence.

Table 3.1(1). The Puritan and other plays: selected spellings

Texts: (I) Non-Eld	-cst	(')hem	em	'em	e'm	(") has	h'as	ha's	doe(')s	do(')s	thou'rt	th'art	you're	y'are	they're	th'are
Phoen.	.	.	1_b	20	17[a]	23	.	23	3	15	4	.	7	16	2	3
MT	.	.	4	14	28	27	1	15	10	12	.	.	13	12	9	.
MWM	1	.	20	8	38	42	4	8	.	17	7[c]	1	6	10	26	.
GC	12	.	4	2	31	10	5	25	.	8	3	.	5	5	5	.
(II) Eld																
Trick	3	.	4	4	28	39	.	5	.	7	9	.	9	7	1	.
YFG	3	.	38	20	1	42	2	.	6	6	3	2	20	22	20	.
Pur.	2	.	7	32	2	36	2	9	2	6[d]	2	1	5	10	6	.
RT	5	.	5	21	12	38	3	4	5	23	8	1	3	8	4	.
D.Ch.	.	.	.	.	.	.	.	.	.	.	.	1	.	.	1	.
Ling.	.	.	.	.	.	1	.	.	1	.	.	5	.	.	.	2
N.Ho	.	.	4	15	.	25	.	.	15	1	.	.	.	5	.	.
Volp(Q)	.	52	.	.	.	45	.	4	1	18	.	.	.	.	.	.
WYW	.	.	.	.	.	12	.	.	2	3	.	.	.	.	.	.

Notes   Texts as in Table I.1 except as follows:
N.Ho = Northward Ho, from Dram. Works, II; Volp(Q) = Volpone, from
Q 1607, ed. in type-facsimile by Henry De Vocht, in Materials for the
Study of the Old English Drama, 13 (1937).   Occurrences:
[a] Once as a'm. [b] Once as am. [c] Once as thu'rt. [d] Once as doos.

It is clear from the table that Eld's compositors were following
copy fairly faithfully. Among the texts of undoubted authorship set
by them, -cst, e'm, h'as, thou'rt, and you're appear exclusively in
plays by Middleton. Volpone has both ha's and do(')s, but Table I.1
shows that these are genuine Jonsonian spellings evident in his other plays;
similarly, in Volpone Eld's workmen faithfully reproduced Jonson's
invariable 'hem. The rarest spelling in the table is probably e'm; this
does not appear at all in any play printed by Eld in 1607-08 except in
Middleton's plays Trick and Your Five Gallants, and those claimed for
Middleton, The Puritan and The Revenger's Tragedy.[1] It is also clear that
Eld's men did not introduce contractions not found in copy--hence the dearth

[1] This statement includes Eld's quartos of Travails of Three English
Brothers (Q 1607) and Byron (Q 1608), where 'em does not appear in any
spelling.

of contractions in such plays as Devil's Charter, Lingua, and What You
Will. From the evidence it would seem that The Puritan was printed from
a Middleton autograph.

3.1.5. Survey of scenes

It is literally true that Middleton's style is visible on every page
of The Puritan; nor is there any convincing sign of a collaborator.[1]
Table 3.1(2) will display the distribution of those features which are
used in the statistical argument of the following section (3.1.6). In
the present survey of the various scenes of the play I shall mention
mostly the more distinctive features: mainly parallel collocations which
I have noticed in the course of this study.

I.i. The first sign of Middleton occurs in the initial stage-direction with the phrase Sonne and heyre. In the dialogue of the first
page (A3) we find comfort, the interjection why twice, 'em once, the
spelling ha's, and the phrase give him his due (the latter noted as a
Middletonism by Eccles; see Table I.1). By the middle of A3 we are
clearly in the atmosphere of Michaelmas Term: Edmond, who is called
sonne and heyre again (this time by his mother) is a lively embodiment
of a stock Middleton joke,[2] well expressed by Fitsgrave in Your Five
Gallants (H3; IV.viii.288): Are your fathers dead, gentlemen, y'are so
merry [?]. On A4 there is another collocational parallel--that's the
properer phrase, which occurs also in identical form in Your Five
Gallants, F4v (IV.v.21). Before the scene ends we have another instance
of "son and heir" (A4v), and one of by my Fathers Copy (B1).

I.ii. In Pyeboard's first speech there is a past participle in -cst:
licenc'st (B1). Ha's occurs twice on B1v, "sons and heirs" twice more
(B1v, B2). The scene also includes one instance of the Middletonian
contraction sh'as (B2v), as well as one of she'as (B2; not included in
the statistical argument).

I.iii. On B3 we have Middleton's prefix for a chorus speech--All,
not Omnes. The hypocrisy of Puritans (and others) is a favorite Middleton
theme, and here and in the next scene it evokes some favorite phrases.

---

[1] I argued in "Middleton's Hand in The Puritan" that woult in this play
suggested a minor collaborator; but I now think otherwise; see below,
s.v. I.iv.

[2] This "death of father" joke in Michaelmas Term was noted by W. D.
Dunkel, in "The Authorship of The Puritan," PMLA, 45 (1930), 807.

Nicholas' what an oath was there (B3) is exactly paralleled in No Wit
(G5v; V.i.183): What an oath was there Sir?--and closely in More Dissemblers
(C6v; II.iii.40): What a word was there?

    I.iv. On B3 in the previous scene Nicholas had warned Corporal Oath:
if you sweare once, wee shall all fall downe in a sowne presently. Now,
when Captain Idle says bluntly "Wilt soon at night steal me thy master's
chain?" Nicholas replies: Oh, I shall sowne! (C1).   This has very close
parallels: in Your Five Gallants (E3v; III.v.3) the Courtesan deceitfully
welcoming Pursenet exclaims: thy arme bound in a scarfe, I shall sowne
instantly; and in Hengist (V.i.185) the Puritan Oliver, forced to witness
a play, says Oh I shall swound. This simple phrase is not common in early
Jacobean drama: indeed, I cannot recall any instance of it used in a
context of hypocrisy outside Middleton's plays.   There is another instance
in More Dissemblers (D2v; III.i.168), where Lactantio says If woman be
amongst it, I shall swoun.

    On C2 occurs the first instance of the contraction upo'th' (/vpp'oth/)
which in the 132-play corpus is used only by Middleton and once by Dekker
(see Table I.1: Jonson in his later plays uses upo'the). In the last line
of C2 occurs the Middletonism sauing my selfe harmlesse.

    In this scene, however, there also occur features which seem unlike
Middleton's usual habits. The oath grace of God (C2; I.iv.233) contains
the undisguised divine name; of course, it is a stroke of excellent
theatre to put this oath in the mouth of Nicholas, of all people. There
are also two instances of woult (C1, I.iv.135; C1v, I.iv.167), the variant
of "wilt" with lip-rounded vowel which is much more commonly contracted to
wou't. Neither woult nor wou't occurs in undoubted Middleton. It is
possible to postulate the hand of a collaborator in this scene; however, the
oath with God and the form woult are more likely to be merely very rare
Middletonian usages, since, as we shall see (3.2.6.2, 3.3.5.1), there are
parallels in other problem plays of this period.

    II.i. On D1 (II.i.179) occurs the exclamation tuh, which I have found
elsewhere only in Phoenix (F1v; II.iii.159-60), where Tangle says tuh tuh,
tuh, tuh, tuh. This is not merely a variant spelling of tut, but an
audibly distinct utterance. Another rare link with Middleton is possibly
the exclamation vff on D1v (II.i.235), paralleled by Ough in Your Five
Gallants (B3; I.ii.67); however, Ough is phonetically ambiguous. On D2

occurs the rare construction "can possible": Ile speake as much as euer I can possible (II.i.285-86), which is found also in Phoenix (G4v; IV.i. 88) and Your Five Gallants (H3v; IV.viii.313), but only once in the 132-play corpus outside Middleton (in Fletcher's Island Princess, F 1647, 111a).

II.ii. This ten-line scene is clearly marked as Middleton's by two instances of I'me, and ha's in when ha's mist it, which is two Middletonian features at once--the spelling ha's and the ellipsis for "he has".

III.i. This scene is marked as Middleton's by spellings--dos (D3; III.i.4), ha's (D3v; III.i.29), which is also the ellipsis--and linguistic features (see Table 3.1(2), below).

III.ii. At lines 80-81 occurs the clause that would fetch['] t againe with a Sesarara. The collocation "fetch .. again" is a Middletonism which occurs in Michaelmas Term (A3v; I.i.32), Your Five Gallants (E4; III.v.4), The Widow (B1v; I.i.48-49), and in a section of The Family of Love which I have attributed mainly to Middleton (B1v; I.iii.27). Non-Middletonian instances are rare (see Table I.1). Sesarara, a corruption of the legal term Certiorari, occurs three times in Phoenix in slightly less debased forms: Sursurrara (C1; I.iv.121), Sursurarers (F2v; II.iii.238), Sursararaes (G4v; IV.i.82). The only parallel that I have found outside Middleton is the uncorrupted form Certiorare in Ram Alley (H1v).

At line 86 (E1) we have the form exlent, the dissyllabic contraction of "excellent", noticed as a Middletonism above (2.1.4.2, s.v. 1 Honest Whore, I.v.a).

III.iii. This scene is marked as Middleton's by oaths and other linguistic features (see Table 3.1(2), below).

III.iv. Masse here[he comes] (E3; III.iv.39-40) is a collocation commoner in Middleton than in most other authors (see Table I.1); it is normally used (as here) to mark an entrance. In the next speech (line 43) is the phrase You're kindly welcome. Adverbs in -ly followed by welcome constitute another collocation of which Middleton is unusually fond, especially in his early period.

III.v. There is another instance of the "death of father" joke on F2 (III.v.106-110). When Pyeboard suggests to Captain Idle that during the planned "conjuring" he can keep a straight face by thinking of "the death of thy Father ithe Country," Idle replies that this would have the opposite effect: I should nere lin laughing. Lin is a rare word used much more often by Middleton than by other authors: it occurs five times in his plays from Your Five Gallants onwards (Your Five Gallants, I.i.292; Chaste Maid, III.ii.131; More Dissemblers, III.i.75; Hengist, I.i.2; Widow, V.i.203), and always in the phrase never lin.

The collocation Troth and you say true (F2v; III.v.122) is another Middletonism noted both by Eccles and in another problem play by Oliphant.[1] There is only one instance of Troth .. say true in the Table I.1 corpus outside Middleton (in Robert Armin's Two Maids of Moreclacke, F3); Middletonian instances occur in No Wit, B5v, B7v (I.iii.79, 179) and More Dissemblers, F4 (V.i.156).

On F4 (from line 287 onwards) is the almanac passage that both dates the play and resembles the similar passage in No Wit, I.i.259-62. This kind of thing could well be imitated in general terms; but it is highly significant, as Dunkel remarks,[2] that both the Puritan and No Wit passages begin with the identical phrase Stay, stay, stay.

There is another instance of woult on F3v, in a scene which otherwise seems purely Middletonian.

IV.i. This scene of 44 lines is shown to be Middleton's by linguistic evidence (see Table 3.1(2)), including three instances of the interjection why on G1, and yet another instance of the "death of father' joke, when Penny-dub brings merry newes of my fathers death (G1; IV.i.24-25).

IV.ii. This scene is full of Middletonisms. Exlent occurs three times (G1, IV.ii.13; G4, IV.ii.264; G4v, IV.ii.316); fetch . . . agen once more (G1; IV.ii.9-10). On G1v occurs the exclamatory oath Coades, the euphemistic deformation of "God's" which Middleton uses in Trick (Coades Nigs, C4; II.i.329) and in Women Beware Women (Coads-me, H1; I.ii.105); there is no instance in the Table I.1 corpus unconnected with Middleton. A few lines further on we have Why la you now (G1v; IV.ii.40), which, as mentioned above (2.1.4.2, s.v. 1 Honest Whore, I.iii), occurs also in Michaelmas Term (V.iii.33). On G2 there is vpp'oth once more (IV.ii.92).

The pseudo-conjuring passage which follows, like the similar one in Family of Love, III.vi, is a favorite Middleton device. This one has an

---

[1] "The Authorship of The Revenger's Tragedy," p.161.

[2] "The Authorship of The Puritan," p.806.

exact parallel in More Dissemblers, for the nonsense words in The Puritan
(G2v; IV.ii.123) begin with Rumbos--ragdayon, and in More Dissemblers,
Elv (IV.i.129), we have Rumbos stragadelion. In The Puritan the pseudo-
Greek also includes the word vmbrois (IV.ii.129); Umbra occurs in More
Dissemblers (E2; IV.i.124). In both plays the gibberish changes to
approximations of English; in The Puritan, very amusingly, it turns into
the names of highwayman-haunted spots, doubtless well known to Captain
Idle. One of these is coome park, the scene of Pursenet's robbery of
Tailby in Your Five Gallants, III.ii.

On G3 there are the spellings gracst (line 171) and e'm (twice,
line 188); the form woult occurs again at line 167. In view of the
clear signs of Middleton's autograph at this point, it is after all
likely that Middleton did write woult.

IV.iii. The oaths Zounes and Sbloud uttered by Corporal Oath
(H1) are unusual for Middleton, but easily explained by the need for
characterization here; indeed, their occurrence in this passage shows
that they are not regarded as normally acceptable language by the
author of The Puritan. Exlent occurs again at line 92 (H1v).

V.i and V.ii. These scenes are indicated as Middleton's by linguistic evidence, and by a parallel noted by Eccles ("Middleton's Birth and
Education," p. 439).

V.iii. This short scene (42 lines) contains 'em and troth.

V.iv. The scene opens (lines 2-3) with the Middletonism your
honour is most chastly welcome. On H4 there occurs the exclamation pah
(twice, line 110); pah occurs also in Phoenix (H4v; IV.iii.35), but is
very rare elsewhere.

From this brief survey of the text, it is clear that we can be
confident that Middleton wrote the whole of The Puritan.[1] What statistical value we can attach to our confidence will be discussed in the
next section.

---

[1] Eld's attribution to "W.S." must remain a mystery; it does not seem
likely that it was an attempt at fraud, in view of the other honest and
correct attributions of Eld publications about this time. Possibly
there was a "W.S." involved, who was "revised out".

Table 3.1(2). The Puritan:
distribution of features used in the statistical argument.

Segment 1

Scene	sigs.	push	puh, pah	tut, tuh	hum	coad's	'sfoot, 'slid	faith	troth, mass	ay: yes	among: amongst
1.1	A3-B1	.	.	1,	.	.	.	1	1,	1:	.
1.2	B1-B2v	.	2,	.	.	.	.	.	1,	1:	1:
1.3	B2v-B3v	.	.	.	.	.	.	.	.	6:	.
1.4	B3v-C3	2	1,	.	.	.	.	4	2,2	7:	.
2.1	C3-D3	.	.	,1	.	.	.	2	2,	8:	:1
2.2	D3	.	.	.	.	.	.	.	.	.	2:
3.1	D3-D4	.	.	.	2	.	.	.	,1	3:	1:
3.2	D4-E1	.	.	.	.	.	.	.	.	1:	.
3.3	E1-E2v	..	.	.	.	.	1,2	3	4,1	9:2	1:1
3.4	E3-F1	.	1,	.	.	.	3,	4	3,3	5,2	.
3.5	F1-F4v	.	4,	2,	.	.	5,	7	5,1	11:4	.
4.1	F4v-G1	.	.	.	.	.	.	2	.	1:	.
4.2	G1-G4v	1	1,	.	.	1	3,1	8	5,1	3:1	1:
4.3	G4v-H1v	.	.	.	.	.	2,	2	,1	2:	.
5.1	H1v-H2	.	.	.	.	.	,1	2	.	.	.
5.2	H2-H2v	.	.	.	.	.	.	4	.	.	.
5.3	H2v-H3	.	.	.	.	.	.	.	1,	.	.
5.4	H3-H4	.	,2	.	.	.	1,	.	.	.	:1
Totals:		3	9,2	3,1	2	1	15,4	39	24,10	58:9	6:3

Table 3.1(2). The Puritan. Segment 2

Scene	sigs.	beside: besides	between: betwixt	toward: towards	'em: them	has: hath	does: doth	I'm: I am	I'd	sh'as
1.1	A3-B1	1:	1:1	.	2:	2:1	.	1:2	1	.
1.2	B1-B2v	.	.	1:	4:	6:	1:	:2	.	1
1.3	B2v-B3v	.	.	.	.	1:	1:	:2	.	.
1.4	B3v-C3	.	.	.	2:	2:	2:	:6	.	.
2.1	C3-D3	.	1:	.	12:3	4:	.	:3	3	.
2.2	D3	.	1:	.	.	1:	.	2:	.	.
3.1	D3-D4	.	.	.	5:	1:	1:	1:1	.	.
3.2	D4-E1	1:1	.	.	.	5:	.	1:1	.	.
3.3	E1-E2v	:1	.	.	2:1	5:	.	1:3	.	.
3.4	E3-F1	.	.	.	4:2	2:	.	3:4	1	.
3.5	F1-F4v	1:1	2:	.	1:2	7:	.	:2	3	.
4.1	F4v-G1	.	.	.	.	.	.	.	.	.
4.2	G1-G4v	2:	1:	1:	3:	8:	2:	2:	2	.
4.3	G4v-H1v	.	.	.	1:	.	.	:1	.	.
5.1	H1v-H2	.	.	.	5:2	1:	.	.	.	.
5.2	H2-H2v	.	.	.	.	.	.	.	.	.
5.3	H2v-H3	.	.	.	1:	.	.	:1	.	.
5.4	H3-H4	.	2:	.	:2	2:1	1:	.	.	.
Totals:		5:3	8:1	2:	41:12	42:2	8:0	11:28	10	1

Segment 3

Scene	sigs.	t'as, t'ad	we're, they're	you're, y'are	i'th', i'the	a'th', a'the	upo'th; on't	exlent, woult	comfort, 'Has
1.1	A3-B1	.	.	,3	.	.	,2	.	3,
1.2	B1-B2v	.	.	.	.	.	,2	.	1,
1.3	B2v-B3v	.	.	.	.	.	,1	.	.
1.4	B3v-C3	.	.	,2	1,	.	1,8	,2	.
2.1	C3-D3	,2	.	1,1	1,	1,	,3	.	2,
2.2	D3	.	.	.	.	.	.	.	,1
3.1	D3-D4	.	.	.	1,	1,	,1	.	1,1
3.2	D4-E1	.	.	.	.	.	.	1,	1,2
3.3	E1-E2v	1,	,1	1,	1,	.	.	.	,1
3.4	E3-F1	.	,1	1,	.	1,	,3	.	.
3.5	F1-F4v	,1	,1	1,1	1,1	.	,6	,1	1,1
4.1	F4v-G1	.	.	.	.	1,1	,1	.	.
4.2	G1-G4v	,1	,2	,3	9,	4,1	1,	3,1	2,1
4.3	G4v-H1v	.	1,	.	1,	1,	.	1,	.
5.1	H1v-H2	.	,1	.	.	.	.	.	.
5.2	H2-H2v	.	.	1,	.	.	.	.	.
5.3	H2v-H3	.	.	.	.	.	.	.	.
5.4	H3-H4	.	.	.	.	.	.	.	.
Totals:		1,4	1,6	5,10	15,1	9,2	2,27	5,4	11,7

3.1.6. The Puritan: a statistical argument

It must be obvious that no known Jacobean dramatist is as good a candidate as Middleton for the authorship of The Puritan. But what of the possibility that the author is someone unknown to us by name, whose style resembles Middleton's very closely? Intuitively one might decide that this is a virtual impossibility, especially in the light of the many parallels of unobtrusive collocations noted in the previous section. I shall, however, now attempt to quantify this notion of "impossibility"-- which in statistical terms is expressed by a very small probability.

3.1.6.1. The method: general principles

My method is nearly the same as that used by Ellegård to show that the author of the Junius letters is not likely to be anyone other than Sir Philip Francis.[1] The procedure followed can be illustrated with a single feature--for example, the oath faith, which occurs frequently in The Puritan, 39 times in all. First we convert this figure to a relative frequency: I have done so by adjusting, as usual, to a standard play-length of 20000 words. Since The Puritan runs to 19922 words, a simple proportion sum gives the relative frequency of faith as 39.1526.[2] We suspect that this is higher than average--the relevant average being that of authors of plays of comparable genre and date: let us say comedies of about 1600-1612.[3] Now the population of all authors who wrote such comedies must be a fairly large one, including authors who have left no extant plays, or only anonymous ones. All we can handle is a sample, as representative as possible, which must be drawn from undoubted works of known authors. (Anonymous plays must be excluded because if we add these to our sample we do not know how many new authors we are adding.) Since the average is one of authors' styles, all authors chosen must contribute equally to the sample; and since many authors have left only one extant play, this implies that we must choose only one play from each author.[4] My comparison sample for the Puritan

---

[1] A Statistical Method, especially pp. 12-19 and 48-63. My account of the method and the terminology I use are deeply indebted to Ellegård.

[2] In the statistical arguments for The Puritan and The Revenger's Tragedy I have worked to four decimal places, using an electronic desk calculator. See Table 3.1(3) for all statistics concerning faith in the Puritan problem.

[3] Six years either way from the date of The Puritan. If one draws the limit more narrowly, there are not enough plays; if much more widely, theatre conditions begin to change noticeably, affecting especially the occurrence of oaths.

[4] Otherwise statistics for some authors would represent a much more accurate picture of their average usage than those for others(and the volume of calculations would also become very great). I treat each chosen play as an equally valid sample, though of course plays differ somewhat in length.

problem comprises sixteen plays by sixteen authors: Armin's Two Maids of
Moreclacke, Barry's Ram Alley, Beaumont's Knight of the Burning Pestle,
Chapman's May Day, Joshua Cooke's Greene's Tu Quoque, Day's Isle of Gulls,
Dekker's 2 Honest Whore, Field's A Woman is a Weathercock, Fletcher's The
Woman's Prize, Jonson's Volpone, Marston's The Dutch Courtesan, William
Rowley's A Shoemaker a Gentleman, Shakespeare's Coriolanus, Sharpham's
The Fleer, Tomkis' Lingua, and Wilkins' The Miseries of Enforced Marriage.
A few of the plays chosen are not normal comedies, but are included because
they are stylistically not very distant from the colloquial comedy register.
Tomkis' Lingua is chosen although it is probably an academic rather than a
commercial comedy, because it is not entirely uncolloquial, and because it
was printed, like The Puritan, by George Eld in 1607. Coriolanus is chosen
for Shakespeare because although it is a tragedy it is statistically the
nearest of Shakespeare's plays to the style of The Puritan (mainly because
of its very high frequencies of i'th' and o'th'). In choosing the sixteen
plays I have, indeed, taken some care to weight the argument as far as
possible against myself; when there was a choice of plays for any given
author, more than one being equally possible on grounds of date and genre,
I chose the one nearest to The Puritan in style--hence, for instance,
Chapman's May Day rather than his less colloquial All Fools or Monsieur
D'Olive.[1]   A few authors, such as Daniel and Heywood, I have rejected
altogether as very uncolloquial and therefore distant from the style of
The Puritan.

The comparative sample being chosen, the next step is to calculate the
relative frequency of faith in each of the sixteen plays, and to take the
mean of these rates. The mean ($\bar{X}_{16}$) happens to be 25.7538. We thus verify
that our impression was correct: faith is considerably more frequent in
The Puritan than "on average". In Ellegard's terminology, we may call faith
a "plus" feature. If we plot the faith scores (relative frequencies) of
The Puritan and of the sample plays on a graph, the vertical axis representing "number of plays" and the horizontal axis "score", The Puritan will lie
on the right or "plus" side of the sample mean, as in Diagram 1, below:

---

[1]   This weights the argument against myself by reducing the stylistic gap
between The Puritan (and Middleton) on the one hand and the sample mean
on the other.

122

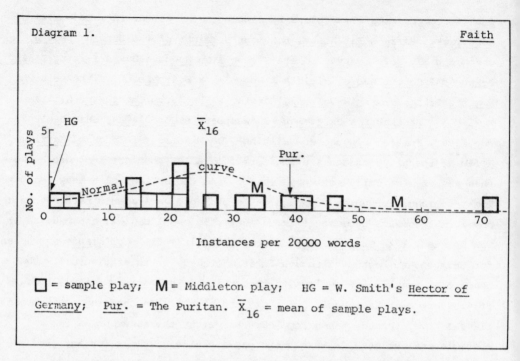

Diagram 1.   Faith

Instances per 20000 words

◻ = sample play; M = Middleton play; HG = W. Smith's Hector of Germany; Pur. = The Puritan. $\overline{X}_{16}$ = mean of sample plays.

To proceed with the method we must now assume some model for the distribution of the scores of the sample and of the population from which the sample is drawn. The natural assumption is that the scores are distributed along the bell-shaped "normal" curve which fits so many quantities such as the heights of people or marks in examinations. Sixteen scores are much too few to verify that the distribution is a normal one; but at least the actual distribution does not contradict that assumption: it clusters towards the mean and tails out above and below roughly as we might expect. Assuming the normal distribution, then, we can use a normal-curve area table to derive the probability at any distance from the mean: that is, the fraction of the total population of authors that is likely to be found at or beyond that distance from the mean. So, in the case of faith, we proceed as follows: the score for The Puritan is 39.1526 - 25.7538 = 13.3988 above the sample mean; since the standard deviation of the sample scores is 16.9106, the Puritan score lies at 0.7923 standard deviations from the mean, for which distance a normal-curve area table gives a probability of .2141; thus, slightly more than one-fifth of all early Jacobean comedy authors might be expected to use faith as frequently a or more frequently than the author of The Puritan. In our sample, three authors do so--Chapman in May Day, Marston in Dutch Courtesan, and Sharpham in Fleer--and three out of sixteen is so close to the fraction predicted by the normal curve model that we are thereby encouraged to continue using this model.

We can now check our opinion that Middleton wrote The Puritan by plotting the faith scores of Middleton's five early comedies on the same graph. The five scores cannot all be shown in Diagram 1, because most are too high--but the lowest score (that for Phoenix) is lower than The Puritan's, so that the latter play clearly falls within the range of Middleton's stylistic variation. Middleton, then, on the evidence of faith, could have written The Puritan. But so could several of the higher-scoring authors. How many, precisely, are as good candidates as Middleton? We can only answer this question if we can fix on some point along the horizontal axis to define the limit of the quality of being "as good" as Middleton: the point I have chosen is the lowest score among Middleton's five plays[1]--for faith, therefore, the score of Phoenix, which is 33.5892, or .4633 standard deviation from the sample mean, yielding a probability of .322. About a third, then, of all authors will be as good candidates as Middleton, judging only from the frequency of faith. This is not strong evidence, but we have much more to be considered, and even this is interesting. The oath faith alone enables us to check the candidature of the only W.S. other than Shakespeare who has left us an extant Jacobean play--the W. Smith who wrote The Hector of Germany (Q 1615).[2] Smith turns out to be a very bad candidate, since there is no instance of faith in the whole of his play. I have calculated his scores for all the other features used in the argument (see Table 3.1(4)), but his candidature is obviously hopeless: his scores are merely average or much worse than average in all three main groups of features.

In principle, we could repeat the procedure as for faith for all features separately, and combine probabilities by multiplication--since a candidate "as good"as Middleton might be defined as one who is at least

---

[1] My procedure here differs from Ellegård's: he used the mean of his problem text (the Junius letters) minus two standard deviations; but The Puritan is too short a text to yield a realistic standard deviation; a figure could only be calculated on a priori assumptions which would not be justified. (See A Statistical Method, pp. 107-08).

[2] For Smith, see Chambers, Elizabethan Stage, III, 493.

as "good" as Middleton's "worst" score in every feature.   But there are
difficulties.   <u>Faith</u> is a high-frequency feature, and the score for its
use over the length of a whole play is a fairly reliable measure of the
author's usage.   But some of our most distinctive evidence consists
of very rare features.   Not only would the frequencies of these, in
isolation, not provide reliable measures; they would not produce normal
curves.   For an item like <u>upo'th'</u> or <u>ex'lent</u>, used by hardly any one
except Middleton, the sample scores would cluster closely about zero,
with one or two authors' scores lying higher and producing a positive
skewness.[1] The same difficulty occurs, to a noticeable extent, with
what Ellegård calls "minus" features--features for which the problem
text, in our case <u>The Puritan</u>, scores distinctly lower than the sample
average; such as <u>ye</u>, <u>'a</u>, and oaths containing the form <u>God's</u>.   For
these features, the <u>Puritan</u> and Middleton scores are near zero, but so
are those of several sample authors, so that the evidence is not very
powerful; and the distribution is positively skewed by a few authors who
make great use of <u>ye</u>, <u>'a</u>, or <u>God's</u>, so that one cannot use the normal-
curve assumption with any confidence.   I have therefore discarded "minus"
features altogether from the statistical argument; and "plus" features
I have dealt with by grouping.

As Ellegård remarks (p.18), for low frequency features some grouping
is always desirable--not only, I would add, to reduce chance variations,
but also to approximate a normal curve.   In allotting features to groups,
Ellegård follows the principle that features of similar distinctiveness
should be grouped together.   Distinctiveness is measured by the
"distinctiveness ratio", which is the ratio of the absolute or relative
frequency of the feature in the problem text and the corresponding mean
frequency of all the sample plays.   It is convenient to use absolute
(or "raw") frequencies when investigating the usefulness of features
for the first time, and thus to classify them roughly by their "raw"
distinctiveness ratios; only the borderline features may need to have
their ratios corrected for play-length.   Thus <u>faith</u> has a "raw"

---

[1]   These distributions are not Poisson distributions either, since I
have found that they always show more dispersion than the Poisson formula
predicts.   For this formula, see Ellegård, p.14.

distinctiveness ratio of 39 x 16/446, since there are 39 instances in
The Puritan and 446 instances in the 16-play sample. This reduces to
very nearly 1.4, which shows that faith is a borderline case, since it
is inadvisable to waste effort on features too near the ratio 1.0; I
have, in fact,adopted a limit of 1.5, below which I discard the feature
from the argument. However, when we compare the frequencies per 20000
words, the corrected ratio is 39.1526/25.7538 = just over 1.52; hence
faith ought to be used. This example illustrates what is probably the
most essential use of the distinctiveness ratio: it provides an objective
criterion for the selection or rejection of features.[1] Ellegård has
used it also to divide features into groups of similar distinctiveness.
I, too, have done this in one method used for the Revenger's Tragedy
problem (see below, 3.2.7.2); but now for The Puritan the principle need
be invoked only to a limited extent. I have divided the plus features
into two groups only--the oath faith, and all other items. Faith needs
to be segregated not merely, or not so much, because it has the lowest
distinctiveness ratio of any used feature, but because it is obviously
the most frequent feature, with a mean relative frequency in the sample
of 25.7538, as compared to 7.954 for the next most frequent feature, i'th'.
If faith were lumped in with the other plus features, its influence would
overwhelm that of much more significant items, and markedly weaken the
argument. Initially I grouped with faith another high-frequency feature,
the exclamation why; but the distributions both of why alone and of why
+ faith showed a clear positive skewness, and I therefore thought it best to
exclude why altogether from the argument. This decision certainly does
not favour Middleton, since he is noted for his high frequency of why.[2]
Luckily, faith can stand by itself: its high frequencies are
reliable and well distributed.   For the rest of the plus features,
I have totalled each play's "raw" score for the whole

---

[1] With a limit of corrected ratio 1.5, it is clear that one need not
examine further any feature whose raw ratio is less than 1.0, since
the highest factor by which the raw ratio can be corrected is 28790/
19922 (= 1.45), the length of the longest play in the sample divided
by that of the problem play. The same is true for the Revenger's Tragedy
problem, where the highest possible correction factor is 28790/21268
(= 1.354).

[2] I would claim that the discarding of why is carried out on an objective
principle, namely, that being of such high frequency, higher even than
faith, with 550 instances in the sample, it could only be grouped with
faith, even though its distinctiveness is higher (raw ratio, 1.92); but
it would then render the method inoperable; hence it cannot be used.

group of items, then corrected for play-length, and then proceeded as for <u>faith</u> to find the sample mean and standard deviation, and Middleton's lowest score; whence a probability can be derived. Table 3.1(3), below, shows the distinctiveness ratios of all marginal plus features.

Table 3.1(3). <u>Puritan</u> problem: distinctiveness ratios (plus features).

<u>Note:</u> The number before the colon in each non-zero cell of the table is the raw or absolute frequency; that after the colon is the frequency per 20000 words.

Play	Length (words)	Excluded (corr.rat.< 1.5)		Included (corr. rat. ≥ 1.5)	
		byrlady	thou'rt+ th'art	tut	a'the+ o'the
TMM	18972	0	0	3: 3.1625	0
RA	22419	0	4: 3.5684	10: 8.921	1: .8921
KBP	21423	0	1: .9335	0	0
MD	23568*	5: 4.243	11: 9.3346	0	1: .8486
GTQ	25231	0	1: .7926	0	0
IG	21351	0	2: 1.8734	0	2: 1.8734
2HW	24832*	0	9: 7.2487	0	2: 1.6108
WW	17772	2: 2.2507	3: 3.376	0	0
W.Pr.	24472*	4: 3.269	0	0	1: .8172
Volp.	28790	0	0	3: 2.084	6 4.1681
DC	19049	1: 1.0499	0	0	7: 7.3494
Sh.G	22745	1: .8793	4: 3.5172	2: 1.7586	0
Cor.	28547*	0	2: 1.4011	0	0
Fl.	16832	1: 1.1882	3: 3.5646	0	0
Ling.	26179	0	5: 3.8198	8: 6.1117	1: .7639
Mis.	25068*	1: .7978	0	7: 5.5848	0
Totals:		15:13.6779	45: 39.4299	33: 27.6226	21: 18.3235
Mean ($\bar{X}_{16}$):		<1: .8548	<3: 2.4643	<3: 1.7264	<2: 1.1452
Pur.	19922*	1: 1.0039	3: 3.0117	3: 3.0117	2: 2.0078
corr. ratio:		1.1744	1.2221	1.7444	1.7532

<u>Other marginal excluded features:</u> raw totals & ratios ---

<u>marry</u> 16-play total: 115.   <u>Puritan:</u> 7.   Raw ratio: < 1.0
<u>ha'</u>   16-play total: 288.   <u>Puritan:</u> 18. Raw ratio: 1.0000

<u>Included features:</u> all in Table 3.1(4) have raw ratios > 2.0, except the following: --- <u>faith</u> (raw ratio, 1.4; corr., 1.52); <u>i'th'</u> (raw ratio, 1.58; corr., 1.8932); <u>a'th'</u> (raw ratio, 1.5; corr., 1.898).

<u>Not considered for the statistical argument:</u> spellings; "miscellaneous words and collocations" (other than <u>comfort</u> and '<u>Has</u>).

<u>Note:</u> Sample plays are listed in alphabetical order of authors.

3.1.6.2. Synonyms

Synonym ratios have great virtues for authorship work: they do not
require a knowledge of text-length, and they are not much affected by
content--in the case of synonyms like between and betwixt, they are
probably not affected by anything except personal preference. But low-
frequency synonyms show the same failings as low-frequency plus features.
The synonymous connectives--between, betwixt, and the rest--are too
infrequent to provide reliable ratios in isolation; and the more distinctive pairs, such as I'm: I am and 'em: them do not in isolation produce
normal curves--the sample scores cluster towards zero, with a strong
positive skewness formed by such authors as Fletcher and the later Dekker.
Grouping is therefore essential to produce both reliability and normality;
the latter is best ensured by eliminating, as far as possible, the
occurrence of zero scores. I have used two methods of grouping: first,
to achieve reliable ratios I have pooled instances of synonymous connectives; after that, to achieve a better approximation to normal distribution
I have averaged percentages of the connective group and of the synonym pairs
listed in Table 3.1(4)--six percentages in all. For convenience, I have
turned all synonym ratios into the equivalents of plus feature scores
by arranging that The Puritan shall have a higher score for every synonym
feature than the mean of the sample plays. This is done by expressing
each feature as a fraction, the numerator of which is provided by the
synonym preferred in The Puritan,[1] and the denominator by the same synonym
plus its alternative. Thus in the case of ay and yes, the fraction is
formed by instances of ay divided by instances of ay + yes; for The Puritan,
58/(58 + 9) = 58/67, which converts to 86.5671 per cent. In connectives,
the same principles apply: the forms preferred in The Puritan are among,
beside, between, and toward (while and whilst being discarded because
no preference for either appears; see Table I.1). Instances of these are
pooled to form the numerator (6+5+8+2 = 21), and instances of the same
words plus amongst, besides, betwixt and towards (21+3+3+1+0 = 28)

---

[1] With one exception: I'm forms the numerator of I'm/(I'm + I am) because
the frequency of I'm relative to that of I am is decidedly higher in
The Puritan than in the 16-play sample. I'm is not actually preferred
to I am in any play used for this argument.

are pooled to form the denominator, so that the fraction is 21/28, or 75 per cent. This pooling of the connectives is strictly necessary, since the ratios of such synonyms as toward and towards may be unreliable not only because of low frequency, but possibly through corruption from the preferences of compositors (though the very consistency of the ratios of some authors shows that such corruption was in fact quite rare).

The method of combining the percentages--by averaging--tends to give each synonym-pair, and the connective group as a whole, about equal weight in determining the final score in the overall synonym group. From the scores in the overall group(the mean percentages) a sample mean and standard deviation, and the probability at the distance of Middleton's lowest-scoring play, are derived in exactly the same way as for plus features (see Table 3.1(4)).

Distinctiveness ratios can be calculated for synonyms as well as for plus features. The only difference is that there is nothing corresponding to the "raw" ratio. The distinctiveness ratio for any synonym feature is found by dividing the sample mean percentage for that feature into the Puritan percentage. The ratios for the features chosen are as follows: ay/(ay + yes), 1.6632; connective group, 3.101; 'em/('em + them), 2.4495; has/(has + hath), 1.7812; does/(does + doth), 1.7605; I'm/(I'm + I am), 4.6356. One synonym pair seemed obviously useless, and this was verified by checking its ratio: 'tis/('tis + it's) has a ratio of 1.0632, and is therefore not used.

When probabilities have been calculated from the three overall groups, (I) plus features, (II) synonyms, and (III) faith, the final probability for the whole argument is achieved by multiplying the three probabilities together.

3.1.6.3. Bias

I have taken great care, in choosing features for statistical treatment, not to favour Middleton's candidature. Every feature in Table I.1, with the exceptions noted at the foot of Table 3.1(3), has been tested separately by examining its distinctiveness ratio. Those with a corrected ratio of 1.5 or higher have been included in the argument (except why, for the reason explained above); all others have been excluded. Middleton's plays do not have any part in this initial screening procedure. For the purposes of this argument items were defined strictly according to the form found in The Puritan; thus, for instance, coads does not

include cuds nor does 'sfoot include Ud's foot. The argument is therefore not consciously biased in favour of Middleton. Of course, there
is a possibility of statistical bias in the choosing of features for
Table I.1 itself. Ellegård made elaborate calculations to allow for bias,
but I have not done so, because I believe that the bias involved in my
work must be very small. First, Table I.1 was drawn up long before the
statistical analyses for the Puritan and Revenger's Tragedy problems
were begun, and it serves not one but twelve authorship problems; any
feature registered for its usefulness in one problem is registered also
for every other problem--which reduces the possibility of selectional
bias very greatly. Nevertheless, some of the features registered in
this automatic way proved useful: for instance, the ay:yes ratio was
included initially because it had been used by MacDonald Jackson as an
argument for Middleton's authorship of The Revenger's Tragedy (see above,
1.1.5.1.1.3). The ay:yes ratio of The Puritan turns out to be even
higher than that of The Revenger's Tragedy. Thus this feature, which
favours Middleton's authorship of The Puritan, was not actually selected
in the course of work on this problem at all. The same is true of all
the connectives, which I first investigated in The Revenger's Tragedy,
but later found significant also for the problems of Blurt and The Puritan.
I have also minimized bias by recording, if only in notes, all types
of evidence that have been used in Jacobean authorship problems in the
past; Table I.1 comprises a selection of useful evidence, but nothing
distinctive in any direction (favorable or unfavorable to my arguments)
has been suppressed.[1] My coverage of oaths, exclamations, and contractions (except those of pronoun + will) has been total. The only area
where bias is obviously possible--collocations and miscellaneous words--
has been excluded from the statistical argument. Finally, to provide a
margin of safety, I have introduced some bias against my argument,
reducing the distinctiveness of The Puritan and Middleton by my selection
of the sixteen sample plays, as explained above (3.1.6.1).

---

[1] Thus, for instance, I am the first investigator to report definite
linguistic evidence which may suggest Middleton's presence in Blurt
(see 2.2.4.6-7) and The Spanish Gipsy (see 4.5.4), a presence which,
however, I argue against in both plays.

3.1.6.4. Substance and spelling

I have used no distinction between features which seems to be a matter of spelling rather than substance. The criterion must be . pronunciation: if a difference could be heard on stage, then the difference is substantial; otherwise, not. In dubious cases I have treated the difference as one of spelling so as to err on the side of safety (see above, 1.1.5.2). I regard as merely spelling variants, and therefore lump together for statistical purposes, the following pairs of forms: thou'rt + th'art; we're + w'are; you're + y'are; a'th' + o'th'; a'the + o'the. But i'th': i'the (etc.) I treat as substantially different. Thus in this argument i'th', a'th' + o'th', i'the, and a'the + o'the are counted as four plus features.[1]

3.1.6.5. Counts of play length.

Most of the plays in Table I.1 and in the 16-play sample for this argument have had their lengths estimated from a random sample of twelve or more quarto pages or sections of equivalent length in non-quarto texts. The estimated length is expressed statistically by 95% confidence limits and these two values $c \pm r$ where c is a central value and r a radius of error or variation about c. There is then 95% probability that the (actually unknown) true length lies between these limits. Essentially r is calculated from the internal variation between the 12, say, page (or section) lengths counted.[2] The radius of error at this confidence level was not more than 7 per cent. of the estimated length for any play in Table I.1, and not more than 6 per cent. for any play used in statistical argument. As a check on the possible error introduced into the final result from these uncertainties, some of the plays with high scores in the 16-play sample (and the 23-play sample for the Revenger's Tragedy problem) were later fully counted. The true errors thus disclosed were all much smaller than the estimated confidence radius, and affected the final probability only slightly (actually, it was slightly decreased, that is, the result was slightly improved). There can be very little uncertainty in the final result due to small uncertainties in the lengths of the other sample plays.

---

[1] Surprisingly enough, the single i'the and two instances of a'the in The Puritan turn out to be distinctive, with corrected ratios greater than 1.5.

[2] The calculations of estimated radius of error and play length were carried out on an Olivetti Programma 101 desk-model computer using a program written by Henry M. Finucan of the Department of Mathematics, University of Queensland. The same computer program also provided means and standard deviations for the Middleton and sample plays in Tables 3.1(4) and 3.2(3).

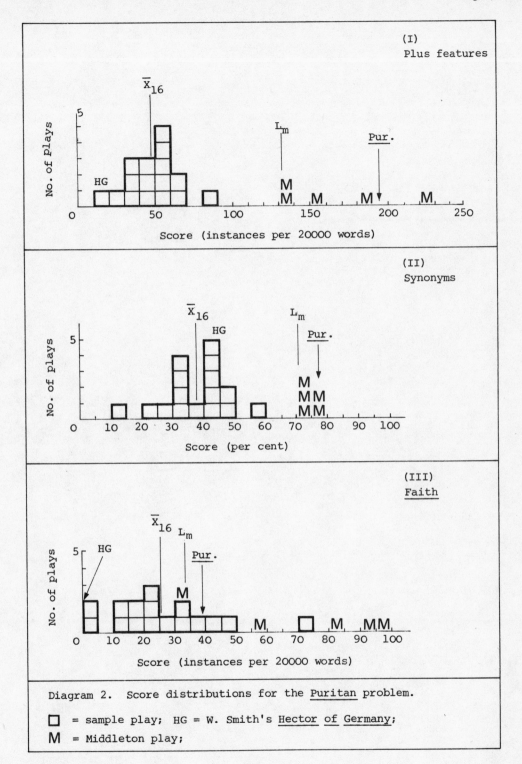

Diagram 2. Score distributions for the Puritan problem.

▢ = sample play; HG = W. Smith's Hector of Germany;

M = Middleton play;

3.1.6.6.   Results

The score-distributions in the three major feature-groups are
shown graphically in Diagram 2 opposite, and numerically in Table 3.1(4)
below. We notice from the diagram that The Puritan seems to be an
average Middleton comedy: in each of the feature-groups it is flanked
on each side by higher and lower scores of the Middleton range. In plus
features and synonyms the separation between the sample range and the
Middleton-Puritan range is complete. Middleton's lowest score (L_m)
lies at 5.0414 standard deviations of the sample distribution in the
plus-feature group; at 3.1373 standard deviations in the synonym group;
and at .4633 standard deviations for faith. The corresponding probabilities are .000,000,233, .000853, and .322.   When multiplied, these
yield the very small figure of .000,000,000,064, or 1 in 15625 million.
Only this fraction of the population of Jacobean dramatists, it seems,
writes a linguistic style as nearly resembling The Puritan as Middleton
does.

There is one more stage necessary to this argument. Ellegård has
outlined (pp. 60-63) the theory required to convert a low probability
of this nature to a belief with 99 per cent confidence that the excellent
candidate already found (in our case, Middleton) is the actual author
of the problem text. I shall not attempt to analyse this mathematical
theory; it is sufficient for our purposes to note that when the probability
obtained is small, certainly when it is less than .00001, the Poisson
series required reduces, for all practical purposes, to its first term,
and the equation given by Ellegård (p.62) becomes

$$P_r = 1 - x/4n \qquad \text{or} \qquad x = 4n \, (1 - P_r)$$

where P_r is the required confidence-level (99%), n is the reciprocal
of the probability (15625 million) and x is the size of the total
population for which this confidence-level will be operative. The
equation for the 99 per cent confidence level reduces to

$$x = .04n$$

so that the population in question is 1/25 of the probability-reciprocal;
for the Puritan problem, therefore, the population is more than 600
million authors. Since this is a population greater than the total
population of the British Isles (indeed, probably greater than the total

population of the earth) in the seventeenth century, we certainly can be confident that Middleton is the actual author of The Puritan. It is difficult to be exact about the number of potential Jacobean dramatists, but 600 million is surely too large by a factor of at least one thousand. Thus the true confidence level is much higher than 99 per cent: there cannot be as much as one chance in a hundred thousand that the author of The Puritan is not Middleton but someone who writes just like him. These figures may seem exaggerated, but I would suggest, on the contrary, that they are a gross under-estimate, since the resemblances between Middleton and The Puritan include many convincing items which have been excluded from the argument--such as collocations and spellings. Moreover, my handling of the statistical data in only three major groups has produced a less powerful conclusion than would have resulted from a subdivision, say, of the plus features into several groups of higher and lower distinctiveness, the method, that is, employed by Ellegard to attack the Junius problem with all available power.[1]   But such refinements are quite unnecessary for our purposes.

I submit, therefore, that Middleton's authorship of The Puritan is now proved beyond reasonable doubt.

---

[1] That this method is more powerful than the grouping by frequency (isolating merely faith) is shown below (3.2.7), where I use both methods as alternatives in the Revenger's Tragedy problem.

Table 3.1(4). Puritan: statistical argument. (I) Plus features
[Group (I) includes all plus features except faith]

Play	Length (words)	push, puh, pah, tut tuh hum	coads, 'sfoot, 'slid	troth, mass	I'd, sh'as, t'as, t'ad, we,you, they+are	i'th(e), a'th(e), o'th(e), upo'th' on't, ex'lent	woult, comfort, 'Has	Tot-al	Total per 20000 words
TMM	18972	5	1	4	6	13	6	35	36.8964
RA	22419	10	.	7	19	2	10	48	42.8208
KBP	21423	.	.	6	8	19	4	37	34.5423
MD	23568*	.	18	9	23	23	4	77	65.3428
GTQ	25231	2	4	8	23	21	8	66	52.3165
IG	21351	.	1	3	1	19	2	26	24.3548
2HW	24832*	.	3	17	25	24	3	72	57.9896
WW	17772	3	3	14	4	17	3	44	49.516
W.Pr.	24472*	.	1	2	9	54	17	83	67.8326
Volp.	28790	7	.	6	6	23	2	44	30.5661
DC	19049	3	.	15	5	15	5	43	45.1467
Sh.G.	22745	2	3	4	12	21	19	61	53.6381
Cor.	28547*	.	.	4	11	94	8	117	81.97
Fl.	16832	.	.	7	11	22	4	44	52.2813
Ling.	26179	13	1	1	3	3	1	22	16.8073
Mis.	25068*	7	12	13	7	11	17	67	53.4546
Phoen.	20840*	12	13	24	41	29	19	138	132.4376
MT	20570*	10	5	22	49	57	15	158	153.6217
MWM	19098*	24	19	24	59	78	13	217	227.2489
Trick	19268*	14	3	31	30	34	19	131	135.9767
YFG	21878*	18	17	32	76	44	13	200	182.832
Pur.	19922*	20	20	34	38	61	22	195	195.7634
HG	16666	.	.	.	2	7	3	12	14.4005

Middleton's mean ($\overline{X}_m$) = 166.4233; his standard deviation (s_m) = 39.4173; his lowest score (L_m) = 132.4376.

Mean of 16 comparison plays ($\overline{X}_{16}$) = 47.8422; standard deviation of 16 comparison plays (s_{16}) = 16.7802.

Distance of Middleton's lowest score from the 16-play mean, in terms of the 16-play standard deviation, =

$(L_m - \overline{X}_{16})/s_{16}$ = 5.0414 standard deviations.

Probability at this distance (from tables of normal-curve area)
= .000,000,233

Table 3.1(4). <u>Puritan</u>: statistical argument. (II) Synonyms

C group = <u>among+beside+between+toward</u>/(same forms + <u>amongst+besides +betwixt+towards</u>).

Play	ay/ay+yes	%	C group	%	'em/'em+them	%	has/has+hath	%
TMM	18/40	45	0/10	0	2/43	4.6511	9/25	36
RA	19/24	79.1666	2/19	10.5263	3/49	6.1224	57/68	83.8235
KBP	24/38	63.1578	11/30	36.6666	13/50	26	21/58	36.2068
MD	8/14	57.1428	1/22	4.5454	47/66	71.2121	30/45	66.6666
GTQ	16/72	22.2222	2/17	11.7647	4/44	9.0909	58/72	80.5555
IG	13/28	46.4285	1/19	5.2631	56/95	58.9473	10/58	17.2413
2HW	13/61	21.3114	6/28	21.4285	9/83	10.8433	45/62	72.5806
WW	18/39	46.1538	10/21	47.619	26/43	60.4651	25/36	69.4444
W.Pr.	5/65	7.6923	8/13	61.5384	66/72	91.6666	42/46	91.3043
Volp.	32/71	45.0704	11/27	40.7407	53/86	61.6279	47/83	56.6265
DC	22/37	59.4594	0/6	0	1/24	4.1666	34/53	64.1509
Sh.G.	19/34	55.8823	1/15	6.6666	23/57	40.3508	35/62	56.4516
Cor.	21/28	75	18/29	62.0609	15/148	10.1351	35/86	40.6976
Fl.	38/60	63.3333	5/12	41.6666	28/81	34.5679	37/77	48.0519
Ling.	20/35	57.1428	6/38	15.7894	0/118	0	1/56	1.7857
Mis.	31/35	88.5714	6/29	20.6896	19/123	15.4471	26/65	40
Phoen.	33/38	86.8421	15/21	71.4285	38/49	77.551	46/49	93.8775
MT	15/22	68.1818	12/26	46.1538	46/54	85.1851	43/46	93.4782
MWM	24/34	70.5882	11/19	57.8947	66/74	89.1891	54/56	96.4285
Trick	28/39	71.7948	23/29	79.3103	36/44	81.8181	44/47	93.617
YFG	19/30	63.3333	27/37	72.9729	59/80	73.75	44/48	91.6666
Pur.	58/67	86.5671	21/28	75	41/53	77.3584	47/49	95.9183
HG	2/3	66.6666	2/9	22.2222	0/58	0	47/53	88.6792

Play	does/does+doth	%	I'm/I'm+I am	%	Mean of all percentages
TMM	25/32	78.125	5/90	5.5555	28.2219
RA	18/25	72	0/42	0	41.9398
KBP	4/16	25	11/75	14.6666	33.6163
MD	20/21	95.238	1/39	2.5641	49.5615
GTQ	18/27	66.6666	2/72	2.7777	32.1796
IG	0/15	0	2/50	4	21.98
2HW	46/48	95.8333	21/59	35.5932	42.9317
WW	14/32	43.75	3/52	5.7692	45.5335
W.Pr.	16/17	94.1176	0/99	0	57.7198
Volp.	18/35	51.4285	2/57	3.5087	43.1671
DC	17/26	65.3846	0/51	0	32.1935
Sh.G.	11/15	73.3333	7/48	14.5833	41.2113
Cor.	19/28	67.8571	0/41	0	42.6251
Fl.	8/24	33.3333	4/48	8.3333	38.2143
Ling.	1/18	5.5555	0/52	0	13.3789
Mis.	14/34	41.1764	0/79	0	34.314
Phoen.	18/19	94.7368	28/61	45.9016	78.3895
MT	22/23	95.6521	25/64	39.0625	71.2855
MWM	17/18	94.4444	26/61	42.6229	75.1946
Trick	7/8	87.5	7/55	12.7272	71.1279
YFG	12/13	92.3076	25/60	41.6666	72.6161
Pur.	8/8	100	11/39	28.2051	77.1748
HG	8/9	88.8888	4/38	10.5263	46.1638

$\bar{X}_m$ = 73.7227

s_m = 3.0758

L_m = 71.1279

$\bar{X}_{16}$ = 37.4242

s_{16} = 10.7428

$(L_m - \bar{X}_{16})/s_{16}$

= 3.1373

standard deviations

Probability at this distance (from tables of normal curve area) = .000853

Table 3.1(4).   The Puritan: statistical argument.(III) Faith

Play	Length (words)	faith	per 20000 words	Play	Length (words)	faith	per 20000 words
TMM	18972	19	20.0295	W.Pr.	24472*	2	1.6345
RA	22419	35	31.2235	Volp.	28790	24	16.6724
KBP	21423	36	33.6087	DC	19049	43	45.1467
MD	23568*	47	39.8845	Sh.G.	22745	25	21.9828
GTQ	25231	41	42.4997	Cor.	28547*	6	4.2035
IG	21351	16	14.9875	Fl.	16832	60	71.2927
2HW	24832*	32	25.7731	Ling.	26179	19	14.5154
WW	17772	18	20.2565	Mis.	25068	23	18.35
Phoen	20840*	35	33.5892	Pur.	19922*	39	39.1526
MT	20570*	58	56.5928				
MWM	19098*	88	92.1562	HG	16666	0	0
Trick	19268*	79	82.0012				
YFG	21878*	109	99.6434				

$\bar{X}_m$ = 72.7565 s_m = 27.3247 L_m = 33.5892

$\bar{X}_{16}$ = 25.7538 s_{16} = 16.9106

Distance of Middleton's lowest score (for Phoenix) from 16-play mean, in terms of 16-play standard deviation, =

$(L_m - \bar{X}_{16})/s_{16}$ =0.4633 standard deviations.

Probability at this distance (from tables of normal-curve area) = .322

Combined probability

The probability of an unknown author's attaining values as high as or higher than Middleton's lowest score in each of the three major feature-groups--(I) plus features (II) synonyms (III) faith--is obtained by multiplying the probabilities for each of these groups:

.000,000,233 x   .000853   x   .322

=   .000,000,000,064

i.e. 1 in 15625 million.

3.2. The Revenger's Tragedy

The authorship of The Revenger's Tragedy is a problem which, in my
opinion, it might be reasonable to regard as already solved. So much
evidence, both linguistic and bibliographical, has been adduced for
Middleton's authorship by Oliphant, Barker, Schoenbaum, Price, and Murray
that the conclusion must by now be almost irresistible that the copy for
the substantive early quarto was a Middleton holograph. I can, however,
report a little additional evidence which points in the same direction,
and I have carried out a statistical analysis (3.2.7, below), on the
same principles as that for The Puritan, which yields overwhelming odds
against the authorship of any one but Middleton.

3.2.1. Text

The Stationers' Register entry for The Revenger's Tragedy is an
important document for our purposes. It is dated 7 October 1607, and
reads as follows:

George Elde   Entred for his copies under th[e h]andes of Sir
              GEORGE BUCK and th[e] wardens. Twoo plaies
              th[e] one called the revengers tragedie th[e] other.
              A trick to catche the old one . . . . xij^{d}

                                          (Arber, III, 360.)

This is the only contemporary external evidence which has any direct
bearing on the authorship of The Revenger's Tragedy, for Q 1607, which
was printed and published by Eld towards the end of the year (some copies
being dated 1608), bore no author's name, the title page reading as
follows:

The Revengers Tragædie. As it hath beene sundry times Acted,
by the Kings Maiesties Seruants. [Eld's device and imprint.]

As we have seen (3.1.1), Eld printed no less than ten other plays in 1607 -
08, so that comparative materials for textual study are copious; the most
useful spelling evidence will be found in Table 3.1(1) above. The most
detailed bibliographical study of Q 1607 is that of George Price ("The
Authorship and Bibliography of The Revenger's Tragedy"). Price decides,
from a scrutiny of omitted and misleading entrances (pp. 263-65), that the
copy for the quarto was probably an authorial fair draft.

3.2.2. Date of composition

The Revenger's Tragedy was probably written about 1606-07. The terminus a quo depends chiefly on apparent influences from Marston, in particular the borrowing of the name Dondolo for the Fool, from Marston's The Fawn (published 1606).[1] I do not find the Marstonian influence otherwise very striking or fundamental, but Dondolo in Revenger's Tragedy is such a perfunctory character that he cannot be an original invention, and thus the direction of borrowing and hence the date of the problem play is indicated.

If both The Puritan and The Revenger's Tragedy are accepted as Middleton's, then there are linguistic indications that the tragedy is the later of the two works;[2] but this cannot be assumed at the present stage of the argument.

3.2.3. Authorship controversy

The first explicit recorded attribution of Revenger's Tragedy is that of the Archer play list of 1656, which has the entry:

| Revenger | T | Tournour | [Item 493] |

This was accepted and clarified by Kirkman in 1661 with his own entry:

| Cyrill Tourneur | | Revengers Tragedy. | T | [Item 540] |

However, it is clear that Kirkman's entry has no independent authority, since he follows Archer in a great many false attributions; even to the point of reproducing absurd errors when he has no evidence to enable him to reject them—and sometimes even when such evidence was available. For instance, he repeats Archer's attribution of The Arraignment of Paris to "Will. Shakespear", even though the play had been correctly ascribed to Peele by Nashe in 1589 and in England's Helicon in 1600.[3] Kirkman also repeats Archer's ascription of The Puritan to Shakespeare. Evidently, where his testimony differs from Archer's it carries some weight; where

---

[1] This was pointed out by E. E. Stoll, in John Webster (Cambridge, Mass.: Harvard Co-operative Society, 1905), p. 212.

[2] The Puritan has no instance of the oath heart, which appears in Middleton's undoubted plays only in 1607-16 (in Your Five Gallants, No Wit, Chaste Maid, and The Widow); Revenger's Tragedy has 11 instances.

[3] See Greg, "Authorship Attributions," p. 322, and Chambers, Elizabethan Stage, III, 458-59.

it agrees, it does not.

The repetition of the Tourneur attribution by Gerard Langbaine the younger[1] is even more obviously valueless, since Langbaine's Account is fundamentally and often fatally dependent on existing printed sources (for instance, he is frequently unable to date plays because the title pages are missing in the copies owned by him), and his main authority in cases of doubtful attribution is Kirkman. Thus the whole case for Tourneur's authorship of The Revenger's Tragedy rests ultimately on the shaky authority of Archer's Item 493. As has often been suggested,[2] it is quite possible that Archer's attribution was merely a guess from the similarity of the play's title to that of Tourneur's genuine Atheist's Tragedy (Q 1611). A guess of this kind is certainly the explanation of Archer's attribution of the anonymous play Every Woman in her Humour quite falsely to Ben Jonson.[3]

After Archer, Kirkman, and Langbaine, the attribution to Tourneur became accepted tradition, until doubts began to be voiced in the later nineteenth century. Critics were struck by the enormous discrepancy between the literary brilliance and flexibly free versification of The Revenger's Tragedy and the relative crudity and stiff verse of The Atheist's Tragedy, Tourneur's one extant undoubted play. At first the difficulty was met by supposing that the order of composition of the two plays was the reverse of that of publication, but Stoll (John Webster, pp. 210-13) showed that there was no sound basis for this theory. The natural supposition is that Atheist's Tragedy dates from not long before 1611.

The obvious alternative solution was to deny the common authorship of the two plays. Fleay (Biographical Chronicle, II, 264, 272) found The Revenger's Tragedy to be more like Webster than Tourneur; Chambers, without favouring any candidate, regarded Tourneur's authorship as not

---

[1] An Account of the English Dramatick Poets (1691; rpt. Hildesheim: Georg Olms, 1968), pp. 505-06.

[2] First, apparently, by Mincoff, according to Schoenbaum, Internal Evidence, p.201, fn.

[3] See Greg, "Authorship Attributions," p. 314.

proven, and listed the play as anonymous in The Elizabethan Stage (IV, 42).
Oliphant first noted the resemblance to Middleton in 1911,[1] but did not
definitely propose Middleton's authorship until his article of 1926
("The Authorship of The Revenger's Tragedy") initiated the present
phase of the controversy. Since 1926 Middleton has been the only serious
contender against Tourneur. Oliphant's case was based mainly on parallels; more parallels, and metrical evidence, were added by Barker.[2]
Linguistic evidence for Middleton, including statistics of oaths and
exclamations, was supplied by Schoenbaum (Middleton's Tragedies,
pp. 153-82); Charles Barber added a distinctive usage;[3] and finally
contractions and spellings were exhaustively tabulated by Murray (Cyril
Tourneur, pp. 144-89), who used a Chi-Squared test of significance, and
found the agreement between the features of The Revenger's Tragedy and
Middleton's early plays so close that "we may reject the hypothesis that
this correlation is caused by chance with a confidence of greater than
99.5 per cent" (p.172).[4] Murray tabulated spellings, but his statistical argument was based only on substantive differences between contractions.

Attempts by defenders of Tourneur's authorship to rebut this mass
of evidence have been meagre, vague, and at times textually inaccurate.
The most notable champions, probably, have been two editors of The
Revenger's Tragedy, Allardyce Nicoll and R. A. Foakes. Nicoll claimed [5]
that spelling evidence supported Tourneur's claim--"y for i" in words
such as poysoned; bould; reuennewe; and "frequent use of wear or weare
for were". I have shown elsewhere[6] that the first three items do not
survive a negative check (all appearing in Middleton), while wear(e) for
"were" does not in fact occur at all in The Revenger's Tragedy. Foakes

---

[1] "Problems of Authorship in Elizabethan Dramatic Literature,"
Modern Philology, 8 (Jan. 1911), 427-28.

[2] "The Authorship of The Second Maiden's Tragedy and The Revenger's
Tragedy"; and Thomas Middleton, pp. 70-71.

[3] "A Rare Use of the Word Honour as a Criterion of Middleton's
Authorship," English Studies, 38 (1957), 161-68.

[4] The figure is given as 99.95 per cent on p. 167, where it is supported
by the phrase "one time in two thousand".

[5] Cyril Tourneur, Works, ed. Nicoll (London: Fanfrolico Press, 1929),
introduction, pp. 36-37.

[6] "The Revenger's Tragedy: Internal Evidence for Tourneur's Authorship
Negated," NQ, 216 (Dec. 1971), 455-56.

in his edition[1] repeated Nicoll's weak or baseless arguments, and added some more weak ones of his own, which, as I have demonstrated (op. cit.), are equally vulnerable to negative checks. Foakes' arguments elsewhere[2] on versification are dealt with in Appendix II.

3.2.4. External evidence for Middleton's authorship

The Stationers' Register entry recorded in 3.2.1, above, couples the two plays Revenger's Tragedy and Middleton's Trick in the same clause. Trick was also published anonymously in the first issue, but when a cancel title-page claimed a recent performance before the King, the phrase "Composde by T. M." was inserted on it. There was no second issue of the tragedy: the date "1608" in some copies was only a stop-press correction of the final digit.[3]

Murray has noticed the interesting fact that about the year 1607 it was not customary to couple plays by different authors in the same clause in the Stationers' Register (Cyril Tourneur, p. 146). He cites Eld's adjacent but separate entries on 6 August 1607 of The Puritan and Northward Ho; and, in fact, there is no instance of the coupling of plays known to be by different authors through the entire Elizabethan and Jacobean periods. But there are several couplings of plays by the same author; for instance, in 1600-1612 there are the following:[4]

23 Augusti ⌈1600⌋

Andrew Wyse Willm Aspley Entred for their copies under the hands of the wardens. Twoo books. the one called: Muche a Doo about nothinge. Thother the second pte of the history of kinge henry the iiij wth the humors of Sr Iohn ffallstaff : Wrytten by mr Shakespere

---

[1] Cyril Tourneur, The Revenger's Tragedy (London: Methuen, 1966), introduction, xlviii-liv.

[2] "On the Authorship of The Revenger's Tragedy."

[3] Price, "The Authorship and Bibliography of The Revenger's Tragedy," pp. 270-71.

[4] This evidence, negative and positive, is drawn from Greg's exerpts of drama items in the S. R., Bibliography, I, 1-34. Quotations are from Greg.

3° Octobr. [1610]

Walter Burre Entred for his Copyes by assignmente. from
Thomas Thorpe & wth the consente of Th'wardens under their
hands. 2 books, thone called Seianus his fall, thother,
Vulpone or the ffoxe

17mo April: [1612]

m[r] Browne. Entred for his Copy under th'ands of Sr. Geo: Buc
& mr warden Lownes, Twoo play books, th'one called, The revenge
of Bussy D'Amboys, beinge a tragedy, thother called, the
wydowes teares, beinge a Comedy, bothe written by Geo: Chapman

It will be noted that the 1610 entry does not mention the author, who
is, of course, Jonson. If we examine the period before 1600, we find
similar things. Three plays of Lyly share an anonymous co-entry on
4 October 1591; Greene's James IV and The Famous Victories of Henry V
(anonymous; not by Greene) receive separate adjacent entries to Thomas
Creede on 14 May 1594. It is hard to see why, in our period, co-entry
should imply common authorship; but so, evidently, it did. If The
Revenger's Tragedy is not by the same author as A Trick to Catch the
Old One, then it is the sole exception to this rule in the reigns of
Elizabeth and James.

There is one other suggestion of Middleton's authorship of The
Revenger's Tragedy in the seventeenth century. Nathaniel Richards, in
his commendatory verses to Women Beware Women, uses the phrase Drabs
of State in line 2. This is a quotation from The Revenger's Tragedy
(H2v; IV.iv.80[1]), and Richards must have known it to be a quotation, since
he lifted the entire line (A drab of State, a cloath a siluer slut) for
use in his own tragedy Messalina,[2] where it appears as

a drab
Of state, a cloth of Silver slut   (lines 1778-79)

Now in the heading of the commendatory verses Richards claims to have
been a "Familiar Acquaintance" of Middleton, and in the ensuing poem

---

[1] Line references to The Revenger's Tragedy are to the edition by
Nicoll in the Works of Cyril Tourneur.

[2] Ed. A. R. Skemp, in Materialien, 30 (1910); my quotation is from this
edition. Skemp, pp. 136-37, lists several other uses by Richards of
the same line from Revenger's Tragedy. It is interesting to note the
change from cloath a to cloth of in Richards' adaptation: this is the
kind of difference one often finds when a parallel does not imply
common authorship, but merely borrowing.

goes on to say of him:

> He knew the rage,
> Madness of Women crost; and for the Stage
> Fitted their humors   (lines 7-9)

--which seems to imply a knowledge of Middleton's life as well as of
his work. It is certain that if Middleton wrote The Revenger's Tragedy
such a "Familiar Acquaintance" would have known the fact; and it seems
to me therefore likely that Drabs of State in the commendatory poem
(and possibly also venom kiss, in line 4) is intended as an allusion to
another play of the same author's which had greatly impressed Richards.
Of course, this is not strong evidence; but it is something. The Richards
poem and the Stationers' Register entry are the only external testimonies
from trustworthy seventeenth century sources concerning The Revenger's
Tragedy; and both provide definite if ambiguous links with plays of
Middleton, not of Tourneur.   The case for Middleton's authorship does
not, therefore, rest solely upon internal evidence.

3.2.5. Spelling evidence

Since Murray and Price have so thoroughly explored the spelling
evidence for Middleton, I shall touch on it only very briefly. The
salient evidence is summarized in Table 3.1(1) above; most convincing of
all are the rare spellings in -cst and e'm, unparalleled in the contemporary work of Eld's shop except in the Middleton plays and The Puritan.
The total spelling evidence is so striking that the conclusion is ines-
capable that The Revenger's Tragedy was printed from a Middleton holograph. Since there is no reason to suspect that Middleton ever worked
as a scribe, this implies his authorship of the play--especially as the
spelling evidence is supported by copious parallels of phrase and by
linguistic evidence of every other variety.

3.2.6. Survey of scenes

I attribute every scene of The Revenger's Tragedy to Middleton:
there is no convincing suggestion of any collaborator. The linguistic
evidence is given in Table 3.2(1) below; as in the case of The Puritan,
the features tabulated are restricted to those which are used in the
statistical argument (of 3.2.7). In the following survey I shall mention
only those items which I have noted for the first time myself, or on
which I can throw some fresh light.

3.2.6.1. The first fifteen lines

To illustrate the copiousness of the evidence for Middleton, I will begin by examining the first fifteen lines of Vindice's opening quasi-soliloquy.

> DVke: royall letcher; goe, gray hayrde adultery,
> And thou his sonne, as impious steept as hee:
> And thou his bastard true-begott in euill:
> And thou his Dutchesse that will doe with Diuill,
> Foure exlent Characters--   (A2; I.i.4-8)

This opening is already very much in Middleton's manner. First of all, Middleton is fond of beginning a play with a soliloquy or a substantial speech by an important character touching on a main theme of the play--for example, Wit-good's soliloquy in Trick, Vortiger's in Hengist, and Ignatius' speech in the Induction to A Game at Chess.[1] Again, the rhyme euill--Diuill, though not in itself rare, occurs interestingly enough in precisely the same position in Michaelmas Term (Induction, lines 3-4). And exlent, as we have seen before (2.1.4.2, 3.1.5), is a rare contraction outside Middleton's plays.

> ---O that marrow-lesse age,
> Would stuffe the hollow Bones with dambd desires,
> And stead of heate kindle infernall fires,
> Within the spend-thrift veyne of a drye Duke,
> A parcht and iuicelesse luxur.   (A2; I.i.8-12)

One notices here Middletonian spellings (dambd, and the suffix -lesse), but above all the word luxur,[2] which occurs outside this play only in Middleton pamphlets, The Black Book (D3; Bullen, VIII, 28) and Father Hubburd's Tales (D4; Bullen, VIII, 86); it is probably a coinage of Middleton's.

---

[1] This habit and the parallel in Trick were noted by W. D. Dunkel in "The Authorship of The Revenger's Tragedy,' PMLA, 46 (1931), 783.

[2] Luxur and its parallels were noted by Barker, in "The Authorship of The Second Maiden's Tragedy and The Revenger's Tragedy," p. 126.

O God! one

That has scarce bloud inough to liue vpon.

And hee to ryot it like a sonne and heyre?

O the thought of that

Turnes my abused heart-strings into fret.

Thou sallow picture of my poysoned loue,

My studies ornament, thou shell of Death . . . (A2; I.i.12-18)

The exclamation O God is not like Middleton's usual practices, but it is to be remembered that we have no undoubted tragedy from his early period, and the phrase here is half an invocation, very much in the manner of Hamlet's first soliloquy.[1] Sonne and heyre we have noted before as a favorite Middleton phrase. The rhyme that--fret, linking a half-line with a full pentameter, is typical of Middleton's versification, which abounds in half-lines, occasionally placed in rhyme (e.g. sale-- raile, in Phoenix, C2, which Bullen re-lineates, I.iv. 200-01). Lastly, we have the phrase My studies ornament, which is very similar to My studies ornaments[2] (More Dissemblers, B2; I.ii.4). This, the first parallel noted for Middleton by Oliphant ("The Authorship of The Revenger's Tragedy, p. 160), I have found not to be matched anywhere in the 132-play corpus, nor, indeed, anywhere else.

Thus already in the first fifteen lines of The Revenger's Tragedy we have two items which point uniquely to Middleton (luxur and studies ornament), as well as several other features of varying rarity: exlent is very rare, and not found in Tourneur. It is true, of course, that between Middleton and Tourneur the contest is not a fair one, since Middleton has a far greater body of work in which parallels may be found. That is so; but here I am not so much arguing against Tourneur as for Middleton against the entire field of early Jacobean playwrights, which constitutes a perfectly fair contest. A reasonable criterion between Middleton and Tourneur alone is that of versification, which is dealt with mainly in Appendix II.

---

[1] I agree with David L. Frost's judgment, in The School of Shakespeare, pp. 36-47, that the main literary influence on The Revenger's Tragedy is that of Hamlet.

[2] The plural form in More Dissemblers is dictated by vertues in the previous line.

3.2.6.2.   The rest of the play

I.i.

I.i.46 (A2v): <u>giue</u> <u>Reuenge</u> <u>her</u> <u>due</u>. The collocation <u>give</u> .. <u>due</u> is noted as a Middletonism by Oliphant ("The Authorship of <u>The Revenger's Tragedy</u>," p. 163); it occurs in each of the five early plays (<u>Phoenix</u>, B1, I.ii.14-15; <u>Michaelmas</u> <u>Term</u>, B2v, I.i.211; <u>Mad World</u>, F1, III.iii.121; <u>Trick</u>, C2v, II.i.179; <u>Your</u> <u>Five</u> <u>Gallants</u>, A4v, I.i.207) and in <u>The Puritan</u> (A3); it is not common elsewhere, and not found in <u>The</u> <u>Atheist's Tragedy</u>.

I.iii.

I.iii.33, 147 (B3, B4v): <u>exlent</u> twice more.

I.iii.132 (B4v): <u>gint</u>, in the expression <u>You</u> <u>haue</u> <u>gint</u> [= given it] the <u>Tang</u> <u>yfaith</u>. Gi(')n(')t is an extremely rare contraction: the only instances I have noticed in plays of undoubted authorship are two in <u>Mad World</u> (gi'nt, C1v, II.ii.17; <u>gin't</u>, D4v, III.ii.49), and the only other instances are in plays with which Middleton may have been concerned (see Table I.1).

II.i.

II.i.19 (C2v): <u>cut</u> <u>of</u> <u>a</u> <u>great</u> <u>deale</u> <u>of</u> <u>durty</u> <u>way</u>. This striking parallel to <u>Mad World</u>, I.i.75 (A3), noted by Oliphant ("The Authorship of <u>The</u> <u>Revenger's</u> <u>Tragedy</u>," p. 162), is not matched by anything even remotely similar in the comparative corpus. (See Table I.2.)

II.i.62 (C3v): <u>Masse</u> <u>fitly</u> <u>here</u> <u>she</u> <u>comes</u>. Middleton's use of <u>mass</u> .. <u>here</u> to mark an entrance has been noted before (3.1.5, s.v. <u>Puritan</u>, III.iv). There is an instance in <u>Phoenix</u> (I1; IV.iii.66).

II.i.129-30 (C4): <u>no</u> <u>man</u> . . . <u>common</u>. This rhyme occurs also in <u>Mad World</u>, I.ii.87-88 (B2), but nowhere else in the 132-play corpus.

II.i.228 (D1v): <u>Nine</u> <u>Coaches</u>. This is matched by <u>nine</u> <u>Coaches</u> <u>shall</u> <u>not</u> <u>stay</u> <u>me</u>, in <u>No</u> <u>Wit</u>, V.i.355 (H1). Another unique parallel.

II.i.256 (D2): <u>Troth</u> <u>he</u> <u>sayes</u> <u>true</u>. A Middletonism noted by Oliphant: see above, 3.1.5, s.v. <u>Puritan</u>, III.v.

II.ii.

II.ii.14 (D2v): <u>Masse</u> <u>here</u> <u>he</u> <u>comes</u>. See above, II.i.

II.ii.75 (D3): <u>giue</u> <u>'em</u> <u>their</u> <u>due</u>. See above, I.i.

II.ii.95 (D3v): <u>an</u> <u>vnknowne</u> <u>thing</u>. This matches the same phrase, which certainly is not common, in <u>Trick</u>, II.i.108 (C1v).

II.ii.129 (D3v): <u>Luxur</u>. See above, 3.3.6.1.

II.ii.156 (D4): <u>Lets in her friend by water</u>. Compare the same method of assignation described by Francisca in <u>The Witch</u>, lines 500-01. She uses the same word "friend"; he will <u>come by water to the Back-dore</u> at <u>Midnight</u>.

III.iii.

III.iii.18 (E3v): <u>Troth you say true</u>. See above, II.i.

III.iii.20 (E3v): <u>The third part of a minute</u>. Oliphant remarks ("The Authorship of <u>The Revenger's Tragedy</u>," p. 163) "Middleton had a strange fancy for thirds," and lists several instances. I have totalled the instances of the collocation <u>third part of</u> in Table I.1; I have not found any in the 132-play corpus outside Middleton.

III.v.

III.v.78 (Flv): <u>bewitching minute</u>. Oliphant, reading wrongly <u>bewilder-ing minute</u>, seems to have missed the exactness of this parallel to <u>Mad World</u>, IV.v.18 (G2v).

III.v.86 (Flv): <u>giue vs our due</u>. See above, I.i.

III.vi.

III.vi.57 (F4): <u>giue him his due</u>. See above, I.i.

III.vi.87-88 (F4v): <u>O death and vengeance</u> . . . <u>Hell and torments</u>. These balanced outcries, distributed between different speakers, are a Middletonian device. We may compare: <u>All</u>. <u>Death and vengeance!</u> <u>Go</u>[ldstone]. <u>Hell, darkenesse</u>, in <u>Your Five Gallants</u>, II.iii.198-99 (D2v); also, perhaps, <u>death and darkenesse</u> in <u>Trick</u>, III.iii.86 (E3).

III.vi.102 (F4v): <u>Darkenesse</u>. Compare this exclamation with the instances just quoted in <u>Your Five Gallants</u> and <u>Trick</u>.

IV.i.

IV.i.101 (G2): <u>Tis Oracle</u>. This, I would suggest, is the only really good parallel in <u>Revenger's Tragedy</u> to <u>Atheist's Tragedy</u>, which has <u>T'is Oracle</u> (Blv; I.i); and even here we notice a significant difference of spelling, since <u>Tis</u> without apostrophe is the form almost invariably used by Middleton in <u>A Game at Chess</u>, <u>T'is</u> the form used by Tourneur both in <u>Atheist's Tragedy</u>[1] and in his poems.[2] The phrase <u>T(')is Oracle</u> does not occur in Middleton's plays; but if an extensive search is made for parallels

_____

[1] See Murray's Table I, in <u>Cyril Tourneur</u>, p. 177.

[2] In Allardyce Nicoll's edition of Tourneur's <u>Works</u>, we find in <u>The Trans-formed Metamorphosis</u> <u>t'is</u> twice (pp. 53, 68), <u>tis</u> once (p.66); in <u>A Grief for Prince Henry</u>, <u>T'is</u> only (p. 267). <u>Metamorphosis</u> was printed by Valen-tine Simmes in 1600, <u>Henry</u> by Nicholas Okes in 1613; <u>Atheist's Tragedy</u> by Thomas Snodham in 1611. The <u>t'is</u> spelling, transmitted by three printers, is clearly authorial; its virtual absence from <u>Revenger's Tragedy</u> is inex-plicable on the theory of Tourneur's authorship, since the text is not scribal.

through a full-length play, it is normal to find one or two which point
in a wrong direction; as, perhaps, in the case of I love alife in Blurt
(see above, 2.2.4.6-7). This is why single parallels prove nothing; it
is the weight of numbers that counts. Tis Oracle occurs also in Fletcher's Valentinian (F 1647, 16b); but this is not sufficient reason for
crediting Fletcher with a share in The Revenger's Tragedy.

IV.ii.

IV.ii.68 (G3): sasarara. This corruption of certiorare, as was
noted in 3.1.5, occurs only in Puritan, III.ii, and three times in
Phoenix. The verb fetch occurs in association with both the Puritan
and Revenger's Tragedy instances.

IV.ii.91,97 (G3v): sonne and Heire, sonne and heire. Two more
instances of this favorite Middleton phrase. The first occurs in
another "death of father" joke (see above, 3.1.5, s.v. Puritan, I.i).

IV.ii.227-28 (H1), 225 (H1v): thankes, thankes to any spirit,/
That mingled it mongst my inuentions . . . Nay . . . tis in graine, I
warrant it hold collour. This double parallel to exactly the same two
sentences in the same sequence in Mad World, III.iii.70-71, 81-82 (E4,
E4v), noted by Barker in Thomas Middleton (pp. 70-71), is surely the
most striking of the resemblances in The Revenger's Tragedy to Middleton's works; it has no counterpart in any other play that I have read.
I would suggest that the way these two sentences occur, in close proximity in a single scene in each play, is very strong evidence that one
mind is responsible for both, for what we observe here is a sequence of
verbal ideas retrieved intact by the memory of an author. The only
other possible theory would be plagiarism by Middleton or the author of
Revenger's Tragedy at a time when neither play was in print: an uncon-
vincing explanation unless the author of Revenger's Tragedy was the
actor who played Follywit in Mad World. But this actor must have been
a boy, one of the Children of Paul's.

The form mongst in IV.ii.228, which matches exactly mongst in Mad
World, III.iii.71, also happens to be the connective (a)mongst which
on the whole Middleton prefers to among. Tourneur clearly prefers among;
he has, in Atheist's Tragedy, among six times (C2v, D2v, E4v, H3v, I4v,
K2), amongst once (H4). In his poems and prose he has among three times
(Works, ed. Nicoll, pp. 170, 266, 267), amongst once (p. 172). Overall,

therefore, the probability of Tourneur writing amongst rather than among
is 2/11 per instance. But there are six instances of amongst in Revenger's Tragedy, none of among. Hence the probability of Tourneur writing
all those instances, and of being the author of The Revenger's Tragedy,
must be rather small.

IV.iii

IV.iii.10 (H1v): Woult. This is the only instance in Revenger's
Tragedy of this form, which occurs four times in Puritan (see above,
3.1.5), and, as we shall see (3.3.5.1), once in A Yorkshire Tragedy, but
elsewhere only in Marston's What You Will (C3) among the corpus plays.
The instance in A Yorkshire Tragedy, printed by Richard Braddock, suggests
that the form is not due to Eld's compositors: it is probably a very rare
usage of Middleton's, appearing only in a few plays of doubtful authorship.

V.i.

V.i.51 (H4v): let him reele to hell. A favorite Middleton idea;
compare A Drunckard now to Reele to the Devill, in Witch, lines 442-43.
The early poem The Ghost of Lucrece (O 1600) has the exact phrase reele
to hell at line 450[1] (C4), though in a different context.

V.iii.

V.iii.102 (I4): Law you now. A Middletonism; see 2.1.4 (s.v.
1 Honest Whore, I.iii), and 3.1.5 (s.v. Puritan, IV.ii), above. Middleton's usual spelling seems to be la, but in More Dissemblers we have Lo
in Lo you there Sir (E4; IV.i.272) and in Lo you (F3; V.i.100), which
implies a rounded vowel that could be spelt Law.

3.3.6.3. Summary

In this brief survey of the text of The Revenger's Tragedy I have
been forced to omit many interesting parallels to Middleton. However,
it should be clear from this selection that Oliphant's and Barker's
intuitions of distinctiveness were largely justified: the evidence did
point uniquely to Middleton. Moreover, I have noticed and checked out
several more items (exlent, gint, the rhyme no man--common, the phrase
nine coaches, and less distinctive features such as son and heir) which

---

[1] According to the lineation in the edition of the poem by Joseph
Quincy Adams (New York: Scribner's, 1937).

all point in the same direction. This is one of the exacting tests of an
authorial hypothesis: that it should be confirmable by fresh evidence
not noticed by the original proposer. There are doubtless other points
of resemblance between The Revenger's Tragedy and Middleton which have
escaped me, too, but may be found by others or by a computer analysis
of the total vocabulary of the play. If, on the other hand, there were
anything at all to be said for the theory of Tourneur's authorship, it
is strange that it has not been discovered since Sykes' rather poor
article which raked together a few unimpressive Tourneur parallels in
1919.[1]

---

[1] "Cyril Tourneur: The Revenger's Tragedy: The Second Maiden's Tragedy,"
NQ, 12th ser., 5 (Sept. 1919), 225-29. Sykes' parallels between
Revenger's Tragedy and Atheist's Tragedy are mostly not very parallel
or occur also in Middleton, such as serious business, Revenger's Tragedy,
I.ii.108 (B1), which occurs also in Women Beware Women, II.ii.18 (I2) and
IV.i.182 (M7). Tis Oracle, noted by Sykes, has been dealt with above.

Table 3.2(1). The Revenger's Tragedy:
distribution of features used in the statistical argument

Segment 1

Scene	sigs.	push, puh	tut	'sfoot, 'slid	'slud, 'sblood	heart, death	faith	troth	mass	ay: yes
1.1	A2-A4	,1	.	.	.	1,	4	.	.	1:
1.2	A4-B2v	,1	.	.	.	.	5	2	.	1:
1.3	B2v-Clv	2,	.	2,	1,	.	3	3	.	2:
1.4	Clv-C2v	.	.	.	.	,1	1	.	.	.
2.1	C2v-D2	.	2	,1	.	.	4	1	1	7:
2.2	D2-E2v	,1	.	1,	,1	3,	6	1	1	:1
3.1	E2v-E3	.	.	.	.	.	1	1	.	.
3.2	E3	.	.	.	.	.	.	.	.	.
3.3	E3-E3v	.	.	.	.	.	1	1	.	1:
3.4	E3v-E4v	.	.	.	1,	.	1	.	.	1:
3.5	E4v-F3v	1,1	1	.	.	.	4	1	1	1:1
3.6	F3v-Gl	.	.	1,	.	1,1	3	.	.	5:
4.1	Gl-G2	1,	.	1,	.	1,	2	.	.	1:1
4.2	G2-Hlv	.	.	2,	.	1,	3	.	.	4:1
4.3	Hlv	.	.	1,	.	,1	.	.	.	.
4.4	Hlv-H4	1,	.	.	.	.	1	1	.	1:
5.1	H4-I2v	1,2	.	.	.	1,	2	1	2	4:1
5.2	I2v	.	.	.	.	.	.	.	.	.
5.3	I2v-I4v	.	.	1,	1,1	3,	3	.	.	.
Totals:		6,6	3	9,1	3,2	11,3	44	12	5	29:5

Segment 2

Scene	sigs.	among: amongst	beside: besides	between: betwixt	while: whilst	'em: them	has: hath	does: doth	I'm: I am
1.1	A2-A4	.	.	.	.	.	3:	1:	.
1.2	A4-B2v	.	.	.	:1	1:1	5:1	1:	1:2
1.3	B2v-Clv	.	.	.	.	3:	.	4:	1:1
1.4	Clv-C2v	:2	.	.	.	1:	1:.	.	.
2.1	C2v-D2	.	.	.	:2	2:	5:	5:	2:
2.2	D2-E2v	:1	1:	.	.	11:3	4:2	3:1	1:5
3.1	E2v-E3	.	.	.	.	.	.	.	:1
3.2	E3	.	.	.	.	.	.	.	:1
3.3	E3-E3v	.	.	.	.	.	.	.	.
3.4	E3v-E4v	.	.	.	:1	5:	.	.	:1
3.5	E4v-F3v	.	:1	1:	.	4:2	3:1	5:	3:
3.6	F3v-Gl	.	.	.	.	1:	1:	.	1:3
4.1	Gl-G2	.	.	1:1	.	1:	4:	2:	3:
4.2	G2-Hlv	:1	.	.	.	1:	6:1	1:	3:1
4.3	Hlv	.	.	.	.	:1	.	.	1:
4.4	Hlv-H4	:1	.	.	.	.	4:1	1:	3:4
5.1	H4-I2v	.	.	.	.	1:1	7:1	2:1	3:1
5.2	I2v	.	.	.	.	.	.	.	.
5.3	I2v-I4v	:1	1:	.	.	7:1	2:	3:	:3
Totals:		0:6	2:1	2:1	0:4	38:9	45:7	28:2	22:23

Table 3.2(1).   The Revenger's Tragedy

Segment 3

Scene	sigs.	I'd	I've	we're	thou'rt, th'art	sh'as	t'as, t'ad	you're, y'are	y'ave, they're
1.1	A2-A4	.	.	.	1,	1	.	.	2,
1.2	A4-B2v	3	.	3	,1	.	.	.	.
1.3	B2v-Clv	1	2	.	3,	.	.	.	.
1.4	Clv-C2v	1	.	.	.	1	.	.	.
2.1	C2v-D2	2	1	.	.	.	1,	1,2	,1
2.2	D2-E2v	1	.	1	1,	.	1,	,1	,1
3.1	E2v-E3	.	.	.	1,	.	.	.	.
3.2	E3	.	.	.	.	.	.	.	.
3.3	E3-E3v	.	.	.	.	.	.	.	.
3.4	E3v-E4v	1	.	.	.	.	.	.	,1
3.5	E4v-F3v	.	.	2	2,	1	1,	.	1,1
3.6	F3v-Gl	.	.	2	.	.	.	,1	.
4.1	Gl-G2	.	.	.	.	.	.	.	.
4.2	G2-Hlv	.	1	.	.	.	1,	,4	1,
4.3	Hlv	.	.	.	.	.	.	.	.
4.4	Hlv-H4	.	1	.	.	.	.	.	.
5.1	H4-I2v	.	1	3	.	.	1,	1,	.
5.2	I2v	.	.	1	.	.	.	.	.
5.3	I2v-I4v	.	.	3	.	.	,1	1,	.
Totals:		9	6	15	8,1	3	5,1	3,8	4,4

Segment 4

Scene	sigs.	gint	i'th'	a'th', a'the	on't	exlent	woult	comfort	'Has
1.1	A2-A4	.	1	1,	.	1	.	1	.
1.2	A4-B2v	.	1	1,1	1	.	.	2	1
1.3	B2v-Clv	1	3	4,	1	2	.	.	.
1.4	Clv-C2v	.	.	.	1	.	.	2	.
2.1	C2v-D2	.	.	3,	2	.	.	2	.
2.2	D2-E2v	.	5	2,	2	.	.	3	.
3.1	E2v-E3	.	1	.	.	.	.	.	.
3.2	E3	.	.	.	.	.	.	.	.
3.3	E3-E3v	.	.	.	.	.	.	.	.
3.4	E3v-E4v	.	.	.	.	.	.	4	.
3.5	E4v-F3v	.	.	2,	1	.	.	1	.
3.6	F3v-Gl	.	.	.	2	.	.	.	.
4.1	Gl-G2	.	1	.	2	.	.	.	1
4.2	G2-Hlv	.	.	1,	2	.	.	.	4
4.3	Hlv	.	.	.	.	.	1	.	.
4.4	Hlv-H4	.	1	.	1	.	.	.	.
5.1	H4-I2v	.	1	3,	1	.	.	1	1
5.2	I2v	.	.	.	1	.	.	.	.
5.3	I2v-I4v	.	.	.	1	.	.	1	.
Totals:		1	14	17,1	18	3	1	17	7

3.2.7. The statistical argument

The principles of the statistical argument of the Revenger's Tragedy problem are exactly those of the corresponding argument for The Puritan. However, there are naturally differences of detail .

3.2.7.1. Comparative sample

The plays and authors I have chosen for the comparative sample are both twenty-three in number, comprising the following: Armin, Two Maids of Moreclacke; Barnes, The Devil's Charter; Barry, Ram Alley; Beaumont, The Knight of the Burning Pestle; Brewer, The Lovesick King; Chapman, May Day; Chettle, Hoffman; Cooke, Greene's Tu Quoque; Day, Isle of Gulls; Dekker, 2 Honest Whore; Field, A Woman is a Weathercock; Fletcher, Bonduca; Jonson, Volpone; Marston, The Fawn; Mason, The Turk; William Rowley, A Shoemaker a Gentleman; Shakespeare, Coriolanus; Sharpham, Cupid's Whirligig; Smith, The Hector of Germany; Tomkis, Lingua; Webster, The White Devil; and Wilkins, The Miseries of Enforced Marriage. None of these plays, probably, differs in date of composition from The Revenger's Tragedy by more than ten years.

In the choice of the comparative sample there was a perplexing problem of genre to be considered. When one asks what is the genre of The Revenger's Tragedy, in spite of the title the answer is not immediately obvious. The play is not a tragedy in the genre of Chapman's, Jonson's, and Marston's tragedies, perhaps not even in the genre of Shakespeare's, though it bears some kind of relationship to Hamlet.[1] With its colloquialisms and its two-word rhymes ("undo 'em--through 'em," and so forth), it sounds in many places more like a comedy than a tragedy: perhaps we should say, a satirical or "black" comedy. For statistical purposes I have thought it best, therefore, to compare this anomalous play with a mixture of tragedies and comedies, preferably of a satirical kind. Since Chapman's and Jonson's tragedies, and Marston's Sophonisba, are so very different in style from The Revenger's Tragedy, I have rejected them in favour of the comedies May Day, Volpone, and The Fawn. To have used Sophonisba, Sejanus, and one of the Byron plays might have helped the statistical argument by swinging the sample mean away from the The Revenger's Tragedy and the Middleton plays, but the strength gained thus

---

[1] David L. Frost says amusingly "The Revenger's Tragedy might well have been written by Hamlet" (The School of Shakespeare, p.41).

would have been slightly spurious, since choice of genre is no part of my argument for authorship. Besides, a sample consisting only of tragedies could not have numbered enough authors unless the date limits had been widened unacceptably. As it is, the heterogeneity of the sample also works against Middleton's candidature, since it tends to increase the sample's standard deviation.[1]

Many of the plays used for this problem were also used for the Puritan problem; in three cases, the same author appears in both, but represented by a different play. For the present problem Bonduca and The Fawn are preferred to The Woman's Prize and The Dutch Courtesan for reasons of genre (Fawn also for date). Cupid's Whirligig replaces The Fleer not because there is much to choose between the kinds of Sharpham's two plays, but because Whirligig is the later,[2] and Revenger's Tragedy was entered in the Stationers' Register two months later than Puritan (see above, 3.1.1, 3.2.1), and is possibly nearer in date of composition to Whirligig than to Fleer (see above, 3.2.2).

It must be stressed that no play was added to or rejected from the comparative sample once statistical analysis had been begun. The samples for the Revenger's Tragedy and Puritan problems were chosen at the same time, so that experience gained in the first problem did not affect the conditions of the second.

3.2.7.2. Features

The bulk of the features used are the same as those used for The Puritan. This is a consequence of the fact that Revenger's Tragedy and Puritan are very similar in linguistic style.

One minor difference occurs in the synonymous connectives. Since Revenger's Tragedy has among, O: amongst, 6, and while, O: whilst, 4, it is clear that in all the plays used in the argument amongst and whilst must contribute to the numerator of the connective group, whereas among, while, and whiles must contribute to the denominator (see above, 3.1.6.2). Middleton's usages of among: amongst and while: whilst are so variable

---

[1] This point occurs to me now; I was unaware of such statistical subtleties when I chose the Puritan and Revenger's Tragedy comparative samples.

[2] The Fleer was entered in the Stationers' Register on 13 May 1606, and Cupid's Whirligig on 29 June 1607 (Chambers, Elizabethan Stage, III, 490-91).

that these changes hardly affect his candidature. Since there is no preference in Revenger's Tragedy for either toward or towards, this synonym-pair is dropped from the argument. Other pairs remain the same: 'tis/('tis+it's) is excluded (distinctiveness ratio, 1.07), whereas ay/(ay+yes), with the next lowest ratio (1.565), is included, as are the 'em, has, does, and I'm synonym-pairs, all with higher ratios.

Among plus features, in this problem why is excluded strictly on the basis of distinctiveness ratio, its corrected ratio being only 1.27. There are, in fact, no really marginal features: the excluded feature of highest ratio other than why is marry (corrected ratio, 1.134), whereas the included feature of lowest ratio is a'the+o'the (corrected ratio, 1.9812). Thou'rt+th'art, which had to be excluded from the Puritan argument because of low distinctiveness (see Table 3.1(3)), in the present problem has a corrected ratio of 3.77, and is therefore included.

The treatment of faith is not quite such an obvious matter in this problem as it was in that of The Puritan, since this time it is more distinctive (corrected ratio, 2.47). Because of its high frequency I have, nevertheless, thought it best to place it in a group apart from the majority of the plus features. This decision once made, the exact grouping of the less distinctive plus features does not affect the outcome of the argument, though it does affect the size of the probability achieved. I have therefore calculated the final probabilities by two alternative methods, "A" and "B". Method A is the method of the Puritan argument, the two plus groups being (I) all plus features except faith (II) the high-frequency feature faith alone. Method B closely follows Ellegård in defining the two groups strictly by corrected distinctiveness ratios: Group (I) comprises plus features of ratio 2.5 or more, and Group (II) comprises plus features of ratio less than 2.5 but more than 1.5--faith (2.47), you're+y'are (2.32), tut (2.02), i'th' (1.995), and a'the+o'the (1.9812). Group (III) for this problem--the overall group of synonyms-- remains the same in both methods, A and B.

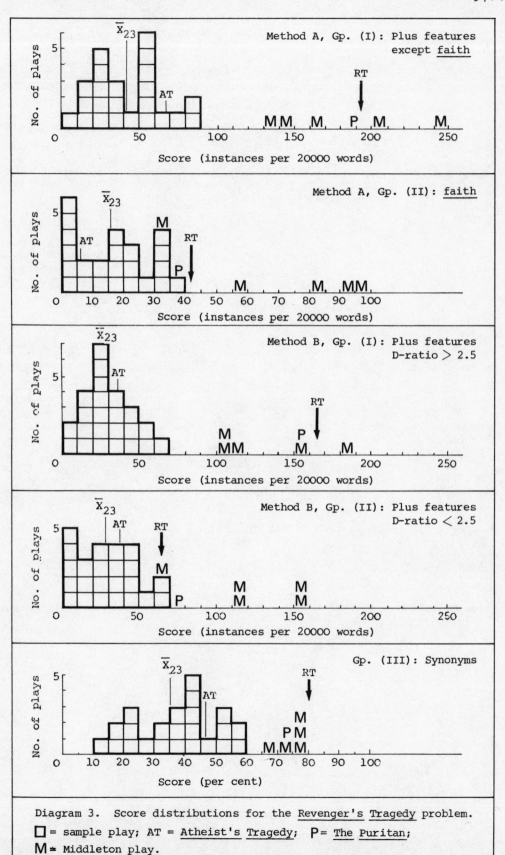

Diagram 3. Score distributions for the Revenger's Tragedy problem.
□ = sample play; AT = Atheist's Tragedy; P = The Puritan;
M = Middleton play.

3.2.7.3. Results

The results of the statistical calculations are set out graphically
in Diagram 3 (facing this page) and numerically in Table 3.2(3).   The
Revenger's Tragedy's score falls within the Middleton range in all feature
groups except that of synonyms (Group III), and even here it fits easily
into the positive tail of the Middleton distribution, as it lies no more
than 1.57 standard deviation (of the Middleton plays: 1.57 s_m) above the
Middleton mean, clearly a possible Middleton score. The Atheist's Tragedy's
scores, on the other hand, are far distant, lying not far from the sample
mean in most groups--a little higher in synonyms, but decidedly lower in
faith. Tourneur, indeed, in every group is a worse candidate than Chapman
as well as Middleton. Incidentally, I have given also the scores for
likeness to Revenger's Tragedy obtained by The Puritan: it appears to be
a very typical Middleton play, lying always within the Middleton range,
and always close to The Revenger's Tragedy.

With 23 plays, the sample is just large enough for us to be able
to check whether the distributions differ significantly from normal ones.
It appears that they do not. The check which I have used is a Chi-Squared
test, as follows:

The sample range, in each group, is divided into four classes, chosen
so that, on the normality hypothesis, E (the expected number of play-scores)
is never less than 5 in any class. This condition is necessary, because
the test is nor accurate when E is less than 5. I have chosen to make the
divisions conveniently at the mean $(\overline{X})$, and .75 standard deviation above and
below the mean; thus the four classes are: (1) zero to $[\overline{X} - .75s]$; (2)
$[\overline{X} - .75s]$ to $\overline{X}$; (3) $\overline{X}$ to $[\overline{X} + .75s]$; (4) $[\overline{X} + .75s]$ to plus infinity.
From the normal-curve area table it is easily found that E for these classes
is 5.29, 6.21, 6.21, and 5.29 respectively. If O is the observed number
of scores in a class, then the sum of $(O - E)^2/E$ for all the four classes
gives us Chi-Squared; whereupon, entering the Chi-Squared table at one
degree of freedom, we can derive a probability. If this probability (p)
is less than .05, then the discrepancy would not occur by chance more
often than one time in twenty, and may therefore be considered statistically
significant. Table 3.2(2), below, sets out the results of the test.

Table 3.2(2)
Chi-Squared test of Revenger's Tragedy 23-play sample distributions

Data for four range-classes, divided at $\bar{X}$, $\bar{X}$-.75s, $\bar{X}$+ .75s. Total no. of scores = 23. E in the four classes, in direction of increasing score: 5.29, 6.21, 6.21, 5.29. Chi-Squared has one degree of freedom.

Feature group	Observed no. of scores per class				Chi-Squared	Probability	Statistical significance
Method A, Gp. (I)	5,	7,	6,	5	.1391	>.5	None
" A, Gp. (II)	7,	4,	7,	5	1.4553	>.1	"
" B, Gp. (I)	6,	7,	4,	6	1.0772	>.25	"
" B, Gp. (II)	5,	7,	6,	5	.1391	>.5	"
[Synonym] Gp. (III)	7,	3,	7,	6	2.4075	>.1	"

From the tabulated data it will be seen that even the greatest recorded discrepancy between expectation and observation would be likely to occur by chance more often than once in ten times. (I have, in fact, experimented with various other groupings of plus features and other methods of combining the synonyms, and yet have never produced a distribution with p less than .1.) The probabilities above .5 in cases A(I) and B(II) have the interpretation that the data are more than usually concordant with the assumption of normality. In other words, given the grouping into broad classes and the smallness of the number in the sample, no better agreement with normality could reasonably be expected. This is not to say that a larger sample might not reveal subtle discrepancies from normality. But though it is not possible to prove that the distributions are in fact normal, at least on the evidence there is no reason to suspect that they are not.

Turning now to Table 3.2(3), and multiplying the probabilities yielded by the three overall feature-groups, we achieve the following final probabilities: by Method A, .000,000,00799, or less than 1 in 100 million; by Method B, .000,000,000,064, or less than 1 in 15,000 million. As in the case of The Puritan, these large numbers are almost certainly gross underestimates, since the argument has excluded the evidence of minus features, spellings, parallel collocations, and versif-ication. However, taking the figures as they stand, they give us estim-ates for the fraction of the population of Jacobean dramatists who write as much like The Revenger's Tragedy as Middleton does: one hundred-millionth or one fifteen-thousand-millionth. By applying Ellegard's formula reduced to one term (see above, 3.1.6.6), we take 1/25 of these probability-reciprocals to be the populations of authors up to which we can be 99 per cent confident that Middleton is the actual, nor merely the potential, author of The Revenger's Tragedy.

By Method A that population is almost exactly 5,000,000 authors; by Method B it is over 600,000,000 authors. There were certainly not as many as five million adult Englishmen alive in 1606-07; and six hundred million probably exceeds the early seventeenth century population of the whole earth.[1] Whichever figure and whichever method one accepts, I submit that Middleton's authorship of The Revenger's Tragedy is proved beyond reasonable doubt.

---

[1] Curiously enough, this Method B result is exactly the same as that for The Puritan (see above, 3.1.6.6).

Table 3.2(3) Revenger's Tragedy: statistical argument
Method A for plus features. Group (I): all except faith.

Play	Length (words)	'sfoot, 'slid, 'slud, 'sblood, heart, push, puh, tut	death, troth, mass	I'd, I've, we're, w'are	sh'as, t'as, t'ad, y'ave, thou, you, they+ art, are	i'th', a'th(e), o'th'(e), on't, ex'-lent, gi'n't	woult, com-fort, 'Has	Tot-al	Total per 20000 words
TMM	18972	5	6	1	5	13	6	36	37.9506
D.Ch.	25183	1	.	.	2	1	6	10	7.9418
RA	22419	10	7	4	21	1	10	53	47.2813
KBP	21423	.	6	.	9	19	4	38	35.4758
LK	18015	.	2	5	9	21	9	46	51.0685
MD	23568*	.	39	4	32	23	4	102	86.558
Hoff.	20491	1	7	4	4	1	11	28	27.329
GTQ	25231	2	13	4	20	21	8	68	53.9019
CTT	20016	.	6	1	6	7	9	29	28.9768
IG	21351	.	4	1	2	19	2	28	26.2282
2HW	24832*	.	24	.	34	24	3	85	68.46
WW	17772	.	26	2	5	17	3	53	59.6443
Bon.	21049	.	.	2	5	30	18	55	52.259
Volp.	28790	4	12	6	.	17	2	41	28.4821
Fawn	22717	.	5	.	3	6	4	18	15.8471
Turk	18519	1	6	4	8	.	3	22	23.7593
Sh.G.	22745	2	7	7	9	21	19	65	57.1554
Cor.	28547*	.	4	6	7	94	8	119	83.3712
CW	24854	3	17	.	2	9	7	38	30.5785
HG	16666	.	1	2	1	6	3	13	15.6006
Ling.	26179	8	3	1	7	2	1	22	16.8073
WD	26285*	.	2	5	15	63	7	92	70.0019
Mis	25068*	7	32	2	5	10	17	73	58.2415
Phoen	20840*	2	38	16	41	28	19	144	138.1957
MT	20570*	10	28	14	44	55	15	166	161.4
MWM	19098*	24	43	18	63	74	13	235	246.099
Trick	19268*	10	34	10	35	34	19	142	147.3946
YFG	21878*	18	63	14	76	44	13	228	208.4285
RT	21268*	15	46	30	37	54	25	207	194.6586
AT	22122*	.	5	6	30	29	5	75	67.8057
Pur.	19922*	15	54	11	30	58	22	190	190.7439

$\bar{X}_m$ = 180.3035; s_m = 45.6439; L_m = 138.1957. $\bar{X}_{23}$ = 42.7356; s_{23} = 22.2021

$(L_m - \bar{X}_{23})/s_{23}$ = 4.2996 standard deviations.

Probability at this distance (from tables of normal-curve area)

= .0000086

Table 3.2(3) Revenger's Tragedy: statistical argument.

Method A for plus features. Group (II): faith

Play	Length (words)	faith	per 20000 words	Play	Length (words)	faith	per 20000 words
TMM	18972	19	20.0295	2HW	24832*	32	25.7731
D.Ch.	25183	7	5.5593	WW	17772	18	20.2565
RA	22419	35	31.2235	Bon.	21049	2	1.9003
KBP	21423	36	33.6087	Volp	28790	24	16.6724
LK	18015	18	19.9833	Fawn	22717	20	17.6079
MD	23568*	47	39.8845	Turk	18519	2	2.1599
Hoff.	20491	2	1.952	Sh.G.	22745	25	21.9828
GTQ	25231	41	32.4997	Cor.	28547*	6	4.2035
CTT	20016	0	0	CW	24854	43	34.602
IG	21351	16	14.9875	HG	16666	0	0
Phoen.	20840*	35	33.5892	Ling.	26179	19	14.5154
MT	20570*	58	56.5928	WD	26285*	12	9.1306
MWM	19098*	88	92.1562	Mis.	25068*	23	18.35
Trick	19268*	79	82.0012				
YFG	21878*	109	99.6434				
RT	21268*	44	41.3767				
AT	22122*	8	7.2326				
Pur.	19922*	39	39.1526				

$\overline{X}_m = 72.7565 \quad s_m = 27.3247$

$L_m = 33.5892$

$\overline{X}_{23} = 16.8209 \quad s_{23} = 12.2538$

$$(L_m - \overline{X}_{23})/s_{23} =$$

1.3684 standard deviations.

Probability at this distance (from tables of normal-curve area)

= .086

Table 3.2(3)   Revenger's Tragedy: statistical argument.

Method B for plus features.   Group (I): Distinctiveness Ratio ⩾ 2.5

Play	Length (words)	push, puh	'sfoot, 'slid, 'slud, 'sblood, heart, death, troth, mass	I'd, I've, we're, w'are	sh'as, t'as, t'ad, y'ave, thou, they+ art,are	a'th', o'th', on't ex'- lent, gi'n't	woult, com- fort, 'Has	Tot- al	Total per 20000 words
TMM	18972	2	6	1	.	2	6	17	17.9211
D.Ch.	25183	.	.	.	2	1	6	9	7.1476
RA	22419	.	7	4	11	.	10	32	28.5472
KBP	21423	.	6	.	2	11	4	23	21.4722
LK	18015	.	2	5	8	17	9	41	45.5176
MD	23568*	.	39	4	14	15	4	76	64.4942
Hoff.	20491	.	7	4	1	1	11	24	23.4249
GTQ	25231	2	13	4	4	9	8	40	31.707
CTT	20016	.	6	1	2	6	9	24	23.9808
IG	21351	.	4	1	2	15	2	24	22.4813
2HW	24832*	.	24	.	10	5	3	42	33.8273
WW	17772	.	26	2	4	10	3	45	50.6414
Bon.	21049	.	.	2	3	16	18	39	37.0563
Volp.	28790	1	12	6	.	8	2	29	20.1458
Fawn	22717	.	5	.	3	6	4	18	15.8471
Turk	18519	.	6	4	3	.	3	16	17.2795
Sh.G.	22745	.	7	7	4	10	19	47	41.3277
Cor.	28547*	.	4	6	2	52	8	72	50.4431
CW	24854	1	17	.	1	9	7	35	28.1644
HG	16666	.	1	2	1	2	3	9	10.8004
Ling.	26179	.	3	1	7	1	1	13	9.9316
WD	26285*	.	2	5	7	30	7	51	38.8054
Mis.	25068*	.	32	2	1	4	17	56	44.6784
Phoen.	20840*	2	38	16	18	19	19	112	107.4856
MT	20570*	7	28	14	19	25	15	108	105.0072
MWM	19098*	16	43	18	47	40	13	177	185.3597
Trick	19268*	7	34	10	19	18	19	107	111.0649
YFG	21878*	13	63	14	34	32	13	169	154.493
RT	21268*	12	46	30	26	39	25	178	167.3876
AT	22122*	.	5	6	18	6	5	40	36.163
Pur.	19922*	12	54	11	15	41	22	155	155.6068

$\overline{X}_m = 132.682$; $s_m = 35.7725$; $L_m = 105.0072$. $\overline{X}_{23} = 29.8105$; $s_{23} = 14.8865$

$(L_m - \overline{X}_{23})/s_{23} = 5.0513$ standard deviations.

Probability at this distance (from tables of normal-curve area)

= .000,000,22

Table 3.2(3) Revenger's Tragedy: statistical argument.

Method B for plus features. Group (II): Distinctiveness ratio $<$ 2.5

Play	Length (words)	tut	faith	you're+ y'are	i'thi	a'the+ o'the	Total	Total per 20000 words
TMM	18972	3	19	5	11	.	38	40.059
D.Ch.	25183	1	7	.	.	.	8	6.3534
RA	22419	10	35	10	.	1	56	49.9576
KBP	21423	.	36	7	8	.	51	47.6123
LK	18015	.	18	1	4	.	23	25.5342
MD	23568*	.	47	18	7	1	73	61.9484
Hoff.	20491	1	2	3	.	.	6	5.8562
GTQ	25231	.	41	16	12	.	69	54.6946
CTT	20016	.	.	4	1	.	5	4.996
IG	21351	.	16	.	2	2	20	18.7344
2HW	24832*	·	32	24	17	2	75	60.4059
WW	17772	.	18	1	7	.	26	29.2595
Bon.	21049	.	2	2	14	.	18	17.1029
Volp.	28790	3	24	.	3	6	36	25.0086
Fawn	22717	.	20	.	.	.	20	17.6079
Turk	18519	1	2	5	.	.	8	8.6397
Sh.G.	22745	2	25	5	11	.	43	37.8105
Cor.	28547*	.	6	5	42	.	53	37.1317
CW	24854	2	43	1	.	.	46	37.0161
HG	16666	.	.	.	4	.	4	4.8001
Ling.	26179	8	19	.	.	1	28	21.3911
WD	26285*	.	12	8	32	1	53	40.3271
Mis.	25068*	7	23	4	6	.	40	31.9131
Phoen.	20840*	.	35	23	9	.	67	64.2994
MT	20570*	3	58	25	28	2	116	112.7856
MWM	19098*	8	88	16	34	.	146	152.8955
Trick	19268*	3	79	16	16	.	114	118.3309
YFG	21878*	5	109	42	12	.	168	153.5789
RT	21268*	3	44	11	14	1	73	68.6477
AT	22122*	.	8	12	7	16	43	38.8753
Pur.	19922*	3	39	15	15	2	74	74.2897

$\overline{X}_m$ = 120.378; s_m = 36.6276; Lm = 64.2994. $\overline{X}_{23}$ = 29.7461; s_{23} = 17.9133

$(L_m - \overline{X}_{23})/s_{23}$ = 1.9289 standard deviations.

Probability at this distance (from tables of normal-curve area)

= .0269

Table 3.2(3) <u>R</u>evenger's <u>T</u>rage<u>dy</u>: statistical argument. (III)   Synonyms.

C group = <u>amongst</u>+<u>beside</u>+<u>between</u>+<u>whilst</u>/(same forms + <u>among</u>+<u>besides</u>+<u>betwixt</u> +<u>while</u>+<u>whiles</u>).

Play	ay/ ay+yes	%	C group	%	'em/ 'em+them	%	has/ has+hath	%
TMM	18/40	45	3/24	12.5	2/43	4.6511	9/25	36
D.Ch.	7/8	87.5	11/28	39.2857	0/78	0	0/43	0
RA	19/24	79.1666	6/26	23.0769	3/49	6.1224	57/68	83.8235
KBP	24/38	63.1578	31/55	56.3636	13/50	26	21/58	36.2068
LK	16/26	61.5384	11/19	57.8947	28/47	59.5744	35/45	77.7777
MD	8/14	57.1428	8/39	20.5128	47/66	71.2121	30/45	66.6666
Hoff.	36/43	83.7209	7/34	20.5882	2/36	5.5555	16/49	32.653
GTQ	16/72	22.2222	15/24	62.5	4/44	9.0909	58/72	80.5555
CTT	6/14	42.8571	8/19	42.1052	31/90	34.4444	1/53	1.8867
IG	13/28	46.4285	18/31	58.0645	56/95	58.9473	10/58	17.2413
2HW	13/61	21.3114	16/28	57.1428	9/83	10.8433	45/62	72.5806
WW	18/39	46.1538	9/25	36	26/43	60.4651	25/36	69.4444
Bon.	3/16	18.75	8/18	44.4444	95/101	94.0594	38/39	97.4358
Volp.	32/71	45.0704	17/34	50	53/86	61.6279	47/83	56.6265
Fawn	15/36	41.6666	7/11	63.6363	1/46	2.1739	44/82	53.6585
Turk	7/10	70	11/17	64.7058	0/30	0	0/28	0
Sh.G.	19/34	55.8823	17/25	68	23/57	40.3508	35/62	56.4516
Cor.	21/28	75	15/30	50	15/148	10.1351	35/86	40.6976
CW	44/66	66.6666	8/25	32	0/47	0	4/70	5.7142
HG	2/3	66.6666	13/19	68.421	0/58	0	47/53	88.6792
Ling.	20/35	57.1428	12/43	27.9069	0/118	0	1/56	1.7857
WD	4/34	11.7647	20/32	62.5	0/72	0	3/45	6.6666
Mis.	31/35	88.5714	10/34	29.4147	19/123	15.4471	26/65	40
Phoen.	33/38	86.8421	13/19	68.421	38/49	77.551	46/49	93.8775
MT	15/22	68.1818	19/27	70.3703	46/54	85.1851	43/46	93.4782
MWM	24/34	70.5882	16/23	69.5652	66/74	89.1891	54/56	96.4285
Trick	28/39	71.7948	21/28	75	36/44	81.8181	44/47	93.617
YFG	19/30	63.3333	18/38	47.3684	59/80	73.75	44/48	91.6666
RT	29/34	85.2941	14/16	87.5	38/47	80.851	45/52	86.5384
AT	3/20	15	13/26	50	18/30	60	48/62	77.4193
Pur.	58/67	86.5671	17/28	60.7142	41/53	77.3584	47/49	95.9183

$\overline{X}_m$ = 73.8215; s_m = 4.2247; L_m = 68.3487. $\overline{X}_{23}$ = 36.7441; s_{23} = 13.7584

$(L_m - \overline{X}_{23})/s_{23}$ = 2.2971 standard deviations.

Probability at this distance (from tables of normal-curve area)
= .0108

Combined probabilities

METHOD A: .0000086 x .086 x .0108   = .000,000,00799

METHOD B: .000,000,22 x .0269 x .0108 = .000,000,000,064

i.e., by Method A, less than 1 in 100 million;
    by Method B, less than 1 in 15,000 million.

Revenger's Tragedy: statistical group (III).   Synonyms.

Play	does/ does+doth	%	I'm/ I'm+I am	%	Mean of percentages
TMM	25/32	78.125	5/90	5.5555	30.3052
D.Ch.	0/22	0	0/16	0	21.1309
RA	18/25	72	0/42	0	44.0315
KBP	4/16	25	11/75	14.6666	36.8991
LK	7/11	63.6363	4/38	10.5263	55.1579
MD	20/21	95.238	1/39	2.5641	52.2227
Hoff.	2/15	13.3333	1/61	1.6393	26.2483
GTQ	18/27	66.6666	2/72	2.7777	40.6354
CTT	0/25	0	0/65	0	20.2155
IG	0/15	0	2/50	4	30.7802
2HW	46/48	95.8333	21/59	35.5932	48.8841
WW	14/32	43.75	3/52	5.7692	43.597
Bon.	13/13	100	1/50	2	59.4482
Volp.	18/35	51.4285	2/57	3.5087	44.7103
Fawn	21/29	72.4137	0/53	0	38.9248
Turk	0/15	0	0/53	0	22.4509
Sh.G.	11/15	73.3333	7/48	14.5833	51.4335
Cor.	19/28	67.8571	0/41	0	40.6149
CW	2/57	3.5087	0/55	0	17.9815
HG	8/9	88.8888	4/38	10.5263	53.8636
Ling.	1/18	5.5555	0/52	0	15.3984
WD	1/18	5.5555	0/54	0	14.4144
Mis.	14/34	41.1764	0/79	0	35.7682
Phoen.	18/19	94.7368	28/61	45.9016	77.8883
MT	22/23	95.6521	25/64	39.0625	75.3216
MWM	17/18	94.4444	26/61	42.6229	77.1397
Trick	7/8	87.5	7/55	12.7272	70.4095
YFG	12/13	92.3076	25/60	41.6666	68.3487
RT	28/30	93.3333	22/45	48.8888	80.4009
AT	16/26	61.5384	3/38	7.8947	45.3087
Pur.	8/8	100	11/39	28.2051	74.7938

3.3. A Yorkshire Tragedy

A Yorkshire Tragedy represents a problem for which the evidence I
shall cite (with the exception of a few parallel phrases) can contain
no bias whatever, since I did not regard the play as a problem of
the Middleton canon when I began this study. I had no views on the
authorship of the play, but had hoped to use it as a comparison text for
The Family of Love, with which it shares the printer and year of publication. The linguistic data for A Yorkshire Tragedy were recorded fairly
early in the investigation, but were not inserted in Table I.1. It was
only when I had assembled the whole corpus of Table I.1 plays that I
re-examined the data for A Yorkshire Tragedy, and then realised with
surprise that its pattern of exclamations, oaths, and contractions so
closely approximated Middleton's that the question of his authorship was
clearly raised.

3.3.1. Text

A Yorkshire Tragedy was entered in the Stationers' Register for the
copy of Thomas Pavier on 2 May, 1608. The entry reads: "A booke Called
A Yorkshire Tragedy written by Wylliam Shakespere" (Arber, III, 377). The
quarto was printed the same year; the title page reads:

> A Yorkshire Tragedy. Not so New as Lamentable and true. Acted
> by his Maiesties Players at the Globe. Written by W. Shakspeare.
> [Device] . . . Printed by R. B. for Thomas Pavier . . . 1608.

The head title (on sig. A2) is "ALL's ONE. OR, One of the foure
Plaies in one, called a York-shire Tragedy: as it was plaid by the Kings
Maiesties Plaiers". The shortness of the text (6230 words) fits this
description; obviously it was one item in a four-item program at the Globe.
The printer, identified by initials and device, was Richard Braddock, who
in 1608 also printed The Family of Love and Day's Humour Out of Breath
(see above, 2.3.1).

3.3.2. Source and date of composition

The story told in A Yorkshire Tragedy is that of the murders by
Walter Calverley of two of his sons in April 1605. Calverley was tried,
and on refusing to plead was pressed to death, at York on 5 August 1605.
The play is largely based on a pamphlet, Two Most Unnatural Murthers,
which was entered in the Stationers' Register on 12 June 1605 (Arber, III,
292), dating, therefore, from before Calverley's execution.

Baldwin Maxwell argues, quite reasonably, that since the Husband's fate is left doubtful in the last scene, the play also is probably earlier than the execution, for "few Elizabethan chroniclers, ever eager to underscore a moral, would have deliberately omitted the wages exacted for such a crime".[1] On this assumption, the date of composition must have been June-August 1605. In any case, the play must surely have been on the stage well before the end of 1605, or else topicality would have been lost.

3.3.3. Relationship to other plays

A Yorkshire Tragedy was acted with three other short plays now lost. It also bears some relationship to George Wilkins' The Miseries of Enforced Marriage (Q 1607), which is a free adaptation of the earlier part of Calverley's career--the "pre-contract" and "riotous living" noted in Two Most Unnatural Murthers (pp. 4-7). It has often been argued that:

(1) the three other short plays of the four-in-one program also dealt with the Calverley story;

(2) these three plays, possibly by George Wilkins, were later re-modelled by him as one play with a tacked-on "happy ending"--the extant Miseries.

I agree with Maxwell that the first of these suppositions (on which the second depends) is highly unlikely. In view of the Elizabethan-Jacobean appetite for variety even within a single play it is not probable that four separate pieces would have concentrated doggedly on one grim story. Nor, as Maxwell says (Apocrypha, pp. 170-71), would there have been any point in breaking up such a story into four plays; nor does A Yorkshire Tragedy require any knowledge on the part of the audience of any previous pieces, whereas if there had been four Calverley plays, the extant Tragedy could not have been the first one.

The first scene of A Yorkshire Tragedy requires a special explanation. Structurally, it does not belong with the following nine scenes of the Tragedy proper; it seems rather to be an alternative version of part of

---

[1] Studies in the Shakespeare Apocrypha (New York: Columbia Univ. Press, 1956), p. 177. This work is cited hereinafter as Apocrypha.

Miseries, Scene iv (sig. C3v, the Clown's return from London). Maxwell
conjectures (Apocrypha, pp. 152-53) that the scene is a late addition
to the Tragedy, designed to relate the play to Miseries, also acted by
the King's Men about 1606-07.

3.3.4. Authorship controversy

Pavier published a second quarto of the Tragedy in 1619, again with
a title-page ascription to "W. Shakespeare", and the play entered the
Shakespeare Apocrypha via the Third Folio (1664). But since the early
nineteenth century very few critics have been willing to credit Shakespeare with anything but a minor share in the play, if that.

The only full-scale argument for another author has been that of
H. Dugdale Sykes, who attributes the play to Wilkins.[1] Sykes argues
from parallels, most of which fail to survive the negative check: for
instance, tricks, which he claims (p.83) as a favorite word of Wilkins,
is also very common in other dramatists of the period, notably Middleton.
Moreover, the linguistic evidence recorded in Table I.1 shows that
Wilkins cannot possibly be the principal author of the final text, since
Wilkins in Miseries prefers them, hath, doth to 'em, has, does, and has
I'm, O: I am, 79; between, 2: betwixt, 14, in contrast to the Tragedy's
use of I'm and preferences for 'em, has, does, and between.

Middleton's authorship was suggested by Oliphant in 1927. A propos
of Wit at Several Weapons, he wrote: "Act V, scene 1, bears certain
resemblances to that powerful playlet A Yorkshire Tragedy--not least of
all in its doublings ('see, see him, see him deceived'; 'shelter,
shelter'; 'nothing else, nothing else'). Act I, scene 2, it may be
remarked, has much the same short, sharp style of sentence that meets us
in A Yorkshire Tragedy--a play which I am not at all sure that we do not
owe to Middleton."[2] In this passage it is not quite clear which problem
play is being cited to prove the authorship of the other. Oliphant had
a keen appreciation of Middleton, and a flair for detecting his presence;
but his evidence here is weak, and he did not pursue this matter further.

---

[1] Sidelights on Shakespeare (Stratford on Avon: Shakespeare Head Press,
1919), pp. 77-98.

[2] The Plays of Beaumont and Fletcher, p. 457.

No one has elaborated the case since. Thus the authorship of A Yorkshire Tragedy has remained an unsolved mystery till now.

3.3.5. Evidence of Middleton's presence

I propose to cite two categories of evidence for Middleton's presence in the Tragedy: (1) linguistic evidence which is positively probative because it has been subjected to the "negative check" through the Table I.1 corpus; (2) other kinds of evidence which I shall offer merely as a defence against the argument that the Tragedy is not Middleton's because it differs from Middleton's work in one way or another. This latter "defensive" evidence need not have been subjected to the negative check, since mere agreement between the Tragedy and Middleton is a sufficient refutation of the charge of difference; and it justifiably includes some literary arguments.

3.3.5.1. Probative evidence

The essential evidence which furnishes a high probability of Middleton's presence in A Yorkshire Tragedy is the pattern of contractions, taken together with the pattern of exclamations and oaths. To go no further than three contractions, t'as, upo'th', and 'em, I can state that the class of known authors writing in 1600-1620 for the London commercial stages who use t'as and upo'th' even once as well as 'em more often than them[1] in even one play is a class with one member only-- Middleton. This is true not only of the authors tabulated in Table I.1, but for all authors, since those whom I have excluded, such as Daniel and Samuel Rowley, make little or no use of 'em. A Yorkshire Tragedy has five instances of 'em (sigs. A2, A2v, B1, Clv, D1) beside four instances of them (A3v, B1, Blv, C2); Ta's occurs on B2, and vppot'h on A4. Upo'th' is a contraction so rare that I have found it only in Middleton and once in Dekker (Satiromastix, IV.ii.56.)[2]

---

[1] I do not in fact recall having found any author except Middleton who uses both t'as and upo'th'. I include the 'em preference merely as a precaution, since I have not made detailed notes on authors who differ very much from Middleton in linguistic style, and place the date limit at 1620 because I have not made an exhaustive study of such late authors as Shirley and Davenant.

[2] The upo'the in Jonson's plays from Alchemist (acted 1610) onwards I regard as a different contraction, just as o'the is different from o'th'.

Moreover, these forms in the Tragedy are not likely to be compositorial:
in Humour Out of Breath (printed by Braddock in the same year as the
Tragedy), there is no instance of 'em, t'as, or upo'th'. Interestingly
enough, the form Ta's in the Tragedy is not only a Middletonian contraction but also a Middletonian spelling: the same spelling (related
to Middleton's favorite ha's) occurs in Michaelmas Term, H2. The Tragedy's vppot'h also reflects Middleton's spelling habits, since in the
holograph Game at Chess the double -pp- is invariable in uppon, and
vppo'th occurs three times in Mad World (C3; Fl, twice) and once in
Michaelmas Term (D4v). The late placing of the apostrophe in the Tragedy's
vppot'h may be a compositor's aberration, or again it may derive ultimately from Middleton's habit of writing apostrophes rather beyond their
logical position, as in /e'm/ or even/em'/for 'em (see 1.2.2.2).[1]

The linguistic agreements between Middleton and A Yorkshire Tragedy
include many more items, some of them fairly rare ones. The following
occur in the Tragedy and in every one of Middleton's five undoubted early
plays:

Rarer contractions: I'm, y'ave.

Other contractions: I'd, y'are, i'th', o'th' (treating this as a
variant spelling of a'th'), on't, ha' (and other very common ones).

Exclamations: puh. (Tut occurs in Tragedy and in all the early
Middleton plays except Phoenix.)

Oaths: 'sfoot, 'slid, faith, mass.

Affirmative particles: preference for ay over yes.

Connectives: non-preference for betwixt over between. (This is the
only connective feature worth considering, as there are too few
instances of the others to provide ratios.)

Colloquialisms: preferences for has and does over hath and doth.

Single words: comfort (twice in 6230 words in Tragedy).

Ellipsis: 'Has for "he has" (twice in 6230 words in Tragedy).

Items which occur in the Tragedy and in some of Middleton's early
plays include the contraction thou'rt and the exclamation hum.

---

[1] I am, however, doubtful as to the nature of the copy for Q 1608:
there seem to be too many disagreements from Middleton's spellings
for it to have been a Middleton autograph.

There is one other item in the Tragedy which is perhaps strictly inadmissible, but to my mind constitutes the clinching piece of evidence: the word woult on B2v. We have seen that this very rare feature occurs both in The Puritan and in The Revenger's Tragedy, plays for which we have better than 99 per cent confidence that the author is Middleton. Of course, it is not therefore certain that woult is a Middletonian form: it might conceivably be compositorial, since it occurs also in the Eld text of Marston's What You Will (C3). But here it is again, in a play which we suspect is Middleton's (it does not occur in Braddock's other 1608 printings, Family of Love or Humour Out of Breath); and the coincidence is highly suggestive.

3.3.5.2. Defensive evidence

3.3.5.2.1. Collocations and single words in unusual meanings

If Middleton is the principal author of A Yorkshire Tragedy, we might expect to find a few parallels of collocations and word-usage to his undoubted plays (though not very many, perhaps, since the Tragedy is only about one-third the length of an average full-length play). And expectation is not disappointed: I have noted the following items, none of which occurs in the source-pamphlet, Two Most Unnatural Murthers.

(1) A sight able to kill a mothers brest (Tragedy, C4). Compare a sight able to make an olde man shrinke (Mad World, D4; III.ii.26); the sight of these iewells is able to cloy me (Your Five Gallants, F4; III.iv.9); also, it would kill his heart (Your Five Gallants, Flv; III.v.120). The phrase in Tragedy combines two Middletonian collocations: sight .. able to and kill .. "heart" or "breast".

(2) An vnderputter, a slaue pander (Tragedy, A4). Here also there are probably two Middletonisms. For "slave pandar", see below. With vnderputter, in this sense, compare vnderput, "concubine", in Michaelmas Term, E2v (III.i.80).

(3) I haue consumd all, plaid awaie long acre (Tragedy, Blv). Compare the same use of "Long Acre" as a pseudo-proper noun for "estate" in but where's Long-acre? in Trick, A3 (I.i.7-8), part of Wit-good's similarly rueful meditation on his losses.

(4) Is the rubbish sold, those wiseakers your lands (Tragedy, B3v). Compare rubbish, "land", in foure hundred a yeare in good Rubbish (Trick, C4v; II.i.366-67).

Compare also the pun on Acres and Wise-acres in Women Beware Women, L3v (III.ii.114).

There are also at least two parallels to The Revenger's Tragedy:

(1) slaue pander (A4); compare Revenger's Tragedy, slaue-pander
(El; II.ii.245), slaue Pandar (G4, IV.ii.135; G4v, IV.ii.201);

(2) broke custom (Bl); compare Revenger's Tragedy, broke custome
(A2; I.i.27).

3.3.5.2.2. Namelessness

The characters in A Yorkshire Tragedy, after the anomalous and detachable first scene, are all nameless. This may not be merely discretion
as regards the powerful Calverley family; after all, the dramatist could
have bestowed fictitious names (as Wilkins does in Miseries), Christian
names at least. But namelessness of main characters is a well-known
Middleton characteristic: one need only cite, in Women Beware Women, the
Duke, the Cardinal, the Mother, and the Ward.[1] Among the early plays,
in Phoenix we have the Duke, the Captain, the Knight, the Jeweller's Wife,
and the Niece; in Michaelmas Term, the Country Wench, her father, and
Lethe's mother; in Your Five Gallants, the various Courtesans. The namelessness of the characters in A Yorkshire Tragedy is a very striking feature
of the play, which can be easily explained on the theory of Middleton's
authorship.

3.3.5.2.3. The opening

The true beginning of the play, as we have seen, is Scene ii: thus
it is reasonable to suppose that the Tragedy originally opened with the
stage-direction Enter Wife (A3v). What follows, occupying the rest of
A3v, is the Wife's soliloquy, which establishes the situation and paints
the character of the Husband. We have seen above (3.2.6.1) that Middleton
likes to begin a play with a soliloquy or quasi-soliloquy from an important
character. The Wife's soliloquy contains a possibly significant parallel
to Revenger's Tragedy: Forgetting heauen looks downward, with which we
may compare looke downe-ward (Revenger's Tragedy, D2; II.i.274), which has
similar "hellish" connotations.

---

[1] Middleton's liking for namelessness seems to have been first pointed out
by Oliphant (The Plays of Beaumont and Fletcher, pp. 442-43).

3.3.5.2.4. Literary considerations

It is interesting to read the comments of critics who pass no judgment on the authorship of A Yorkshire Tragedy: several of these comments point to Middleton. Thus, Baldwin Maxwell notes (Apocrypha, pp. 180-81) that the Tragedy is "remarkably free" of oaths including the name of God. He also judges (op.cit., p. 183) that the play's "powerful effect" is due "in large part to the play's brevity and to the swiftness with which it reaches its climax". Speed of action is an important aspect of Middleton's art, both in comedy and tragedy. Most interesting of all, perhaps, is the analysis by A. C. Cawley of the type of tragedy embodied in the play.[1] Cawley maintains (accurately, in my opinion), that in A Yorkshire Tragedy we have a rare instance in English domestic drama of genuine Christian tragedy--the tragedy of a soul's damnation, since in the last scene the Husband is not truly repentant, but merely despairing. Now, this is as good a description of Middleton's usual tragic formula as one can get: Hengist, Women Beware Women, and The Changeling are all essentially damnation tragedies--Middleton's heroes and heroines are people who are shown up in Acts II-III and sent to the Devil in Act V. In A Yorkshire Tragedy things move faster, but the process is the same.

3.3.5.2.5. Versification

In the last category of defensive evidence I would place the versification of the play. Tucker Brooke (The Shakespeare Apocrypha, p. xxxv), gives the following figures for A Yorkshire Tragedy:

End-stopped lines: 88 per cent.

Rhyming lines: 20 per cent.

End-stopping and fairly abundant rhyme are features of Middleton's early style; as Brooke remarks, they rule out Shakespeare as the principal author of the play at this date. (However, some of the verse of the Tragedy strikes me as non-Middletonian: see below.)

3.3.6. Signs of plural authorship

If it is accepted that Middleton is the main author of the Tragedy, I think there are also signs that he is not the only one. The most suspicious circumstance, perhaps, is the total absence of the oath troth, one of Middleton's early favorites: in the most appropriate comparison

---

[1] English Domestic Drama: A Yorkshire Tragedy (Leeds: Leeds Univ. Press, 1966), pp. 10-12.

play, The Revenger's Tragedy, troth is wholly absent from no more than
four scenes in sequence (III.vi-IV.iii, F3v-Hlv: see Table 3.2(1)),
totalling 12 quarto pages; A Yorkshire Tragedy contains ten scenes,
28 quarto pages. The fact, too, that on't occurs only once in the
Tragedy (A3v) is suspicious. There are also positive non-Middletonisms:
O God, twice (Cl, C3v; Scenes iv, v); wud, once (Blv; Scene ii); and
the exclamation vm, twice, in the phrase Hum, vm vm (Cl; Scene iv).
These items faintly suggest that the collaborator may have been Dekker;
on the other hand, Sykes may have been right in thinking that Wilkins
had at least something to do with the play.   One of his parallels--
thy hasty news? (B4; Scene iii) is matched by the identical phrase in
the Wilkins collaboration The Travails of Three English Brothers,[1] though
here direct borrowing is certainly possible. I do not think the evidence
allows us to fix on the identity of the collaborator; but several scenes
or parts of scenes (which I shall detail below, (3.3.7), seem to me to
lack any convincing trace of Middleton, the verse especially moving to
a different rhythm.

The attribution to Shakespeare, so often repeated by Pavier, and
including the entry in the Stationers' Register where it could have had
no motivation as an advertisement, may suggest that the play did receive
some slight touches from the hand of the master. Many critics have
wanted to give him the prose speech in Scene iv that begins:

> Oh thou confused man, thy pleasant sins haue vndone thee
>
> thy damnation has beggerd thee, that heauen should say we
>
> must not sin, and yet made women . . .   (Clv)

There are certainly Shakespearean echoes here; most obviously,
pleasant sins parallels Edgar's phrase pleasant vices in the last scene
of Lear. But the speech turns into non-Shakespearean (and probably
non-Middletonian) verse on C2 after the stage-direction Teares his haire.
Probably Shakespeare's part in the play (if it is not a mirage) is
confined to a single insertion of a few lines in the prose speech above.

3.3.7. Authorship divisions

I must stress that I do not have much confidence in the authorship
divisions which follow; possibly there is a fair amount of mixed writing

---

[1] Sykes, Sidelights on Shakespeare, p.89.

in the play. In the survey of scenes I shall account merely for those
sections which I consider non-Middletonian; the attribution of the
Middletonian sections is covered by the general argument of 3.3.5.1
above and by the linguistic features displayed in Table 3.3, below.

3.3.7.1. Summary of attributions

In the summary below, "X" stands for an unknown collaborator who
is neither Shakespeare nor Middleton.

Middleton: Scenes i-iii.a (to the end of the Husband's first speech on
B4), vi-x.a (to S.D. Children laid out, D2v).

X: Scenes iii.b, v, x.b.

Mixed (Middleton, X, perhaps Shakespeare): Scene iv.

3.3.7.2. Survey of non-Middletonian sections

iii.b. (X.) The Wife's speech beginning Oh heauen knowes (B4)
contains no Middletonian feature, and soon afterwards the Husband
exclaims thy hasty news?. The Wife's last speech (B4v) sounds more like
Wilkins than Middleton.

iv. (Mixed.) The first part of the scene (to the exit of the Master
of the College) is perhaps partly Middletonian: it contains y'are (B4v),
em (C1v), and y'aue (C1v), but also O God (C1) and Hum, vm vm (C1). Oh
thou confused man . . . (C1v) may be Shakespeare's. The verse speech
of the Husband, C2-C2v, is irregular enough for Middleton, but And I
in want, not able for to lyue seems too crude for Middleton in 1605.

v. (X) I cannot detect any trace of Middleton here. The scene
contains the other instance of O God (C3v) as well as one of Sbloud
(C3v), which Middleton normally avoids.

x.b. (X) The verse from Children laid out to the end of the play
seems to me to be non-Middletonian: in particular, there is only one
feminine ending (D3, last line) in over forty lines, whereas Middleton
averages about 25 per cent feminine endings in his early period (see
above, 1.2.4).

3.3.8. Conclusion

I have suggested (3.3.5.1) that there is a "high probability" of
Middleton's presence in A Yorkshire Tragedy: but I will not pretend
that the probability at all approaches the probabilities of Middleton's
presence in The Puritan or in The Revenger's Tragedy. It is conceivable

(though I think not likely) that all the resemblances to Middleton in
A Yorkshire Tragedy are due to coincidence or borrowing, and that the
true author is an unknown dramatist who happens to share a great many
usages with Middleton. It is just possible to make a rough evaluation
of this possibility, by calculating the various scores of A Yorkshire
Tragedy in those feature-groups used for the Revenger's Tragedy problem.[1]
The assumption relied on here is that The Revenger's Tragedy represents
Middleton's early linguistic style in tragedy, which is probably near
enough to the truth for our purposes.[2] Thus, high scores mean wide
divergences from the Jacobean norm in the direction of the Middletonian
manner. On Method B (the more powerful of the two methods used for the
Revenger's Tragedy problem), A Yorkshire Tragedy has the following scores
(corrected for play length) in plus features: Group (I), 70.626; Group
(II), 57.7848. For Synonyms (Group III), its score is 63.0277 per cent.
These scores yield probabilities of .0031, .0588, and .0291 respectively,
which multiplied together give .0000051, or 1 in 196,000. This is
the fraction of the population of Jacobean dramatists who write a
linguistic style as closely approaching Middleton's as that of A Yorkshire
Tragedy. These figures are enough, according to this method, to give us
99 per cent confidence in Middleton's authorship if the population of
dramatists was no larger than 7800. This may sound fairly impressive,
but I think this argument should be regarded as merely suggestive: for
one thing, it is based on a risky extrapolation, since A Yorkshire
Tragedy is less than one-third normal play-length, and the plus feature
scores above are therefore obtained by multiplying by a factor greater
than 3. Moreover, there are features in the play, as we have seen, that
do not square with Middleton's sole authorship. Considering the problem
as a whole, I will claim merely that it is more likely than not that
A Yorkshire Tragedy is a play written mainly by Middleton with some
assistance from others, who may include Shakespeare.

---

[1] For Group (I) I count hart, of chance (Yorkshire Tragedy, C4v; Scene
viii) as an instance of the oath heart.

[2] Results are much the same if one calculates the scores of A Yorkshire
Tragedy as for the Puritan problem.

Table 3.3. A <u>Yorkshire</u> <u>Tragedy</u>: significant features

Segment 1

Sect-ion	sigs.	puh, tut	hum, um	why	Oh God	'sfoot 'slid	'sbl-ood	faith, mass	ay: yes	betw-een	'em: them	has: hath
1	A2-A3v	1,	.	8	.	,1	.	6,1	5:	.	2:	2:
2	A3v-B3	1,	.	.	.	.	.	.	2:	.	1:3	6:1
3.a	B3-B4	.	.	1	.	.	.	1,	.	1	.	1:
3.b	B4-B4v	.	.	1	.	.	.	.	.	1	.	.
4	B4v-C2v	1,	1,2	.	1	.	.	1,	:1	.	1:1	2:
5	C3-C3v	.	.	.	1	.	1	.	.	1	.	.
6	C3v-C4	.	.	.	.	.	.	.	.	.	.	.
7	C4-C4v	.	.	.	.	.	.	.	.	.	.	5:
8	C4v-D1	.	.	2	.	1,	.	.	.	.	1:	1:
9	D1v-D2	.	.	.	.	.	.	.	.	.	.	.
10.a	D2-D2v	,1	.	.	.	.	.	1,	.	.	.	.
10.b	D2v-D3v	.	.	.	.	.	.	.	.	.	.	.
Totals:		3,1	1,2	12	2	1,1	1	9,1	7:1	3	5:4	17:1

Segment 2

Sect-ion	sigs.	does: doth	ha'	I'm: I am	thou'rt, t'as	,y'are, y'ave	i'th', o'th'	upo'-th', on't	woult, wud	com-fort, 'Has
1	A2-A3v	1:	.	:2	.	.	2,	,1	.	.
2	A3v-B3	1:1	1	4:6	1,1	2,	,1	1,	1,1	.
3.a	B3-B4	.	.	1:1	.	.	2,1	.	.	1,
3.b	B4-B4v	.	.	.	.	.	.	.	.	.
4	B4v-C2v	.	1	:2	.	1,1	1,	.	.	.
5	C3-C3v	.	.	:2	.	.	.	.	.	.
6	C3v-C4	.	.	.	.	.	.	.	.	.
7	C4-C4v	.	.	:2	.	.	.	.	.	,1
8	C4v-D1	.	.	:1	.	.	,1	.	.	,1
9	D1v-D2	.	.	1:2	.	.	,1	.	.	.
10.a	D2-D2v	.	.	:1	.	.	.	.	.	.
10.b	D2v-D3v	.	.	.	.	.	.	.	.	1,
Totals:		2:1	2	6:19	1,1	3,1	5,4	1,1	1,1	2,2

4. Later Middleton

4.1. Anything for a Quiet Life

Throughout Section 4 the basis of comparison will be all of Middleton's undoubted unassisted post-1610 plays, including The Widow. Before we examine the possible additions to the post-1610 canon, it is necessary to settle the question whether Anything for a Quiet Life[1] is an unassisted Middleton play or not. An affirmative answer to this question would stretch the range of Middleton's known usage quite considerably, and therefore make later negative decisions more hazardous.

4.1.1. Text

The quarto of 1662, published by Francis Kirkman, bears the title page attribution "Written by Tho. Middleton, Gent." The text of this normal-length comedy is crammed into 52 pages, nearly all the verse being printed as prose. In so late an edition we cannot hope to use spelling evidence for authorship, and in fact Middleton's spellings are hardly anywhere detectable.

4.1.2. Date of composition

There is general agreement that Anything for a Quiet Life is shown by topical allusions to have been written in or shortly after 1621.[2] Such a date is supported by the evidence of the style of those portions of the play universally attributed to Middleton.

4.1.3. Authorship controversy

The first suggestion that Anything was not wholly Middleton's seems to have been Bullen's remark (I, lxxxvii-lxxxviii) "I suspect that the play in its present shape has been revised by another hand. The character of Lady Cressingham is drawn very much in the manner of Shirley." But the present controversy dates from the work of Sykes (1921).[3] Arguing from parallels, Sykes gave more than half the play to Webster; he convinced Webster's editor, F. L. Lucas, and many other scholars.

---

[1] Scene divisions and line-references for Anything for a Quiet Life in this study are based on the Works of John Webster, ed. F. L. Lucas (London: Chatto and Windus, 1927), IV. Quotations are from Q 1662.

[2] This date was established by Lucas (Webster's Works, IV, 65).

[3] "A Webster-Middleton Play: Anything for a Quiet Life," in Sidelights on Elizabethan Drama, pp. 159-72; reprinted from NQ, 12th ser., 9 (1921), 181-83, 202-04, 225-26, 300.

Bentley roundly condemned the theory of Webster's collaboration, as well as the variant suggested by Dunkel,[1] that of revision (Jacobean and Caroline Stage, IV, 860); but later comments by those who have made close studies of Middleton and Webster show that Bentley's rather general strictures have not quite carried the day.[2] Finally, Murray attempted to resolve the question with a brief study of contractions,[3] but achieved no decisive result. To some slight extent he was deceived by relying on Lucas' text. This is not in general bad (it is a vast improvement on Bullen's), but it is based on a single copy of Q 1662--the British Museum copy 162.d.31--which unfortunately is defective in a vital reading, and is probably the only extant copy that is so defective.[4] But a more fundamental reason for Murray's lack of success is that Middleton and Webster, about 1621, were not grossly different in their linguistic styles, and therefore a much more searching analysis was needed.

---

[1] "The Authorship of Anything for a Quiet Life," PMLA, 43 (1928), 793-99.

[2] See, for example, the observations of Barker, Thomas Middleton, p 192; and R. W. Dent, John Webster's Borrowing (Berkeley: Univ. California Press, 1960), pp. 60-61.

[3] A Study of John Webster (The Hague: Mouton, 1969), Appendix I, pp. 261-63.

[4] The reading in question is in V.i. 67, F4v. I have collated the two British Museum copies, shelf-marked 162.d.31 and 644.f.11, the two National Library of Scotland copies shelf-marked Bute 381 and H 28e. 6a (2), and one copy each from the Dyce Collection (Victoria and Albert Museum), the Chapin, Folger, and Huntington Libraries, and the libraries of Harvard and Yale Universities--10 copies in all. Sig. F4v is clearly invariant, and in all copies except Br. Mus. 162.d.31 the eighteenth line of text has George begin his speech with I am. In 162.d.31, probably as a result of a paper flaw, only the right hand top corner of the a in I am is visible. Lucas evidently mistook this mark for an apostrophe, since his edition reads I'm. This is an unfortunate error for our purposes, since Middleton favours I'm but Webster never uses it at all; and V.i.67 is part of a section claimed by Sykes for Webster. (I owe the explanation of the defective a to the Head of the Antiquarian Division, The British Museum.)

4.1.4. Evaluation of external evidence

Kirkman's attribution of 1662 is based on no known previous authority, and therefore must be allowed to carry some weight, especially as Middleton is undisputedly the author of nearly half the play. But the interpretation of the attribution is highly doubtful: does "written by Middleton" necessarily mean "written by nobody but Middleton"? It is worth noticing in this connection that Kirkman in his catalogue of 1661 gives the entire Beaumont and Fletcher canon to "John Fletcher" alone, and similarly omits an undoubted collaborator in the cases of Ferrex and Porrex and Fortune by Land and Sea.[1] Moreover, even if we assume that Kirkman would have been less casual in a title-page attribution, we have seen (2.2.4.1) that the probability of his being correct is only about 50 per cent or less. All in all, the external evidence may be said to favour the attribution of Anything for a Quiet Life to Middleton alone, but not to provide an unambiguous contrary argument if we find substantial reasons for allotting part of the play to a second author.

4.1.5. Tests of the collaboration theory
4.1.5.1. Middleton and Webster: the evidence of play totals

It is a fortunate circumstance that Sykes' case for Webster was based entirely on parallels, because the linguistic evidence of colloquialisms and affirmative particles can supply an independent check on his claim. As a preliminary, we may examine the feature totals for Anything in Table I.1 and compare them with the corresponding totals for late Middleton and for Webster, especially for Webster's tragi-comedy The Devil's Law Case (Q 1623), his only unassisted play comparable in genre, and possibly the nearest in date.[2] Middleton and Webster contrast sharply in their ratios I'm:I am, 'em:them, and ay:yes. As regards I'm, the difference is not one of degree: Middleton uses it often, Webster never. Webster uses 'em only in The Duchess of Malfi, and there only three times; Middleton prefers 'em to them in all of his plays except Chaste Maid. Webster's overall ratio of ay:yes is 16:88, or 1:5½; Middleton in his later period uses yes only slightly more often than ay.

---

[1] Greg, "Authorship Attributions," p.323, fn.1.

[2] The date of composition of Devil's Law Case is controversial: Lucas (II,216) favours c. 1620, Bentley (V, 1250-51) prefers 1610. Unless Webster had an overwhelming sense of linguistic decorum (which is unlikely, since he prefers hath in comic scenes in his early Ho plays), the difference in has:hath ratio between his tragedies and Devil's Law Case suggests that Lucas is nearer the truth.

Now the totals of these three features in <u>Anything</u> are all strongly
deviant from the Middleton norm in the direction of Webster's practices.
The play's <u>I'm</u>:<u>I am</u> and '<u>em</u>:<u>them</u> ratios are lower than those of any
undoubted Middleton play, and its <u>ay</u>:<u>yes</u> ratio of 6:35 is a trifle lower
even than Webster's overall ratio, and sharply divergent from anything
by Middleton.[1]　　We may say that the Sykes theory has prima facie
corroboration: if it were a false hypothesis we would have to believe
that these three features, the best discriminators between late Middleton
and Webster, all independently and by chance varied far from the Middleton
norm in the Websterian direction. A rough calculation suggests that the
odds against such a coincidence are at least 700 to one.[2]　 It is possible
of course, that the depletions of <u>I'm</u> and '<u>em</u> are not independent, since
they could have been altered by scribal transmission to <u>I am</u> and <u>them</u>,
but such an ad hoc theory fails to explain the low frequency of <u>ay</u>.
Altogether, we are encouraged to take the case for Webster seriously
enough to put it to the crucial test, namely, an examination of the distribution of these and other significant features through the text of the
problem play.

4.1.5.2. Distribution of significant features

　　　　Sykes made definite claims that certain scenes or parts of scenes
in <u>Anything</u> were the work of Webster alone--the sections marked "W" in
Table 4.1(3), below. If his theory is correct, these sections should
be noticeable by their lack of Middletonian linguistic features. But
as a preliminary the value of this test had better be checked by applying
it to some of Middleton's undoubted plays. <u>Chaste Maid</u> and <u>Trick</u> are both
somewhat lacking in typical Middletonian contractions: <u>Chaste Maid</u> has
rather low figures for <u>I'm</u> and '<u>em</u>, and <u>Trick</u> has the very low <u>I'm</u>: <u>I am</u>
ratio of 7:48. It will be useful to note how many scenes of substantial
length occur in these plays without definite indicators of Middleton's
style. Only those indicators which persist in Middleton's later period

---

[1] The <u>Second Maiden's Tragedy</u>, which will be claimed as Middleton's below
(4.2), has one instance of <u>ay</u> to five of <u>yes</u>; but this low ratio is
presumably due to chance variation over small numbers.

[2] There are eight late Middleton plays (including <u>Widow</u>); adding <u>Anything</u>,
we have nine plays. If we arrange their feature-scores for <u>I'm</u>: <u>I am</u>,
'<u>em</u>:<u>them</u>, and <u>ay</u>:<u>yes</u> in series, ordering them in terms of likeness to
Webster's mean ratios, then <u>Anything</u> is the end play of nine in each
series in the Webster direction. The probabilities of this happening by cha
are roughly 1/9 for each series, or $(1/9)^3$ for all three independently,
i.e. 1/729.

are worth considering, since we could not expect high frequencies of puh,
tut, 'sfoot, or faith in a play as late as Anything. The evidence is
displayed in Tables 4.1(1) and 4.1(2) below. (Scenes and line counts
follow Bullen.)

Table 4.1(1). Chaste Maid: distribution of Middletonisms

Scene	Length (lines)	M markers			M pointers			yes	them	I am	
		push	cuds	I've	I'm	'em	ay				
1.1	211	.	.	.	.	3	2	5	.	.	Scenes
1.2	131	.	.	.	.	1	.	1	1	4	without M
2.1	191	.	1	.	.	.	.	1	3	5	features
2.2	178	.	.	.	1	1	2	.	.	7	(II.iv,
2.3	42	.	.	.	.	1	1	1	.	1	IV.ii-iii)
2.4	16	.	.	.	.	.	.	1	.	.	Total: 122
3.1	59	.	.	.	.	.	1	.	.	2	lines
3.2	206	.	.	.	3	2	4	3	9	1	
3.3	145	.	.	.	4	1	2	.	1	.	
4.1	267	.	.	.	3	4	2	.	4	1	
4.2	9	.	.	.	.	.	.	.	.	.	
4.3	97	.	.	.	.	.	.	1	2	2	
5.1	169	1	.	.	.	.	.	2	3	6	
5.2	100	.	.	1	.	.	1	.	.	2	
5.3	31	.	.	.	.	.	1	.	.	1	
5.4	116	.	.	.	.	4	.	.	4	2	
Total:	1968	1	1	1	11	17	16	15	27	34	

Table 4.1(2). Trick: distribution of Middletonisms

Scene	Length (lines)	M markers			M pointers			yes	them	I am	
		push	cuds, coads	we're	I'm	'em	ay				
1.1	145	.	.	.	.	2	1	.	.	1	
1.2	66	.	.	.	.	.	.	.	.	1	Scenes
1.3	80	.	.	.	1	1	1	2	1	1	without
1.4	76	.	.	.	.	2	2	.	.	1	M features
2.1	402	2	1.1	.	3	9	4	4	1	8	(I.ii,
2.2	80	.	.	.	.	.	1	.	.	3	III.ii,iv,
3.1	281	1	1,	1	1	5	2	.	1	7	V,i)
3.2	21	.	.	.	.	.	.	.	.	3	total:
3.3	126	.	.	.	1	1	2	1	.	1	183
3.4	77	.	.	.	.	.	.	.	.	4	lines
4.1	111	.	.	1	.	1	7	1	1	2	
4.2	96	.	.	.	.	.	3	.	1	1	
4.3	69	.	.	1	.	.	.	.	.	1	
4.4	307	.	1,	.	1	7	3	1	1	5	
4.5	205	1	.	.	.	4	1	.	.	4	
5.1	19	.	.	.	.	.	.	.	.	.	
5.2	207	.	.	.	.	4	1	2	2	5	
Total:	2368	4	3,1	3	7	36	28	11	8	48	

We see that in Chaste Maid the longest continuous series of scenes without any of the tabulated Middletonisms is the sequence IV.ii-iii, 106 lines long; the only other such scene, II.iv, adds a mere 16 lines. In Trick, the "featureless" scenes are short and scattered, and in fact lack all the useful indicators except I am. In neither play does the total of featureless scenes exceed 200 lines, or 1/12 of the text. We may therefore expect a similar pattern in Anything if it is really a play wholly by Middleton. In particular, the scenes claimed by Sykes for Webster should be covered, to the extent of perhaps 11/12 of their total length, with Middletonisms, and very long scenes especially should not "survive" the test. The actual pattern in Anything is shown in Table 4.1(3), below.

Table 4.1(3). Anything for a Quiet Life: distribution of Middleton/ Webster discriminators (a test of the Sykes claim for Webster).

Sections after Sykes (W = section claimed). Scenes & lines as in Webster's Works, ed. Lucas. IV.ii is divided at George's entrance; V.i. after lines 117 and 270 at the Exeunts (V.i.a,b,c correspond to V.i, ii, iii of Dyce's edition, used by Sykes).

Sect- ion	Length (lines)	Claim	push, cuds, I've, we're	M markers betw- ixt	I'm	'em	M Pointers ay	yes	them	I am	Webster markers of't	Pue wawe
1.1	371	W	.	.	.	.	.	6	17	10	.	.
2.1	183	W	.	.	.	.	.	6	.	6	.	1
2.2	245		.	.	2	5	1	3	1	2	.	.
2.3	87		.	.	.	.	1	1	.	2	.	.
3.1	173	W	.	.	2	1	.	1	2	6	.	.
3.2	200		.	.	.	4	3	1	.	4	.	.
4.1	297	W	.	.	.	.	.	3	6	5	.	.
4.2.a	44	W	.	.	.	.	.	.	.	3	.	.
4.2.b	90		.	.	1	1	.	.	.	1	.	.
4.3	88		.	1	.	1	.	1	.	2	.	.
5.1.a	117	W	.	.	.	1	.	3	2	5	.	.
5.1.b	153	W	.	.	.	.	.	4	1	5	2	.
5.1.c	358		.	2	2	3	1	6	1	10	.	.
Total:	2306		.	3	7	16	6	35	30	61	2	1

Sections without M features (I.i, II.i, IV.i, ii.a, V.i.b) Total: 948 lines

Obviously, the results are very different from expectation on the hypothesis that the Sykes claim is false. Of the 1238 lines claimed wholly for Webster, only III.i and V.i.a are invaded by Middletonisms; these two scenes total 290 lines, not quite one-quarter of the claimed

sections. Five sections, totalling 948 lines, survive the test, most
notably the entire continuous block of I.i and II.i, the first 554 lines
of the play. In this block there are 16 I am, 17 them, and 12 yes,
without one single instance of I'm, 'em, or ay--a phenomenon quite
unparalleled in Middleton's undoubted plays. The only section for which
Sykes' claim seems to be certainly wrong is III.i. V.i.a[1] has one 'em
(sig. F4v; V.i.78), but Webster did write 'em in The Duchess of Malfi,
so that the claim is not certainly disproved here. The connective betwixt,
which is never used by Webster (see Table I.1), occurs three times towards
the end of the play, but always in scenes admitted by Sykes to be wholly
or partly Middleton's (IV.iii, V.l.c).

There is, moreover, positive linguistic evidence for Webster's
presence. The exclamation Pue wawe in II.i (Clv; II.i.64) is one never
used by Middleton; with it we may compare Pew wew in The White Devil (B3),
and perhaps also Pew in Devil's Law Case (Ll) and in Webster scenes of
Westward Ho (III.ii.8, IV.i.24).[2] Better still are the two instances
of of't in V.i.b (G2; V.i.223, 225). Middleton has 287 instances of on't
in his thirteen plays, but no of't in any play either undoubted or claimed
for him alone in this study. Of't is a rare contraction in the period,
as Table I.1 shows: only five of the thirty-three tabulated authors use
it at all,[3] and only one uses it in all of his undoubted plays. That
one is Webster. With this piece of evidence I submit that Webster's hand
in Anything for a Quiet Life is established beyond reasonable doubt.

The clear separation between the two authors' shares through most
of the play suggests collaboration rather than revision; in any case,
collaboration is the simpler hypothesis, which I will therefore adopt.

4.1.6. Authorship divisions

On the basis of the tests used above, it is possible to divide
Anything in accordance with Sykes' claim with the exception of III.i,

---

[1] Sykes, following Dyce's scene divisions, calls this section "V.i,"
V.i.b "V.ii," and V.i.c "V.iii." Thus the only scene which he divided
between Webster and Middleton was IV.ii.

[2] Pue and Pew were presumably pronounced /pju:/, whereas Middleton's
puh must have been pronounced differently, as /pu:/.

[3] Daborne, Davenport, Dekker, Massinger, Webster. I say "Davenport" here
for convenience; a very complicated problem surrounds Davenport, Dick of
Devonshire, and The Bloody Banquet, but probably only one individual is
responsible for the of't in these three sets of texts: see below, 5.1.4.2.

which must be either Middleton's or of mixed authorship; I shall allot it to Middleton, since he is the play's undoubted author. Sykes is probably right in thinking that both authors contributed to V.i.c: apart from the Middletonian features tabulated above, the section contains Tush (H1), the prefix Omnes twice (H2, H2v), and God-a-mercy twice (H2; V.i.573, 575), all features which are rare or not found at all in undoubted Middleton. However, since Middleton's hand seems to be the principal one here, I shall for the sake of simplicity allot the scene to him, and divide the play into two authorial shares as follows:

Middleton: II.ii-iii, III, IV.ii.b-iii, V.i.c. Total: 1241 lines
Webster: I, II.i, IV.i-ii.a, V.i. a-b. Total: 1065 lines.

For convenience of reference, I shall henceforth abbreviate the two shares as defined above as follows: Middleton's share = AQL(M); Webster's share = AQL(W).

4.1.7. Corroborative evidence

There are five contractions, in addition to I'm, 'em, and of't, for which Middleton and Webster have notably different relative frequencies. Table I.1 shows that in his later plays Middleton makes much more use than Webster does of you're+y'are and on't, whereas Webster clearly exceeds Middleton in his use of i'th', a'th' + o'th', and especially of 's (= his). I have calculated the mean frequencies, corrected for play-length, of late Middleton and of Webster for all these features, and have similarly corrected the frequencies in the shares of Anything defined above.[1] The results are set out in Table 4.1(4) below.

---

[1] The absolute frequencies in the shares have been converted to relative frequencies by means of the line counts, as follows (20677 = length of Anything in words):
r.f., AQL(M) = abs.freq. x 2306/1241 x 20000/20677
r.f., AQL(W) = abs.freq. x 2306/1065 x 20000/20677
The mean Middleton and Webster frequencies are calculated by averaging the relative frequencies of the individual plays.

Table 4.1(4). Anything for a Quiet Life: relative frequencies of
distinctive contractions in Middleton, Webster, AQL(M) and AQL(W).

	you're+ y'are	on't	i'th'	a'th'+ o'th'	's
Middleton, 8-play mean ($\overline{X}_m$)	18.53	22.19	13.52	6.43	4.05
Webster, 3-play mean ($\overline{X}_w$)	3.41	8.77	29.23	15.78	13.90
Ratio, $\overline{X}_m/\overline{X}_w$	5.44	2.53	.46	.40	.29
AQL(M), absolute frequency	8	6	6	1	1
AQL(W), absolute frequency	1	0	16	6	4
AQL(M), relative frequency	14.38	10.79	10.79	1.80	1.80
AQL(W), relative frequency	2.09	0	33.51	12.57	8.38
Ratio, r.f., AQL(M)/AQL(W)	6.87	∞	.32	.14	.21

The relative frequencies of each contraction are clearly very
different in the two authorial shares of Anything for a Quiet Life. As
we expect, Middleton has many more you're+y'are and on't in his portion
of the play, and Webster many more i'th', a'th' + o'th', and 's. What
is a little surprising is that the authors' linguistic styles are even
more distinct within the collaborate play than in their unaided works,
as one sees by comparing the two series of ratios. This is perhaps a
linguistic confirmation of Sykes' observation "Until the final scene is
reached the shares of the two authors are quite distinct" (Sidelights on
Elizabethan Drama, p. 159). Certainly the great differences between the
frequencies in the two shares, in every one of five features, is strong
confirmation of Webster's presence in AQL(W).[1]

Finally, I have checked three of Sykes' parallels between Anything
and Devil's Law Case throughout the Table I.1 corpus, and have not found
anything like them elsewhere. They are listed in Table I.2, along with
another parallel briefly mentioned by Lucas (IV, 67)-- I heard one in
England (Clv; II.i.68-69).   This, too, is matched by a collocation in
Devil's Law Case: like one I haue heard of in England (Flv; III.ii).

---

[1] At a very rough (under)estimate, the evidence of these five contractions
strengthens the case for Webster's presence at least 30 times. For the
distribution of each contraction between AQL(M) and AQL(W) has, on the
contrary hypothesis, a probability of ½ of chance agreement (to any
extent) with the Webster theory. The probability of five chance agreements is only $(\frac{1}{2})^5 = 1/32$.

What makes this parallel interesting is that references to what goes on in England, which are fairly common in Webster's plays set in Italy, are appropriate there but not really so in <u>Anything</u>, which is set in England itself: it reads very oddly in the context, suggesting that the author used a favorite expression without noticing its illogicality. This, then, and the other three parallels, all confirm the identification of the second hand in <u>Anything</u> <u>for</u> <u>a</u> <u>Quiet</u> <u>Life</u> as the hand of Webster.

Table 4.1(5), below, lists by sections the occurrences of the contractions used for the argument of Table 4.1(4).

Table 4.1(5). <u>Anything</u> <u>for</u> <u>a</u> <u>Quiet</u> <u>Life</u>: distinctive contractions.

Section	Length (lines)	you're, y'are	on't	i'th'	a'th' o'th'	's
1.1	371	•	•	5	,2	•
2.1	183	,1	•	3	,1	3
2.2	245	1,	1	3	•	1
2.3	87	•	•	1	•	•
3.1	173	2,3	3	•	•	•
3.2	200	•	•	•	•	•
4.1	197	•	•	3	,1	•
4.2.a	44	•	•	•	•	•
4.2.b	90	,1	•	2	•	•
4.3	88	•	1	•	•	•
5.1.a	117	•	•	4	1,	1
5.1.b	153	•	•	1	1,	•
5.1.c	358	,1	1	•	,1	•
Totals:	2306	3,6	6	22	2,5	5

4.2. The Second Maiden's Tragedy

4.2.1. Text and date of composition

The play here dealt with is so totally anonymous that it lacks even a title: the one used today is a makeshift invented by the Master of the Revels, Sir George Buc,[1] who, after censoring the manuscript, wrote at the end of the text, below the word "ffinis":

> This second Maydens tragedy (for it hath
> no name inscribed) may with the reformat-
> ions bee acted publikely.   31. Octobr.
> 1611. /.   G. Buc.

The play was not printed till the nineteenth century, but the manu-script, formerly part of the Warburton collection, has survived (British Museum MS. Lansdowne 807); the Malone Society edition by W. W. Greg (Oxford: 1910) is the basis of this study.

Greg distinguishes four hands in the text:[2]

(1) The principal hand, that of the scribe who made a fair copy of the play from the author's rough draft.

(2) The hand of the "literary corrector", whom Greg surmises to have been the author. This person seems often to have been trying to produce metrically smoother verse.

(3) The hand of a prompter or playhouse corrector.

(4) The hand of Sir George Buc.

However, it is not always possible to allot responsibility for the cor-rections, and above all for the deletions, many of which must have been directly or indirectly due to censorship. In these circumstances, I have taken the work of the scribe, including words or passages later deleted, as the only basis of this study. The literary corrector may or may not have been the author (I believe not);[3] hence the only stratum of the text which is certainly derived from the author is the original work of the scribe.

We are fortunate in that the date of the play is for once precise and certain: October 1611.

---

[1] Presumably Buc was thinking of The Maid's Tragedy, by Beaumont and Fletcher, which he must have censored shortly before.

[2] Introduction to the Malone Society edition, pp. vi-xii.

[3] The hand of the literary corrector is not Middleton's.

4.2.2. Authorship controversy

The authorship of Second Maiden seems to have been a mystery already in the mid-seventeenth century: three attributions appear on the verso of the last leaf of the manuscript, the second and third each cancelling the preceding one. The first reads:

The Second Maydens Tragedy

October 31th [sic]

1611

By Thomas Goff

A Tragedy indeed

The second attribution consists of the cancelling of the name "Thomas Goff" and the substitution of "George Chapman". The third consists of the cancelling of "George Chapman" in favour of "Will Shakspear". According to Greg (Malone Society edition, p. v), the Goffe attribution is probably earlier than 1650, while the others are probably later than 1700. None have any likelihood whatever: Thomas Goffe was an Oxford undergraduate in 1611, and his extant tragedies, all written for academic performances, are composed of the stiffest sub-Marlovian or English Senecal rant. Most probably the attribution to him is due to a mis-interpretation of the stage direction inserted by the prompter at line 1723, "Enter Mr Goughe". This must in fact refer to Robert Gough, an actor of the King's Men's company; another member of the same company, Richard Robinson, is named by the prompter at line 1921. Obviously, Second Maiden was a King's Men's play, and was not the kind of work that Thomas Goffe would be likely to write. The eighteenth century suggestions of Chapman and Shakespeare are obviously very wild surmises, and have properly found no favour with critics.

Schoenbaum (Middleton's Tragedies, p. 185) lists the attributions made by scholars from the early nineteenth century onwards; these comprise the names of Massinger, Tourneur, and Middleton,[1] and since 1900 only Tourneur and Middleton seem to be serious contenders. More-over, the Tourneur claim[2] is based almost wholly on parallels, especially of situation, between Second Maiden and The Revenger's Tragedy; these

---

[1] Middleton was first suggested by Swinburne; see his Complete Works, ed. Sir Edmund Gosse and T. J. Wise, 20 vols. (London: Heinemann, 1925-27), XII, 182-88; also XI, 398-99, and XVIII, 153, 375.

[2] Advanced principally by Sykes, "Cyril Tourneur: The Revenger's Tragedy: The Second Maiden's Tragedy."

are indeed striking,[1] but, since we have seen that not Tourneur but
Middleton was the author of The Revenger's Tragedy, they do not support
Tourneur's candidature.

In this century the claim of Middleton has been supported most
notably by Barker ("The Authorship of the Second Maiden's Tragedy and
The Revenger's Tragedy") and Schoenbaum (Middleton's Tragedies, pp.183-
202), who have assembled an impressive number of verbal parallels to
Middleton's undoubted plays, as well as metrical and linguistic evidence.

4.2.3. Authorship

I believe that Barker and Schoenbaum are completely correct, and
that Second Maiden is a play of Middleton's sole authorship. I have not
made any special attempt to supplement or to investigate the distinctiveness
of their phrase parallels, but I have checked and supplemented some of
their linguistic evidence.

Schoenbaum noted (op.cit., p. 196) that "the not very common oath
cuds me" is used in Second Maiden and in Middleton; I have found that
neither cuds me nor any other oath including the form cuds occurs in
the unassisted work of any other known author between 1600 and 1627,
whereas there are 13 instances of cuds in Middleton's undoubted unassisted
plays (see Table I.1), including 10 of cuds me (twice in No Wit, and
every instance of cuds in Phoenix, Michaelmas Term, Mad World, and
Trick). This oath is much more distinctive than even the exclamation
push for which Middleton is so famous. There are also three instances of
push in Second Maiden, whereas no author in 1600-1627 other than Middleton
has more than one push per play. Another highly significant marker is
the contraction I've, of which there are eight instances in Second Maiden;
such a frequency of I've is not equalled, apart from Middleton, by any
seventeenth century dramatist before Davenant, the highest frequency in
Table I.1 of an author other than Middleton being the four instances in
William Sampson's The Vow Breaker (Q 1636; composed perhaps as early as
1625[2]). With the co-occurrence of these three unique indications--of
cuds, 3 push, 8 I've--the author of Second Maiden is clearly identified as

---

[1] They are summarized by Schoenbaum, Middleton's Tragedies, pp. 186-87.

[2] See Bentley, V, 1043-45.

Middleton. I shall now briefly review the other features included in Table I.1 which support the Middleton claim.

4.2.3.1. Exclamations

There are no exclamations except the Middletonian push and pish, and the frequency of why (19 in 20014 words) is not high; but Middleton's later plays are quite sparing in exclamations, and the frequency of why is only 15 instances (in 20052 words) in More Dissemblers.

4.2.3.2. Oaths

Apart from cuds me, it is significant that the text contains five instances of heart and no less than thirteen of life.[1] These are the favorite oaths of what we might (somewhat improperly) call Middleton's middle period, 1607-1616 (Your Five Gallants to The Widow). High frequencies of life are found uniquely in Middleton in Table I.1: no other author has more than two instances per play, whereas Middleton has eight in No Wit, eleven in Chaste Maid, and seven in The Widow. Faith, troth, marry, mass, and byrlady, all Middletonian oaths, do occur in Second Maiden, but none with remarkable frequency; nor are they very frequent in Middleton's later plays. The single instance of I hold my life (line 1721) also links Second Maiden with No Wit, Chaste Maid, and The Widow, though the oath is not very rare.

4.2.3.3. Connectives

Middleton's most distinctive preferences, those for beside and toward, are clearly evident.

4.2.3.4. Other synonyms

The ay:yes ratio of 1:5 instances is not like Middleton, but with such small numbers variations of this magnitude are quite likely. In the more frequent pairs, 'em, has, does, and even I'm are preferred to their alternatives. Such a high I'm: I am ratio (31:24) is another unique indicator of Middleton in the period 1600-1625; and even Middleton has more I'm than I am in only two plays--The Widow and A Game at Chess. Presumably the scribe of Second Maiden made a very faithful copy of his author's papers.

4.2.3.5. Contractions, spellings, and speech-prefixes

Typical of Middleton are the forms thou'rt rather than th'art, we're rather than w'are, they're rather than th'are; t'as, you're,

---

[1] Schoenbaum has noted the use of life in Second Maiden, but has counted only 10 instances (Middleton's Tragedies, p. 196).

y'ave; and the high frequency (22 instances) of on't. The only anomalies
here are the shortages of i'th' and a'th' + o'th'; but these contractions
are also rare in Chaste Maid and Game at Chess. Curiously enough, there
is even a little evidence which is undoubtedly a mere matter of spelling:
the -cst forms forcst (line 361), forc'st (line 1281), plac'st (line 1895),
and grac'st (line 1897). Chorus speeches take the Middletonian form All,
not the Latin form Omnes (lines 1436, 1789, 1804, 2416).

4.2.3.6. Miscellaneous words and collocations

Fairly high frequencies of comfort (7 instances; r.f. 6.995)[1] and
'Has (9 instances) again accord with Middleton's authorship. I have also
recorded the following Middletonian collocations:

Line 392: masse here he comes too. (See 3.1.5, s.v. Puritan, III.iv.)
Line 533: I would faine leaue yor sight and I could possible. (3.1.5, II.i.)
Line 1340: neuer more deerly wellcome. (3.1.5, III.iv.)
Line 1406: Spoke like an honest subiect. (2.1.4.2, III.i.a.)
Line 1999: troth he saies true ther. (3.1.5, III.v.)

Since all these collocations were first noted in other problem plays,
this evidence is completely unbiased.

There is no need to survey the text by scenes, since every scene
shows abundant signs of Middleton's hand, as Table 4.2 below will
demonstrate. Reference to Table I.1 will reveal the baselessness of all
the other attributions, since the features of Second Maiden do not match
well those of Chapman, Goffe, Massinger, Shakespeare, or Tourneur.

In conclusion, I think it may be agreed that the evidence for Middleton's authorship is very strong. It is not quite as strong as the
evidence for The Puritan and The Revenger's Tragedy, because those texts
obviously reflect very clearly Middleton's autograph, whereas Second
Maiden does not quite do that. Moreover, with the decline in Middleton's
use of oaths and exclamations, and the paucity of i'th' and o'th', I
doubt whether it would be possible to offer a statistical proof of
Middleton's authorship of Second Maiden as powerful as those given above
for Puritan and Revenger's Tragedy, unless one were to make a much more
searching inquiry into vocabulary than there has been scope for in this

---

[1] Cf. the mean r.f. of comfort in the Revenger's Tragedy problem 23-play
sample: 4.6.

study. Nevertheless, I think Middleton's authorship of The Second Maiden's Tragedy is beyond reasonable doubt.

Table 4.2. The Second Maiden's Tragedy: distribution of significant features.

Segment 1

Scene[1]	Lines	push, pish	cuds me	heart	ud's life, life	faith, troth	mass, byr-lady	ay: yes	beside: besides	to-ward
1.1	1-255	.	.	.	.	.	1,	.	1:	.
1.2	256-635	.	.	2	,3	5,1	1,	1:	.	.
2.1	636-818	1,	.	.	.	,1	.	.	2:	.
2.2	819-1025	,1	.	.	,1	2,	.	.	.	1
2.3	1026-1169	1,	.	.	.	,1	.	.	:1	.
3.1	1170-1461	.	.	1	,2	4,1	.	:2	.	.
4.1	1462-1654	,1	1	.	,1	9,	.	.	.	.
4.2	1655-1724	.	.	.	,1	1,	.	.	.	.
4.3	1725-1876	.	.	.	,3	1,	1,	.	.	.
4.4	1877-1983	.	.	.	.	1,	.	.	.	.
5.1	1984-2210	1,	.	2	1.2	1,2	,1	:1	.	.
5.2	2211-2456	.	.	.	.	1,2	.	:2	2:	1
Totals:		3,2	1	5	1,13	25,9	3,1	1:5	5:1	2

Segment 2

Scene[1]	Lines	'em: them	has: hath	does	I'd	I'm: I am	I've	thou'rt	shee'-as	t'as
1.1	1-255	5:	3:2	3	.	3:3	.	.	.	.
1.2	256-635	4:3	7:	3	4	4:3	.	2	.	1
2.1	636-818	1:	2:	2	3	:2	.	2	.	.
2.2	819-1025	4:1	6:	2	.	3:	1	1	1	.
2.3	1026-1169	9:1	2:	.	1	1:	.	.	.	.
3.1	1170-1461	4:	4:	1	1	3:3	1	3	.	.
4.1	1462-1654	2:	1:	1	1	5:3	2	1	.	.
4.2	1655-1724	1:	2:	1	.	1:	1	.	.	.
4.3	1725-1876	1:1	2:	1	.	4:1	1	1	.	.
4.4	1877-1983	2:	2:	.	1	2:2	.	.	.	.
5.1	1984-2210	1:2	6:	1	1	2:5	2	1	.	2
5.2	2211-2456	1:1	7:1	2	2	3:2	.	1	.	.
Totals:		35:9	44:3	17	14	31:24	8	12	1	3

Note: [1] Act IV Scene ii includes the 11-line insertion after line 1724.

Table 4.2. The Second Maiden's Tragedy. Segment 3

Scene	Lines	we're	you're, y'are	y'ave	they're, th'are	i'th'	o'th'	on't	com-fort	'Has
1.1	1–255	1	1,3	.	2,	.	.	2	.	.
1.2	256–635	1	1,2	1	.	1	.	4	3	3
2.1	636–818	1	,1	1	.	.	.	2^a	.	.
2.2	819–1025	.	1,1	.	2,	.	.	1	.	1
2.3	1026–1169	.	.	.	2,	.	.	.	.	.
3.1	1170–1461	.	,1	1	,1	.	1	4	2	2
4.1	1462–1654	1	,4	3	1,	.	.	1	.	.
4.2	1655–1724	.	.	.	.	.	.	.	1	.
4.3	1725–1876	.	.	.	.	.	.	2	.	.
4.4	1877–1983	.	.	.	.	.	.	.	.	.
5.1	1984–2210	.	,2	.	.	1	.	3	.	3
5.2	2211–2456	.	.	.	.	.	.	3	1	.
Totals:		4	3,14	6	7,1	2	1	22	7	9

Note: [a] Occurs once as an't

4.3   The Nice Valour

4.3.1.   Text

The Nice Valour is the sixteenth play of the Beaumont and Fletcher
Folio published in 1647.   It had not been previously entered in the
Stationers' Register, and, as Bentley remarks, [1] "there seems to be no
reliable evidence of any kind about this play before the closing of the
theatres".   The play is the shortest in the 1647 Folio, occupying only
16½ pages, but it does have a Prologue "at the reviving of this Play",
and an Epilogue which names "nicer valour" and "Cupid in's Petticoat":
both, therefore, must genuinely belong to The Nice Valour.   Both refer
to "our Poet" in the singular.

4.3.2.   Date of composition

Baldwin Maxwell, after a detailed study of allusions in the text,
decides in favour of 1615-16 as the date of first preparation of the play
for performance. [2]   This dating is uncertain, but probably not badly
wrong.

4.3.3.   Authorship controversy

As a "Beaumont and Fletcher" play, the authorship of The Nice Valour
has always been doubtful.   Many critics have held theories of revision,
which are plausible enough in that, from the evidence of character names
and other details, it is clear that the scene of action must originally
have been France, though it is referred to by the Duke in IV.i (page 159,
column a) as "Genoa".   The claims of Beaumont, Fletcher, Middleton, and
Rowley, mostly in collaborative or revisional combination, have all been
supported over the past century or so. [3]   Middleton is now probably the
leading candidate for the main share in the authorship since Cyrus Hoy
supported his claim with linguistic evidence ("Shares," SB, 13 [1960],
92-96].   However, Hoy found the Middleton claim to be "beyond final proof"
(p. 96).

4.3.4.   Authorship

I am sure that Middleton is the main author of The Nice Valour in its
extant state, and I agree with Hoy that Fletcher is probably present also.

---

[1] Jacobean and Caroline Stage, III, 382.

[2] Studies in Beaumont, Fletcher, and Massinger, pp. 116-137.

[3] See Oliphant, The Plays of Beaumont and Fletcher, p. 449, for the
nineteenth-century attributions.

Hoy's division of the play seems to me the best possible one; it is as follows:

Fletcher and Middleton: I.i, II.i, IV.i, V.ii-iii.
Middleton: III, V.i.

The scenes indicated as "Fletcher and Middleton" are in fact mainly Middleton with traces of Fletcherian syntax appearing here and there-- perhaps a substratum nearly buried by a thorough-going Middletonian revision, since the linguistic style of the play is almost pure Middleton. It will be my purpose now to supply decisive proof of Middleton's presence.

The most obvious feature, probably, which points to Middleton is the very high (absolute and relative) frequency of the contraction I've-- 19 instances in all (r.f. 25.91), beginning as early in the text as the Duke's second speech, I've enough to hear on't (149a), and continuing with instances in every act (see below, Table 4.3). As we have seen (4.2.3), such a frequency of I've belongs in this period uniquely to Middleton--in fact, the relative frequency in Nice Valour is higher even than those in No Wit (12.273) and The Widow (22.643).

A further convincing sign of Middleton is the I'm:I am ratio of 32:25, very similar to those found in Second Maiden (31:24) and in A Game at Chess (27:22). Preference for I'm over I am, as we have seen (4.2.3), is found among Jacobean dramatists only in Middleton. There are also in Nice Valour 6 instances of I'd. Table I.1 shows that the combin- ation of I'd, I'm, and I've distinguishes Middleton very clearly from Beaumont, Fletcher, and Massinger, who make little use of I'd or I'm, and none whatever of I've.[1] Rowley also uses I'm sparingly, and I've not at all.

Another tell-tale feature is on't, which also occurs in the Duke's second speech, quoted above. There are 26 instances in Nice Valour altogether (r.f. 35.46), a rate not equalled elsewhere in the plays of Table I.1, and approached only by Middleton in Mad World with 29 instances (r.f. 30.37) and in The Witch with 22 instances (r.f. 26.09). No other Jacobean dramatist comes anywhere near Middleton's steady late-period

---

[1] There is no instance of I've in Massinger's later plays, and only one doubtful instance of I'm, spelt /I'em/, in The Guardian (O 1655, I3). Massinger's eight later unassisted plays (not in Table I.1) comprise: The Emperor of the East (Q 1632), The Maid of Honour (Q 1632), A New Way to Pay Old Debts (Q 1633), The Great Duke of Florence (Q 1636), The Unnatural Combat (Q 1639), The Bashful Lover (O 1655), The Guardian (O 1655), and The City Madam (Q 1658).

frequency of about 20 or more on't per 20000 words--certainly not
Beaumont, Fletcher, Massinger, or Rowley. (Fletcher's highest rate
of on't is only 14.69 per 20000 words in Humorous Lieutenant.)

I will now briefly review the other evidence for Middleton.

4.3.4.1. Exclamations

Exclamations include Puh (156b), noted by Hoy; and Hay-day (161a),
which is rather more frequent than puh in Middleton's later plays. Pah
(157b) occurs also in Phoenix (H4v; IV.iii.35). Pish (161a) is used
by Middleton, but is not rare elsewhere.

4.3.4.2. Oaths

Death (157b, 158b), is not a rare oath, but the first instance
occurs in a string of imprecations which (as we have seen, 3.2.6.2,
s.v. Revenger's Tragedy, III.vi) is thoroughly Middletonian: Death,
Hell, fiends, and darkenesse; with which we may compare especially Death
and vengeance . . . Hell, darkenesse in Your Five Gallants (D2v; II.iii.
198-99).

The low frequencies of faith and troth, and the absence of mass,
are not valid evidence against Middleton; there are even lower
frequencies in The Witch (Table I.1). Upon my reputation (158b) is
paralleled by Upon my reputation with your Excellence in More Dissemblers (C2v; II.i.10), and vpon my love to reputation in The Witch (line
96); and, as in Second Maiden, there is one instance of I hold my life
(158a). There are also fairly rare oaths which have parallels in collaborate plays of Middleton's late period, in scenes usually acknowledged
to be Middleton's: Birlakin (155a), paralleled by birlakins in Anything
for a Quiet Life, IV.ii.b (F2v; IV.ii.109); I fex (160b), which is
matched by three oaths in Anything--by my facks, by my fack (C4, C4v;
II.ii.107, 134), and by my fecks, IV.ii.b (F2v; IV.ii.97)--and by one
in Wit at Several Weapons: y'feck, III.i (80a).

4.3.4.3. Affirmatives

The ratio ay, 9:yes, 15 is just about what one might expect from
a collaboration by Middleton and Fletcher about 1615--or a later
revision by Middleton of a Fletcher original of this date.[1]

---

[1] By pooling instances of ay and ay+yes in Middleton's later plays, one
can obtain his overall percentage of ay/(ay+yes), which is 54.67. The
corresponding figure for Fletcher, for the plays Woman's Prize through
Loyal Subject in Table I.1, is 17.47%. Assuming an equal contribution
from each writer, one can take the mean of these figures, 36.07, as
the "expected" percentage for Nice Valour. The observed percentage is
37.5.

4.3.4.4. Connectives

There is little significant evidence in this category, mainly because Fletcher's and Middleton's usages are variable and not very different from each other. But the ratio between, 0:betwixt, 8 is more like late Middleton (compare the ratio 1:10 in Women Beware Women) than like Fletcher.

4.3.4.5. Colloquialisms and contractions

I have nothing to add to the remarks of Hoy on 'em, has, or does; or on the significant dearth of ye, which must prove that Fletcher's hand in the play has been over-written by Middleton. The 21 instances of ha' (23 if one counts ha't) are, as Hoy says, a sign of Middleton, but this feature is not very distinctive: it could not be used in either the Puritan or Revenger's Tragedy arguments above, because even with 18 instances of ha' in Puritan, the "raw" distinctiveness ratio was no higher than 1.0. In particular, ha' is not a safe discriminator between Middleton and Beaumont, who has 10 instances in Knight of the Burning Pestle.

Hoy has noted the two instances of t'as and one of t'ad, and also the fourteen instances of y'are and four of y'ave, which contrast clearly with Fletcher's much lower frequencies. Apart from the evidence of I'd, I'm, I've, and on't, already mentioned, another sign of Middleton is the occurrence of we're (/wee're/), in 164b, and w'are in 157a--there being only one instance of we're (none of w'are) in Fletcher's unassisted plays, in Bonduca (55a), nor any of either form in Beaumont, Massinger, or Rowley. Again, the fairly high frequency of they're+th'are (11 instances altogether) is a clear sign of Middleton, the contraction being rare in Beaumont, Fletcher, and Rowley, and never used by Massinger (see Table I.1). Another interesting Middleton pointer is i' (see 1.3.3): there are 3 instances in Nice Valour, i'your twice (160b, 163b) and i'this (156b); the contraction is rare in Beaumont, Fletcher, and Massinger, and never used by Rowley.

4.3.4.6. Collocations

I.i (151a): 'Tas almost kil'd my heart. A favorite Middleton expression, which, as we have seen (3.3.5.2.1), occurs as kill his heart in Your Five Gallants, III.v.120. Still closer in form is Why 'twould ha' kill'd my heart, in Widow, III.iii.6 (F1); compare also t'as almost broke my heart, in Your Five Gallants, II.i.163 (Clv).

III.i (154b): Faithfully welcome.

IV.i. (159a): Like a soule fetch'd agen.

IV.i, V.iii (160a, 163b): "Italian joke". One of Middleton's favorite jokes (see Appendix III) is the supposed propensity of Italians to anal intercourse. This appears twice in <u>Nice</u> <u>Valour</u>:

(I) Lap[et.] All in Italica, your Backward blowes

All in Italica, you Hermophrodite:

When shall I teach you wit?   (160a)

(This is quite similar to the passage in <u>More</u> <u>Dissemblers</u>, I.iv. 85-86, where, once the Page has pronounced the key word "backward", Dondolo replies "The fitter for the Italian; thou'st no wit Boy".)

(2) [Lapet]   And shall my elaborate Kick come behinde think you?

Clow[n]. Yes, it must come behinde, 'tis in <u>Italica</u> too . . .

(163b)

V.iii (163a): <u>An</u> <u>unknowne</u> <u>thing.</u> Another Middletonism, which occurs in <u>Revenger's</u> <u>Tragedy</u>, II.ii.95, and <u>Trick</u>, II.i.108 (see 3.2.6.2).

The conclusion one may draw from these turns of phrase is that if Middleton was only a reviser, his revision must nevertheless have been a very thorough one: there is very little of Fletcher left in the substance of the play. It may be that Middleton is the single "Poet" referred to in the Prologue and Epilogue; certainly he has a much better claim to the principal authorship than Fletcher. But whatever the history of the text may be, I submit that the evidence here presented-- especially that of <u>I've</u>, <u>I'm</u>, <u>I'd,</u> and <u>on't</u>--leaves no reasonable doubt of Middleton's presence.

The distribution of those features not cited by Hoy in "Shares" is given by Table 4.3, below.

Table 4.3. The Nice Valour: distribution of significant features

Segment 1

Scene	Page and column	i fex	faith, troth	bir- lakin	ay: yes	betwixt	I'd	I'm: I am	I've
1.1	149a-51b	.	1,1	.	:1	.	1	9:5	3
2.1	151b-54b	.	,2	.	:1	1	.	3:2	3
3.1	154b-55a	.	.	1	1:	2	.	1:3	.
3.2	155a-57a	.	.	.	4:3	.	3	7:1	7
3.3	157a-57b	.	.	.	.	.	.	:1	.
3.4	157b-58a	.	1,	.	.	.	.	:1	.
4.1	158a-61a	1	3,3	.	2:8	2	1	7:5	6
5.1	161a-62b	.	.	.	1:	1	.	1:1	.
5.2	162b-63a	.	.	.	1:	1	1	3:2	.
5.3	163a-65b	.	1,2	.	:2	1	.	1:4	.
Totals:		1	6,8	1	9:15	8	6	32:25	19

Segment 2

Scene	Page and column	we're, w'are	you're, y'are	y'ave	they're, th'are	i'	on't
1.1	149a-51b	.	,3	1	,1	.	4
2.1	151b-54b	.	,4	2	,6	.	3
3.1	154b-55a	.	,1	.	.	.	2
3.2	155a-57a	.	,1	1	,1	1	6
3.3	157a-57b	,1	.	.	.	.	.
3.4	157b-58a	.	,1	.	,1	.	.
4.1	158a-61a	.	1,3	.	2,	1	6
5.1	161a-62b	.	.	.	.	.	.
5.2	162b-63a	.	.	.	.	.	3
5.3	163a-65b	1,	,1	.	.	1	2
Totals:		1,1	1,14	4	2,9	3	26

4.4. Middleton and Rowley: Wit at Several Weapons

4.4.1. Wit at Several Weapons: introductory

4.4.1.1. Text

Wit at Several Weapons is the thirtieth play in the Beaumont and
Fletcher Folio of 1647. There is an Epilogue "at the reviving of this
play" which foreshadows the present authorship controversy:

> 'Twould be but labour lost for to excuse
>
> What Fletcher had to do in; his brisk Muse
>
> Was so Mercuriall, that if he but writ
>
> An Act, or Two, the whole Play rise up wit. (Lines 3 - 6)

Reading through the ambiguities (and faulty grammar, or textual corruption)
of these lines, one detects an attempt to suggest that Fletcher did write
as much as two acts of this play; which, however, the author of the
prologue has not explicitly claimed.

As in the case of The Nice Valour, there is no trace of Wit at Several
Weapons in any records before 1647.

4.4.1.2. Date of composition

The date of composition can be fixed with fair assurance at late
1613, because of three very pointed references (85a, IV.i; 86b, 88b, V.i)[1]
to the "New River", which is the conduit from Amwell Head to the Islington
cistern opened 29 September 1613, an occasion with which three Middletons
were concerned.[2] It is possible that the original play was earlier,
and that the 1613 version was a revision, but, as Oliphant remarks
(Beaumont and Fletcher, p. 453), there is no really good evidence for this
independent of evidence for authorship. There is no evidence whatever
for a date after 1613: the New River references would have had no
topicality once the River had ceased to be new.

---

[1] Noticed by Oliphant in The Plays of Beaumont and Fletcher, p. 452.

[2] Sir Thomas Middleton, Lord Mayor elect of London; Hugh Middleton,
goldsmith, who created the "River"; and Thomas Middleton, poet, who
composed the speech called The Running Stream Entertainment for delivery
at the opening ceremony. (See 1.2.1.2, above, and Appendix III.
The Running Stream Entertainment is appended to the Mayoral pageant
The Triumphs of Truth.)

4.4.1.3. Authorship controversy

The authorship of Wit has always been doubtful. Fleay (Biographical
Chronicle, I, 218) suggested Middleton, Rowley, and Fletcher as possible
authors, but decided in favour of Rowley and Fletcher only. Oliphant
(Beaumont and Fletcher, p. 453) lists several attributions which have
included both Middleton and Rowley; he himself suggests Beaumont, Fletcher,
Middleton, and (doubtfully) Rowley. Finally, Hoy has produced linguistic
evidence for dividing the play between Middleton and Rowley only, though
he recognizes traces of what may be Fletcher's hand ("Shares" [V], SB,
13 [1960], 89-92).

4.4.2. Middleton and Rowley: three undoubted collaborations

I believe that Hoy's attribution is correct, and I propose to support
it with additional evidence. But first it will be necessary to show that
this additional evidence performs well in distinguishing the shares of
Middleton and Rowley in their collaborate dramatic works.[1]

In pursuing this method, it is important to avoid circularity of
argument. As we have seen (2.1.1.4.3), features to be tested in a
given play must not be used to prove authorship in the same play. I shall
therefore proceed as follows:

(1) The features I've and we're + w'are, which occur frequently in
Middleton's unaided plays but never in Rowley's, will be used to prove
authorship in the collaborations.

(2) Other features will be tested against the authorship divisions
established by the use of I've and we're + w'are, and also against
divisions established in two previous studies--those of Hoy ("Shares" [V],
SB, 13 [1960], 84-88) and of Pauline Wiggin (An Inquiry),[2] which are
seldom in conflict with each other, and which correspond in general to a
consensus of scholarly opinion.

4.4.2.1. Testable Middleton/Rowley discriminators

Possible Middleton/Rowley discriminators to be tested fall into two
categories: oaths and contractions.

4.4.2.1.1. Oaths

'Slight or light should be Middleton's rather than Rowley's; still
more so any form of cuds; 'slid may be less reliable, since it occurs

---

[1] I am here closely following the method used by Hoy to establish the
reliability of his own evidence ("Shares" [V]).

[2] Wiggin's is the best of the older studies based on versification and
literary considerations.

only in Middleton's earlier undoubted plays. On the other hand, <u>Lord</u> and oaths including the form <u>God's</u> should be pointers to Rowley. <u>Faith</u> and <u>troth</u> are not likely to be reliable indicators of Middleton at this period, but the question is worth testing, since these oaths have been cited as evidence for Middleton's presence in Act I of <u>The Old Law</u>.[1]

4.4.2.1.2. <u>Contractions</u>.

Apart from <u>I've</u> and <u>we're</u>+<u>w'are</u>, the following contractions are likely to be pointers to Middleton's presence in collaborations with Rowley: <u>I'm</u>, <u>y'ave</u>, <u>y'ad</u>,[2] <u>they're</u> + <u>th'are</u>, <u>i'</u>, and <u>on't</u>. Table I.1 shows that Rowley has only one instance of <u>y'ave</u> and one of <u>th'are</u> in his three plays, whereas Middleton has many <u>y'ave</u> and <u>they're</u> (which latter may be spelt <u>th'are</u> in late texts). There are also six instances of <u>y'ad</u> in Middleton--one in <u>No Wit</u>, two in <u>More Dissemblers</u>, and three in Hengist (see 1.2.3.6)--but none in Rowley. <u>I'</u> occurs in <u>The Inner Temple Masque</u>, <u>The Widow</u>, <u>The Family</u> of Love, and in <u>The Nice Valour</u>, but not in Rowley. The <u>I'm</u>:<u>I am</u> ratio and the relative frequency of <u>on't</u> are higher in Middleton than in Rowley, and so may provide weak Middleton pointers.

4.4.2.2. <u>The canon of collaborations</u>

Of the five dramatic works attributed in the seventeenth century to Middleton and Rowley, one, <u>The Spanish Gipsy</u>, is itself a problem play (to be treated in 4.5). <u>The Old Law</u> is semi-problematic, since the possible co-authorship of Massinger must be reckoned with; it will therefore be examined last of the undoubted collaborations (in 4.4.3). The remaining three works comprise the theatre-masque <u>The World Tossed at Tennis</u> (Q 1620; composed 1619-20[3]), and the plays <u>A Fair Quarrel</u> (Q 1617; composed 1615-16) and <u>The Changeling</u> (Q 1653; composed 1622).[4] These will now be examined in order of composition.

4.4.2.3. A Fair Quarrel

The earliest of the undoubted collaborations, <u>A Fair Quarrel</u>, went through two early editions, Q 1617 and Q 1622, and there were two

---

[1] By Price, in "The Authorship and Manuscript of <u>The Old Law</u>," <u>Huntington Library Quarterly</u>, 2 (Feb. 1953), 117-39; see especially p. 126.

[2] I include <u>y'ave</u> and <u>y'ad</u> in my evidence even though they were used by Hoy under the heading <u>y'</u>, because they are much more distinctive than <u>y'are</u>.

[3] See Bentley, IV, 907-09.

[4] For the dates of composition of <u>Fair Quarrel</u> and <u>Changeling</u> see 1.2.5.3 and 1.2.5.4, above.

issues of Q 1617; in the second issue (Q 1617b) the "roaring school" scene was added as an appendix, and in Q 1622 it was inserted in its proper place in the play, as IV.iv. Following the example of Hoy, I base my study of this scene on Q 1622; for the rest of the play I use Q 1617a.

Table 4.4.(1), below, gives the distribution of I've and of features tested (we're+w'are does not occur).

Table 4.4(1). A Fair Quarrel: Middleton/Rowley discriminators

Scene divisions: I.i is divided after Bullen's line 90 (Russell: Nay good sir), in general agreement with Hoy; V.i is divided at the entrance of Captain Ager, etc., in agreement with Wiggin.
Attributions: these follow Hoy for I.i.a; elsewhere, Wiggin.

Sect-ion	Attrib-ution	Length (lines)	I've	'sli-ght	y'ave, y'ad	they're	i'	I'm: I am	on't	faith, troth	Lord
1.1.a	M	90	1	.	.	.	1	.	.	1,	.
1.1.b	R	341	.	.	.	.	.	:7	3	6,1	.
2.1	M	252	3	.	1,1	1	1	3:2	2	3,	.
2.2	R	242	.	.	..	.	.	1:6	3	5,1	1
3.1	M	185	1	1	3,	.	.	2:2	1	1,1	.
3.2	R	176	.	.	1,	.	.	:2	1	1,	.
3.3	M	44	.	.	.	.	.	.	.	.	.
4.1	R	253	.	.	.	.	.	:5	1	14,	.
4.2	M	120	1	.	.	.	1	1:	.	1,	.
4.3	M	123	.	.	1,	2	1	3:3	2	.	.
4.4	R	242	.	.	.	.	.	:4	1	1,	.
5.1.a	R	395	.	.	2,	.	.	5:6	7	9,2	.
5.1.b	M	52	.	.	.	.	.	.	1	1,	.
Totals, M:		866	6	1	5,1	3	4	9:7	6	7,1	0
Totals, R:		1649	0	0	3,0	0	0	6:30	16	36,4	1
Play totals:		2515	6	1	8,1	3	4	15:37	22	43,5	1

For the purpose of feature-testing I have accepted the Wiggin attribution of the last part of V.i to Middleton: my general impression of this section is that it sounds more like Middleton than Rowley,

---

[1]In this and subsequent tables of 4.4 (except 4.4(5)), Middletonisms are placed on the left and Rowleyisms on the right, with features likely to be more distinctive at the extremities.

though there is no strong evidence either way.[1]   For I.i.a, Hoy's
attribution, based on the occurrence of four '_em_ (sigs. Bl-B2), is
confirmed by I've (Bl; I.i.26); there is also the Middletonian _pish_
(B2; I.i.57).[2]   I have fixed the limit of I.i.a at line 90 after the
y'are in line 86, which may be Middleton's, and before the Death in Line
92 (since Death occurs three more times further on in I.i, it is
likely that the oath in line 92 is due to the author of the rest of
the scene).

Apart from the first and last scenes, there are no difficult
problems of author-discrimination. Three instances of I've confirm the
Wiggin-Hoy attribution of II.i to Middleton; the scene contains also a
trace of spelling evidence, forc'st in line 148 (Dlv). Also marked by
I've are III.i and IV.ii. The very short III.iii, in which Hoy has
noted ha', is indicated as Middleton's also by entrancst in line 3 (F4v).

The features tested function, for the most part, as might have been
expected. Lord occurs in a Rowley scene, and 'slight in a Middleton one,
while the relative frequencies of faith and troth are actually higher
in Rowley's share of the play than in Middleton's. Y'ave has a relative
frequency in Middleton's share at least three times as high as in Rowley's;
y'ad, they're, and i' occur only in Middleton scenes. The I'm:I am
ratio is clearly quite a good discriminator: as it happens, there is no
overlap in the two authors' ratio ranges--Middleton's ratio is never
less than 1.0, Rowley's never as much as 1.0. Only on't is disappointing,
with a slightly lower relative frequency in Middleton's share (6 per
866 lines, or .69 per 100) than in Rowley's (16 per 1649 lines, .97
per 100). But this may be partly due to the difference of register, since
Middleton's share is mostly serious, Rowley's mostly comic.

---

[1]
 One pointer to Middleton is the speech-prefix 1. for Ager's friend at
lines 413, 435 (sigs. Klv, K2). Ager's two friends were labelled
consistently 1. and 2. through Middleton's III.i (22 instances). The
use of 1. is illogical in V.i.b, since here it contrasts not with 2.
but with Colo. [nel's] frie. [nd] in line 415 (Klv); its appearance can
only be explained by common authorship for III.i and V.i.b.

[2] And the collocation give .. due (I giue you all your due), I.i.80
(B2); but this is not safe evidence for Middleton, since giue desert
his due occurs in A Shoemaker a Gentleman, C2v.

4.4.2.4. The World Tossed at Tennis

The theatre masque The World Tossed at Tennis is divided by Wiggin at the entrance of the Starches on sig. D2; she gives the whole of the masque before this point to Rowley, and everything after it to Middleton (Inquiry, p.40). Hoy is in general agreement, with the exception of one speech and perhaps neighbouring lines occupying E4v and adjoining portions of E4 and F1, which he gives ("Shares" [V,] p. 87) to Rowley on the evidence of two instances of vm (lines 773, 776; E4v). Hoy's refinement is unnecessary for my purposes: I shall divide the masque into two sections, "R" and "M", at the Starches' entry, postulating merely that "R" is mainly Rowley and "M" mainly Middleton. Table 4.4(2), below, gives the feature-distribution.

Table 4.4(2). The World Tossed at Tennis:
Middleton/Rowley discriminators

Sect-ion	sigs.	Length (lines)	I've	'slid	they're, th'are	i'	I'm: I am	on't	faith	troth
					Tested		features			
"R"	B2v-D2	471	.	.	.	.	:6	.	5	1
"M"	D2-F2v	515	2	2	2,1	5	8:3	8	.	3
Totals:		986	2	2	2,1	5	8:9	8	5	4

Wiggin's general authorship division is clearly confirmed by the distribution of I've; also perhaps by one very Middletonian passage on sig. E4, the Flamen's attack on Deceit's hypocrisy. He mentions

> thy nine Lectures weekely,
> Thy sowning at the hearing of an oath,
> Scarce to be fetch't agen . . .   (lines 718-20)

Fetch't agen is a common Middletonism (see 3.1.5, s.v. III.ii); and we have met the "sowning at the hearing of an oath" in The Puritan (B3; see 3.1.5, s.v. I.iv). But this passage is uncontroversially Middleton's, and so is the verse of E1v, where both instances of I've occur. The prose speeches of Simplicity in section "M" have been claimed for Rowley,[1] but they are full of features which the distribution in A Fair Quarrel confirmed as Middletonisms--they're (D4, E3), i'their (E4), I'm (D3v;

---

[1] By Stork, in his edition of All's Lost and Shoemaker a Gentleman, p.41; and by Dewar M. Robb, "The Canon of William Rowley's Plays," MLR, 45 (1950), p. 138.

D4v, twice). (One can avoid circularity here, perhaps, by pointing out that th'are, i', and I'm occur also in the verse of the "M" section, but nowhere in the 471 lines of Rowley's "R" section.) On't occurs 3 times in Simplicity's prose, 5 times elsewhere; but the conclusion from this distribution is uncertain, as is that from the distribution of troth (once in Simplicity's prose: E2). Faith, however, clearly belongs to Rowley, not Middleton. 'Slid is used twice by Simplicity, once at the bottom of E4 (line 745; verse), and once on F1v (line 836; prose): the authorship of both passages is uncertain.

4.4.2.5. The Changeling

In The Changeling, I follow Hoy's division of IV.ii, and his attribution of the first 17 lines of the scene to Rowley; otherwise, I follow Wiggin's attributions, which are accepted by nearly all scholars.

Table 4.4(3). The Changeling: Middleton/Rowley discriminators

Attributions: these follow Hoy for IV.ii.a; elsewhere, Wiggin.

Section	Attribution	Length (lines)	I've	w'are	cuds, 'slid	y'ave, th'are	I'm: I am	on't	faith, troth	Lord, God's
1.1	R	240	.	.	.	.	3:5	.	.	1,1
1.2	R	237	.	.	.	.	2:4	.	.	.
2.1	M	154	.	2	.	.	1:3	.	,1	.
2.2	M	167	.	1	.	2,1	5:1	4	.	.
3.1	M	10	2	.	.	.	.	.	.	.
3.2	M	27	.	.	.	.	:2	.	.	.
3.3	R	292	.	.	.	1,	2:3	3	.	.
3.4	M	177	1	.	.	.	4:3	5	1,	.
4.1	M	131	1	.	1,	.	3:2	1	,1	.
4.2.a	R	17	.	.	.	.	:1	.	.	.
4.2.b	M	134	1	.	.	,1	4:5	1	1,	.
4.3	R	222	.	.	.	.	1:5	3	.	.
5.1	M	125	1	.	,1	1,1	2:1	.	,1	.
5.2	M	87	1	.	.	.	:1	.	,1	.
5.3	R	231	.	.	.	.	1:7	1	.	.
Totals, M:		1012	7	3	1,1	3,3	19:18	11	2,4	0,0
Totals, R:		1239	0	0	0,0	1,0	9:25	7	0,0	1,1
Play totals:		2251	7	3	1,1	4,3	28:43	18	2,4	1,1

The Changeling has been so well attributed in the past that there is little need of the confirmatory evidence of I've and w'are; nevertheless, their confirmation is available for no less than eight scenes,

in fact for all but the very short III.ii of the scenes attributed to
Middleton.[1]   It is especially gratifying that the 10-line III.i is
now shown by linguistic evidence to be Middleton's.

Of the tested features, possibly the most interesting, and certainly
the rarest item, is Cuds, Diaphanta's exclamatory oath in IV.i.55 (F2v).
This is Middleton's euphemism for God(')s, which he more commonly employs
in combinations such as cud's me; but we have seen that the variant Coades
can occur alone, as in Puritan, Glv (compare Women Beware Women, Coads-
me, Hl), so we need not be surprised at the similar uncombined occurrence
of Cuds.

As to the other oaths, 'slid appears to be Middleton's, and Lord
and a Gods name in I.i (both on Blv) are certainly Rowley's.   Faith
and troth this time appear only in Middleton scenes, but very infrequent-
ly; two years later, in A Game at Chess, they do not appear at all.

The contractions y'ave and th'are perform in a familiar way. Once
again, the relative frequency of y'ave is about three times as high in
Middleton's share as it is in Rowley's: and the they+are contraction
occurs only in Middleton's scenes. I'm: I am fulfils expectation in the
share totals, though the ratios in Middleton's II.i and III.ii show
that it is not always a safe discriminator; and on't performs much better
than in Fair Quarrel, since this time its relative frequencies are 1.09
per 100 lines and .56 per 100 lines in Middleton's and Rowley's shares
respectively.

4.4.2.6. Test results: summary

To sum up the results of our feature-tests in Fair Quarrel, World
Tossed, and Changeling, it would seem that, as discriminators between
Rowley and late Middleton:

(1) faith and troth are useless;

(2) I'm and on't are weak pointers to Middleton, y'ave being somewhat stronger;

(3) y'ad, they're+th'are, and i' are all excellent, apparently as
reliable as I've and we're+w'are, since they never occur in Rowley scenes;

(4) the oaths cuds, 'slid, and 'slight seem also to point unambiguously to Middleton, and Lord and God's to Rowley.

---

[1] W'are is presumably a scribal transformation of Middleton's we're,
as th'are is of his they're.

4.4.3. The Old Law

The Old Law (Q 1656) dates probably from 1618, according to Baldwin
Maxwell (Studies in Beaumont, Fletcher, and Massinger, pp. 138-146).
The publisher, Edward Archer, is presumably responsible for the attribution to Massinger, Middleton, and Rowley, whose names occur, in that
order, on the title page. Probably all critics are sure of the presence
of Middleton and Rowley, but Massinger's contribution has been difficult
to trace. Exceptionally, George Price, in the most elaborate recent
study of the play's authorship ("The Authorship and Manuscript of The Old
Law"), has postulated revisions by Massinger in I.i, II.i, III.ii, IV.ii,
and V.i--that is, in more than half of the play's eight scenes; all this,
as Barker objects (Thomas Middleton, p. 186), on very little evidence.
The fundamental fault of Price's study is suggested by the order of words
in its title: it assumes what it purports to prove--the authorship of the
play--and then explains (or explains away) the details of the text in
accordance with the initial assumptions: that Massinger did participate,
that he participated only as a reviser, and that the copy for the quarto wa
largely his autograph. In fact, there is no safe evidence for any of
these assumptions. In any case, Price is obviously badly wrong in some
of his assignments of scenes to Middleton: Barker's corrections
(Thomas Middleton, pp. 187-89) are invariably sound, even when he is
hesitant about them.

I shall deal with the problem of The Old Law in two stages. First,
I shall show that Massinger has probably made no substantial contribution to any scene except (possibly) the first part of V.i; secondly, I
will divide the rest of the play between Middleton and Rowley, and this
division will provide another test of some Middleton/Rowley discriminators.

4.4.3.1. Massinger's share

Massinger's linguistic style has been thoroughly analysed by Hoy
("Shares" [I], SB, 8 [1956], 129-146). He is very sparing of contractions, even of such common ones as 's for "us" in let's;[1] he shows a
strong preference for hath, but uses does rather than doth. I have discovered some further points of interest: first, that Massinger has no
instance of I'd or I've in any play, and only 8 instances of I'm (including /I'em/ in The Guardian, I3) in all his unassisted plays; second, that

---

[1] In his early work (collaborations with Fletcher) he makes little use of
'em; but contrast the later (unassisted) plays in Table I.1.

he has very strong preferences in affirmatives and connectives, using yes, among, and while rather than ay, amongst, and whilst—his totals for all 15 unassisted plays being as follows: ay, 12: yes, 128; among, 58; amongst, 2; while, 81; whilst, 2.

Table 4.4(4) shows the distribution of Massinger indicators and counter-indicators through The Old Law, synonyms preferred by Massinger being placed first.

Table 4.4(4). The Old Law: tests for Massinger

Scene divisions: V.i. is divided as suggested by Barker (Thomas Middleton, p. 189), after line 431 at the entry of Gnotho etc.

Section	Length (lines)	yes: ay	among: amongst	while: whilst	them: 'em	hath: has	does: doth	I am: I'm	I'd, I've	let's
1.1	488	1:2	1:2	1:	3:7	3:8	3:	3:3	1,	2
2.1	272	1:1	.	1:	4:9	:3	2:1	3:5	4,2	1
2.2	204	1:	.	1:	1:1	:1	1:	2:5	.	1
3.1	356	2:7	.	1:	1:5	1:3	.	8:2	.	1
3.2	318	4:3	:1	.	:9	:11	.	2:7	1,3	.
4.1	177	2:2	:1	:1	1:5	:2	.	4:1	.	1
4.2	284	1:2	.	.	:6	:6	3:	4:5	2,2	2
5.1.a	431	1:1	:2	:2	13:	9:	:7	6:	.	.
5.1.b	282	2:1	.	.	2:5	1:6	3:	4:2	.	1
Total:	2812	15:19	1:6	4:3	25:47	14:40	12:8	36:30	8,7	9

I do not propose to consider in detail Price's "Massinger" parallels: They are mostly unparallel in expression, and none are accompanied by satisfactory negative checks. Moreover, it will be clear from the linguistic evidence of the table—especially the abundance of has, I'm, I'd, and I've—that Massinger cannot be a substantial contributor to any section except possibly V.i.a (the "trial scene"), and even here the hypothesis of his authorship poses difficulties. Certainly the sudden disappearance of 'em, has, and I'm, which are present in every other section, is very striking, and together with the equally sudden appearance of a strong preference for doth irresistibly suggests a change of authorship: but one wonders whether the author of the section is Massinger. The ratios here of among: amongst; while: whilst, and does:doth do not fit his known usage at all well. Now two solutions present themselves: either Archer was quite wrong about Massinger's presence in the play, and the authors concerned are Middleton, Rowley, and an unknown dramatist who uses amongst, whilst, and doth (Daborne, Day, and Heywood are

possible candidates); or else V.i.a is a specimen of Massinger's very
early work, even earlier than the collaborations with Fletcher in which
he already prefers <u>does</u> to <u>doth</u> (hence, much earlier than 1618), over-
written or transcribed by either Middleton or Rowley, who presumably
altered Massinger's <u>among</u> and <u>while</u> to <u>amongst</u> and <u>whilst</u>. The lack of
'<u>em</u> in V.i.a also suggests that if Massinger is involved at all, his
share is likely to be earlier than 1623, the date of publication of his
<u>Duke</u> <u>of</u> <u>Milan</u> (see Table I.1).

Other features in V.i.a may have some bearing on the authorship
problem. The oath '<u>slight</u> (Klv; V.i.266) is not likely to be Rowley's,
but may be Massinger's or Middleton's (or, for that matter, Day's).
Three instances of <u>y'are</u> (I2v, K1, Klv), one of <u>i'th'</u> (I3v), and one of
<u>on't</u> (I2v) do not sound like Massinger, and suggest, if any one, Middle-
ton. The problem is made more difficult by the really vile printing of
this part of the play: we may have to reckon with some serious textual
corruption. But unless this section is actually a reported text, the
<u>does</u>:<u>doth</u> ratio, at least, should be authentic: which rules out
Massinger as a reviser. I will leave the question of the authorship of
V.i.a open, merely accepting the possibility that it may be very early
Massinger revised by Middleton and Rowley; in which case, the whole
play may once have been Massinger's, just as <u>The</u> <u>Nice</u> <u>Valour</u> may once
have been Fletcher's. But a triple collaboration between Middleton,
Rowley, and the unknown author of V.i.a is a simpler hypothesis.

4.4.3.2. <u>Middleton/Rowley</u>

For the rest of <u>The</u> <u>Old</u> <u>Law</u>, (other than V.i.a), Table 4.4(5),
below, will suggest the correct authorship divisions. In this play I
propose to test the performances only of <u>they're</u>+<u>th'are</u>, <u>y'ave</u>, <u>y'ad</u>,
<u>i'</u>, and <u>on't</u>: the rest of the linguistic evidence will be needed to
prove authorship. Since Hoy has not examined this play, I include many
more features than in the cases of the other Middleton-Rowley collaborations. A brief survey of scenes may now be useful.

Table 4.4(5). The Old Law: Middleton/Rowley

Features: more distinctive Middletonisms are placed near the top. Authorship attributions: those symbolized are the ones suggested by the data here tabulated. Key: M = Middleton; R = Rowley; MR = Middleton and Rowley; X = neither Middleton nor Rowley.

Section:	1.1	2.1	2.2	3.1	3.2	4.1	4.2	5.1 a	5.1 b	Tot-al, M	Tot-al, R	Play Total
Authorship:	R	M	M	R	M	MR	M	X	R	M	R	Total
Length: (lines)	488	272	204	356	318	177	284	431	282	1078	1126	2812
M features												
push	.	2	.	.	.	.	.	.	.	2	0	2
pish	.	.	.	.	1	.	.	.	.	1	0	1
psha	.	.	.	.	.	.	1	.	.	1	0	1
pup	.	.	.	.	1	.	.	.	.	1	0	1
cud so	.	.	.	.	.	1	.	.	.	0	0	1
'slight	.	.	.	.	1	.	.	1	.	1	0	2
light	.	.	.	.	1	.	.	.	.	1	0	1
I've	.	2	.	.	3	.	2	.	.	7	0	7
we're	.	.	1	.	1	.	5	.	.	7	0	7
w'are	.	.	1	.	.	.	.	.	.	1	0	1
t'as	.	.	.	.	2	.	.	.	.	2	0	2
t'ad	.	.	.	.	1	.	1	.	.	2	0	2
ha'	.	1	1	.	3	.	.	.	.	5	0	5
you're	.	.	.	.	1	.	1	.	.	2	0	2
y'are	.	2	1	.	1	1	.	3	2	4	2	10
i'th'	.	5	2	.	2	.	.	1	.	9	0	10
a'th'	.	1	.	.	.	.	1	.	.	1	0	2
o'th'	.	.	2	.	.	.	.	.	.	2	0	2
I'm	3	5	5	2	7	1	5	.	2	22	7	30
I am	3	3	2	8	2	4	4	6	4	11	15	36
Tested												
y'ave	.	2	.	.	2	.	2	.	.	6	0	6
y'ad	.	.	.	.	.	.	2	.	.	2	0	2
they're	.	2	.	.	.	.	.	.	.	2	0	2
th'are	.	1	.	.	.	.	1	.	.	2	0	2
i'	.	1	.	.	2	.	1	.	.	4	0	4
on't	3	2	2	1	1	.	2	1	1	7	5	13
R feature												
tush	3	.	.	1	.	.	.	.	.	0	4	4

4.4.3.2.1. Survey of scenes

I.i. (R.) Since Rowley's relative frequency of faith is higher than Middleton's in Fair Quarrel (composed 1615-16) and World Tossed (1619-20), the 5 instances of faith here (the highest frequency of any scene in this play) would tend to suggest Rowley's authorship rather than Middleton's; but they provide very dubious evidence either way. The best evidence for Rowley is supplied by the 3 instances of tush.

II.i. (M.) Middleton's authorship is certified by push, I've, and ha', which latter contraction has been shown by Hoy to occur only in Middleton scenes in the other Middleton-Rowley collaborations. A'th' is a form used by Middleton but not by Rowley in unaided plays, though it must be admitted that semi-spelling evidence of this nature is not very safe in so late a text. Y'are and i'th' are usually somewhat more frequent in Middleton than in Rowley: in this play they are very clearly more frequent in scenes marked as Middleton's by more reliable indicators.

II.ii. (M). Middleton's authorship is indicated by we're, w'are, ha', and the high I'm: I am ratio.

III.i. (R). The lack of contractions, the low I'm: I am ratio, and one instance of tush all suggest Rowley. The only hint of Middleton is the collocation Troath he sayes true (E4v; III.i.145), and this by itself is not strong enough evidence. To my mind a convincing argument for Middleton's absence is the fact that the "Italian joke' is not made , though the right context presents itself twice--the back side of your booke (E3v; III.i.72), and cannot write backward (F2v; III.i.351).

III.ii. (M). The many Middletonian contractions make the authorship here obvious. The exclamation pup on F4 (III.ii.75) also appears in Mad World (D1v, five times), Trick (H1v, four times), and Chaste Maid (D1v, twice); I have not found it elsewhere.

IV.i. (M. and R.) Apart from V.i.a, this is the only scene of doubtful authorship; both Price and Barker give it to Rowley. The low I'm:I am ratio and the scarcity of contractions other than 'em do suggest Rowley; however, a'th' (G3v; IV.i.8) and above all Cud so (H1; IV.i.136) point to Middleton's presence. Probably the scene is a mixed one, with Rowley's hand predominating.

IV.ii. (M.) I've, we're, and t'ad clearly indicate Middleton's authorship. Psha (H1v; IV.ii.15) is paralleled by Pshaw in The Puritan (B1v); there is nothing similar in Rowley.

V.i.a. (X.) See above, 4.4.3.1.

V.i.b. (R.) Rowley's authorship is indicated by the low I'm: I am ratio and the lack of Middletonian contractions. ('T had, not t'ad, is found on K4v, in V.i.588.)

4.4.3.2.2. Feature-test results

Table 4.4(5) clearly confirms the reliability of y'ave, y'ad, they're + th'are, and i', which occur in The Old Law exclusively in Middleton scenes. The relative frequency of on't is slightly higher in Middleton's share of the play (.649 per 100 lines) than in Rowley's (.444 per 100 lines).

4.4.4. Wit at Several Weapons: authorship

Table 4.4(6), below, displays the authorship evidence in Wit at Several Weapons provided by features tested in 4.4.2-4.4.3, and by other items not cited by Hoy. Attributions are those of Hoy, with which I concur.

Table 4.4(6). Wit at Several Weapons: authorship indicators

| Scene | Page and col. | Author-ship | M features | | | | | | | | R markers |
			cuds, 'snigs	light, 'slid	I've, we're	they-'re, gi'n't	y'ave, i'	on't	I'm: I am	I'd	Lord, 'snails
1.1	69a-71b	M	1,	1,1	1,	,1	1,3	2	15:2	1	.
1.2	71b-73b	R	.	,1	.	.	.	1	1:3	.	.
2.1	74a-74b	M	.	.	.	.	.	3	:1	.	.
2.2	74b-77a	R	.	.	.	.	.	1	1:9	1	.
2.3	77a-77b	R	.	.	.	.	.	3	3:1	.	.
2.4	77b-78a	R	.	.	.	.	.	.	1:2	1	.
3.1	78b-81b	M	1,1	1,	3,	2,	,1	4	10:3	6	.
4.1	81b-85a	M	.	1,3	1,1	.	,5	8	6:2	2	.
4.2	85a-86a	M	.	.	.	.	.	1	4:	.	.
4.3	86a	M	.	.	.	.	.	2	3:	.	.
5.1	86b-89b	R	.	,1	.	.	.	2	3:8	3	,2
5.2	89b-92b	R	.	.	.	.	.	1	4:6	2	1,
Totals, M (11 pp.):			2,1	3,4	5,1	2,1	1,9	20	38:8	9	0,0
Totals, R (12 pp.):			0,0	0,2	0,0	0,0	0,0	8	13:29	7	1,2
Play totals (23 pp.):			2,1	3,6	5,1	2,1	1,9	28	51:37	16	1,2

4.4.4.1. Survey of scenes

I.i. (M.) This scene is clearly Middletonian; the most distinctive features are the oath cuds and the contraction gin't, both in the same speech by Witty-pate's father, which is full of Middletonisms:

> O[ld]. K[night]. Has gin't me twice now,
> All with a breath, I thank him; but that I love a wit
> I should be heartily angry; cuds, my Neece . . .   (70b)

Other rare features pointing to Middleton are the oath Light (70b), which outside Middleton I have found only once in the Table I.1 corpus, in Jonson's Devil is an Ass, II.vi.15; I've (70a); and i' in Father i'Law (70a) and i'my (70a, 70b).

I.ii. (R.) Rowley's authorship is most clearly shown by three instances of tush (72a, twice; 73b) noted by Hoy. Hoy has also cited the five /um/ spellings of 'em, which do distinguish Rowley from Middleton, but are perhaps not very secure evidence for Rowley in a play in which Fletcher may have participated, since in the quarto first edition of Fletcher's Rule a Wife (Q 1640) 'em is spelt /um/ 30 times, /'um/ twice, beside /em/ three times.

II.i. (M.) The best evidence for Middleton is provided by the three instances of ha', cited by Hoy (74a, twice; 74b). The high frequency of on't--three instances in this short scene of 60 lines--constitutes supporting evidence.

II.ii-iii. (R). Hoy gives no linguistic evidence for attributing these scenes to Rowley: the four instances of 'em in II.ii are spelt /'em/. The attribution is in fact based on literary similarity to Rowley's undoubted work. For II.ii, at least, it can be supported with the low I'm: I am ratio and the low frequency of on't.

II.iv. (R.) Rowley's authorship is suggested by two instances of tush on 78a.

III.i. (M.) Evidence for Middleton is superabundant. The following are the most interesting items:

Sniggs (80b). The closest parallel to this oath that I have found-- indeed, the only good one--is Coades-Nigs in Trick, C4 (II.i.329).

Cuds me (81a). Occurring only a few lines after Push, this is a certain mark of Middleton's presence.

I love⌈a man that lives by his wits⌉ alife (81b). This collocation occurs once in Fletcher (Monsieur Thomas, Elv), never in Rowley, but often in Middleton.

There is also some semi-spelling evidence--7 instances of you're, which occurs only in Middleton scenes in the Middleton-Rowley collabor-ations (Fair Quarrel, II.i, III.i; Changeling, II.ii; Old Law, III.ii, IV.ii). Sir Gregory's oath y'feck (80a) is matched by similar oaths in Middleton scenes of Anything for a Quiet Life and The Nice Valour (see 4.3.4.2, above).

IV.i. (M.) The most conclusive evidence for Middleton is provided
by the oath Light (83b) and the contractions I've (84a) and we're (82b).
The contraction and collocation Le'me see (82a) occurs also four times
in The Widow (see above, 1.3.3).

IV.ii-iii. (M.) Middleton's authorship of these short scenes is
suggested by their high I'm:I am ratios.

V.i. (R.) Besides one instance of Tush (87a), the oath 'snails
occurs twice (86b, 88a). This is not found in Rowley's unassisted plays,
but does occur (twice) in Rowley's share of Fair Quarrel, V.i (Ilv,
I3v; V.i.110, 274). Ud'so, which occurs on 87a, has occurred also in
Rowley's II.ii (75a). The low I'm:I am ratio and lack of Middleton
contractions also suggest Rowley. There is one instance of 'Slid (88a),
but this has occurred also in Rowley's I.ii (72a); it is more likely
that Rowley for once has adopted a Middletonian oath than that we have
a mixed-authorship scene. The same consideration is probably true of
the Puh which occurs on 87b.

V.ii. (R.) Rowley's authorship is shown by Lord (89b) and another
instance of Ud'so (91a). There is also the spelling evidence of wo'd
(91a), with which we may compare the plentiful l-less spellings of
"would" in Rowley's All's Lost and Shoemaker a Gentleman; though this
is not safe evidence against Fletcher (see Table I.1).

4.4.4.2. Corroborative evidence

4.4.4.2.1. Middleton/Rowley

If we total the scenes allotted to Middleton and then again those
allotted to Rowley, we find that both the I'm:I am ratios and the relative frequencies of on't support very well the Hoy attributions: the
rate of occurrence of on't in Middleton's 11 pages is about 2.7 times
the rate in Rowley's 12 pages, and Middleton's percentage of I'm/I'm +
I am (82.61) is higher than Rowley's (30.95) by about the same factor
(2.67 times).

4.4.4.2.2. Middleton-and-Rowley/Fletcher and others

I agree with Hoy and with Oliphant (Beaumont and Fletcher, p. 454)
that Fletcher is probably present in V.i; which suggests that the extant
text of Wit may represent a revision by Middleton and Rowley of an original by Fletcher and one or more collaborators. But Hoy is also right
in stressing that the play in its present form is essentially by Middleton and Rowley only. Good evidence for Middleton and Rowley rather

than Beaumont, Fletcher or Massinger are the 16 instances of I'd, 7 in
Rowley's share and 9 in Middleton's, whereas I'd is not found more than
onee in any unassisted play of Fletcher, and never in those of Beaumont
or Massinger. Similar considerations are true of I'm and I've, which
are rare or altogether absent in Fletcher and his main collaborators;
yet I'm occurs fairly steadily through the text of Wit, with 13 instances
in Rowley's share alone. The frequency of on't is also considerably
higher in Wit than in Beaumont, Fletcher or Massinger (see Table I.1),
but is similar to that in Fair Quarrel. Finally, the ay:yes ratio in
Wit (21:24) resembles those of Fair Quarrel (22:20) and Changeling (21:22),
and contrasts with the strong preferences for yes of Fletcher and Massinger

 I submit that Hoy's division of Wit at Several Weapons between
Middleton and Rowley is now confirmed, by fresh evidence, beyond reasonable
doubt.

1
 I have not tabulated ay:yes in Fair Quarrel, Changeling, and Wit
at Several Weapons because this ratio is useless as a discriminator
between Rowley and late Middleton. Here, however, are the numbers of
instances of ay and yes in the various sections of these three plays.
Numbers of instances are placed within parentheses.
 Fair Quarrel. Ay: I.i.b (2), II.ii (3), III.i (1), III.ii (1),
IV.i (4), IV.iii (2), IV.iv (6), V.i.a (3). Yes: I.i.b (1), II.i
(7), II.ii (1), III.i (1), III.ii (4), IV.i (2), IV.iv (1), V.i.a (3).

 Changeling. Ay: I.i (3), I.ii (7), II.ii (3), III.ii (1), III.iii
(1), IV.i (3), IV.iii (2), V.i (1). Yes: I.i (1), I.ii (4), II.ii
(1), III.i (1), III.ii (1), III.iii (3), III.iv (1), IV.ii.b (1),
IV.iii (4), V.iii (5).

 Wit at Several Weapons. Ay: I.i (1), II.ii (4), III.i (1), IV.i
(5), V.i (6), V.ii (4); Yes: I.i (1), I.ii (1), II.ii (3), III.i (4),
IV.i (1), IV.ii (2), IV.iii (3), V.i (2), V.ii (7).

4.5. The Spanish Gipsy

4.5.1. Text

The first quarto of The Spanish Gipsy was published in 1653 by
Richard Marriott, with a title-page attribution to "Thomas Midleton and
William Rowley". This volume was also advertised (without authorial
ascription) among plays "in the Press" on the last page (I3v) of The
Changeling (Q 1653), a Moseley publication; in fact, there are several
bibliographical links, which have been listed by George Price,[1] between
The Spanish Gipsy and The Changeling; and possibly the present authorship
problem is in some way due to this connection. A second quarto of Gipsy
(1661) has no textual authority (Price, op.cit., pp. 121-25).

Q 1653 of Gipsy has not, to the best of my knowledge, been satis-
factorily examined in detail by any expert bibliographer.[2] Price's
study is vitiated by his seeming unawareness that the authorship of the
play has ever been called in question; his decision that the printer's
copy was scribal rests on the assumption of Middleton-Rowley authorship,
and is therefore as dubious as the authorship itself. However, my own
observations lead me to agree with Price that the copy was not a prompt-
book, since there are no convincing examples of entrances brought forward
to allow time for walking on: for the most part oncoming characters speak
in the line immediately below their entries. The general tidiness of
the text and the full marking of entrances and exits would seem to rule
out foul papers. Mentions of properties in stage-directions--Enter Soto,
with a Cornet in his hand, E2; A Picture, H1v; Two Swords, I3; A Casket,
I4v--suggest an authorial fair draft lightly annotated for theatrical use,
or a scribal copy of such a draft.

The Dyce copy of Q 1653 contains manuscript insertions and corrections which probably derive from an authentic source (Price, pp. 120-21);
however, these contain no feature which affects the authorship problem,
so for the sake of simplicity I have based this study wholly on the
printed quarto text.

---

[1] "The Quartos of The Spanish Gypsy and Their Relation to The Changeling,"
PBSA, 52 (1958), 111-125; see especially pp. 115-17.

[2] Kate P. Smith, in her unpublished critical edition of Gipsy (Diss.
Northwestern, 1944), gives little useful information on the text.

4.5.2. Date of composition

The date of composition must have been 1623, since the play was
"allowed" by Sir Henry Herbert, Master of the Revels, on 9 July 1623,
and the mention of "elephants and camels" (D3v; II.ii.179) and again
of "camels . . . elephant" (G1; IV.i.98-99) seems to fit the arrival
of five camels and one elephant in London about the early part of July
1623 (Bentley, IV, 893-94). A performance at Court before Prince Charles
is recorded for 5 November 1623 "by the Cockpitt company"--that is, Lady
Elizabeth's men.[1]   There is, furthermore, an obvious advertisement in
the text of Gipsy for the same company's play of the previous year, The
Changeling (Constanza's speech, C3-C3v; II.i.104-112).

4.5.3. Authorship controversy

Marriott's attribution to Middleton and Rowley was accepted by Kirkman in his catalogue of 1661,[2] and remained unquestioned till the present
century. Various attempts have been made to divide the play between the
two traditional authors, but none of these are very convincing.[3] Pauline
Wiggin's attempt (Inquiry, pp. 40-42) is a remarkable contrast to her
detailed and successful divisions of Fair Quarrel, World Tossed, and
Changeling: it is brief, vague, and general, assigning Act II to Rowley
and the rest of the play to Middleton. If this division were true, it
would be an anomaly, since in each of the other Middleton-Rowley plays
Rowley's share exceeds Middleton's, and in World Tossed it is only a
few lines shorter (see 4.4). The unsatisfactory nature of Wiggin's and
all the other divisions is easily explained if neither Middleton nor
Rowley is in fact present in Gipsy.

That suggestion was first made by Sykes ("John Ford the Author of
The Spanish Gipsy") in 1924. Sykes based his case for Ford's authorship

---

[1]
Sir Henry Herbert, Dramatic Records, ed. Joseph Q. Adams (1917; rpt.
New York: Blom, n.d.), p. 51

[2] Rogers-and-Ley gives no author for Gipsy, and Archer does not list
the play.

[3]
For a survey of several attempts, see Barker, Thomas Middleton,
pp.208-09; also, Bentley, IV, 895. Bentley notes that the division has
"clearly baffled the critics".

on (1) word and phrase parallels, (2) two-word rhymes such as <u>without</u> <u>me</u>--
<u>about</u> <u>me</u> (B3v; I.iii.104-05), and (3) the contraction '<u>ee</u> (for "ye") in
the combinations <u>d'ee</u> and <u>t'ee</u> (a Ford characteristic); on the strength
of these three classes of evidence he gave Ford the whole play.

He also attempted to account for the attribution to Middleton and
Rowley as a deliberate fraud, pointing out that Richard Marriott was
certainly guilty of deliberate fraud the following year (1654) when he
published <u>Revenge</u> <u>for</u> <u>Honour</u> as by Chapman, although he had entered it in
the Stationers' Register correctly as by Glapthorne.[1] A weakness of this
argument is that while Chapman may have been more attractive to buyers
than Glapthorne, it is not clear that Middleton and Rowley would have
been more attractive than Ford. However, I believe that Sykes' argument
is defensible: it is quite possible that Marriott was attempting to
profit by the recent publication of <u>The</u> <u>Changeling</u>. If this had sold
well, there would obviously be good prospects for another soi-disant
Middleton-and-Rowley play; whereas no Ford play had been published since
1640.[2] In any event, Sykes' authorship case does not stand or fall
by Marriott's dishonesty: if there is good internal evidence for Ford,
and none for Middleton or Rowley, then it is perfectly possible that
Marriott's attribution was based on a mistake, possibly a mistake origin-
ating at the time when the copy for <u>Gipsy</u> was so closely associated with
that for <u>The</u> <u>Changeling</u> that it attracted the mistaken place-specification
"The Scene, <u>Allegant</u>" (below the list of "Drammatis Personae") obviously
from the same specification in <u>The</u> <u>Changeling</u> (Price, op.cit., pp.115-116).

There has been little satisfactory criticism of Sykes' case for
Ford in the fifty years since it was published. The outright rejections
have been many but vague, in the usual fashion of doxolatry; but serious

---

[1] See Bentley, IV, 489-93 for the soundness of the attribution to
Glapthorne.

[2] Unless we count <u>The</u> <u>Queen</u>, now universally attributed to Ford, but
published anonymously in 1653 by Alexander Gough. Since Gough was
concerned, perhaps fraudulently, in the part-attribution of <u>The</u> <u>Widow</u>
to Jonson and Fletcher (see 1.3.1), his silence on the authorship of
<u>The</u> <u>Queen</u> may indicate his low opinion of the selling-power of Ford's
name.

students of linguistic evidence in Jacobean drama are aware that neither Middleton nor Rowley can easily be found in The Spanish Gipsy. Hoy therefore excludes the play from his study of the Middleton-Rowley collaborations, with the observation that the lack of Middleton-Rowley features "may support the view that the play has been revised by Ford" ("Shares" [V], SB, 13 [1960], 88). The one really useful contribution to the solution of this problem has been the demonstration by M. Joan Sargeaunt that Sykes' case for Ford is weakest as regards the gipsy scenes;[1] while accepting Ford's authorship of the main plot, she quotes extensively from IV.i and then concludes: "I think any candid critic must allow that while this scene might conceivably have been written by Peele, Dekker, Gay, Peacock or W. S. Gilbert, it cannot possibly have been written by John Ford" (p. 52).

The only one of Sargeaunt's authorial candidates who is chronologically possible is, of course, Dekker. His name seems to have been first mentioned in connection with Gipsy by Oliphant, who in 1929 remarked of this play "it certainly seems in the main to be from the workshop of Ford and Dekker".[2]

4.5.4. Authorship

I have followed up the suggestions of Oliphant and Sargeaunt, and I find that the gipsy scenes of The Spanish Gipsy are indeed by Dekker, and that the play can be divided without much uncertainty between Dekker and Ford. Whether Dekker and Ford were the original authors, or the revisers of a Middleton-Rowley play, cannot be certainly determined. I have found in the text just one feature that points unambiguously to Middleton--the contraction gin't in the expression I ha gin't him (E3v; III.ii.146); but an attribution based on only one feature is too weak to be taken seriously. Probably the best theory, because the simplest, is that the play was first written by Dekker and Ford in 1623, and never subjected to major revision; then fraudulently or mistakenly attributed to Middleton and Rowley.

It is, of course, a priori quite likely that a play written partly by Ford in 1623 should have Dekker as its second author, since 1623-24

1
John Ford (1935; rpt. New York: Russell and Russell, 1966), pp. 41-52.

2
Shakespeare and His Fellow Dramatists (New York: Prentice-Hall, 1929), II, 18.

is known to be the period in which Dekker and Ford collaborated in
several dramatic works, as follows:

Date of composition[1]	Authorship status	Title	Text category
1623	Doubtful	The Welsh Ambassador	Play
1623-24	Undoubted	The Sun's Darling	Theatre masque
1624	Undoubted	The Fairy Knight	Play (lost)
1624	Undoubted	The Bristow Merchant	Play (lost)

Dekker and Ford also worked together about this time on two plays of
undoubted multiple authorship: The Witch of Edmonton (1621) with Rowley,
and The Late Murder of the Son upon the Mother (1624; lost) with Rowley
and Webster. Unfortunately for comparison purposes, none of these works
is an extant play undoubtedly by Dekker and Ford only; hence it is not
possible to follow the method of 2.1 and 4.4 and check out Dekker-Ford
features on the collaborations before applying them to the problem of
The Spanish Gipsy. Instead, I will first examine Gipsy, and then (in
4.5.4.5) see what light is thrown upon any difficulties by evidence
derived from the collaborations.

I shall defend my attribution to Dekker and Ford first by estab-
lishing the apparent absence of Middleton and Rowley; secondly, by
justifying Sykes' claim for the presence of Ford; thirdly, by establish-
ing the presence of Dekker; and finally, by dividing the play between
Dekker and Ford.

4.5.4.1. The absence of Middleton and Rowley

The differences between The Spanish Gipsy and the genuine Middleton-Rowley collaborations--especially the nearly contemporary Change-
ling--are easily seen from Table I.1. Gipsy has no push or tush, no
cuds, 'slid, or any other oath typical of Middleton or Rowley, and only 8
instances of why; which low figure resembles rather the rates of why
in Dekker's later plays and in several of Ford's. The ay:yes ratio of

---

[1] For the dates of the six collaborations by Dekker and Ford, alone or
with others, see Bentley, IV.
My studies of the extant collaborations are based on Dekker's Dram.
Works, ed. Bowers, III,IV.

only 6:21 is wrong for Middleton-Rowley, though very reasonable for Dekker-Ford. There is no I've, sh'as, sh'ad, t'as, t'ad, we're, w'are, or i', and perhaps most strikingly of all only 2 instances of on't, and only 2 I'm beside 70 I am. These deficiencies, especially of such frequent contractions as on't and I'm, add up to an impossibility: there is simply no parallel in Table I.1 among plays in which Middleton had at least a major share. Nor are there any spellings which suggest either Rowley or Middleton--no 'um for "'em", and no you're or they're.

Apart from gin't (noticed above), the few features which might suggest the presence of Middleton or Rowley ('em, has, ha', y'ave, and the l-less spellings of woult and would) are also compatible with the authorship of Dekker and Ford.

The distribution of significant features will be given in Table 4.5(1).

4.5.4.2. The presence of Ford

I have, first of all, verified that some of Sykes' parallels of phrase are truly distinctive, and point to Ford alone. The best parallels are those given in Table I.1--the exclamatory phrase 'deed la and the expressions the float of (for "the flood of") and undertake a voluntary exile.[1] These three features occur in Ford and in Gipsy, but nowhere else in the Table I.1 plays. As to Sykes' other types of evidence, his attempt to use the broad category of two-word rhymes is ridiculous, since these are very frequent also in Middleton and other authors (as Sargeaunt has pointed out, pp. 42-43). But the evidence of d'ee and t'ee is perfectly sound: as Sargeaunt remarks (pp. 44-45), few other authors use d'ee and t'ee except in very colloquial prose, whereas in Ford and in Gipsy they occur in serious blank verse.[2]

The best proof that Sykes is right about Ford's presence is the fact that further evidence, not noticed by Sykes, also points to Ford. The following features are given in Tables I.1 and 4.5(1):

---

[1] Less useful is the forfeit of, which occurs also in Hengist, IV.ii.178.

[2] Ronald M. Huebert, in "On Detecting Ford's Hand: a Fallacy" (The Library, 26 [1971], 256-59), has argued that d'ee is equally frequent in James Shirley's plays. But t'ee, on Huebert's evidence, quite clearly is rare in Shirley. In any case, Shirley is not a candidate for Gipsy: his versification is very different, and very distinctive.

(1) Two instances of <u>whiles</u> (F2, III.iii.27; I2v, V.i.173). Ford
is uniquely fond of this form, which occurs abundantly in all his
plays;[1] it occurs only very rarely in Middleton, and never more than
once per play; Rowley does not use it at all.

(2) Five instances of the pronoun '<u>a</u> (= "he"; B3v, twice; C1,
D1v, I3). This pronoun is quite rare in Middleton or Rowley, but is
much used by Ford.

Two <u>whiles</u> and five '<u>a</u> may not seem much, but since, as we shall
see, Ford wrote less than 1000 lines of this play, they represent
normal relative frequencies for Ford in both <u>whiles</u> and '<u>a</u>, but very
abnormal rates for Middleton or Rowley. Both features occur exclusively in main-plot scenes, where Ford's presence is suggested by Sykes'
evidence.

4.5.4.3. <u>The presence of Dekker</u>

A conviction of Dekker's presence is most easily attained in the
manner outlined by Sargeaunt: if one accepts that the main author, or
the author of the main plot, is Ford, then it becomes obvious that he
had a collaborator for the gipsy scenes. Dekker's style, I think,
first becomes unmistakable in II.i, with the occurrence in close sequence
of <u>ha'</u>, <u>Omnes</u>, the spelling /wud/ (C4v; II.i.197), and the vocative
phrases in Sancho's speech:

> Farewel old Gray-beard, adue Mother mumble-crust, morrow
> my little Wart of beauty.   (C4v; II.i.225-27)

The phrase <u>Mother</u> <u>mumble-crust</u> is a theatrical allusion used as a
vocative alias, which as we have seen (2.2.4.6, s.v. <u>Blurt</u>, I.i. 72-73)
is a Dekker device, used with especial frequency in <u>Satiromastix</u>. The
identical phrase, <u>mother</u> <u>Mumble-crust</u>, occurs in <u>Satiro-mastix</u>,
III.i.139-40; <u>Madge-mumble-crust</u> in <u>Shoemaker's</u> <u>Holiday</u>, I.iv.5, indicates the derivation from the character Madge Mumble-crust in Udall's
<u>Ralph</u> <u>Roister</u> <u>Doister</u>. I have not found <u>mumble-crust</u> outside Dekker
in the late-Elizabethan-Jacobean period.[2]

A fair number of other Dekker phrases occur in <u>Gipsy</u>, as will be
noted in the survey of scenes (4.5.4.4.2). For the present I will merely

---

[1] The <u>whiles</u> in Ford's plays are certainly authentic: the seven plays
(from their title pages) had at least five different printers; and
<u>whiles</u> occurs also in Ford's commendatory poem prefixed to <u>The</u> <u>Duchess</u>
<u>of</u> <u>Malfi</u>. There is only one <u>whilst</u> (F1, III.ii.255), no <u>while</u> in
sections of <u>The</u> <u>Spanish</u> <u>Gipsy</u> which I attribute to Ford.

[2] <u>Old</u> <u>mumble</u> <u>crust</u> <u>lord</u> occurs in a Dekker scene of <u>The</u> <u>Welsh</u> <u>Ambassador</u>
(IV.ii.4-5). Ford wrote only V.i and possibly III.iii of this play:
see below, 4.5.4.5.3.

point out <u>Grave</u> <u>Mother</u> <u>Bumby</u> earlier in II.i (C3v, II.i. 140), another
theatrical-alias-vocative, this time a reference to the fortune-teller
who is the title character of Lyly's <u>Mother</u> <u>Bombie</u>. The same vocative,
<u>Mother</u> <u>Bumby</u>, in the same spelling, occurs in what is assuredly a
Dekker scene in <u>The</u> <u>Witch</u> <u>of</u> <u>Edmonton</u> (IV.i.197).[1]

It should be noted also that, contrary to traditional Middleton-
Rowley theories, the best linguistic suggestions of Middleton's
presence are not found in the main plot but in the gipsy scenes. In
the main-plot scenes the <u>has</u>:<u>hath</u> ratio is much too low for Middleton,
whereas the gipsy scenes include the single <u>gin't</u>, plenty of <u>has</u> and
<u>'em</u>, and nearly all the instances of <u>ha'</u>. But in fact the manner of
these gipsy scenes is quite different from Middleton's--one has only
to look at the gipsy scenes in <u>More</u> <u>Dissemblers</u> to become aware of
the difference.

Brome's gipsies in <u>A</u> <u>Jovial</u> <u>Crew</u> (acted 1641) are very different
also, being much more realistic; in any case, Brome's linguistic style,
as exemplified by his earliest play <u>The</u> <u>Northern</u> <u>Lass</u> (Q 1632; acted
1629; see Table I.1), resembles his master Jonson's, and is not to be
found in <u>The</u> <u>Spanish</u> <u>Gipsy</u>. I have, indeed, examined every dramatist
writing in the period 1620-27, and I find that only Dekker's manner
and linguistic style match those of the sub-plot of <u>The</u> <u>Spanish</u> <u>Gipsy</u>.

4.5.4.4. <u>Authorship divisions</u>

4.5.4.4.1. <u>Summary of attributions</u>

    Dekker: I.i; II.i; III.i-ii.a (to <u>Exit</u> <u>Gipsies</u> <u>Dancing</u>, E4v); IV.
    Ford: I.iii-v; II.ii; III.ii.b-iii; V.
    Doubtful: I.ii.

4.5.4.4.2. <u>Survey of scenes</u>

    I.i. (D.) Dekker's authorship of this main-plot scene is indicated
as early as line 3 by the contraction <u>it's</u>, which Ford never uses. The
sobriety of Spaniards (I.i.3-5) is noted by Bullen as an idea favoured
by Dekker in <u>A</u> <u>Strange</u> <u>Horse-Race</u>. Again, the two instances of <u>ha'</u>
(B1), a contraction very seldom used by Ford, point to Dekker.

---

[1] IV.i is the only scene of <u>The</u> <u>Witch</u> <u>of</u> <u>Edmonton</u> which can be
confidently ascribed to Dekker: see below, 4.5.4.5.

I.ii.   I classify this 14-line scene as "doubtful" because it contains the phrase the forfeit/Of thine own life (B2), which suggests Ford, whereas the evidence of I'm, has, and does suggests Dekker.

I.iii. (F.)   The best evidence for Ford is the has:hath ratio of 0:3; as Table I.1 shows, Ford, unlike Middleton, Rowley, and the later Dekker, prefers hath to has in every one of his undoubted plays.   The exclamation Phew (B2v; I.iii.21) was noted by Sykes as common in Ford; it does, indeed, occur 10 times in his seven plays, but also once in a Rowley scene of Fair Quarrel (I3v; V.i.269).   The phrase forfeits of (B2; I.iii.18) may be weak evidence for Ford.

I.iv. (F.)   Two instances of 'a in the serious verse of B3v clearly point to Ford.

I.v. (F.)   The evidence for Ford's presence includes another 'a (Clv; I.v.74), and the following phrases noted by Sykes:

I.v.29 (B4v): The float of those desires; paralleled by the float/ Of the vnruly faction in my bloud (Love's Sacrifice, C2), and the float/ Of infinite desires (Love's Sacrifice, E4v-F1).

I.v.68 (C1): I undertake this voluntary exile; paralleled by he vndertooke/ A voluntary exile (Lover's Melancholy, C3v), and I vndertake a voluntary exile (Broken Heart, B2).

II.i. (D.)   The main evidence for Dekker has been noted above (4.5. 4.3).   In addition, there are the following items.

II.i.9-10 (C2): our stile has higher steps to climbe over. Compare the same pun on "style/stile" in Satiromastix, I.ii.270-73.

II.i.28 (C2v): Grandos.   The same incorrect plural occurs in The Noble Spanish Soldier (II.i.163, 184), which is most probably Dekker's.

II.i.51 (C2v): we Spaniards are no great feeders.   Another aspect of Spanish temperance also mentioned by Dekker in Strange Horse-Race (see Bullen's note to I.i.4); also in Blurt, especially I.ii.200-16.

II.i.95 (C3): a Parrot I am.   Compare Match Me, II.i.120, where yonder parrot also refers to a girl (Tormiella).   Almond for Parrat occurs in Old Fortunatus, I.i.53.

II.ii. (F.)   Ford's authorship is indicated by the has:hath ratio of 1:4, the 'a on Dlv (II.ii.22), and perhaps also by the form Deede for "indeed" on D2 (II.ii.46):   Ford has the aphetic deed in Lady's Trial, B2v, and elsewhere (see below).   Y'ad (D3v; II.ii.168) occurs in Love's Sacrifice, Klv (as /y'had/).

III.i. (D.) Dekker's authorship is strongly suggested by the form
wut on D4v (III.i.64) followed by it's (III.i.89) and Omnes (III.i.95).
The whole scene, with its references to the Muses, Helicon, Parnassus,
and Constanza-Pretiosa's welcome to smooth queint Romances (D4v; III.
i.98), is very much in Dekker's manner--the manner of II.i--and not
in that of Middleton. Grandoes occurs again on E1 (III.i.105). The
concluding song is full of Dekkerisms:--

III.i.115 (E1): Pindy Pandy. Compare the same phrase in Shoemaker's
Holiday, IV.iv.133. It is extremely rare elsewhere, and does not occur
in Middleton, Rowley, or Ford.

III.i.135 (E1v): Welcome Poet to our Ging. This line sums up the
simple romantic flavour of the whole scene; Ging occurs in Dekker's
pamphlet Penny-wise, Pound-foolish, B4v (A Ging of good fellowes).

III.i.139 (E1v): Peter see me (for the wine "Pedro Ximenes"). Peter
sa meene, with the same meaning, occurs in 2 Honest Whore, IV.iii.
49-50. I have found nothing similar elsewhere.

III.ii.a. (D.) III.ii appears to be of mixed authorship, with
Dekker's hand dominant till the exit of the "gipsies". Ford may be
present at the very beginning of the scene, as Sykes points out a parallel in lines 1-2, circled [with] friends. Thereafter, the steady use
of chorus speeches headed Omnes indicates Dekker's technique. The song
(E2v-E3), based on a prolonged military metaphor, is very much in Dekker's
manner. Wud occurs five times (E3, once; E4, four times). The phrase
A crack rope (E4; III.ii.215) occurs also in Match Me. I.iii.7, and
is rare elsewhere (no instance in Middleton or Rowley; one instance
in Ford's The Fancies, B2). The two instances of ha' (E3, E3v) also
point to Dekker rather than Ford.

III.ii.b. (F.) There are no very good authorship indicators here,
but there are two instances of comfort on F1v, and this word is much
more frequent in Ford than in Dekker.

III.iii. (F.) Comfort occurs again in line 2; thereafter whiles
(F2; III.iii.27) and d'ee (F2v; III.iii.40) indicate Ford's authorship,
which is confirmed by has, O:hath, 2.

IV.i. (D.) The scene begins with two Omnes speeches (F3v) and two
Dekker phrases:--

IV.i.6 (F3v): 'Tis Musick to me. Compare Match Me, IV.iii.14:
it's musick to them. I have found no other instance of "music to".

IV.i.10 (F3v): your Oysters, no opening. Compare If This Be, III.
ii.106: heres the oyster opend. The association of "oysters" and
"opening' is surprisingly rare: there is no instance in Middleton,
Rowley, or Ford.

I count one more Omnes on F4v (IV.i.82), since this is distin-
guished from the song by Roman type; in any case the three ha' (F4v;
Glv, twice) provide clear evidence of Dekker's presence. The vocative
pretty Soule (G2; IV.i.175) occurs also in Match Me, II.ii.7 (and
Westward Ho, II.ii.64, in a Dekker scene); there is no instance in
Middleton, Rowley, or Ford.

IV.ii. (D.) The indications of authorship here are faint; I give
the scene to Dekker because of the it's on G3 (IV.ii.34).

IV.iii. (D.) The pattern of ha', has, and Omnes points to Dekker;
on Hlv wud occurs in the same speech as two instances of ha' (IV.iii.
115-16). The phrase make buttons (= be in great fear) on H2v (IV.iii.
166) is paralleled in If This Be Not, IV.ii.89, but nowhere in Middleton,
Rowley, or Ford.

V.i. (F.) The linguistic evidence for Ford is fairly strong, including whiles, 'a, d'ee, and t'ee, and there is another instance of the
forfeit of (H4; V.i.43). On Il (V.i.95) occurs the asseveration by
Constanza Deede la I am. This, as Sykes has noted, is paralleled by No,
no deed la (Fancies, D4); perhaps also by In good deed la (Fancies, I3v).
I have found no instance of deed la except in Gipsy and in Ford.

V.ii. (F.) There is no good evidence here, but the manner seems to
be Ford's rather than Dekker's.

V.iii. (F.) In the last scene the evidence for Ford is clear, with
three instances of 'ee (d'ee, I4v, twice; t'ee, Kl). It is possible
that Dekker has returned before the end (perhaps at the entrance of
Alvarez and the rest at the bottom of Kl), since there are two Omnes
on Klv and one ha' on K2 (V.iii.105), but Ford does use these forms
occasionally, so I have preferred to leave the scene undivided.[1]

---

[1] One minor piece of evidence in favour of my authorship division of
Gipsy is the distribution of ye, which Ford tends to use more often
than Dekker. See Table 4.5(1), below.

Table 4.5(1). **The Spanish Gipsy**: significant features

Authorship attributions: those symbolized are the ones suggested by the data here tabulated. Key: D = Dekker; F = Ford.

Segment 1: Dekker/Ford discriminators

Section	Attribution	Length (lines)	D features					F features			
			it's	ha'	Omnes	does	has:hath	comfort	whiles	'a	ye,'ee
1.1	D	58	1	2	.	.	1:	1	.	.	.
1.2		14	.	.	.	1	1:	.	.	.	.
1.3	F	106	.	.	.	.	:3	.	.	.	.
1.4	F	22	.	.	.	.	.	.	.	2	.
1.5	F	122	.	.	.	1	1:2	1	.	1	3,
2.1	D	268	.	2	2	3	3:	.	.	.	1,
2.2	F	179	.	.	.	1	1:4	.	.	1	.
3.1	D	142	1	.	1	.	1:	.	.	.	.
3.2.a	D	236	.	2	8	1	5:2	.	.	.	.
3.2.b	F	68	.	.	.	.	.	2	.	.	.
3.3	F	107	.	.	.	1	:2	1	1	.	,1
4.1	D	211	.	3	3	.	2:	.	.	.	1,
4.2	D	107	1	.	.	2	1:	.	.	.	.
4.3	D	235	.	2	2	.	6:	.	.	.	.
5.1	F	208	.	.	.	1	4:2	1	1	1	1,2
5.2	F	57	.	.	.	.	1:1	.	.	.	1,
5.3	F	112	.	1	2	.	1:	1	.	.	1,3
Totals, D:		1257	3	11	16	6	19:2	1	0	0	2,0
Totals, F:		981	0	1	2	4	8:14	6	2	5	6,6
Play totals:		2252	3	12	18	11	28:16	7	2	5	8,6

Segment 2: other features

Section	Attribution	Length (lines)	I'm:I am	y'are	y'ave,y'ad	th'are	gi'n't	i'th'	o'th'	on'
1.1	D	58	:3	.	.	.	.	.	.	.
1.2		14	1:2	.	.	.	.	.	.	.
1.3	F	106	:6	1	.	.	.	.	.	.
1.4	F	22	:1	.	.	.	.	.	.	.
1.5	F	122	:2	3	.	.	.	.	.	.
2.1	D	268	:9	1	1,	1	.	.	1	1
2.2	F	179	:1	.	,1	.	.	.	.	.
3.1	D	142	:1	1	.	.	.	.	.	.
3.2.a	D	236	1:3	.	.	.	1	1	.	.
3.2.b	F	68	:3	1	.	.	.	.	.	.
3.3	F	107	:5	.	.	.	.	.	.	.
4.1	D	211	:5	1	.	.	.	.	.	.
4.2	D	107	:1	.	.	.	.	.	.	.
4.3	D	235	:7	.	.	.	.	.	.	.
5.1	F	208	:11	2	.	.	.	.	.	1
5.2	F	57	:5	.	.	.	.	.	.	.
5.3	F	112	:5	.	.	.	.	.	.	.
Play totals:		2252	2:70	10	1,1	1	1	1	1	2

4.5.4.5. Difficulties and the Dekker-Ford collaborations

It must be admitted that there are some difficulties in my propos-
ition that Dekker wrote more than half of The Spanish Gipsy. Most
important are the deficiencies in what might be the expected totals
of I'm and i'th'. Dekker was using both contractions freely in his
later years, yet there are only two instances of I'm and one of i'th'
in the whole of Gipsy. A possible explanation that suggests itself
is that some scenes which I have allotted to Dekker are in fact partly
also by Ford; Sykes, indeed, notes some parallels to Ford in the
dialogue of the gipsy scenes. But I cannot believe that Ford had any
but a very minor share in these scenes, because there is a difficulty
in the opposite direction: we find no doth in Gipsy, whereas we should
expect some from Ford (see Table I.1). As it is, my theory of the
collaboration, which reduces Ford's share of the does:doth total to
4:0, would seem to be a necessary one. (The Middleton-Rowley attribution would explain the lack of doth, but certainly not the lack of I'm
or i'th'.)

Collaboration sometimes produces unexpected results; let us therefore see what light is shed on our problem by the Dekker-Ford collaborations. It is reasonable to begin with The Sun's Darling, since this is
the sole extant dramatic work undoubtedly written (in its original form)
by Dekker and Ford only.

4.5.4.5.1. The Sun's Darling.

This theatre-masque was licensed by Herbert on 3 March 1623/4; it
was acted by the same "Cockpit Company" that produced The Spanish Gipsy
(Herbert, Dramatic Records, p.27). The text of The Sun's Darling
as we have it (in Q 1656) has been revised for performance in 1638-39,
either by Ford or by someone other than Ford or Dekker, since the last
three lines of Act IV and much of the first 190 lines of Act V refer
obviously to Charles I's preparations against the rebel Scots; I.i.137
also mentions the date "1538", which suggests that the actual date was
1638/9. However, it is likely that the revision substantially affected
only V.a (lines 1-190).[1]   As for the rest of the masque, there is
now, I think, some degree of critical agreement on the authorial division.
I shall follow Price's assignment (Thomas Dekker, p. 110) of Acts I,
IV, and V.b (lines 191-342) to Ford, and Acts II-III to Dekker: this
assignment is supported by the distribution of ha' and of has:hath.
Table 4.5(2), below, gives the data for these and other features of

---

[1] I am here following Bowers' account, in Dekker's Dram. Works, IV,
10-12. The last three lines of Act IV contain no significant feature.

228

interest.

Section	Attribution	Length (lines)	ha'	'em: them	has: hath	does: doth	I'm: I am	i'th'
Table 4.5(2). The Sun's Darling: significant features								
Attributions follow Price (Thomas Dekker, p. 110).								
I	F	212	.	5:2	1:1	1:	:6	1
II	D	323	1	2:4	1:	4:	:8	.
III	D	296	2	1:5	10:	3:	1:5	1
IV	F	299	.	:5	1:2	:2	2:6	.
V.a		190	.	1:1	.	8:2	2:4	.
V.b	F	152	.	2:3	:3	6:1	:2	.
Totals, D:		619	3	3:9	11:0	7:0	1:13	1
Totals, F:		663	0	7:10	2:6	7:3	2:14	1
Masque totals:		1472	3	11:20	13:6	22:5	5:31	2

Because of the difference of genre one cannot be sure that the linguistic pattern of The Sun's Darling would be very similar to that of a normal Dekker-Ford play of 1623-24. However, the pattern of The World Tossed at Tennis is fairly similar to that of the Middleton-Rowley plays; and there are indications in the table above that the linguistic styles in The Sun's Darling are not greatly different from those of plays by the authors involved. The ratios 'em:them and has:hath are often sensitive to genre; yet here the 'em:them ratios of the two shares are within the range of what we might expect in Ford or late Dekker plays (the Dekker ratio of 3:9 is a little low, but one must allow for variation in such low numbers); and the has:hath ratio functions very well in distinguishing between Ford and Dekker.

Assuming, then, that the evidence of The Sun's Darling may be applicable to the problem of The Spanish Gipsy, we notice that there are only two instances of i'th' in the whole masque; Dekker's rate of one i'th' in 619 lines is not totally incompatible with his rate of one in 1257 lines in Gipsy. Similarly, his I'm:I am ratio in the masque (1:13) is not too different from his ratio in the play (1:29). And Ford's does:doth ratio in the masque (7:3) suggests that 4:0, as in Gipsy, would be a perfectly possible ratio for him. Hence it would appear from the evidence of the contemporary Sun's Darling that there are no serious linguistic objections to the theory that The Spanish Gipsy is a collaboration of Dekker and Ford only.

4.5.4.5.2. The Witch of Edmonton

Not much useful evidence can be gleaned from The Witch of Edmonton
because of uncertainties of authorship: the title-page of the first
edition (Q 1658) attributes the play to Rowley, Dekker, Ford, "&c".
The '&c" is usually ignored today; even so, the shares of the three
named authors are not very distinct. Rowley's presence is indicated
by two instances of Tush (III.ii.46, III.iii.9) and one 'um for "'em"
(V.i.87). I.i is agreed by most critics to be Ford's; it contains the
speech I have a suit t'ye (line 133), which matches I may be bold/To
make a suite t'ee in Gipsy, K1 (V.iii.54-55).[1]

IV.i is the only scene of The Witch of Edmonton that can be
confidently claimed as Dekker's, on the evidence of 2 it's and 8 Omnes
(compared with only 4 Omnes in all the rest of the play). Another mark
of Dekker are the theatrical-alias-vocatives: Gammer Gurton (IV.i.251);
and Mother Bumby (IV.i.197), which has been mentioned above (4.5.4.3).
For what the evidence is worth, IV.i. contains 2 i'th', and 10 I am but
no I'm. It also contains one instance of Hoyda (IV.i.177), with which
we may compare Hoyday in Gipsy (E4, III.ii.199; H2, IV.iii.159).

4.5.4.5.3. The Welsh Ambassador

The Welsh Ambassador is a manuscript play dating possibly from
1623, since this is the last date in a list of prophecies in V.iii.96.
It was attributed to Dekker by Abraham Hill, a book collector, between
1677 and 1703,[2] and apparently independently by Bertram Lloyd in 1945.[3]

On internal evidence, Lloyd gave Dekker the whole play except III.iii
and V.i, which he allotted to Ford.

Lloyd's attribution is almost certainly correct in essentials. The
share which he gives to Dekker (wholly on word, phrase, and passage
parallels) contains 4 it's: 64 'tis; 11 /wud/, 1/wutt/, 18 ha'; 33 has:
1 hath; and 15 Omnes: altogether, a typical Dekker pattern. III.iii
contains very little useful linguistic evidence (1 has:1 hath), but V.i
must be Ford's, since, as Lloyd has noted, it contains d'ee and t'ee

---

[1] There is no instance of does or doth in I.i.

[2] See Bentley, III, 267-68; IV, 864-66.

[3] "The Authorship of The Welsh Ambassador," RES, 21 (1945), 192-201.

(twice each), 'a (6 times), and deed la (V.i.47). The attribution is corroborated by 2 has: 4 hath; 0 it's: 12 'tis, and all the instances of ye (9) in the whole play.[1]   I shall therefore assume that V.i is Ford's, III.iii of doubtful authorship, and the rest of the play Dekker's.

In Ford's V.i there are 2 does:1 doth; 1 I'm: 10 I am; and no i'th'. In Dekker's share there are 15 does: 0 doth; 21 I'm: 41 I am; and 12 i'th'. Thus the Dekker I'm:I am ratio and i'th' frequency in this play are very different from those in The Sun's Darling and The Spanish Gipsy. Presumably what we see in these works are the extremities of a range, Sun's Darling and Gipsy illustrating the lowest possible Dekker values of I'm and i'th', and The Welsh Ambassador a high value for each feature, or perhaps the norm.

Dekker's share of The Welsh Ambassador also contains parallels to the gipsy scenes of The Spanish Gipsy. Logger-head Elephant occurs twice (III.i.20, III.ii.64); compare Elephant with growte head (Gipsy, G1; IV.i.99). The "style/stile" pun is made in IV.ii.41; and mumble crust has been noted above (4.5. 4.3).

4.5.5. Conclusion

I submit that a strong case has been made out for the presence of both Ford and Dekker in The Spanish Gipsy; that there are no clear traces of Rowley in the play; and only one feature (gin't) that suggests Middleton. Moreover, the difficulties of the theory are eased by the rather similar linguistic pattern in The Sun's Darling. On the available evidence, it is best to attribute The Spanish Gipsy to Ford and Dekker alone.

---

[1] In V.i there are also two instances of Omnes.

5. A problem play of doubtful date

5.1. The Bloody Banquet

The method of determining the authorship of plays by comparison of internal features works brilliantly in some cases, delivering a single clear solution where the data are abundant and unambiguous; in other cases, the method may not work at all, or rather it may point to several different solutions, all equally possible, just as an equation in algebra may have several different but equally valid roots.

The Bloody Banquet constitutes the last and by far the most baffling of the major problems which I have felt obliged to attack in this study; and in this particular case I believe that the question of Middleton's presence cannot be decided. It is easy to show that the linguistic usages of the play are grossly unlike those of Middleton's dramatic style in any period after 1603, but since the date of the play is wholly uncertain these considerations do not totally exclude the possibility of a very immature Middletonian tragedy. There are other possibilities, too, not all mutually exclusive: a collaboration, a revision of a Middletonian original, or influence by Middleton on another dramatist. It may or may not be possible for us to identify the "other dramatist". Thus, though I do not know the true solution to this authorship problem, I believe that I can reject some solutions and estimate the likelihood of some others.

5.1.1. Text

The only early edition of The Bloody Banquet is a quarto whose title page reads as follows:

The Bloodie Banqvet. A Tragedie. Hector adest secumque Deos in proelia ducit. Nos haec novimus esse nihil. By T. D. [Device] London Printed by Thomas Cotes. 1639.

It is not clear what class of manuscript served as copy for Q 1639: stage directions contain many references to properties, but several seem to be of a literary character, as though designed for a reader; for instance, Enter Queene sad (B4v; 492[1]). One entrance seems to be timed: that of Mazeres, F1 (1382), which is separated by five lines from his first speech; otherwise, oncoming characters mostly enter and speak immediately.

---

[1] My study of The Bloody Banquet is based on the edition by Schoenbaum (Oxford: Malone Society, 1962), which of course exactly reproduces Q 1639. References are to Q and to the line number of Schoenbaum's edition.

McManaway has suggested ("Latin Title-Page Mottoes,' p. 35) that the
shortness of the text may point to a bad quarto, but, as he also acknowledge
the presence of the title-page mottoes is a counter-indication.[1]
Schoenbaum in his edition (pp. vii-viii) notes several places where
abridgements may have taken place. From the totality of the evidence, I
would conjecture that the copy for the quarto was a scribal manuscript edite
from a prompt-book.

5.1.2. Date of composition.

Banquet was not entered in the Stationers' Register, and the only
information we possess that has any bearing on the question of date is the
inclusion of "The Bloody banquett' in the list of forty-five plays belonging
to the King and Queen's Young Company at the Cockpit, dated 10 August 1639.[2]
Bentley notes that several of the plays in this list were more than twenty
years old; but this is only the flimsiest evidence for dating. Nor does
dramaturgic crudity help at all unless one can identify the author. All
that can be said, therefore, in the absence of topical allusions in the text
or of contemporary references to the play, is that Banquet was written not
later than 1639.

5.1.3. Authorship speculations

In the Archer play-list of 1656, "Bloody banquet" is attributed to
"Thomas Barker" (item 64). Since elsewhere in the Archer list "Thomas
Barker" (who is not otherwise known as a dramatist) is credited with the
authorship of "Fortunatus" (item 210) and "Match me in London" (item 384),
while one "Thomas Darker" is given "Whore of Babylon" (item 594), it has
usually been supposed that "Barker" and "Darker" are compositors' errors
for "Dekker" or, more likely,"Decker".   This interpretation is confirmed
by the evidence of Anthony à Wood, who, in his catalogue of Ralph Sheldon's
library, made probably about 1675-1680, inserted "The bloody Banquet. Tr-
[agedy] . per eund [em]. Lond. 1639' in a series of Dekker plays after Whore
of Babylon and before If This Be Not, "eundem" referring to "Tho. Dekker",
whose name appears in the catalogue above.[3]

---

[1] With 15618 words, Banquet is short, but not excessively so; Nice Valour
is still shorter (14664), yet is not suspected of being a reported text.

[2] Bentley, I, 330-31; III, 282-84.

[3] A. C. Baugh, "A Seventeenth Century Play List," MLR, 13 (1918),
401-11. Baugh reprints Wood's catalogue, the entry for Banquet being on
p. 409.

Anthony à Wood's confirmation does not necessarily mean that Archer's ascription was correct, however. Kirkman in his catalogues of 1661 and 1671 reverted to the initials "T.D." for the author of Banquet; as Greg points out ("Authorship Attributions," p. 317), he was a friend of William Beeston, the manager of the theatre company to whom the play had belonged, so possibly he had good reason to reject the ascription to Dekker. By the same token, he clearly did not know who the author was. Since Kirkman's testimony, The Bloody Banquet has remained a play of doubtful authorship.

The authorship speculations of the nineteenth and twentieth centuries can hardly be called a controversy, since there have been many guesses but no well-developed cases, unless we except Oliphant's (to be described below). The candidates suggested comprise the following:

(1) Dekker. There have been occasional supporters of Archer and Wood, but to the best of my knowledge no internal evidence for Dekker has been cited.

(2) Robert Davenport. According to Schoenbaum (Malone Society edition of Banquet, p. vi), the Davenport attribution was first made by D. E. Baker in 1812; it has since been revived by McManaway ("Latin Title-Page Mottoes," pp. 34-35). The suggestion is that, since "The bloody banquett" occurs in the 1639 Cockpit list after plays by Davenport, the title-page "T. D." may be a mistake for "R. D." McManaway notes that the title-page motto 'Hector adest [etc.]" is used also on the title-page of the anonymous manuscript play Dick of Devonshire, which, with Banquet, he attributes on internal evidence to Davenport.[1] But there has been little development of this case since McManaway's article of 1946.

(3) Thomas Drue. This author was proposed by Fleay (Biographical Chronicle, I, 162), and accepted by Bentley (III, 282-84) because "this attribution seems . . . to raise fewer difficulties than any of the others which have been proposed". No internal evidence has been cited in favour of Drue; the only external evidence is that he is chronologically possible, and that his initials are T. D.

(4) Middleton (in collaboration with Dekker). Oliphant, in a brief article in 1925,[2] accepted the Archer-Wood attribution to Dekker, and then proceeded to assign more than half the play on internal evidence to Middleton. His case relies almost wholly on phrase-parallels and

---

[1] Dick of Devonshire was written probably in 1626 (Bentley, V, 1319); it is extant in the British Museum MS. Egerton 1994. My study of the play is based on the edition by James and Mary McManaway (Oxford: Malone Society, 1955). The editors quote parallels of situation between Dick and Davenport's plays (pp. x-xi).

[2] "The Bloodie Banquet," TLS, 17 December 1925, p. 882.

versification; it has been examined and rejected as at least "not proven" by Schoenbaum (<u>Middleton's Tragedies</u>, pp. 223-26).

5.1.4. Authorship

A curious aspect of this problem is that there are textual links of one kind or another with three of the four authorial candidates listed above. To put it a little differently, we might say that three of the four are rather bad candidates, and one is very bad indeed. I shall consider the cases for the four candidates in turn, beginning with the worst.

5.1.4.1. Drue

I believe that if his only extant play (<u>The Duchess of Suffolk</u>, Q 1631) is a reliable indicator of his usage, Thomas Drue can be eliminated as a candidate for the sole authorship of <u>The Bloody Banquet</u>. I will now review the evidence (from Table I.1).

5.1.4.1.1. Exclamations

Not one of the tabulated exclamations for <u>The Duchess of Suffolk</u> matches any for <u>The Bloody Banquet</u>, except, inevitably, <u>why</u>; and even for <u>why</u> there is a great discrepancy of relative frequency (<u>Duchess</u>, 7.92; <u>Banquet</u>, 47.38). No author of only two plays in Table I.1 shows so great a discrepancy between his plays as regards exclamations.

5.1.4.1.2. Oaths

'<u>Sfoot</u>, <u>heart</u>, <u>death</u>, '<u>slight</u>, '<u>snails</u>, <u>troth</u> and <u>mass</u> all occur in <u>Banquet</u>, but not in <u>Duchess</u>; <u>Lord</u> and <u>I hold my life</u> occur in <u>Duchess</u> but not in <u>Banquet</u>. The only oaths common to the two plays are <u>Heaven</u>, <u>faith</u>, and <u>Marry</u>--all commonplace ones.

5.1.4.1.3. Colloquialisms and contractions

<u>Duchess</u> and <u>Banquet</u> are markedly different in two ratios, <u>does:doth</u> and <u>I'm:I am</u>. Drue's play is stiffly formal, with <u>does</u>, 1: <u>doth</u>, 10, and no <u>I'm</u> beside 36 <u>I am</u>; <u>Banquet</u> has <u>does</u>, 9: <u>doth</u>, 6, and 13 <u>I'm</u> beside 25 <u>I am</u>. Moreover, there is no trace in <u>Duchess</u> of <u>Banquet's</u> very distinctive use of <u>of't</u> rather than <u>on't</u>.

5.1.4.2. Davenport

There are clear linguistic links between <u>The Bloody Banquet</u>, the anonymous manuscript play <u>Dick of Devonshire</u>, and one of Robert Davenport's plays, <u>A New Trick to Cheat the Devil</u> (Q 1639), but not with the other

Davenport plays, The City Nightcap (Q 1661) and King John and Matilda
(Q 1655). The most striking items are listed below.

5.1.4.2.1. New Trick-Dick-Banquet links

5.1.4.2.1.1. Of't

The on't:of't ratio in Banquet, 0:7, is unique in Table I.1; obviously
the nearest resemblances to it are those of Dick of Devonshire (1 : 6)
and of New Trick (1 : 11).

5.1.4.2.1.2. Numbered speech-prefixes

The usual form for a speech-prefix referring to a numbered character
(First Gentleman, First Servant, and so forth) is "numeral, then abbreviation", such as 1 Gent. or 1 Ser. The reversed form, "abbreviation, then
numeral"--Gent. 1, et cetera--is used by Jonson, and in Goffe's Raging Turk,
but only rarely and sporadically elsewhere.

In The Bloody Banquet numbered prefixes appear only in II.i and III.ii.
In the former scene, the Shepherds are Shep. 1 and Shep. 2 exclusively
(18 instances), and in the latter the four Servants are Ser. 1, Ser. 2,
Ser. 3, and Ser. 4 exclusively (4 instances). Similarly, in Dick of
Devonshire the numbered prefixes in II.i (the only ones in the play) are of
the same form, the Soldiers being labelled Sol. 1 and Sol. 2 (4 instances).
In New Trick the two Gentlemen are Gen. 1 and Gen. 2 throughout (35 instances,
in I.ii, IV.ii, and V.ii).

5.1.4.2.1.3. Connectives

Banquet, Dick, and New Trick show preferences for among and while over
amongst and whilst; the other Davenport plays show the opposite preferences.

5.1.4.2.1.4. Ye

Davenport in King John and City Nightcap makes substantial use of ye
(35 and 96 instances respectively); but ye does not occur at all in New
Trick, or in Banquet, and only once in Dick (line 1281).

5.1.4.2.1.5. Contractions

Apart from of't, two other contractions link New Trick with the plays
of doubtful authorship. Th'are appears in Banquet, Dick, and New Trick,
but not in the other Davenport plays; i'th' is fairly frequent in City

Nightcap (20 instances) and King John (14 instances), but rare (2 instances each) in New Trick, Dick, and Banquet.

5.1.4.2.2. Possible explanations

I suggest that the features listed above, and especially the rare of't and abbreviation+numeral prefix form, establish a connection between Banque Dick, and New Trick which must be more than a coincidence. However, it is noticeable that in some other features there is more resemblance between Banquet and the Davenport plays other than New Trick: thus, 'snails (Banque C3v; 696) occurs in City Nightcap (F4), not in New Trick; and Banquet is linked with King John and Matilda by the slight preference of both plays for does over doth.

In the circumstances, it would be highly desirable to seek further dat on Davenport's usages. Unfortunately, the extant non-dramatic texts are all very short; the most useful of these, "A Dialogue between Policy and Piety",[1] contains probably only two items of significance: amongst in the Epistle Dedicatory, and whilst on the second page of text, which tend to confirm the City Nightcap-King John preferences.

Altogether, it seems to me that the evidence is nearly, but not quite, strong enough to force us to disintegrate the Davenport canon. The odd reversals in New Trick of Davenport's preferences can hardly be explained by stylistic development, since New Trick appears to be not very different in date from King John and Matilda (written about 1628-34); moreover, if Dick of Devonshire is really by Davenport, it must have been written by him at nearly the same time as City Nightcap (written 1624).[2] On the other hand, it seems to me that the features which link Banquet, Dick and New Trick are all of a kind that could have been produced by scribal transcript

---

[1] Folger MS. 1919.3. Bentley (III, 228-29) dates this at "c. 1635', and states correctly that the piece is "not really a play". It is in fact a poem, largely in heroic couplets.

[2] See Bentley, III, 227-35, for the dating of Davenport's plays. New Trick must be pre-1639, and was probably written 1624-36. Bentley is inclined to favour the attribution of Dick of Devonshire to Heywood (V,1320 but Table I.1 makes clear that Heywood is not a good candidate, since unlike Dick he has preferences for amongst, whilst, doth, and on't; he makes considerable use of i'th' and o'th'; but very little use of 'em or I'm.

On this theory, we must postulate that a single scribe who favoured th'are but disfavoured ye and i'th', and preferred among, while, of't, and Gen. 1 (etc.) to amongst, whilst, on't, and 1 Gen. (etc.), was employed to produce copies of New Trick, Banquet, and Dick of Devonshire, and to a large extent imposed his own linguistic usages on these texts. The theory requires that all three texts be scribal or printed from scribal copy. Dick probably is a scribal text (James and Mary McManaway, edition, pp. vi-viii), but one copied directly from the author's papers, and, though showing signs of annotation by a prompter, not actually a prompt-book: the continuous writing of speeches throughout the play gives rather a literary impression. New Trick also has many continuously-written speeches, and may well be a text derived from a scribal manuscript. Banquet does not have continuous writing of speeches, [1] but is most likely printed from scribal copy (see above, 5.1.1). As we have seen (2.2.1), the person who wrote out the text of Dick also supplied four missing pages of Blurt in the same hand; the Blurt manuscript regularly has speeches continuously written, though the Blurt quarto has not. I would surmise that the source of the Blurt manuscript may well have been a complete copy of the quarto, and that this scribe was an inveterate "improver", since the Blurt manuscript differs from the quarto by having errors corrected and rough metre converted to smooth, sometimes by the contraction of I am to I'm. Exceptionally, though, at one point (H3; V.iii.137), where Q 1602 reads Oh heer's our other spirits that walke i'th night, the manuscript has the rougher line Oh, here's our other spirits y[t] walke in the night--which agrees with our postulate of a scribe who disfavours i'th'.

The obvious alternative to this scribal theory is the disintegration of the Davenport canon. There is a shred of external evidence in favour of disintegration: the publisher's preface to New Trick (dating, presumably, from 1639) calls the play an Orphant, and wanting the Father which first begot it--words that would normally be interpreted as referring to a post-umous play. Yet Davenport must have been alive in 1655, when the address to the reader (surely authorial, though it uses the third person) in King John and Matilda is signed "R. D." Could there have been two Davenports, one dead before 1639 who was the author of Bloody Banquet, Dick of Devonshire, and New Trick, the other the author of City Nightcap and King John and

---

[1] Lines 692 and 1119 each contain two very short speeches totalling six syllables; these probably represent space-saving devices.

<u>Matilda</u>? This would seem to be a very shaky proposition, since <u>New</u> <u>Trick</u>
bears the title-page attribution "Written by R. D. Gent.," while the
Stationers' Register for 28 March 1639 tells us that the author was "Maste
Damport" (Arber, IV, 462). It is just possible, of course, that this
author is not Robert Davenport, but (shall we say?) a Richard or a Thomas
Damport, whose initials have been wrongly printed on one title page, eithe
that of <u>Banquet</u> or of <u>New</u> <u>Trick</u>. (The latter mistake, by confusion with
Robert Davenport, is the more likely, in which case the hypothetical autho
would be a Thomas Damport.)

However, I do not think this solution is a very plausible one. To be
really confident that linguistic resemblance implies common authorship, we
need to find some parallels of phrase and perhaps similarity in versificati
In the case of the three plays <u>New</u> <u>Trick</u>, <u>Dick</u> <u>of</u> <u>Devonshire</u>, and <u>The</u>
<u>Bloody</u> <u>Banquet</u> I do not perceive any convincing resemblances; even the
situational parallels of the McManaways between <u>Dick</u> and the Davenport pla
(which are hardly compelling) do not include any items from <u>New</u> <u>Trick</u>
(edition of <u>Dick</u>, x-xi). I think, therefore, that the scribal explanation
of the linking linguistic features is preferable to the theory of common
authorship.

5.1.4.3. <u>Dekker</u>

Internal evidence for Dekker in <u>The</u> <u>Bloody</u> <u>Banquet</u> is not easy to fin
Oliphant asserted that "the internal evidence shows that Dekker was mainly
responsible for the Lapirus story"--but he did not cite any details of suc
evidence. There is one instance of <u>Snayles</u> in II.ii (C3v; 696), and Dekke
does use this oath; but so do Davenport and other authors such as Rowley.
Apart from this, I see no linguistic items which point clearly to Dekker
anywhere in the text.

Strangely enough, there is some external evidence for Dekker (if a
title page is "external") which has not, to the best of my knowledge, been
noticed yet by any one. McManaway ("Latin Title-Page Mottoes," p. 35)
remarks "The second motto has not come to my attention on any other title-
page of the period". But <u>Nos</u> <u>haec</u> <u>nouimus</u> <u>esse</u> <u>nihil</u> occurs as the last
clause in the lines <u>Ad</u> <u>Detractorem</u> prefixed to Dekker's <u>Satiromastix</u> (<u>Dram</u>
<u>Works</u>, I, 308). Another item which just possibly may have significance is
the heading of the character list in <u>Bloody</u> <u>Banquet</u> (A1v)--<u>Drammatis</u> <u>Perso</u>

This is not rare in the period,[1] but other formulae such as "The Names of the Persons" are probably somewhat commoner. We may notice that Drammatis Personae occurs so often in Dekker's character lists--in Whore of Babylon, Roaring Girl, Wonder of a Kingdom, and Noble Spanish Soldier (Dramatis Personae in Satiromastix)--that it is probably due to the author. If so, then we have two items in the preliminaries to Bloody Banquet which suggest that the Archer-Wood attribution is not purely a mirage.

5.1.4.4. Middleton

It is clear from the data given for Bloody Banquet in Table I.1--especially the minimal use of 'em, and the strong preference for hath--that the play in its present form cannot be substantially by Middleton if it dates from 1604 or later. Nevertheless, there are some highly' suggestive Middleton parallels. Either the main author of this play was strongly influenced by Middleton--especially, perhaps, by The Revenger's Tragedy--or else he may have been Middleton himself in his earliest period, about 1600-02. On the latter supposition we might postulate a play mainly by Middleton with a little help from Dekker (hence the title-page "T. D."), later revised and/or transcribed by a person or persons including the scribe of Dick of Devonshire. I will now list the features that suggest Middleton.

I.i.

A3v (101-03): Maz⌊eres⌋. . . . remember you are possess'd./ Arm⌊atrites⌋. What, with the Devill?/ Max. ⌊sic⌋ The Devill! the Dukedome, the Kingdome, Lydia. There is in fact no "Dukedom" in question, Lydia being certainly a kingdom in this play; Dukedome has been inserted for the sake of alliteration with Devill. This little trick parallels Revenger's Tragedy: ⌊Vindice⌋ Nine Coaches waiting--hurry, hurry, hurry. /Cast⌊iza⌋. I to the Diuill./Vind⌊ice⌋. I to the Diuill, toth' Duke by my faith. (Dlv; II.i. 228-30).

A4 (131): sh'had. From Table I.1 it will be seen that sh'(h)ad occurs six times in Middleton's late plays, but is rather rare elsewhere.

A4v (172): comfort. Oliphant has noted the four instances of this favorite Middleton word; but he is wrong to think this relative frequency

---

[1] It occurs, for instance, as the heading of the character lists of both The Spanish Gipsy and The Changeling.

(5.12 per 20000) in any way remarkable (compare the mean relative frequency of the 23-play Revenger's Tragedy problem sample: 4.6).

I.iv.

B3 (349-50): Zen[archus]. Come, come, drive away these fits, faith Ile have thee merry./ Tym[ethes]. As your son and heire at his fathers funerall. Tymethes' speech combines two Middletonisms, the phrase son and heire and the "death of father" joke. Compare The Puritan, I.i (3.1.5, above); Revenger's Tragedy, IV.ii (3.2.6.2, above).

B3 (378): Right Oracle. Compare Revenger's Tragedy, Tis Oracle (IV.i; see 3.2.6.2, above).

B4v (491): masse here she comes. A common Middletonism (see Table I.1).

C1 (513): sfoote; C1v (542): Hum. Both common Middletonisms occurring in The Revenger's Tragedy.

II.iii.

C4 (743): Masse here a walkes; I am far enough from my selfe. This speech contains another instance of masse here, as well as a clear resemblance to Revenger's Tragedy, I.iii.3 (B2v)--Vindice's What brother? am I farre inough from my selfe? [= "Am I well enough disguised?"]. This latter parallel was noted by Oliphant.

C4v (768): Sfoote. See above, s.v. I.iv.

IV.i.

E3 (1253): heart of ill fortune. This oath seems to resemble hart, of chance, in A Yorkshire Tragedy, C4v.

IV.iii

F4v (1605): Mysticall Strumpet. Schoenbaum (Middleton's Tragedies, p. 225) remarks that this suggests Middleton, and (p. 197) quotes instances from Middleton plays of "mystical" qualifying nouns of bawdy connotation.

V.i.

G3v (1847-48): Why law you now such geere will nere thrive with you. This speech, followed in the next line by poyson to mine eyes (compare poyson to my Heart, Chaste Maid, Il, V.i.14), does rather support Oliphant's claim that the diction of this play is "markedly" Middletonian; certainly there is no instance of the collocation why law you now outside Middleton (and 1 Honest Whore) in Table I.1 (see 2.1.4.2, s.v. 1 Honest Whore, I.iii;

3.2.6.2, s.v. Revenger's Tragedy, V.iii; the spelling law in Bloody Banquet agrees with that in Revenger's Tragedy rather than that in Michaelmas Term).

Taking the parallels as a whole, I feel that there are so many resemblances to Middleton's manner that Oliphant's case cannot be lightly brushed aside. It cannot, however, be vindicated in the absence of confirming linguistic evidence such as that of contractions. As to the versification, which Oliphant claims as a point in Middleton's favour, I agree with Schoenbaum (Middleton's Tragedies, p. 225) that there are considerable discrepancies. I count 437 rhyming lines in the text, of which only 28 (6.4 per cent) are feminine, whereas in every one of Middleton's undoubted early plays feminine rhyme is at least twice as frequent (12 to 25 per cent; compare Revenger's Tragedy, 13 per cent). However, the verse of Banquet might plausibly be taken as representing the first beginnings of the Middletonian verse style.

5.1.4.5. Conclusion

Two types of solution to the problem of The Bloody Banquet seem to present themselves:

(1) The play is a much-revised one, written originally by Middleton with some help from Dekker about 1600-02.

(2) The play was written in its first form after 1603 by an unknown author much influenced by The Revenger's Tragedy.

For both solutions, we must postulate that the text has passed through the hands of the Dick of Devonshire scribe. I do not know which solution is the more plausible; but at least the case for Middleton's presence in the play remains "not proven". On the whole, the best attribution is still Kirkman's: "T. D."

Table 5.1, below, summarizes the linguistic evidence that may be relevant to this problem.

Table 5.1. The Bloody Banquet: significant features

Segment 1

Sect-ion	Lines	pish, puh	hum	why	'sfoot, 'slight	heart, death	'snails	faith, troth	mass
Ind.& Ch.	1-49	.	.	.	.	.	.	.	.
1.1	50-227	.	.	5	.	.	.	.	.
1.2	228-241	.	.	.	.	.	.	.	.
1.3	242-346	.	.	.	.	.	.	1,	.
1.4	347-594	.	1	11	1,	1,	.	3,1	1
2.1	595-667	.	.	7	.	.	.	.	1
2.2	668-710	.	.	.	.	.	1	.	.
2.3	711-813	.	.	1	1,	,1	.	1,1	1
2.4	814-875	.	.	.	.	.	.	.	.
3.1	876-1011	.	1	4	,1	.	.	4,2	1
3.2	1012-1049	.	.	.	.	.	.	.	.
3.3	1050-1196	.	.	.	.	.	.	1,1	1
4.1	1197-1287	1,	.	3	,1	.	.	1,	.
4.2	1288-1414	,1	.	1	.	.	.	.	.
4.3	1415-1726	.	.	3	.	,1	.	,1	.
5.1	1727-1857	.	.	2	.	.	.	3,	.
5.2	1858-2033	.	.	.	.	.	.	.	.
Play totals:		1,1	2	37	2,2	1,2	1	14,6	5

Segment 2

Sect-ion	Lines	'em: them	has: hath	does: doth	I'm: I am	th'art, y'are	th'are, sh'had	i'th'	of't	com-fort
Ind.& Ch.	1-49	:1	.	.	.	.	.	.	.	.
1.1	50-227	:3	:5	1:	1:2	,1	,1	.	.	1
1.2	228-241	.	.	.	.	.	.	.	.	.
1.3	242-346	:2	:2	:1	:1	1,	1,	.	.	.
1.4	347-594	1:3	2:3	2:	:7	,2	.	1	2	.
2.1	595-667	:6	1:	1:	.	.	.	.	1	.
2.2	668-710	.	.	:1	:4	.	.	.	.	.
2.3	711-813	:3	2:	2:	1:3	.	1,	.	.	.
2.4	814-875	:3	.	.	.	,2	.	.	.	.
3.1	876-1011	:1	1:	.	1:1	.	.	1	.	.
3.2	1012-1049	.	:2	.	.	.	.	.	.	.
3.3	1050-1196	1:3	:1	1:1	.	.	.	.	.	.
4.1	1197-1287	:3	:1	:1	1:	1,	.	.	2	.
4.2	1288-1414	.	:3	1:	2:1	.	.	.	1	.
4.3	1415-1726	1:4	:2	:1	5:3	,1	.	.	.	3
5.1	1727-1857	:2	1:1	1:1	2:2	.	.	.	1	.
5.2	1858-2033	:2	:3	.	:1	.	.	.	.	.
Play totals:		3:36	7:23	9:6	13:25	2,6	2,1	2	7	4

6. Summary of conclusions

It may now be useful to present a summary classification of Middleton's extant plays, based on the evidence presented in Sections 1-5. In the last category, "exclusions from the canon", I will place those plays where the evidence is not decisively in favour of Middleton's presence. Listings will approximate to order of composition.

6.1. The canon of Middleton's plays

6.1.1. Plays by Middleton alone (16 plays)

The Phoenix; Michaelmas Term; A Mad World, my Masters; A Trick to Catch the Old One; The Puritan; The Revenger's Tragedy; Your Five Gallants; The Second Maiden's Tragedy; No Wit, No Help like a Woman's; A Chaste Maid in Cheapside; More Dissemblers Besides Women; The Widow; The Witch; Hengist, King of Kent; Women Beware Women; A Game at Chess.

6.1.2. Collaborate plays of Middleton (10 plays)

The Family of Love (with Dekker; revised by Barry); 1 Honest Whore (with Dekker); A Yorkshire Tragedy (with one or more collaborators unknown: Wilkins? Shakespeare?); The Roaring Girl (with Dekker); Wit at Several Weapons (with Rowley); The Nice Valour (with, probably revising, Fletcher); A Fair Quarrel (with Rowley); The Old Law (with Rowley and one other dramatist: Massinger?); Anything for a Quiet Life (with Webster); The Changeling (with Rowley).

6.1.3. Plays excluded from the canon (3 plays)

Blurt, Master Constable (by Dekker); The Spanish Gipsy (by Dekker and Ford); The Bloody Banquet (by T. D.).

Appendix I

Main data tables

I.1.   Introduction to Table I.1: feature totals for 133 plays

I.1.1.   General arrangement

Table I.1 has been arranged so that, as far as possible, the essential
data relevant to a particular authorship problem may be available at one
view: hence the repetitions of all the undoubted Middleton plays on Bands
1 and 2, and the partial repetition of the Fletcher plays on Bands 2 and 3.
All the problem plays are given on Band 1 beside the undoubted Middletons;
some are repeated on the other Bands so that each Band can be used for
comparison purposes.

The order of plays within the sections of each author is the order
of composition as far as this is known or can be plausibly guessed.

Very seldom has use been made of the principle of alphabetical order;
indeed, only when no other principle of ordering presented itself.
Features are tabulated in a conventional order, the main groups as follows:
(1) Exclamations; (2) Oaths; (3) Affirmatives; (4) Connectives; (5) Pronouns
(6) Verbs; (7) Pronoun + verb contractions; (8) Other contractions; (9)
Contraction-spellings (woult, wou't, wou'd); (10) Spellings; (11) Prefixes;
(12) Selected words and collocations, in three sub-groups: (12a) Middletonisms; (12b) Dekkerisms; (12c) Other items. Feature groups (1)-(2) are
contained in Segment 1; groups (3)-(11) in Segment 2; and group (12) in
Segment 3.

I.1.2. Corpus

I.1.2.1.   Inclusions and exclusions

Band I

The Middleton and Dekker corpora are discussed in 1.2, 1.3, and 2.1.

The Barry, Ford, and Rowley sections contain all the undoubtedly
unassisted plays of those authors. Hoy has shown clearly ("Shares" [V],
SB, 13 [1960], 82-83, 104) that A Match at Midnight (Q 1633) cannot with
any confidence be attributed to Rowley, and I have therefore omitted this
play.

Band 2

The Tourneur, Goffe, Beaumont, and Webster sections contain all the
undoubted plays of these authors.

For Shakespeare only a very small sample is offered, comprising two
late plays rather high in colloquialisms such as 'em; data for other late
plays will be found in Appendix V.

For Fletcher I have used the unassisted canon as determined by Hoy ("Shares" [I], SB, 8 [1956], 129-46); excluding only the generically unsuitable Faithful Shepherdess.

For Massinger, only the earlier plays are included in the corpus, but all the unassisted ones have been taken into account in the text of this study.

Band 3

The Marston section contains all the undoubted plays (for Jack Drum, now confirmed as Marston's by external evidence, see 2.2.4.3.1, fn.).

The Chapman section contains all the undoubted Chapman comedies except the early Blind Beggar of Alexandria (Q 1598; probably a reported text).

The Jonson section contains all the Jonson comedies contemporary with Middleton's dramatic career, plus The Case is Altered, of uncertain but probably early date, which is included as an example of a play omitted by Jonson from his 1616 Folio, and therefore perhaps relevant to Jonson's performance in unacknowledged works of doubtful authorship. For the exclusion of tragedies by Chapman and Jonson, see 3.2.7.1.

Band 4

Most of the minor dramatists in this Band are represented by their complete extant plays. Only small samples are given for Heywood and Brome, however.

In the case of Heywood, three late plays are given, including the holograph The Captives, to show that he is not a good candidate for the authorship of Dick of Devonshire; his earlier plays do not differ greatly from his later in linguistic style.

Brome's Northern Lass is included to show the contrast between the linguistic style of the author of A Jovial Crew and that of The Spanish Gipsy.

Sampson is included because his only extant play, The Vow Breaker, may date from as early as about 1625 (Bentley, V, 1043-45), and because this play contains the then rare contraction I've.

I.1.2.2. Textual policy

For problem plays I have in every case used the first seventeenth century edition or a Malone society reprint thereof; for Middleton plays, the first seventeenth century edition, or in the case of manuscript texts the best available twentieth century edition; exceptionally, for A Game at Chess I have used two texts, the Trinity manuscript 0. 2. 66 for spellings

of 'em, has, and does, but Bald's edition for other features except the
first word in IV.ii.17 (see 1.2.2, fn.). I have been forced to adopt this
policy in regard to A Game at Chess because Bald's edition is the best
available one, giving a fuller version of Middleton's play than any early
text, and yet is not trust-worthy as to the placing of apostrophes.

For plays other than problem and Middleton plays I have used
scholarly twentieth century editions in most cases where these were
available, but have also checked crucial features against the original
quartos (for instance, the Omnes prefixes in the Dekker plays). In using
modern scholarly editions I am following the practices of Hoy and Murray
(though I have not used Lucas' Webster, since I discovered the error in
his text of Anything for a Quiet Life described in 4.1.3, fn. 4).

I.1.3. Text limits for statistical purposes

Data for plays in Table I.1 are based on the editions listed below
(I.1.6.2), excluding detachable prologues and epilogues and any matter
known certainly to be inauthentic (such as the "ditty" disclaimed by
Webster in The Duchess of Malfi, H2); but including inductions, songs,
speech-prefixes, and stage-directions. A few exceptions or clarifications
to this general statement follow.

(1) In Joshua Cook's Greene's Tu Quoque (H3), a 73-word quotation from
Marlowe's Hero and Leander is excluded from the text studied.

(2) In Dekker's Shoemaker's Holiday, the songs (Dram. Works, I, 20-21)
are excluded, since they are printed separately before the play.

(3) In Dekker's Old Fortunatus, the public theatre Prologue (Dram. Works
I, 115) is excluded, but the Prologue and Epilogue at Court, which are
dramatic in form, are included.

(4) In Beaumont's Knight of the Burning Pestle, the dramatic prologue
and epilogue are included, but the extraneous Q2 prologue is excluded.

(5) In Marston's Malcontent, the Induction (by Webster) is excluded.

I am well aware that by excluding prologues and epilogues I have
often excluded material about which there is no shadow of doubt as to
authorship. Nevertheless, it seemed best to adopt some general rule, and
for this one I have the precedent of Hoy, who also has excluded prologues
and epilogues. I have tried to draw the line, in doubtful cases, between
truly organic dramatic matter and detachable pieces addressed only to the
audience or the reader.

I.1.4. <u>Word counts</u>

I.1.4.1. <u>Rules adopted for counting</u>

The text included in the word-count begins with <u>Act</u> I, <u>Scene</u> I and ends with <u>Finis</u> or <u>The End</u>; if the initial formula is absent, the count begins with the first stage direction, and if the end-formula is absent it ends with the final <u>Exeunt</u>. Between these limits, all Act and Scene formulae are included. So are all stage directions and speech prefixes (since significant features do occur in them).

All abbreviated words are counted as whole words.

Numerals are translated into words and then so counted; for example, <u>1</u> is one word, <u>100</u> ("a hundred", or "one hundred") is two words.

Contractions are subjected to a rule that a "word" for counting purposes must contain at least one syllable. Thus, <u>i'th'</u> is one word (<u>th'</u> constituting no syllable), but <u>i'the</u> is two. Vowelless forms such as <u>'s</u> (="his" or "us") do not, therefore, contribute to the count (I have counted <u>i'</u> as a separate word wherever possible under this rule except in the combination <u>i'faith</u>, which I have counted as one word.)

Hyphens after prefixes which are bound morphemes (<u>con-</u>, <u>pre-</u>, etc.), and hyphens at line-ends, are counted as joining two parts of a single word; all other hyphens (e.g. in <u>Gentle-woman</u>) are counted as dividing separate words.

I.1.4.2. <u>Full counts and sample counts</u>

Word counts in Table I.1 marked with an asterisk are exact counts of the entire text as defined above. All other counts are estimates based on 12 to 30 sections of the text (usually quarto pages or folio columns) selected by means of a table of random numbers.

Before sampling in this way, initial, final, and any other obviously anomalous pages were excluded and fully counted, and the total number of words in these pages was later added to the estimate based on the random sample.

The precise number of randomly-selected sections needed for each play was decided by inspection of the variance in the first twelve sections sampled, more sections being sampled when this appeared to be necessary. By this method the desired accuracy was attained: the estimated error on the final sample, at the 95 per cent confidence level, did not exceed 7 per cent of the total words for any play, nor more than 6 per cent for any play used in the <u>Puritan</u> and <u>Revenger's Tragedy</u> statistical arguments.

Since the word-counts for most plays are only estimates, it might have been reasonable to round the last digits up or down to zero; but since I was constantly using these estimates in statistical arguments, I preferred not to lose any available accuracy, and so have given the counts to the nearest whole number of words, being the best estimates that the sampling technique can provide.

I.1.5. Features

Clarification is needed as to the type-boundaries of some features. Several of these are oaths; and here the term "oath" also needs defining. By an oath I mean an asseveration or exclamation naming some numinous or prized entity; I exclude conjurations (e.g. "swear by my sword"), but include quoted or reported "oaths" as defined above.

1.1.5.1. Exclamations

Why is counted only when an interjection, not when an interrogative.

1.1.5.2. Oaths

Jesu(s), Lord('s), God's, and God are counted whenever these forms occur in what is recognizably an oath, but not in prayers. The plural form gods is not counted.

Heaven(')(s) is counted when it occurs as a possessive (e.g. by Heaven's love) or as head-word in an exclamatory noun phrase (e.g. O Heaven, or good Heaven) or when directly dominated by by (e.g. by the Heavens), but not in a post-nominal qualifier (e.g. by my hopes of Heaven).

Heart and death are counted only when not qualified by any following of phrase. Thus, heart of ill fortune, death of man, and so forth, are not counted.

Faith and troth are counted in all exclamatory or asseveratory phrases except when preceded by the and followed by an of phrase; thus, i'faith, by my faith, and good faith are counted, but by the faith of a gentleman is not.

1.1.5.3. Connectives.

Connectives are never counted when they occur as rhyme words. In the case of beside and besides, the number before the comma in the Table I.1 columns gives the occurrences as adverb, that after the comma the occurrences as preposition. Toward and towards are counted only when prepositions, while, whil(e)st, and whiles only when conjunctions, and not when preceded by the.

I.1.5.4. Colloquialisms and contractions

The pronoun 'a (= "he") is not counted in the form quotha, which I treat as a single word. Ha' is not counted in the combination ha't (often spelt hate), but does't is counted as an instance of does, and has't as an instance of has. The ellipsis 'Has for "he has", however spelt, is counted also an an instance of has (here, therefore, one word counts as two features).

"Jonsonian" elisions, such as I'am, ye'are, and so forth, are not counted at all, and the ye' in ye'are is not counted as an instance of ye.

The column headings thou'rt, we're, you're, and they're include all spellings which clearly preserve the vowel of the pronoun (e.g. their, the're, there) irrespective of the presence or position of the apostrophe; th'art, w'are, y'are, and th'are include all spellings which clearly preserve the vowel of the verb, similarly irrespective of the apostrophe.

I.1.5.5. Speech prefixes

Group speeches exclude utterances that are sung, or are spoken off-stage ('Within'). The column All does not include prefixes where All is followed by another word or numeral, e.g. All Lords or All 3.

I.1.5.6. Ellipsis

The feature which I denote by 'Has is not a contraction or a spelling, but the ellipsis of he before has at the beginning of a clause. This may be spelt in several ways (/'has/, /h'as/, /ha's/, or /has/, with or without initial capital).

I.1.6. List of abbreviations used

I.1.6.1. Problem plays

X Plays is used as an abbreviation of the phrase "problem plays".

I.1.6.2. The 132-play corpus

The list below specifies the text represented by the abbreviation and used as the basis for this study; for full details of the text in question, see the Bibliography of Primary Sources.

AF	All Fools (Chapman's Comedies, ed. Holaday)
AL	Amends for Ladies (Q 1618)
Alb.	Albumazar (Q 1615)
Alch.	The Alchemist (Jonson's Works, ed. Herford and Simpson)
ALL	All's Lost by Lust (Q 1633)
AM	Antonio and Mellida (Q 1602)
AQL	Anything for a Quiet Life (Q 1661)
AR	Antonio's Revenge (Q 1602)
AT	The Atheist's Tragedy (Q 1611)
BB	The Bloody Banquet (ed. Schoenbaum, Malone Society)
Bel.	Believe as you List (ed. Sisson, Malone Society)
BF	Bartholomew Fair (Jonson's Works)
BH	The Broken Heart (Q 1633)
Blurt	Blurt, Master Constable (Q 1602)
Bon.	Bonduca (F 1647)
Bond.	The Bondman (Q 1624)
C.T.	The Courageous Turk (Q 1632)
CA	The Case is Altered (Jonson's Works)
Capt.	The Captives (ed. Brown, Malone Society)
Ch.	The Changeling (Q 1653)
Chan.	The Chances (F 1647)
CMC	A Chaste Maid in Cheapside (Q 1630)
CN	The City Nightcap (Q 1661)
Cor.	Coriolanus (F 1623)
CR	Cynthia's Revels (Jonson's Works)
CTT	A Christian Turned Turk (Q 1612)
CW	Cupid's Whirligig (Q 1607)
D. Ch.	The Devil's Charter (Q 1607)
D.M.	The Duke of Milan (Q 1623)
D. Suff.	The Duchess of Suffolk (Q 1631)
DA	The Devil is an Ass (Jonson's Works)
DC	The Dutch Courtesan (Q 1605)
DD	Dick of Devonshire (ed. McManaway, Malone Society)
DLC	The Devil's Law Case (Q 1623)
DM	The Duchess of Malfi (Q 1623)
EMI	Every Man in his Humour (Jonson's Works)
EMO	Every Man out of his Humour (Jonson's Works)
Eng.	Englishmen for my Money (Q 1616)
Epic.	Epicene (Jonson's Works)
ET	The English Traveller (Q 1633)
Fawn	Parasitaster, or, The Fawn (Q 1606, 2nd edn.)
FCN	The Fancies Chaste and Noble (Q 1638)
FL	The Family of Love (Q 1608)
Fl.	The Fleer (Q 1607)
2FMW	The Fair Maid of the West, Part II (Q 1631)
FQ	A Fair Quarrel (Q 1617a, with IV.iv from Q 1622)
GC	A Game at Chess (ed. Bald; spellings from Trinity MS)
GTQ	Greene's Tu Quoque (Q 1614)
GU	The Gentleman Usher (Chapman's Comedies)
HDM	A Humorous Day's Mirth (Chapman's Comedies)
Heng.	Hengist, King of Kent (ed. Bald)
HG	The Hector of Germany (Q 1615)

HL	The Humorous Lieutenant (F 1647)
HOB	Humour out of Breath (Q 1608)
Hoff.	Hoffman (Q 1631)
1HW	The Honest Whore, Part I (Q 1604, 1st edn.)
2HW	The Honest Whore, Part II (Dekker's Dramatic Works, ed. Bowers)
IG	The Isle of Gulls (Q 1606)
IP	The Island Princess (F 1647)
ITBN	If This Be Not a Good Play, the Devil is in it (Dekker's Dramatic Works)
JD	Jack Drum's Entertainment (Q 1601)
JK	John à Kent (ed. Byrne, Malone Society)
KBP	The Knight of the Burning Pestle (ed. Hoy, in Beaumont and Fletcher, Dramatic Works, ed. Bowers)
KJM	King John and Matilda (Q 1655)
L. Sub.	The Loyal Subject (F 1647)
Law Tr.	Law Tricks (Q 1608)
Ling.	Lingua (Q 1607)
LK	The Lovesick King (Q 1655)
LM	The Lover's Melancholy (Q 1629)
LS	Love's Sacrifice (Q 1633)
LT	The Lady's Trial (Q 1639)
M.Thom.	Monsieur Thomas (Q 1639)
Malc.	The Malcontent (Q 1604 , 3rd edn., excluding Induction)
MD	May Day (Chapman's Comedies)
MDBW	More Dissemblers Besides Women (O 1657)
Mis.	The Miseries of Enforced Marriage (ed. Blayney, Malone Society)
ML	The Mad Lover (F 1647)
MML	Match Me in London (Dekker's Dramatic Works)
Mons.	Monsieur D'Olive (Chapman's Comedies)
MT	Michaelmas Term (Q 1607)
MWM	A Mad World, my Masters (Q 1608)
NL	The Northern Lass (Q 1632)
NTCD	A New Trick to Cheat the Devil (Q 1639)
NV	The Nice Valour (F 1647)
NWNH	No Wit, No Help like a Woman's (O 1657)
Ores.	The Tragedy of Orestes (Q 1633)
Phoen.	The Phoenix (Q 1607)
Pict.	The Picture (Q 1630)
Pilg.	The Pilgrim (F 1647)
PL	The Parliament of Love (ed. Lea, Malone Society)
PMC	The Poor Man's Comfort (Q 1655)
Poet	Poetaster (Jonson's Works)
Pur.	The Puritan (Q 1607)
PW	Perkin Warbeck (Q 1634)
R.A.	The Roman Actor (Q 1629)
R.T.	The Raging Turk (Q 1631)
RA	Ram Alley (Q 1611, 1st edn.)
Ren.	The Renegado (Q 1630)
RT	The Revenger's Tragedy (Q 1607)

RW	Rule a Wife and Have a Wife (Q 1640)
Sat.	Satiromastix (Dekker's Dramatic Works)
Sh.G	A Shoemaker a Gentleman (Q 1638)
Sh.H.	The Shoemaker's Holiday (Dekker's Dramatic Works)
SMT	The Second Maiden's Tragedy (ed. Greg, Malone Society)
SN	The Staple of News (Jonson's Works)
Soph.	Sophonisba (Q 1606)
Span.	The Spanish Gipsy (Q 1653)
STM(S)	Sir Thomas More (ed. Greg, Malone Society; Hand S only)
Temp.	The Tempest (F 1623)
TMM	Two Maids of Moreclacke (Q 1609)
TP	'Tis Pity She's a Whore (Q 1633)
Trick	A Trick to Catch the Old One (Q 1608)
Turk	The Turk (Q 1610)
Valen.	Valentinian (F 1647)
VB	The Vow-Breaker (ed. Wallruth, Materialien)
Volp.	Volpone (Jonson's Works)
W.Pl.	Women Pleased (F 1647)
W.Pr.	The Woman's Prize (F 1647)
WBW	Women Beware Women (O 1657)
WD	The White Devil (Q 1612)
WGC	The Wild Goose Chase (F 1652)
Wh.B.	The Whore of Babylon (Dekker's Dramatic Works)
Widow	The Widow (Q 1652)
Witch	The Witch (ed. Greg and Wilson, Malone Society)
WM	A Wife for a Month (F 1647)
WNV	A New Wonder, a Woman Never Vexed (Q 1632)
WSW	Wit at Several Weapons (F 1647)
WT	The Widow's Tears (Chapman's Comedies)
WW	A Woman is a Weathercock (Q 1612)
WYW	What You Will (Q 1607)
YFG	Your Five Gallants (Q n.d., 1st edn.)
YT	A Yorkshire Tragedy (Q 1608)

Table I.1   /Exclamations
Segment 1
Band 1

		Length (words)	push	pish	puh	pah	pew	p-, other	phew	tut	tush	t-, other	hum(h)	um(h)	h(e/l)yda(y)	why
	Blurt	18037*	.	.	.	.	.	1ᵃ	.	.	2	.	.	2	.	17
lays 1608	1HW	25509	.	.	4	2	.	.	.	.	.	.	4	7	.	47
	FL	22362	.	.	.	.	.	.	.	13	.	.	1	.	.	28
	YT	6230*	.	.	3	.	.	.	.	1	.	.	1	2	.	12
	Pur.	19922*	3	1	9	2	.	1	.	3	.	1ᵇ	2	.	.	66
	RT	21268*	6	.	6	.	.	.	.	3	.	.	1	.	.	32
idd-eton	Phoen.	20840*	.	.	2	1	.	.	.	.	.	5ᵇ	4	.	.	41
	MT	20570*	3	1	4	.	.	.	.	3	.	.	.	.	.	45
	MWM	19098*	6	1	10	.	.	10	.	8	.	.	.	.	.	60
1608	Trick	19268*	4	.	3	.	.	4	.	3	.	.	4	.	1	57
	YFG	21878*	6	.	7	.	.	.	.	5	.	.	.	.	.	76
1610<	NWNH	27703*	5	3	.	.	.	.	.	.	.	.	.	.	5	40
	CMC	18489*	1	3	.	.	.	2	.	.	1	.	.	.	2	28
	MDBW	20052*	.	2	.	.	.	.	.	.	.	.	.	.	2	15
	Witch	16862*	.	.	.	.	.	.	.	.	.	.	.	.	1	25
	Heng.	22037*	.	5	.	.	.	.	.	.	.	.	3	.	1	26
	WBW	26162*	.	5	.	.	.	.	.	.	.	.	.	.	.	33
	GC	19342*	3	.	1	.	.	.	.	.	.	.	.	.	.	16
	Widow	20315*	.	9	1	.	.	.	.	.	.	.	2	.	.	53
lays 1610<	SMT	20014*	3	2	.	.	.	.	.	.	.	.	.	.	.	19
	WSW	21596	1	1	3	.	.	.	.	.	6	.	13	1	.	47
	NV	14664	.	1	1	1	.	.	.	.	.	.	.	.	1	23
	AQL	20677	.	.	.	.	1ᶜ	.	.	.	2	.	.	.	.	41
	Span.	17460	.	1	.	.	.	.	1	.	.	.	.	1	2	8
	BB	15618	.	1	1	.	.	.	.	.	.	.	2	.	.	37
arry ekker	RA	22419	.	.	.	.	.	.	.	10	.	.	.	.	.	50
	Sh.H.	19276	.	.	.	.	.	.	.	.	.	.	1	.	.	23
	OF	25636	.	.	.	.	.	.	.	1	.	.	1	.	.	24
	Sat.	22397*	1	.	1	.	.	1ᵃ	.	1	.	1ᵈ	.	.	.	24
	2HW	24832*	.	3ᵉ	.	.	.	.	.	.	.	.	.	4	.	16
	Wh.B.	21807	.	.	.	.	.	.	.	1	.	.	.	4	.	7
	ITBN	23936	.	.	.	.	.	.	.	1	.	.	8	.	1	3
	MML	19924	.	1	.	.	.	.	.	1	.	.	.	5	.	6
ord	LM	19065	.	2	.	.	.	.	1	1	.	.	.	.	.	4
	BH	17748	.	2	.	.	.	.	1	.	.	.	1	.	2	6
	LS	19061	.	5	1	.	1	.	.	2	.	.	.	3	1	25
	TP	22370	.	1	.	.	.	.	.	.	.	.	.	.	.	37
	PW	19725	.	4	.	.	.	.	1	.	.	.	.	.	.	3
	FCN	18417	.	5	.	.	.	.	2	.	.	.	2	2	1	11
	LT	15997	.	3	.	.	1ᶠ	.	3	.	.	.	1	4	3	12
owley	Sh.G.	22745	.	.	.	.	.	.	.	2	3	.	.	.	2	14
	WNV	22259	.	.	.	.	.	.	.	3	2	.	.	.	.	27
	ALL	17442	.	.	.	.	.	.	.	1	13	.	8	.	.	14
1 + R	FQ	21276	.	2	.	.	.	.	1	.	6	.	1	.	.	42
	Ch.	21143	5	.	1	.	.	1	.	.	5	.	.	.	.	18

* Fully counted. Occurrences: ᵃAs ptrooh. ᵇAs tuh (all instances).
ᶜAs pue waw. ᵈAs tprooth. ᵉOnce as pesh. ᶠAs pew-waw.

Band 1(b)   /Oaths

		Jesu(s)	Lord('s)	God's	God	Heaven(')(s)	Cud(')s, Coad(')s	'snigs	'sfoot	foot	'slid	'slud	'sblood	'swounds, -z	'sheart, heart	'sdeath, death	'slife, life	'slight, light
X Plays >1608	Blurt	1	3	5	5[b]	2	.	.	6[a]	.	2	.	.	1	.	.	.	2,
	1HW	.	5	15	9	1	1[c]	.	21	.	2	.	8[f]	7	1 1	.	1[d]	2,
	FL	.	4	2[e]	2	.	.	.	.	.	.	.	1[f]	.	.	.	.	.
	YT	.	.	.	2	1	.	.	.	.	.	.	1	.	.	.	.	.
	Pur.	.	.	.	1	1	.	.	1	.	.	1	1	.	1[g]	.	.	.
	RT	.	.	.	1	3	,1	.	9	.	.	1	3	2	11	3	.	.
Middleton >1608	Phoen.	.	.	.	.	.	1,	.	10	.	.	3	.	.	.	1	1,	.
	MT	.	.	.	.	2	1,	.	2	.	.	3	1	.	.	1	1,	.
	MWM	.	.	.	.	.	3,	.	14	.	.	5	.	.	.	.	,3	.
	Trick	.	.	.	.	2	3,	1[h]	1	.	.	1	.	.	.	1	,1	.
	YFG	.	.	.	.	1	1,	.	16	.	.	1	1	.	10	3	7,3	1,
1610<	NWNH	.	.	.	.	.	3,	.	.	.	.	.	.	1	2	.	,8	.
	CMC	.	.	.	.	.	1,	.	.	2	.	.	.	1	11	4	,11	.
	MDBW	.	.	.	.	.	.	.	.	.	.	.	.	.	.	.	.	.
	Witch	.	.	.	.	.	.	.	.	.	.	.	.	.	.	.	.	.
	Heng.	.	.	.	.	.	.	.	.	.	.	.	.	.	.	1	.	.
	WBW	.	.	.	.	.	,1	.	.	.	.	.	.	.	.	1	,1	.
	GC	.	.	.	1	.	.	.	1	.	.	.	.	.	.	1	.	,
	Widow	.	.	.	.	.	.	.	.	.	.	.	.	.	1	.	,7	1,
X Plays 1610<	SMT	.	.	.	.	1	1,	.	.	.	.	.	.	.	5	.	1[d]	13
	WSW	.	1	.	.	.	2,	1	.	2	6	.	.	.	.	2	.	,
	NV	.	.	.	.	.	.	.	.	.	.	.	.	.	.	2	.	.
	AQL	.	.	.	.	.	.	.	.	.	.	.	.	.	.	1 2	.	.
	Span.	.	.	.	3	.	.	.	.	1	.	.	.	.	.	1	.	.
	BB	.	.	.	4	.	.	.	2	.	.	.	.	.	.	1 2	.	2,
Barry	RA	.	4	1	3	14	.	.	27	.	.	.	3[j]	2	6	.	.	.
Dekker	Sh.H.	.	9	6	12	.	.	.	.	.	.	.	.	3	1	.	.	.
	OF	1	.	4	4	1	.	.	.	.	.	.	.	1	6 1	.	.	.
	Sat.	19[k]	4	10	11	1	.	.	1	.	.	2	3[m]	11[n]	1	.	.	.
	2HW	.	3	2	1	.	.	.	4[o]	1	.	.	3	7	1	1	.	.
	Wh.B.	.	.	.	.	.	.	.	.	.	.	.	.	.	1	.	.	.
	ITBN	.	.	.	.	.	.	.	.	.	.	.	1	10	.	6	.	.
	MML	.	.	.	.	5	.	.	1	.	.	.	.	.	1	8[p] 1	.	.
Ford	LM	.	.	.	.	.	.	.	1	.	.	.	.	.	.	.	.	.
	BH	.	.	.	.	.	.	.	.	.	.	.	.	.	.	.	.	.
	LS	.	.	.	.	2	.	.	3	.	.	.	.	.	.	1	1,	.
	TP	.	.	.	.	2	.	.	3	.	.	.	.	.	.	1	.	.
	PW	.	.	.	.	.	.	.	.	.	.	.	.	.	.	.	.	.
	FCN	.	.	.	.	1	.	.	.	.	.	.	.	.	.	.	.	.
	LT	.	.	.	.	2	.	.	1	.	.	.	.	.	.	.	.	.
Rowley	Sh.G.	.	.	3	.	1	.	.	3	.	.	.	.	1	.	1	1,	.
	WNV	.	.	.	.	1	.	.	8	1	.	.	.	4	.	.	.	.
	ALL	.	.	.	.	1	.	.	.	.	.	.	.	1	.	1	.	.
M + R	FQ	.	1	.	.	1	.	.	.	1	.	.	.	.	.	4	.	1,
	Ch.	.	1	1	.	2	1,	.	.	.	.	1	.	.	.	.	.	.

Occurrences: [a] Once as vds foote. [b] Once as by gad. [c] As Cods life. [d] As Vds life. [e] Both as Gogs. [f] As blud. [g] As hart, of chance. [h] As Coades-Nigs. [j] 3 times as bloud. [k] 16 times as S(h)esu. [m] Twice as Vds bloud. [n] 10 times as owndes. [o] Once as Vds foot [p] 3 times as vds death.

	'(s) nails	'(s) precious	'Od's	'(Ud)s, other	f(æck(s)[a]	faith	troth	marry	mass	byrlady	my reputation	hold my life
lurt						6	10	11	2			
HW	2					35	20	15	5	1		1
L						25	1	7	1	3		
T						9			1			
ur.						39	24	7	10	1		
T						44	12	6	5			
Phoen.						35	17	3	7	2		
KT						58	17	6	5	3		
WM						88	17	3	7			
Prick						79	19	4	12	1		
FG						109	23	6	9			
WNH						53	11	12	6			2
MC						58	9	4	4			6
DBW						14	7	7	1	4	1	
Witch						2	5	4				
Meng.		1	1[a]			11	2	3		2		
WBW						35	16	9	1	2		
GC							3	2				
Widow			1[b]			41	14	11	4	6		1
SMT						25	9	7	3	1		1
WSW	2			3[c]	1	45	12	5	1	1[d]	1	
WV					1	6	8	10		1[e]	1	1
AQL					3	9	7	8		1		
Span.							3					
BB	1					14	6	2	5			
RA					1	35	6		1			
Sh.H.	4					22	10	7	4			2
DF						15	13	6	1			
Sat.						9	10	6	3			3
2HW				1[c]		32	17	15				1
Wh.B.						1	2	3				
ITBN	1[f]					2	1	8				1
MML						8	4	2				1
LM						2	3	2				
BH						1		1				
LS				1		2	3	5		1		
TP				2		11	11	3		1		
PW						1				2		
FCN							2	6		1		
LT							1	2				
Sh.G.		1[g]				25	2	7	2	1		
WNV						14	9	5				1
ALL						7	1	1				
FQ	2					43	5	6				
Ch.		1				2	4	2				

Occurrences: [a] As Ods pretious.   [b] As 'odds' light.   [c] As Vds so (all instances).   [d] As birlakin.   [e] As birlakins.   [f] As Vds nailes.   [g] As precious coales.

Band 1(d)

Table I.1   Segment 2   /Connectives

		Length (words)	ay	yes	among	amongst	beside adv.,prep.	besides adv.,prep.	between	betwixt	toward	towards	while	whil(e)st	whiles
X Plays >1608	Blurt	18037*	8	7	3	.	.	7,1	4	.	.	.	1	3	
	1HW	25509	52	34	4	5	.	4,2	4	1	.	.	.	7	
	FL	22362	24	8	4	6	,1	2,9	3	4	.	2	4	4	
	YT	6230*	7	1	2	1	.	,1	3	.	.	.	1	.	
	Pur.	19922*	58	9	6	3	3,2	3,	8	1	2	.	1	1	
	RT	21268*	29	5	.	6	1,1	,1	2	1	1	1	.	4	
Middle-ton >1608	Phoen.	20840*	33	5	3	4	1,1	,1	7	.	3	1	2	.	
	MT	20570*	15	7	1	10	6,1	1,1	2	2	2	.	3	.	
	MWM	19098*	24	10	1	5	,6	,1	2	2	2	.	3	3	
	Trick	19268*	28	11	4	5	5,3	.	6	1	5	.	2	2	
	YFG	21878*	19	11	15	8	2,1	,1	7	1	2	.	3	.	
1610 <	NWNH	27703*	12	12	4	6	5,6	1,	8	8	2	.	3	1	
	CMC	18489*	16	15	2	7	.	1,4	3	1	2	2	3	2	
	MDBW	20052*	10	12	.	11	1,1	,1	.	.	.	.	1	3	
	Witch	16862*	8	9	2	3	1,1	1,1	3	4	.	.	1	3	
	Heng.	22037*	7	7	1	10	.	3,1	4	2	.	.	5	1	
	WBW	26162*	17	21	2	10	2,2	2,	1	10	2	1	2	.	
	GC	19342*	10	14	.	8	,2	,1	1	4	1	.	.	4	
	Widow	20315*	37	7	3	3	.	.	7	4	.	.	7	.	
X Plays 1610 <	SMT	20014*	1	5	3	7	2,3	,1	5	2	2	.	3	1	
	WSW	21596	21	24	.	9	1,1	1,1	8	13	2	1	13	.	
	NV	14664	9	15	.	5	,1	,2	.	8	1	1	4	.	
	AQL	20677	6	35	1	3	.	2,1	9	3	1	1	5	2	
	Span.	17460	6	21	.	8	.	,4	1	1	.	.	.	4	
	BB	15618	17	7	2	.	,1	1,5	.	6	1	1	1	.	
Barry	RA	22419	19	5	1	3	.	,4	.	8	1	2	7	3	
Dekker	Sh.H.	19276	21	24	2	3	1,	6,4	.	1	.	1	.	4	
	OF	25636	11	10	9	2	1,	,1	5	.	.	.	.	21	
	Sat.	22397*	19	16	6	6	,1	4,1	3	.	.	.	1	8	
	2HW	24832*	13	48	3	11	.	4,4	3	1	.	2	.	2	
	Wh.B.	21807	9	9	1	5	.	2,1	3	.	.	.	.	18	
	ITBN	23936	4	30	.	6	.	4,2	1	1	.	.	.	6	
	MML	19924	3	37	.	6	.	,2	2	3	.	.	.	4	1
Ford	LM	19065	1	27	.	1	.	.	11	1	.	.	1	7	4
	BH	17748	2	17	1	5	,1	6,	4	3	.	2	.	1	4
	LS	19061	9	26	.	9	1,2	1,2	.	5	.	1	.	.	12
	TP	22370	14	30	.	3	2,	1,	2	8	.	.	1	6	5
	PW	19725	.	5	1	7	.	1,	6	3	1	.	2	3	4
	FCN	18417	1	18	.	17	,2	2,	4	3	.	.	1	1	6
	LT	15997	3	17	.	9	,1	,1	5	4	1	.	.	.	9
Rowley	Sh.G.	22745	19	15	1	11	.	,2	.	1	.	.	4	6	
	WNV	22259	33	24	2	7	.	1,	4	11	.	.	2	6	
	ALL	17442	9	10	.	4	.	2,2	.	1	.	1	1	7	
M + R	FQ	21276	22	20	.	4	.	2,1	3	7	.	3	4	.	
	Ch.	21143	21	22	.	11	1,3	.	4	5	.	.	.	2	

	/Pronouns						/Verbs					/Pronoun + verb contractions							
	ye	'ee	'a [= he]	's [= his]	'em	them	has	hath	does	doth	ha'	I'd	I'm	I am	I've	thou'rt / th'art	sh'as / sh'ad	'tas, / 'tad,	'thas, / 'thad,
lurt	1	.	.	2	.	35	21	11	19	2	3	6	.	70	.	,1	.	.	.
HW	1	.	.	4	40	48	45	12	17	4	43	3	19	49	.	,7	1,	.	1
L	3	2	41	9	21	47	19	29	12	8	8	1	.	48	.	,4	.	.	.
T	2	.	1	1	5	4	17	1	2	1	2	1	6	19	.	1,	.	1	.
ur.	1	.	.	1	41	12	47	2	8	.	18	10	11	28	.	2,1	2,[a]	5	.
RT	.	.	.	2	38	9	45	7	28	2	3	9	22	23	6	8,1	3,	6	.
hoen.	6	.	.	.	38	11	46	3	18	1	17	6	28	33	8	4,	3,	2	.
T	5	.	3	1	46	8	43	3	22	1	33	4	25	39	4	.[b]	2,	3	.
WM	1	.	.	6	66	8	54	2	17	1	4	6	26	35	9	7,[b]1	7,	1	.
rick	1	1	.	1	36	8	44	3	7	1	6	7	7	48	.	9,	1,	2	.
FG	6	1	5	1	59	21	44	4	12	1	8	8	25	40	6	3,2	.	6	.
WNH	7	.	.	7	40	22	57	5	24	1	.	17	31	37	17	5,	3,	2	3
MC	7	.	2	1	17	27	35	13	9	4	14	1	11	34	1	.	.	.	.
DBW	.	.	.	6	36	6	52	1	12	.	.	7	26	35	2	2,1	2,2	1	3
itch	1	.	.	2	35	8	35	14	6	4	4	3	14*	25*	3	8,	7,2	.	.
eng.	1	.	.	3	62	14	42	2	10	.	.	6	28	35	.	.	.	.	.
BW	2	.	.	7	43	10	64	.	20	.	.	6	34	39	.	,2	7[c]2	.	3
C	.	.	.	.	38	5	41	3	8	.	2	8	27	22	2	3,	2,	3	.
idow	3	.	.	10	63	6	54	.	8	.	26	12	62	24	23	7,	4,	3	5
MT	4	.	.	2	35	9	44	3	17	.	10	14	31	24	8	12,	1[a]	3	.
SW	3	1	.	4	50	5	63	2	22	.	32	16	51	37	5	4,	1,1	.	2
V	2	.	.	7	29	6	39	.	13	.	21	6	32	25	19	,2	.	3	2
QL	2	.	.	5	16	30	47	4	14	1	.	1	7	61	.	,2	.	.	.
pan.	8	6	5	.	29	13	28	16	11	.	12	4	2	70	.	,4	.	.	3
B	.	.	1	2	3	36	7	23	9	6	.	2	13	25	.	,2	,1[d]	.	1
A	4	.	80	3	3	46	57	11	18	7	1	4	.	42	.	,4	.	1	.
h.H.	7	.	1	.	.	47	2	24	4	14	.	3	.	45	.	,7	.	.	.
F	.	.	.	.	1	65	20	50	9	23	.	.	.	72	.	,5	.	.	.
at.	6	.	1	10	.	47	37	11	18	2	37	10	1	40	.	1,11	.	.	.
HW	26	.	.	4	9	74	45	17	46	2	49	.	21	38	.	,9	1,	.	.
h.B.	5	.	.	1	7	116	14	21	9	5	10	2	6	11	.	,3	1,	.	1
TBN	4	.	.	8	46	34	38	8	25	1	24	1	13	47	.	,11	1,	.	1
ML	.	1	.	6	15	30	32	6	24	1	14	3	23	44	.	,8	.	.	1
M	52	29	6	4	11	12	15	36	12	9	.	.	4	71	.	,5	.	.	1
H	11	43	25	1	12	13	14	36	6	14	.	2	2	42	3	,3	.	.	1
S	25	12	6	.	17	17	18	22	4	9	2	3	4	64	.	,4	.	.	1
P	11	30	2	1	3	20	2	45	5	10	1	4	11	45	.	,1	.	.	.
W	20	28	28	.	12	35	16	38	1	13	.	.	1	34	1	,3	.	.	.
CN	65	8	30	3	14	22	23	28	11	3	1	3	9	49	1	,10	1,	.	.
T	44	11	14	.	10	19	12	29	9	6	.	1	6	36	.	,4	1,	.	.
h.G.	34	1	.	2	23	34	35	27	11	4	.	7	7	41	.	1[e],3[f]	.	.	.
NV	10	.	.	6	30	46	33	15	14	1	.	15	13	48	.	,4	.	1	.
LL	4	1	.	.	14	17	37	8	14	2	4	2	8	32	.	,3	.	.	.
Q	5	.	1	.	42	8	46	5	9	2	4	11	15	37	6	,2	1,	.	.
h.	1	.	.	1	41	10	31	12	11	.	12	4	28	43	7	,1	.	.	2

Occurrences: [a] Once as she'as. [b] Once as thu'rt. [c] Once as sh'has. [d] As sh'had. [e] As thor't. [f] Once as th'rt.

*Note:—Counts of I'm and I am exclude I'am (18 instances in The Witch).

Band 1(f)

Other contractions

Group	Play	it's	'tis	we're, w'are	you're, y'are	y'(h)ave	they're, th'are	le'me	gi'n't	i'	i'th'	i'the	a'th'	a'the	o'th'	o'the	upo'th'	on't	of't	ex'lent
X Plays >1608	Blurt	7	27	.	,4	.	1,	.	.	.	7	.	2	2	.	.	.	.	.	.
	1HW	10	69	,1	3,32	.	5,1	.	.	.	9	.	2	1	1	.	.	6	.	.
	FL	.	48	.	,5	.	.	.	2	5	5	3	.	.	2	3	.	5	.	.
	YT	.	16	.	,3	1	.	.	.	.	5	.	.	.	.	4	.	1	1	.	.
	Pur.	.	50	1,	5,10	.	6,	.	.	.	15	1	9	2	.	.	2	27	.	5
	RT	.	94	15,	3,8	4	4,	.	1	.	14	.	17	1	.	.	.	18	.	3
Middleton >1608	Phoen.	.	66	2,	7,16	4	2,3	.	.	.	9	1	5	.	1	.	.	.	13	.	.
	MT	1	70	4,2	13,12	5	9,	.	.	.	28	.	7	2	.	.	2	17	.	.
	MWM	1	56	3,	6,10	5	26,	.	2	.	34	.	8	.	1	.	6	29	.	.
	Trick	.	57	3,	9,7	6	1,	.	.	.	16	.	3	.	.	.	.	.	14	.	.
	YFG	1	60	.	20,22	3	20,	.	.	.	12	.	8	.	.	.	.	.	24	.	.
1610<	NWNH	4	81	8,1	6,32[a]	8	15,	.	.	.	22	.	.	.	.	15	.	.	28	.	.
	CMC	2	70	.	4,1	.	6,	.	.	.	1	8	.	.	1	1	1	.	17	.	.
	MDBW	2	54	1,2[b]	6,13[c]	6	5,	.	.	.	14	.	.	.	.	5	.	.	18	.	4
	Witch	1	84	2,	7,5	10	10,	.	.	.	18	.	.	.	.	5	.	.	22	.	.
	Heng.	1	86	,1	,15	15	6,5	.	.	.	17	.	.	.	.	8	.	.	28	.	.
	WBW	2	116	,3	2,33	17	9,	.	.	.	23	.	.	.	.	10	.	.	33	.	.
	GC	.	44	3,	5,5	4	5,	.	.	.	5	.	3	.	.	.	.	.	18	.	.
	Widow	5	77	2,1	9,23	12	25,	4	.	7	18	1	.	.	.	10	.	.	26	.	.
X Plays 1610<	SMT	.	78	4,	3,14	6	7,1	.	.	.	2	.	.	.	.	1	.	.	22[d]	.	.
	WSW	.	93	1,	12,6	1	2,	1	1	9	16	3	2	3	.	.	.	.	28	.	.
	NV	1	60	1,1	1,14	4	2,9	.	.	3	12	.	.	.	.	10	1	.	26	.	.
	AQL	.	67	.	3,6	.	.	.	1	22	.	.	2	.	5	.	.	6	2	.	.
	Span.	3	62	.	,10	1	,1	.	1	.	1	1	.	.	1	.	.	2	.	.
	BB	.	57	.	,6	.	,2	.	.	2	.	.	.	.	.	.	.	.	.	.	7
Barry	RA	.	54	.	,10	2	2,2	.	.	.	.	1	.	1	.	.	.	.	.	.	.
Dekker	Sh.H	3	46	.	,6	.	,1	.	.	.	1	.	.	.	.	.	.	.	1	.	.
	OF	10	78	.	,9	.	.	.	.	.	.	.	.	.	.	.	.	.	.	.	.
	Sat.	10	83	.	1,4	.	6,	.	.	.	6	.	12	7	.	.	1	.	4	.	.
	2HW	29	63	.	,24	.	.	.	.	.	17	.	.	1	1	1	.	.	4	.	.
	Wh.B.	3	41	.	,13	.	,1	.	.	.	7	.	.	.	.	.	.	.	.	.	.
	ITBN	3	52	.	,6	2	,2	.	.	.	23	.	3	.	1	.	.	.	1	1	.
	MML	6	49	.	,9	2	,4	.	.	.	35	.	1	.	.	.	.	.	2	.	.
Ford	LM	.	82	1,	,8	.	.	.	.	.	2	.	.	.	.	.	1	.	3	.	.
	BH	.	60	1,1	,10	1	.	.	.	.	4	.	.	.	.	1	.	.	5	.	.
	LS	.	83	.	,2	1	.	.	.	.	2	.	.	.	.	1	.	.	10	.	.
	TP	.	74	.	,8	.	.	.	.	.	.	.	.	.	.	.	.	.	8	.	.
	PW	.	43	,2	1,7	.	1,	.	.	.	4	.	.	.	.	1	.	.	2	.	.
	FCN	.	56	,1	,6	5	,3	.	.	.	4	.	.	.	.	5	2	.	16	.	.
	LT	.	37	1,	,3	1	,1	.	.	.	4	.	.	.	.	1	.	.	6	.	.
Rowley	Sh.G.	.	76	.	5,	.	.	.	.	.	11	.	.	.	.	3	.	.	7	.	.
	WNV	1	81	.	,11	1	,1	.	.	.	4	.	.	.	.	1	.	.	9	.	.
	ALL	.	57	.	,6	.	.	.	.	.	3	.	.	.	.	1	1	.	1	.	.
M + R	FQ	1	69	.	2,11	8	3,	.	4	10	.	.	1	.	.	.	.	.	22	.	.
	Ch.	1	97	,3	1,20	4	,3	.	.	.	7	.	.	.	.	1	.	.	18	.	.

Occurrences: [a] 11 times as y're. [b] Once as w're. [c] Once as y're. [d] Once as an't.

Column groups: **/Spellings** — *of 'em* — *[of has]* — *of does* — **/Prefixes**

	woult	wou't	wou'd	-cst	(')hem	(')am	(')um	em, |m|	'em, 'm|	e'm	(')has	h'as	ha's	doe(')s	do(')s	otherwise	Total, group sp.	All	Omnes	1. Gent. (&c.)	Gent. 1. (&c.)
lurt	.	1	3	.	.	.	.	.	.	.	21	.	.	19	.	.	20	.	17	+	.
HW	.	3	6	2	.	.	.	39	.	1	43[a]	1[b]	1	17	.	.	26	2	21	+	.
PL	.	2	2	.	21	.	.	.	.	.	19	.	.	7	4	1	3	.	.	.	.
PT	1	.	1	.	.	.	.	5	.	.	15	2	.	2	.	.	6	1	.	+	.
Pur.	4	.	2	.	.	.	.	7	32	2	36	2	9	2	5	1	10	1	.	.	.
KT	1	.	.	5	.	.	.	5	21	12	38	3	4	5	23	.	2	1	.	+	.
Phoen.	.	.	.	.	.	1[c]	.	1	20	16	23	.	23	3	15	.	5	3	.	+	.
MT	.	.	.	.	.	.	1	3	14	28	27	1	15	10	12	.	2	2	.	+	.
TWM	.	.	.	1	.	.	.	20	8	38	42	4	8	.	17	.	3	1	.	.	+[d]
Trick	.	.	.	3	.	.	.	4	4	28	39	.	5	.	7	.	4	3	.	.	.
TFG	.	.	.	3	.	.	.	38	20	1	42	2	.	6	6	.	10	9	.	+	.
JWNH	.	.	.	.	.	.	.	.	40	.	50	7	.	23	1	.	15	6	.	+	.
CMC	.	.	.	.	.	.	.	1	16	.	30	5	.	6	2	1	10	7	.	+	.
MDBW	.	.	.	.	.	.	.	.	36	.	51	1	.	6	6	.	5	3	.	+	.
Witch	.	.	.	.	.	.	.	.	35	.	28	4	3	.	6	.	.	.	.	+	.
Meng.	.	.	.	.	.	.	.	52	10	.	41	1	.	9	1	.	10	8	1	+	.
WBW	.	.	.	.	.	.	.	.	43	.	54	10	.	16	4	.	3	.	1	+	.
GC	.	.	.	12	.	.	.	4	2	31	10	5	25	.	8	.	.	.	.	+	.
Widow	.	.	.	.	.	.	.	.	62	.	45	9[ee]	.	.	8	.	2	.	.	+	.
SMT	.	.	.	4	.	.	.	.	35	.	43	1	.	17	.	.	4	4	.	+	.
NSW	.	.	1	.	.	.	.	7	1	42	63	.	.	20	2	.	2	.	.	.	.
NV	.	.	.	.	.	.	.	.	29	.	36	2	1	13	.	.	2	.	1	+	.
AQL	.	.	.	.	.	.	.	.	16	.	45	1	1	14	.	.	3	.	2	+	.
Span.	.	1	7	.	.	.	.	.	29	.	28	.	.	11	.	.	21	.	18	.	.
BB	.	.	.	.	.	.	.	.	3	.	7[e]	.	.	9	.	.	5	.	2	.	+[f]
RA	.	2	1	.	.	.	.	1	2	.	53	.	4	18	.	.	7	1	3	+	.
Sh.H.	.	.	.	.	.	.	.	.	.	.	2	.	.	4	.	.	20	16	.	.	.
OF	.	.	.	.	.	.	.	.	1	.	20	.	.	8	1[g]	.	25	8	.	.	.
Sat.	.	8	14	.	.	.	.	.	.	.	37	.	.	18	.	.	22	4	10	+	.
2HW	.	4	12	.	.	.	.	1	8	.	45	.	.	46	.	.	47	.	43	+	.
Wh.B.	.	.	.	.	.	.	.	1	6	.	8	.	6	9	.	.	53	.	36	+	.
ITBN	.	7	15	.	.	.	.	3	43	.	36	2	.	25	.	.	101	.	84	+	.
MML	.	.	2	.	.	.	.	1	14	.	32	.	.	24	.	.	15	.	15	+	.
LM	.	.	.	.	.	.	.	.	11	.	11	1	3	10	2	.	2	1	.	.	.
BH	.	.	1	.	.	.	.	.	12	.	13	1	.	6	.	.	4	.	3	.	.
LS	.	.	3	.	.	.	.	.	17	.	18	.	.	3	.	.	3	.	1	.	.
TP	.	4	2	.	.	.	.	.	3	.	2	.	.	5	.	.	8	.	5	.	.
PW	.	.	.	.	.	.	.	2	10[h]	.	5	.	11	1	.	.	4	.	3	.	.
FCN	.	.	1	.	.	.	.	8[j]	6	.	23	.	8	8	3	.	2	1	.	.	.
LT	.	.	.	.	.	.	.	3	7	.	12	.	.	8	1	.	4	.	.	.	.
Sh.G.	.	.	4	.	.	.	.	.	23	.	30	5	.	11	.	.	12	9	.	.	.
WNV	.	.	.	.	.	.	.	.	30	.	33	.	.	14	.	.	1	.	1	.	.
ALL	.	1	33	.	.	.	.	8	.	6	37	.	.	14	.	.	6	.	6	.	.
FQ	.	.	.	3	.	2	34	.	6	.	35	.	11	7	2	.	2	.	2	+	.
Ch.	.	.	.	.	.	.	15	.	26	.	31	.	.	11	.	.	.	.	.	+	.

Occurrences: [a] 7 times as _haz_. [b] As _h'az_. [c] As _a'm_. [d] One instance only. [e] Once, _h'has_. [ee] Once as _'as_. [f] 22 instances. [g] As _dost_ = [does it]. [h] Once as _eem'_. [j] Once as _eem_.

Band 1(h)

Table I.1 Segment /Middletonisms
3

Band 1 /Selected words & collocations

		Length (words)	by..copy	can possible	Chaucer	comfort	fetch..again	give..due	'Has [= he has]	Inn a court [+ noun]	Inns a court [+ noun]	"Italian" joke	la(w) you	la(w) you now	lin	love..alife
X Plays 1608	Blurt	18037*	.	.	.	1	.	.	1	.	.	.	.	.	.	1
	1HW	25509	2	.	.	1	.	.	4	.	.	.	5	3	.	.
	FL	22362	.	.	1	4	1	.	.	1	.	.	.	.	.	.
	YT	6230*	.	.	.	2	.	.	2	.	.	.	.	.	.	.
	Pur.	19922*	1	1	.	11	2	1	7	.	.	.	1	1	1	.
	RT	21268*	.	.	.	17	.	4	7	.	.	.	1	1	.	.
Middle-ton >1608	Phoen.	20840*	1	1	.	7	.	1	12	.	.	.	.	.	.	.
	MT	20570*	.	.	.	11	1	1	4	.	.	1	3	3	.	.
	MWM	19098*	.	.	.	8	.	1	5	1	1	.	1	.	.	.
	Trick	19268*	1	.	.	15	.	1	4	.	.	.	1	1	.	3
	YFG	21878*	.	1	.	8	1	1	5	.	.	.	.	.	1	1
1610	NWNH	27703*	1	.	1	18	.	.	4	.	.	.	3	.	.	.
	CMC	18489*	.	.	.	5	.	.	5	.	.	.	.	.	1	1
	MDBW	20052*	.	.	1	9	.	.	4	.	.	1	2	.	1	.
	Witch	16862*	.	.	.	13	.	.	4	.	.	.	.	.	.	.
	Heng.	22037*	.	.	.	7	.	.	3	.	.	.	.	.	1	.
	WBW	26162*	1	.	.	19	.	.	9	.	.	.	.	.	.	.
	GC	19342*	.	.	.	3	.	.	6	.	.	1	.	.	.	1
	Widow	20315*	.	.	.	17	1	.	9	.	1	.	1	.	1	2
X Plays 1610	SMT	20014*	.	1	.	7	.	.	9	.	.	.	.	.	.	.
	WSW	21596	.	.	.	4	.	.	4	.	.	.	2	.	.	1
	NV	14664	.	.	.	6	1	.	11	.	.	2	.	.	.	.
	AQL	20677	.	.	.	4	.	.	3	.	.	.	.	.	.	.
	Span.	17460	.	.	.	7	.	.	1	.	.	.	.	.	.	.
	BB	15618	.	.	.	4	.	.	1	.	.	.	1	1	.	.
Barry	RA	22419	.	.	.	1	.	.	9	1	.	.	.	.	.	1
Dekker	Sh.H.	19276	.	.	.	.	.	.	.	.	.	.	.	.	.	.
	OF	25636	.	.	.	1	.	.	.	.	.	.	.	.	.	.
	Sat.	22397*	.	.	.	.	.	2	3	.	.	.	.	.	.	.
	2HW	24832*	.	.	.	1	.	.	2	.	.	.	1	.	.	.
	Wh.B.	21807	.	.	.	2	.	.	.	.	.	.	.	.	.	.
	ITBN	23936	.	.	.	4	.	1	2	.	.	.	.	.	.	.
	MML	19924	.	.	.	.	.	.	.	.	.	.	.	.	.	.
Ford	LM	19065	.	.	.	9	.	.	1	.	.	.	.	.	.	.
	BH	17748	.	.	.	17	.	.	1	.	.	.	.	.	.	.
	LS	19061	.	.	.	7	.	1	.	.	.	.	.	.	.	.
	TP	22370	.	.	.	7	.	.	.	.	.	.	.	.	.	.
	PW	19725	.	.	.	13	.	.	.	.	.	.	.	.	.	.
	FCN	18417	.	.	.	6	.	.	.	.	.	.	.	.	.	.
	LT	15997	.	.	.	5	.	.	.	.	.	.	.	.	.	.
Rowley	Sh.G.	22745	.	.	.	11	.	1	8	.	.	.	.	.	.	.
	WNV	22259	1	.	.	15	.	.	2	.	.	.	.	.	.	.
	ALL	17442	.	.	.	.	.	.	.	.	.	.	.	.	.	.
M + R	FQ	21276	.	.	.	6	.	1	1	.	.	.	.	.	.	.
	Ch.	21143	.	.	.	8	.	.	.	.	.	.	.	.	.	.

* Fully counted.

/Dekkerisms

	[adv.] -ly welcome	mass, here	I (do) protest	sasarara	save..harmless	son and heir	spoke like	subaudi	suspectless	third part of	troth..say true	tut, man	Adam/Eve	Garlic/strong	godamercy	hair..an end	lily..hands	make buttons	marry muff
Blurt	.	.	.	.	.	.	.	.	.	.	.	.	1	1	1	2	2	.	2
1HW	1	.	2	.	1	3	1	1	.	.	.	.	.	.	2	.	.	.	2
FL	1	.	.	.	.	.	.	1	1	.	.	3	.	.	.	.	.	.	.
YT	.	.	1	.	.	.	.	.	.	.	.	.	.	.	.	.	.	.	.
Pur.	2	1	8	1	1	5	.	.	.	.	1	.	.	.	.	.	.	.	.
RT	.	2	2	1	.	3	.	.	.	1	2	.	.	.	.	.	.	.	.
Phoen.	6	1	6	3	.	.	.	.	.	.	.	.	.	.	.	.	.	.	.
MT	2	.	4	.	1	6	.	.	.	.	.	.	.	.	.	.	.	.	.
MWM	3	.	4	.	.	1	.	.	.	.	.	1	.	.	.	.	.	.	.
Trick	.	.	4	.	1	.	1	.	.	.	.	.	.	.	.	.	.	.	.
YFG	4	.	4	.	.	.	.	1	3	1	.	1	.	.	.	.	.	.	.
NWNH	1	2	2	.	1	1	3	.	.	3	2	.	.	.	.	.	.	.	.
CMC	.	.	4	.	.	.	.	.	.	.	.	.	.	.	.	.	.	.	.
MDBW	.	.	.	.	.	1	1	.	.	2	1	.	.	.	.	.	.	.	.
Witch	1	.	2	.	.	.	.	.	.	.	.	.	.	.	.	.	.	.	.
Heng.	.	.	.	.	.	.	.	.	.	.	.	.	.	.	.	.	.	.	.
WBW	.	1	1	.	.	.	.	.	.	1	.	.	.	.	.	.	.	.	.
GC	.	.	.	.	.	1	1	.	.	.	.	.	.	.	.	.	.	.	.
Widow	.	2	5	.	.	.	.	.	.	.	.	.	.	.	.	.	.	.	.
SMT	1	1	1	.	.	.	1	.	.	.	1	.	.	.	.	.	.	.	.
WSW	1	.	5	.	.	1	.	.	.	.	.	.	.	.	.	.	.	.	.
NV	1	.	.	.	.	.	.	.	.	.	.	.	.	.	.	.	.	.	.
AQL	.	.	4	.	.	1	.	.	.	.	.	.	.	.	.	2	.	.	.
Span.	1	.	2	.	.	.	.	.	.	.	.	.	.	.	.	.	.	1	.
BB	.	2	1	.	.	1	.	.	.	.	.	.	.	.	.	.	.	.	.
RA	.	.	8	1[a]	1	.	.	.	.	.	.	.	.	.	.	1	.	.	.
Sh.H.	.	.	.	.	.	.	.	.	.	.	.	.	.	.	.	5	.	1	.
OF	.	.	.	.	.	.	.	.	.	.	.	.	.	.	1	.	.	.	.
Sat.	.	.	.	.	.	.	.	.	.	.	.	.	.	1	1	4	4	.	1
2HW	.	.	3	.	.	.	.	.	.	.	1[b]	.	.	.	.	.	.	.	2
Wh.B.	.	.	.	.	.	.	.	.	.	.	.	.	.	.	.	.	.	.	.
ITBN	.	.	1	.	.	.	.	.	.	.	.	.	.	.	.	1	.	1	.
MML	.	.	.	.	.	.	.	.	.	.	.	.	1	.	1	1[c]	.	.	.
LM	1	.	5	.	.	.	.	.	.	.	.	.	.	.	.	.	.	.	.
BH	.	.	.	.	.	.	.	.	.	.	.	.	.	.	.	.	.	.	.
LS	.	.	2	.	.	.	.	.	.	.	.	.	.	2[d]	1	.	.	.	.
TP	.	.	1	.	.	.	.	.	.	.	.	.	.	.	1	.	.	.	.
PW	.	.	.	.	.	.	.	.	.	.	.	.	.	.	.	.	.	.	.
FCN	2	.	4	.	.	.	.	.	.	.	.	.	.	.	.	.	.	.	.
LT	.	.	1	.	.	.	.	.	.	.	.	.	.	.	.	.	.	.	.
Sh.G.	.	.	2	.	.	.	.	.	.	.	.	.	.	.	.	.	.	.	.
WNV	.	.	1	.	.	.	.	.	.	1	.	.	.	.	.	.	.	.	.
ALL	1	.	2	.	.	1	.	.	.	.	.	.	.	.	.	.	.	.	.
FQ	.	.	.	.	.	.	.	.	.	.	.	.	.	.	.	.	.	.	.
Ch.	.	.	.	.	.	.	.	.	.	.	.	.	.	.	.	.	.	.	.

Occurrences: [a] As Certiorare. [b] As troth . . to tell you true.

[c] As foretop . . an end. [d] Both times as strongest . .garlick.

		moon/horn(s)	mumble-crust	no point	oyster/open	parrot [= woman]	puss-cat	rowly-powly	Signior no	snick up	snip snap	stile/style pun	Tamburlaine	wink at small faults	deed la	float of	forfeit of	'tis Oracle	undertake a voluntary exile
X Plays >1608	Blurt	.	.	1	.	.	2	1	6	1	1	.	1	.	.	.	.	.	.
	1HW	1	.	.	.	.	.	.	.	.	.	.	.	.	.	.	.	.	.
	FL	1	.	.	.	.	.	.	.	.	.	.	.	1	.	.	.	.	.
	YT	.	.	.	.	.	.	.	.	.	.	.	.	.	.	.	.	.	.
	Pur	.	.	.	.	.	.	.	.	.	.	.	.	.	.	.	.	.	.
	RT	.	.	.	.	.	.	.	.	.	.	.	.	.	.	.	.	1	.
Middleton >1608	Phoen.	.	.	.	.	.	.	.	.	.	.	.	.	.	.	.	.	.	.
	MT	.	.	.	.	.	.	.	.	.	.	.	.	.	.	.	.	.	.
	MWM	.	.	.	.	.	.	.	.	.	.	.	.	.	.	.	.	.	.
	Trick	.	.	.	.	.	.	.	.	.	.	.	.	.	.	.	.	.	.
	YFG	.	.	.	.	.	.	.	.	.	.	.	.	.	.	.	.	.	.
1610<	NWNH	.	.	.	.	.	.	.	.	.	.	.	.	.	.	.	.	.	.
	CMC	.	.	.	.	.	.	.	.	.	.	.	.	.	.	.	.	.	.
	MDBW	.	.	.	.	.	.	.	.	.	.	.	.	.	.	.	.	.	.
	Witch	.	.	.	.	.	.	.	.	.	.	.	.	.	.	.	.	.	.
	Heng.	.	.	.	.	.	.	.	.	.	.	.	.	.	.	.	1	.	.
	WBW	.	.	.	.	.	.	.	.	.	.	.	.	.	.	.	.	.	.
	GC	.	.	.	.	.	.	.	.	.	.	.	.	.	.	.	.	.	.
	Widow	.	.	.	.	.	.	.	.	.	.	.	.	.	.	.	.	.	.
X Plays 1610<	SMT	.	.	.	.	.	.	.	.	.	.	.	.	.	.	.	.	.	.
	WSW	.	.	.	.	.	.	.	.	.	.	.	.	.	.	.	.	.	.
	NV	.	.	.	.	.	.	.	.	.	.	.	.	.	.	.	.	.	.
	AQL	.	.	.	.	.	.	.	.	.	3a	.	.	.	.	.	.	.	.
	Span.	.	1	.	1	1	.	.	.	.	.	1	.	.	1	1	3	.	1
	BB	.	.	.	.	.	.	.	.	.	.	.	.	.	.	.	.	.	.
Barry	RA	.	.	.	.	.	.	.	.	.	.	.	.	.	.	.	.	.	.
Dekker	Sh.H.	.	1	1	.	.	.	.	.	1	1b	.	1	.	.	.	.	.	.
	OF	.	.	3	.	.	.	.	.	.	1	.	.	.	.	.	.	.	.
	Sat.	.	1	.	.	.	1	1	.	.	.	1	1	.	.	.	.	.	.
	2HW	.	.	.	.	.	.	.	.	.	.	.	.	.	.	.	.	.	.
	Wh.B.	.	.	.	.	.	.	.	.	.	.	.	.	.	.	.	.	.	.
	ITBN	1	.	.	1	.	.	.	.	.	.	.	.	.	.	.	.	.	.
	MML	3	.	1	.	1	.	.	1	.	.	.	.	1	.	.	.	.	.
Ford	LM	.	.	.	.	.	.	.	.	.	.	.	.	.	.	.	.	.	1
	BH	.	.	.	.	.	.	.	.	.	.	.	.	.	.	.	.	.	1
	LS	1c	.	.	.	.	.	.	.	.	.	.	.	.	.	2	1	.	.
	TP	.	.	.	.	.	.	.	.	.	.	.	.	.	.	.	1	.	.
	PW	.	.	.	.	.	.	.	.	.	.	.	.	.	.	.	.	.	.
	FCN	.	.	.	.	.	.	.	.	.	2d	.	.	.	2	.	.	.	.
	LT	.	.	.	.	.	.	.	.	1	.	.	.	.	.	.	1	.	.
Rowley	Sh.G.	.	.	.	.	.	.	.	.	.	.	.	.	.	.	.	.	.	.
	WNV	.	.	.	.	.	.	.	.	.	.	.	.	.	.	.	.	.	.
	ALL	.	.	.	.	.	.	.	.	.	.	.	.	.	.	.	.	.	.
M + R	FQ	.	.	.	.	.	.	.	.	.	.	.	.	.	.	.	.	.	.
	Ch.	.	.	.	.	.	.	.	.	.	.	.	.	.	.	.	.	.	.

Occurrences: [a] Once as Snip-snapper.   [b] As snipper snapper.   [c] As horned Moone.   [d] Once as snipper-snapper.

Table I.1 Segment 1 /Exclamations

Band 2

Group	Play	Length (words)	push	pish	puh	pah	pew	p-,other	phew	tut	tush	t-,other	hum(h)	um(h)	h(ē/ī)o/ yda(y)	why
Tourneur	AT	22122*									9					24
X Play	RT	21268*	6		6					3			1			32
Middleton	Phoen.	20840*			2	1						5	4			41
	MT	20570*	3	1	4					3						45
	MWM	19098*	6	1	10			10		8						60
(1608)	Trick	19268*	4		3			4		3			4		1	57
	YFG	21878*	6		7					5						76
(1610)	NWNH	27703*	5	3											5	40
	CMC	18489*	1	3				2			1				2	28
	MDBW	20052*		2											2	15
	Witch	16862*													1	25
	Heng.	22037*		5									3		1	26
	WBW	26162*		5												33
	GC	19342*	3		1											16
	Widow	20315*		9	1								2			53
X Plays	SMT	20014*	3	2												19
	WSW	21596	1	1	3							6	13	1		47
	NV	14664		1	1	1									1	23
Goffe	C.T.	14794									4					14
	Ores.	20142									9					40
	R.T.	27150									2					3
Beaumont	KBP	21423														30
Fletcher	W.Pr.	24472*														26
	Bon.	21049						2								18
(1618)	Valen.	25783														15
	M.Thom.	18754											2			17
	ML	18964		1									1			34
	Chan.	19060														19
	L.Sub.	21392														14
Massinger	D.M.	21586														6
	Bond.	20937		2								1	3			4
	PL	17129										2	1			3
	R.A.	18932														4
	Pict.	22588										1		1	1	3
	Ren.	20444		1								3	2			4
	Bel.	19200														2
Shakespeare	Cor.	28547*						1a				2				17
	Temp.	17670														9
X Play	AQL	20677					1b					2				41
Webster	WD	26285*					1c					1	1			21
	DM	24790														16
	DLC	24006					1		1						2	42

* Fully counted. Occurrences: a As pow waw. b As Pue wawe. c As Pew wew.

/Oaths

		Jesu(s)	Lord('s)	God's	God	Heaven(')(s)	Cud(')s, Coad(')s	'snigs	'sfoot	foot	'slid	'slud	'sblood	swounds, 'z-	'sheart	heart	'sdeath	death	'slife, life	'slight, light
Tourneur	AT		1	2	4									2			1	1		
X Play	RT				1	3			9		1	3	2			11		3		
Middle-ton	Phoen.						1,		10		3							1	1,	
	MT				2		1,		2		3	1								
	MWM						3,		14		5									,3
>1608	Trick					2	3,1[a]		1		1							1	1,	
	YFG					1	1,		16		1	1				10		3	7,3	1,1
1610<	NWNH						3,			:				1		2			,8	
	CMC						1,			2				1		11		4	,11	
	MDBW																			
	Witch																			
	Heng.																1			
	WBW							,1									1		,1	
	GC					1			1								1		,1	,1
	Widow																1		'7 1,	
X Plays	SMT					1	1,									5			1[b],13	
	WSW		1				2,	1		2	6							2		,3
	NV																	2		
Goffe	C.T.					1														
	Ores.					10														
	R.T.					13														
Beaumont	KBP		1	5	1[c]	2														
Fletcher	W.Pr.		1	1	1	2			1											
	Bon.					6											2			
>1618	Valen.					11														
	M.Thom.		1	2[d]	1	10														
	ML		1	1		12												4		
	Chan.					13								1			1			
	L.Sub.		4			7														
Mass-inger	D.M.					2														
	Bond.					2					1						1		6	
	PL					1											1			
	R.A.																			
	Pict.					2								1					2,	
	Ren.										1			1					2,	
	Bel.																			
Shake-speare	Cor.				1	4											1			
	Temp.		1			5														
X Play	AQL																1	2		
Webster	WD		3	6	3	2			2[e]								5[f]	1		
	DM					4														
	DLC		2			2			2[e]											

Occurrences: [a] As Coades-Nigs. [b] As Vds life. [c] As by Gad. [d] Once as Gogs bores. [e] Twice as Vds foote. [f] 4 times as Vds Death.

	'(s)nails	'(s)precious	'Od's	('Ud)'s, other	f(a/e)ck(s)	faith	troth	marry	mass	byrlady	my reputation	hold my life
AT	.	3	.	1	.	8	4	1	.	.	.	.
RT	.	.	.	.	.	44	12	6	5	.	.	.
Phoen.	.	.	.	.	.	35	17	3	7	2	.	.
MT	.	.	.	.	.	58	17	6	5	3	.	.
MWM	.	.	.	.	.	88	17	3	7	.	.	.
Trick	.	.	.	.	.	79	19	4	12	1	.	.
YFG	.	.	.	.	.	109	23	6	9	.	.	.
NWNH	.	.	.	.	.	53	11	12	6	.	.	2
CMC	.	.	.	.	.	58	9	4	4	.	.	6
MDBW	.	.	.	.	.	14	7	7	1	4	1	.
Witch	.	.	.	.	.	2	5	4	.	.	.	.
Heng.	.	1	1[a]	.	.	11	2	3	.	2	.	.
WBW	.	.	.	.	.	35	16	9	1	2	.	.
GC	.	.	.	.	.	.	.	3	2	.	.	.
Widow	.	.	1[b]	.	.	41	14	11	4	6	.	1
SMT	.	.	.	.	.	25	9	7	3	1	.	1
WSW	2	.	.	3[c]	1	45	12	5	1	.	1	.
NV	.	.	.	.	1	6	8	10	.	1[d]	1	1
C.T.	.	.	.	.	.	.	.	.	.	.	.	.
Ores.	.	.	.	.	.	5	3	.	.	.	.	.
R.T.	.	.	.	.	.	3	.	.	.	.	.	.
KBP	.	.	.	.	.	36	6	7	.	.	.	.
W.Pr.	.	.	.	.	.	2	2	6	.	4	.	.
Bon.	.	.	.	.	.	2	.	1	.	.	.	.
Valen.	.	.	.	.	.	2	2	.	1	.	.	.
M.Thom.	.	1	.	.	.	9	3	4	5	2	.	.
ML	.	.	.	.	.	3	2	2	1	.	.	.
Chan.	.	.	1	.	.	1	1	3	2	.	.	.
L.Sub.	.	.	.	.	.	6	3	2	2	1	.	.
D.M.	.	.	.	.	.	1	2	1	.	.	.	.
Bond.	.	.	.	.	.	2	1	1	.	.	.	.
PL	.	.	.	.	.	2	4	1	.	.	.	.
R.A.	.	.	.	.	.	1	.	.	.	.	.	.
Pict.	.	.	.	.	.	.	.	.	.	.	.	.
Ren.	.	.	.	.	.	1	2	1	.	.	.	.
Bel.	.	.	.	.	.	.	1	2	.	.	.	.
Cor.	.	.	.	.	.	6	4	.	.	.	.	.
Temp.	.	.	.	.	.	2	1	1	.	1[d]	.	.
AQL	.	.	.	.	3	9	7	8	.	1[e]	.	.
WD	.	.	.	.	.	12	1	3	.	.	.	.
DM	.	.	.	.	.	1	.	.	.	.	.	.
DLC	.	.	.	.	.	6	1	7	.	.	.	.

Occurrences: [a] As Ods pretious.
[b] As 'odds' light. [c] 3 times as Vds so.
[d] As birlakin. [e] As birlakins.

Band 2(d)

Table I.1
Band 2 Segment 2

		Length (words)	ay	yes	among	amongst	beside adv.,/prep.	besides adv.,/prep.	between	betwixt	toward	towards	while	whil(e)st	whiles
			/Affirmatives		/Connectives										
Tourneur	AT	22122*	3	17	6	1	.	,1	11	2	.	3	4	1	.
X Play	RT	21268*	29	5	.	6	1,1	,1	2	1	1	1	.	4	.
Middle-ton	Phoen.	20840*	33	5	3	4	1,1	,1	7	.	3	1	2	.	.
	MT	20570*	15	7	1	10	6,1	1,1	2	2	2	.	3	.	.
	MWM	19098*	24	10	1	5	,6	,1	2	2	2	.	3	3	.
>1608	Trick	19268*	28	11	4	5	5,3	.	6	1	5	.	2	2	.
	YFG	21878*	19	11	15	8	2,1	,1	7	1	2	.	3	.	.
1610 <	NWNH	27703*	12	12	4	6	5,6	1,	8	8	2	.	3	1	.
	CMC	18489*	16	15	2	7	.	1,4	3	1	2	2	3	2	.
	MDBW	20052*	10	12	.	11	1,1	,1	.	.	.	.	1	3	.
	Witch	16862*	8	9	2	3	1,1	1,1	3	4	.	.	1	3	.
	Heng.	22037*	7	7	1	10	.	3,1	4	2	.	.	5	1	.
	WBW	26162*	17	21	2	·10	2,2	2,	1	10	2	1	2	.	.
	GC	19342*	10	14	.	8	,2	,1	1	4	1	.	.	4	.
	Widow	20315*	37	7	3	3	.	.	7	4	.	.	7	.	.
X Plays	SMT	20014*	1	5	3	7	2,3	,1	5	2	2	.	3	1	1
	WSW	21596	21	24	.	9	1,1	1,1	8	13	2	1	13	.	.
	NV	14664	9	15	.	5	,1	,2	.	8	1	1	4	.	.
Goffe	C.T.	14794	5	12	1	8	.	,2	.	2	.	3	2	15	.
	Ores.	20142	11	49	1	2	.	,1	.	9	.	2	1	12	1
	R.T.	27150	1	5	1	6	,1	,1	.	5	.	1	1	17	.
Beaumont	KBP	21423	24	14	3	4	,1	9,4	6	1	1	1	6	20	1
Fletcher	W.Pr.	24472*	5	60	3	3	,3	,1	2	1	.	.	5	.	.
>1618	Bon.	21049	3	13	2	3	,2	2,3	1	2	1	.	1	2	.
	Valen.	25783	3	29	1	.	1,1	5,3	.	2	.	.	4	5	.
	M.Thom.	18754	6	14	6	.	,2	2,2	1	.	.	.	1	1	.
	ML	18964	4	27	4	3	1,1	2,1	3	.	1	.	2	1	.
	Chan.	19060	10	22	3	7	,2	,1	2	1	.	1	1	6	.
	L.Sub.	21392	9	24	1	3	,1	1,	3	.	1	1	1	9	.
Mass-inger	D.M.	21586	2	2	3	2	.	2,	8	.	.	1	5	.	.
	Bond.	20937	.	8	7	.	.	2,	1	.	.	.	5	.	.
	PL	17129	2	8	2	.	.	1,2	1	1	.	.	3	1	.
	R.A.	18932	.	12	5	.	.	2,	2	.	.	.	7	.	.
	Pict.	22588	.	7	9	.	.	1,4	3	.	.	.	10	.	.
	Ren.	20444	2	6	7	.	1,	.	1	1	.	1	4	1	.
	Bel.	19200	2	13	5	.	.	2,1	5	2	.	.	3	.	.
Shake-speare	Cor.	28547*	21	7	5	2	1,	2,	9	4	3	3	4	3	1
	Temp.	17670	14	3	1	1	.	,1	3	4	.	2	7	.	5
X Play	AQL	20677	6	35	1	3	.	2,1	9	3	1	1	5	2	1
Webster	WD	26285*	4	30	.	7	.	2,1	10	.	.	3	9	3	.
	DM	24790	3	33	1	4	,1	.	8	.	1	5	5	2	.
	DLC	24006	9	25	4	.	1,	1,4	10	.	.	.	5	1	1

	/Pronouns						/Verbs					/Pronoun + verb contractions							
	ye	'ee	'a = [he]	's = [his]	'em	them	has	hath	does	doth	ha'	I'd	I'm	I am	I've	thou'rt, th'art	sh'as, sh'ad	'tas, 'thas	'tad, 'thad
AT	1	.	.	8	18	12	48	14	16	10	35	2	3	35	2	,10	1,1	.	3
RT	.	.	.	2	38	9	45	7	28	2	3	9	22	23	6	8,1	3,	6	.
Phoen.	6	.	.	.	38	11	46	3	18	1	17	6	28	33	8	4,	3,	2	.
MT	5	.	3	1	46	8	43	3	22	1	33	4	25	39	4	.	2,	3	.
MWM	1	.	.	6	66	8	54	2	17	1	4	6	26	35	9	7[a],1	7,	1	.
Trick	1	1	.	1	36	8	44	3	7	1	6	7	7	48	.	9,	1,	2	.
YFG	6	1	5	1	59	21	44	4	12	1	8	8	25	40	6	3,2	.	6	.
NWNH	7	.	.	7	40	22	57	5	24	1	.	17	31	37	17	5,	3,	2	3
CMC	7	.	2	1	17	27	35	13	9	4	14	1	11	34	1	.	.	.	.
MDBW	.	.	.	6	36	6	52	1	12	.	.	7	26	35	2	2,1	2,2	1	3
Witch	1	.	.	2	35	8	35	14	6	4	4	3	14*	25*	3	8,	7,2	.	.
Heng.	1	.	.	3	62	14	42	2	10	.	.	6	28	35	.	.	.	.	.
WBW	2	.	.	7	43	10	64	.	20	.	.	6	34	39	.	,2	7[b],2	.	3
GC	.	.	.	.	38	5	41	3	8	.	2	8	27	22	2	3,	2,	3	.
Widow	3	.	.	10	63	6	54	.	8	.	26	12	62	24	23	7,	4,	3	5
SMT	4	.	.	2	35	9	44	3	17	.	10	14	31	24	8	12,	1[c],	3	.
WSW	3	1	.	4	50	5	63	2	22	.	32	16	51	37	5	4,	1,1	.	2
NV	2	.	.	7	29	6	39	.	13	.	21	6	32	25	19	,2	.	3	2
C.T.	4	.	.	4	.	59	2	21	1	29	.	.	.	13	.	,1	.	.	.
Ores.	7	.	.	4	5	55	1	56	4	49	1	9	7	14	.	2,1	.	1	.
R.T.	3	.	.	1	.	65	10	59	.	18	2	12	12	50	2	1,4	.	.	1
KBP	3	3	11	7	13	37	21	37	4	12	10	.	11	64	.	,1	.	.	.
W.Pr.	84	.	.	6	66	6	42	4	16	1	.	1	.	99	.	.	.	.	1
Bon.	[352]	.	4	6	95	6	38	1	13	.	.	1	1	49	.	.	.	.	.
Valen.	[412]	.	2	2	71	15	48	4	7	.	.	.	.	93	.	,1	.	.	1
M.Thom.	[343]	.	.	4	27	2	43	6	26	.	1	.	1	67	.	.	.	.	1
ML	[308]	.	15	3	25	4	26	6	30	.	2	.	.	51	.	.	.	.	.
Chan.	[290]	.	4	2	44	6	45	2	5	.	.	.	6	60	.	.	.	.	4
L.Sub.	[424]	.	.	3	133	13	66	3	10	.	2	.	2	64	.	.	.	.	1
D.M.	.	.	.	.	12	24	8	46	13	.	.	.	5	83	.	.	,1	.	.
Bond.	.	.	.	.	15	44	19	8	13	1	.	.	.	76	.	.	.	.	.
PL	1	.	.	.	7	24	17	21	8	.	.	.	2	69	.	.	.	.	.
R.A.	.	.	.	.	14	22	4	28	19	.	.	.	.	42	.	.	.	.	.
Pict.	.	.	.	.	52	10	12	35	10	.	.	.	.	98	.	.	.	.	.
Ren.	.	.	.	.	10	13	15	21	12	.	.	.	.	69	.	.	.	.	.
Bel.	.	.	.	.	26	10	.	38	10	.	.	.	.	65	.	.	.	.	.
Cor.	8	.	3	14	15	133	35	51	19	9	.	6	.	41	.	,2	.	.	.
Temp.	5	.	.	2	17	44	7	26	15	13	.	2	.	33	.	1,	.	.	.
AQL	2	.	.	5	16	30	47	4	14	1	.	1	7	61	.	,2	.	.	.
WD	1	.	.	17	.	72	3	42	1	17	.	4	.	54	.	1,1	.	.	1
DM	2	.	.	15	3	81	3	54	1	28	.	7	.	77	.	1,	.	.	.
DLC	2	.	3	20	.	60	81	1	14	2	1	5	.	77	.	.	.	2	1

Occurrences: [a] Once as thu'rt. [b] Once as sh'has. [c] As shee'as.

*Excludes 18 instances of I'am.

Band 2(f)

/Other contractions

		it's	'tis	we're, w'are	you're, y'are	y'(h)ave	they're, th'are	le'me	gi'n't	i'	i'th'	i'the	a'th'	a'the	o'th'	o'the	upo'th'	on't	of't	ex'lent
Tourneur	AT	.	51	,2	,12	2	,5	.	.	9	7	15	.	.	5	16	.	1	.	.
X Play	RT	.	94	15,	3,8	4	4,	.	1	.	14	.	17	1	.	.	.	18	.	.
Middleton	Phoen.	.	66	2,	7,16	4	2,3	.	.	.	9	1	5	.	1	.	.	13	.	.
	MT	1	70	4,2	13,12	5	9,	.	.	.	28	.	7	2	.	.	2	17	.	.
	MWM	1	56	3,	6,10	5	26,	.	2	.	34	.	8	.	1	.	6	29	.	.
>1608	Trick	.	57	3,	9,7	6	1,	.	.	.	16	.	3	.	.	.	.	14	.	.
	YFG	1	60	.	20,22	3	20,	.	.	.	12	.	8	.	.	.	.	24	.	.
1610<	NWNH	4	81	8,1	6,32[a]	8	15,	.	.	.	22	.	.	.	15	.	.	28	.	.
	CMC	2	70	.	4,1	.	6,	.	.	.	1	8	.	1	1	1	.	17	.	.
	MDBW	2	54	1,2[b]	6,13[c]	6	5,	.	.	.	14	.	.	.	5	.	.	18	.	.
	Witch	1	84	2,	7,5	10	10,	.	.	.	18	.	.	.	5	.	.	22	.	.
	Heng.	1	86	,1	,15	15	6,5	.	.	.	17	.	.	.	8	.	.	28	.	.
	WBW	2	116	,3	2,33	17	9,	.	.	.	23	.	.	.	10	.	.	33	.	.
	GC	.	44	3,	5,5	4	5,	.	.	.	5	.	3	.	.	.	.	18	.	.
	Widow	5	77	2,1	9,23	12	25,	4	.	7	18	1	.	.	10	.	.	26	.	.
X Plays	SMT	.	78	4,	3,14	6	7,1	.	.	.	2	.	.	.	1	.	.	22[d]	.	.
	WSW	.	93	1,	12,6	1	2,	1	1	9	16	3	2	3	.	.	.	28	.	.
	NV	1	60	1,1	1,14	4	2,9	.	.	3	12	.	.	.	10	1	.	26	.	.
Goffe	C.T.	4	32	2,	.	.	.	.	.	.	9	.	.	.	8	.	.	.	.	.
	Ores.	.	45	2,	.	.	.	.	.	.	12	.	4	.	5	.	.	4	.	.
	R.T.	.	58	3,	1,3	2	1,	.	.	.	.	.	.	.	.	.	.	.	.	.
Beaumont	KBP	8	41	.	7,	.	1,	.	.	1	8	.	3	.	2	.	.	6	.	.
Fletcher	W.Pr.	1	54	.	1,7	.	.	.	.	.	20	.	.	.	19	1	.	14	.	.
>1618	Bon.	.	69	1,	,2	1	2,	.	.	.	14	.	.	.	10	.	.	6	.	.
	Valen.	.	63	.	,3	.	.	.	.	.	12	.	.	.	8	.	.	11	.	.
	M.Thom.	.	65	.	1,2	.	.	.	.	1	9	.	.	.	6	.	.	8	.	.
	ML	.	80	.	1,4	.	.	.	.	.	14	1	2	.	5	.	.	8	.	.
	Chan.	.	88	.	,1	1	1,	.	.	.	12	.	.	.	4	1	.	10	.	.
	L.Sub.	.	86	.	,1	.	2,	.	.	.	13	.	.	.	10	.	.	11	.	.
Massinger	D.M.	.	62	.	,2	.	.	.	.	.	.	1	.	.	.	.	.	1	3	.
	Bond.	.	65	.	.	.	.	.	.	.	.	.	.	1	.	.	.	5	.	.
	PL	.	75	.	.	.	.	.	.	.	.	.	.	.	.	.	.	2	1	.
	R.A.	.	67	.	.	.	.	.	.	.	.	2	.	.	.	.	.	.	1	.
	Pict.	.	43	.	.	.	.	.	.	.	5	3	.	.	.	.	.	5	4	.
	Ren.	.	56	.	.	.	.	.	.	.	.	.	.	.	.	.	.	1	2	.
	Bel.	.	46	.	.	.	.	.	.	.	.	1	.	.	.	.	.	2	.	.
Shakespeare	Cor.	3	52	.	,5	.	.	.	.	.	42	.	29	.	16	.	.	7	.	.
	Temp.	.	18	.	1,	.	.	.	.	.	16	.	.	.	21	1	.	8	.	.
X Play	AQL	.	67	.	3,6	.	.	.	.	1	22	.	2	.	5	.	.	6	2	.
Webster	WD	.	55	1,	8,	.	5,	.	.	.	32	.	7	1	11	.	.	12	4	.
	DM	1	54	.	1,	.	,1	.	.	.	31	.	.	.	19	1	.	12	3	.
	DLC	.	65	.	,4	1	1,	.	.	.	46	.	11	.	11	.	.	9	6	.

Occurrences: [a] all times as y're. [b] Once as w're. [c] Once as y're. [d] Once as an't.

/Prefixes

	woult	wou't	wou'd	-cst	(')hem	(')am	(')um	em,'m	'em,'m	e'm	(')has	h'as	ha's	doe(')s	do(')s	otherwise	Total, group sp.	All:	Omnes:	l. Gent. (etc.)	Gent. l. (etc.)
							Spellings of 'em				[of has]			[of does]							
AT		3							18		45	3		16			7	2			
RT	1			5				5	21	12	38	3	4	5	23		2	1		+	
Phoen.						1[a]		1	20	16	23		23	3	15		5	3		+	
MT						1		3	14	28	27	1	15	10	12		2	2		+	
MWM			1					20	8	38	42	4	8		17		3	1			
Trick				3				4	4	28	39		5		7		4	3			+[b]
YFG				3				38	20	1	42	2		6	6		10	9		+	
NWNH									40		50	7		23	1		15	6		+	
CMC								1	16		30	5		6	2	1	10	7		+	
MDBW									36		51	1		6	6		5	3		+	
Witch									35		28	4	3		6					+	
Heng.								52	10		41	1		9	1		10	8	1	+	
WBW									43		54	10		16	4		3		1	+	
GC				12				4	2	31	10	5	25		8					+	
Widow									62		45	9[c]			8		2			+	
SMT				4				35			43	1		17			4	4		+	
WSW			1				7	1	42		63			20	2		2			+	
NV									29		36	2	1	13			2		1	+	
C.T.											1	1			1		3	2		+	
Dres.									5		1			2	2		2		1	+	
R.T.											2	2	6				23	1	10		+[d]
KBP			1		1[e]	2		1	9		21			4			1	1		+	
W.Pr.									66		37	4	1	3	13					+	
Bon.									95		29	9		13			3			+	
Valen.									71		37	5	6	2	5		3	1		+	
M.Thom.									27		41	1	1	1	25		7			+	
IL		1	17						25		24	2		27	3		1			+	
Chan.									43	1	41	3	1	3	2		1			+	
G. Sub.			1						133		63	3		6	4		4	2		+	
O.M.									12		8			7	6		2	1		+	
Bond.								2	13		19			13			5	2			
PL								6[f]		1	17			8			5		1	+	
R.A.									14		3		1	18	1		2	2		+	
Pict.								1	51		12			10			1		1	+	
Ren.									10		15			11	1			1		+	
Bel.							16	10						10			1			+	
Cor.				1				4	11		7		28	13	6		52	34	2	+	
Temp.								1	15	1[g]	4		3	2	13		1				
QL									16		45	1	1	14			3		2	+	
WD											1	2		1			5	2			
M									3		1	1	1		1		8			+	
LC			1								81			14			2			+	

Occurrences: [a] As a'm. [b] One instance only. [c] Once as 'as. [d] 5 instances. [e] As 'ham. [f] Once as e [following letter illegible]. [g] As em'.

Band 2(h)

Table I.1

Band 2   Segment 3

Selected words and collocations

| Group | Play | Length (words) | / Middletonisms | | | comfort | fetch..again | give..due | 'Has = he has | Inn a Court + Noun | Inns a Court + Noun | "Italian' joke | la(w) you | la(w) you now | lin | love alife |
			by..copy	can possible	Chaucer											
Tourneur	AT	22122*	.	.	.	2	.	.	3	.	.	1	.	.	.	
X Play	RT	21268*	.	.	.	17	.	4	7	.	.	.	1	1	.	
Middle-ton >1608	Phoen.	20840*	1	1	.	7	.	1	12	.	.	.	.	.	.	
	MT	20570*	.	.	.	11	1	1	4	.	1	.	3	3	.	
	MWM	19098*	.	.	.	8	.	1	5	1	1	.	1	.	.	
	Trick	19268*	1	.	.	15	.	1	4	.	.	.	1	1	.	
	YFG	21878*	.	1	.	8	1	1	5	.	.	.	.	.	1	
1610<	NWNH	27703*	1	.	1	18	.	.	4	.	.	.	3	.	.	
	CMC	18489*	.	.	.	5	.	.	5	.	.	.	.	.	1	
	MDBW	20052*	.	.	1	9	.	.	4	.	1	.	2	.	1	
	Witch	16862*	.	.	.	13	.	.	4	.	.	.	.	.	.	
	Heng.	22037*	.	.	.	7	.	.	3	.	.	.	.	.	1	
	WBW	26162*	1	.	.	19	.	.	9	.	.	.	.	.	.	
	GC	19342*	.	.	.	3	.	.	6	.	1	.	.	.	.	
	Widow	20315*	.	.	.	17	1	.	9	.	1	.	1	.	1	
X Plays	SMT	20014*	.	1	.	7	.	.	9	.	.	.	.	.	.	
	WSW	21596	.	.	.	4	.	.	4	.	.	.	2	.	.	
	NV	14664	.	.	.	6	1	.	11	.	2	.	.	.	.	
Goffe	C.T.	14794	.	.	.	3	.	.	.	.	.	.	.	.	.	
	Ores.	20142	.	.	.	8	.	.	.	.	.	.	.	.	.	
	R.T.	27150	.	.	.	.	.	.	2	.	.	.	.	.	.	
Beaumont	KBP	21423	.	.	.	3	.	.	1	.	.	.	.	.	.	
Fletcher >1618	W.Pr.	24472*	.	.	.	12	.	.	5	.	.	.	.	.	.	
	Bon.	21049	.	.	.	7	.	.	11	.	.	.	.	.	.	
	Valen.	25783	.	.	.	5	.	.	4	.	.	.	.	.	.	
	M.Thom.	18754	.	.	.	8	.	.	2	.	.	.	.	.	.	
	ML	18964	.	.	.	.	.	.	7	.	.	.	.	.	.	
	Chan.	19060	.	.	.	6	.	.	9	.	.	.	.	.	.	
	L.Sub.	21392	.	.	.	8	.	.	2	.	.	.	.	.	.	
Mass-inger	D.M.	21586	.	.	.	6	.	.	.	.	.	.	.	.	.	
	Bond.	20937	.	.	.	13	.	.	.	.	.	.	.	.	.	
	PL	17129	.	.	.	10	.	.	.	.	.	.	.	.	.	
	R.A.	18932	.	.	.	3	.	.	.	.	.	.	.	.	.	
	Pict.	22588	.	.	.	5	.	.	.	.	.	.	.	.	.	
	Ren.	20444	1	.	.	9	.	.	.	.	.	.	.	.	.	
	Bel.	19200	.	.	.	4	.	.	.	.	.	.	.	.	.	
Shake-speare	Cor.	28547*	.	.	.	5	.	.	3	.	.	.	.	.	.	
	Temp.	17670	.	.	.	9	.	.	.	.	.	.	.	.	.	
X Play	AQL	20677	.	.	.	4	.	.	3	.	.	.	.	.	.	
Webster	WD	26285*	.	.	.	5	.	.	2	.	.	.	2	.	.	
	DM	24790	.	.	.	12	.	.	1	.	.	.	.	.	.	
	DLC	24006	.	.	.	8	.	.	.	.	.	.	1	.	.	

	[adv.] -ly welcome	mass, here	I (do) protest	sasarara	save..harmless	son and heir	spoke like	subaudi	suspectless	third part of	troth..say true	tut, man	Adam/Eve	garlic/strong	godamercy	hair..an end	lily..hands	make buttons	marry muff
AT	1	.	1	.	.	.	.	.	.	.	.	.	.	.	.	1[b]	.	.	.
RT	.	2	2	1	.	3	.	.	.	1	2	.	.	.	.	.	.	.	.
Phoen.	6	1	6	3	.	.	.	.	.	.	.	.	.	.	.	.	.	.	.
MT	2	.	4	.	1	6	.	.	.	.	.	.	.	.	.	.	.	.	.
MWM	3	.	4	.	.	1	.	.	.	.	.	1	.	.	.	.	.	.	.
Trick	.	.	4	.	1	.	1	.	.	.	.	.	.	.	.	.	.	.	.
YFG	4	.	4	.	.	.	.	1	3	1	.	1	.	.	.	.	.	.	.
NWNH	1	2	2	.	1	1	3	.	.	3	2	.	.	.	.	.	.	.	.
CMC	.	.	4	.	.	.	.	.	.	.	.	.	.	.	.	.	.	.	.
MDBW	.	.	.	.	.	1	1	.	.	2	1	.	.	.	.	.	.	.	.
Witch	1	.	2	.	.	.	.	.	.	.	.	.	.	.	.	.	.	.	.
Heng.	.	.	.	.	.	.	.	.	.	.	.	.	.	.	.	.	.	.	.
WBW	.	1	1	.	.	.	.	.	.	1	.	.	.	.	.	.	.	.	.
GC	.	.	.	.	.	1	1	.	.	.	.	.	.	.	.	.	.	.	.
Widow	.	2	5	.	.	.	.	.	.	.	.	.	.	.	.	.	.	.	.
SMT	1	1	1	.	.	1	.	.	.	1	.	.	.	.	.	.	.	.	.
WSW	1	.	5	.	.	1	.	.	.	.	.	.	.	.	.	.	.	.	.
NV	1	.	.	.	.	.	.	.	.	.	.	.	.	.	.	.	.	.	.
C.T.	.	.	.	.	.	.	.	.	.	.	.	.	.	.	.	.	.	.	.
Ores.	.	.	.	.	.	.	2	.	.	.	.	.	.	.	.	.	.	.	.
R.T.	.	.	.	.	.	.	.	.	.	.	.	.	.	.	.	.	.	.	.
KBP	.	.	.	.	.	.	.	.	.	.	.	.	.	.	.	.	.	.	.
W.Pr.	.	.	1	.	.	.	.	.	.	.	.	.	.	.	.	.	.	.	.
Bon.	.	.	.	.	.	.	.	.	.	.	.	.	.	.	.	.	.	.	.
Valen.	1	.	.	.	.	.	.	.	.	.	.	.	.	.	.	.	.	.	.
M.Thom.	1	.	1	.	.	.	.	.	.	.	.	.	.	.	.	.	.	.	.
ML	.	.	.	.	.	.	.	.	.	.	.	.	.	.	3	.	.	.	.
Chan.	.	.	.	.	.	.	.	.	.	.	.	.	.	.	.	.	.	.	.
L.Sub.	2	.	.	.	.	.	.	.	.	.	.	.	.	.	2	.	.	.	.
D.M.	.	.	.	.	.	.	.	.	.	.	.	.	.	.	.	.	.	.	.
Bond.	.	.	.	.	.	.	.	.	.	.	.	.	.	.	.	.	.	.	.
PL	.	.	.	.	.	.	.	.	.	.	.	.	.	.	.	.	.	.	.
R.A.	.	.	.	.	.	.	1[a]	.	.	.	.	.	.	.	.	.	.	.	.
Pict.	.	.	.	.	.	.	.	.	.	.	.	.	.	.	.	.	.	.	.
Ren.	.	.	.	.	.	.	.	.	.	.	.	.	.	.	.	.	.	.	.
Bel.	.	.	.	.	.	.	.	.	.	.	.	.	.	.	.	.	.	.	.
Cor.	.	.	.	.	.	1	.	.	.	.	.	.	.	.	.	.	.	.	.
Temp.	.	.	.	.	.	.	.	.	.	.	.	.	.	.	.	.	.	.	.
AQL	.	.	4	.	.	1	.	.	.	.	.	.	.	.	2	.	.	.	.
WD	2	.	4	.	.	.	.	.	.	.	.	.	.	.	.	.	.	.	.
DM	.	.	.	.	.	.	.	.	.	.	.	.	.	.	.	.	.	.	.
DLC	1	.	10	.	.	.	.	.	.	.	.	.	.	.	.	.	.	.	.

Occurrences: [a] As Spoken like.   [b] As haire stand almost on end.

		moon/horn(s)	mumble-crust	no point	oyster/open	parrot =[woman]	puss-cat	rowly-powly	Signior no	snick up	snip snap	stile/style pun	Tamburlaine	wink at small faults	deed la	float of	forfeit of	'Tis Oracle	undertake a voluntary exile
Tourneur	AT																	1	
X Play	RT																	1	
Middleton	Phoen.																		
	MT																		
	MWM																		
>1608	Trick																		
	YFG																		–
1610<	NWNH																		
	CMC																		
	MDBW																		
	Witch																		
	Heng.																1		
	WBW																		
	GC																		
	Widow																		
X Plays	SMT																		
	WSW																		
	NV																		
Goffe	C.T.																		
	Ores.																		
	R.T.																		
Beaumont	KBP									2									
Fletcher	W.Pr													1					
>1618	Bon.																		
	Valen.																	1	
	M.Thom.			2															
	ML																		
	Chan.				1														
	L.Sub.																		
Massinger	D.M.																		
	Bond.																		
	PL																		
	R.A.																		
	Pict.																		
	Ren.																		
	Bel.																		
Shakespeare	Cor.	1																	
	Temp.																		
X Play	AQL										3[d]								
Webster	WD																		
	DM																		
	DLC																		

Occurrences: [a]Once as Snip-snapper.

Table I.1   Segment 1   Band 3(a)

Band 3   /Exclamations

			push	pish	puh	pah	pew	p-, other	phew	tut	tush	t-, other	hum(h)	um(h)	h(e/o)! yda(y)	why
Chapman	HDM	17210	.	.	.	.	.	.	.	1	1	.	.	.	.	75
	GU	21995	1	.	.	.	.	.	.	.	.	.	.	.	.	33
	AF	19108	.	.	.	.	.	.	.	.	4	.	1	.	.	20
	MD	23568*	.	.	.	.	.	1a	.	.	1	.	.	.	.	36
	Mons.	16636	.	.	.	.	.	.	.	.	8	.	.	.	.	19
	WT	23179	.	.	.	.	.	.	.	.	6	.	.	.	.	7
Marston	AM	14330	.	5	.	.	2b	2c	.	1	1	.	.	1	.	14
	AR	16369	.	5	.	.	.	.	.	3	3	.	.	7	.	20
	JD	17414	.	2	.	.	.	.	.	4	4	1d	.	.	.	27
	WYW	17145	.	5	1	.	1	1	.	4	1	1e	.	.	.	34
	Malc.	18571	.	2	.	.	3	.	1	2	1	.	.	2	.	46
	DC	19049	.	3	.	3	.	1c	.	.	.	.	.	.	.	28
	Fawn	22717	.	5	.	.	.	.	.	.	1	.	.	1	.	44
	Soph.	16653	.	1	.	.	.	.	.	.	1	.	.	2	.	5
X Play	Pur.	19922*	3	1	9	2	.	1	.	3	.	1f	2	.	.	66
Jonson	CA	20058	.	.	1	.	.	.	.	12	1	.	.	.	.	48
	EMI	25664	.	2	.	.	.	.	.	13	.	.	.	.	1	74
	EMO	38248	.	2	1	.	.	.	.	15	2	.	7	.	1	92
	CR	33145	.	.	.	.	.	.	.	8	.	.	.	.	4	35
	Poet.	28727	.	2	.	.	.	.	.	7	.	.	.	.	.	23
	Volp.	28790	.	.	1	.	.	.	.	3	.	.	3	.	.	35
	Epic.	29066	.	.	.	.	.	.	.	5	.	.	.	6	.	50
	Alch.	28537	.	.	.	.	.	.	.	2	.	.	2	1	.	45
	BF	36411	.	.	.	.	.	.	.	1	.	.	3	.	2	58
	DA	28584	.	.	.	.	.	.	.	1	.	.	.	.	.	37
	SN	26688	.	.	.	.	.	.	.	5	.	.	.	.	.	29
	Widow	20315*	.	9	1	.	.	.	.	.	.	.	2	.	.	53
Fletcher	W.Pr.	24472*	.	.	.	.	.	.	.	.	.	.	.	.	.	26
	Bon.	21049	.	.	.	.	.	2	.	.	.	.	.	.	.	18
	Valen.	25783	.	.	.	.	.	.	.	.	.	.	.	.	.	15
	M.Thom.	18754	.	.	.	.	.	.	.	.	.	.	2	.	.	17
	ML	18964	.	1	.	.	.	.	.	.	.	.	1	.	.	34
>1618	Chan.	19060	.	.	.	.	.	.	.	.	.	.	.	.	.	19
	L.Sub.	21392	.	.	.	.	.	.	.	.	.	.	.	.	.	14
1619 <	HL	21789	.	.	.	.	.	.	.	.	.	.	.	.	.	16
	IP	20746	.	.	.	.	.	.	.	.	.	.	.	.	.	9
	Pilg.	20937	.	.	.	.	.	.	.	.	.	.	.	.	.	5
	WGC	22851	.	.	.	.	.	.	.	.	.	.	1	.	.	15
	W.Pl.	20421	.	.	.	.	.	.	.	.	.	.	.	.	.	6
	RW	17641	.	.	.	.	.	.	.	.	.	.	1	.	.	17
	WM	20227	.	.	.	.	.	.	.	.	.	.	.	.	.	8

* Fully counted.   Occurrences: [a]Once as ptrough   (cf. one instance of phtroh).

[b]Once as Pew waw.   [c]As Paugh (all instances).   [d]As toh.   [e]As tit.

[f]As tuh.

Author	Play	Jesu(s)	Lord('s)	God's	God	Heaven(')(s)	Cud(')s, Coad(')s	'snigs	'sfoot	foot	'slid	'slud	'sblood	'swounds, 'z-	'sheart	heart	'sdeath	death	'slife, life	'slight, light
Chapman	HDM	1	5	12	3	5	.	.	.	.	.	.	6	.	.	.	.	.	.	.
	GU	.	6	22[a]	6	13	.	.	.	.	.	1	5	5	9	.	.	.	.	.
	AF	1	1	5	3	16	.	.	9	8	.	.	.	.	1	.	.	.	.	3,
	MD	.	9	19	4	9	.	.	18	.	.	.	12	9	2	.	1	.	4,	9,
	Mons.	.	1	4	1	16	.	.	9	.	.	.	.	.	1	.	.	.	.	11,
	WT	.	.	3	.	9	.	.	3	.	.	.	.	.	.	.	.	.	.	10,
Marston	AM	2	2	5	2	9	.	.	1	3	5	2	.	.	.	.	.	.	.	1,
	AR	1	3	8	3	9	.	1[b]	1	3	2	.	.	.	.	.	.	.	1	.
	JD	5	3	5	10	9	.	.	.	.	.	.	.	.	12	.	2	.	.	.
	WYW	7	5	8[c]	6	5	.	.	7[d]	2	2	.	.	.	.	.	.	.	1	1,
	Malc.	.	3	4	15	10	.	.	.	.	.	.	.	.	.	2	.	4	,2	.
	DC	.	24	8	6	9	.	.	.	.	.	.	.	.	4	.	1	2	1	.
	Fawn	1	5	4	1	12	.	.	.	.	.	.	.	.	.	.	.	.	.	.
	Soph.	.	1	.	1	.	.	.	.	.	.	.	.	.	.	.	.	.	.	.
X Play	Pur.	.	.	.	1	.	,1	.	15	.	4	.	1	1	.	.	.	.	.	.
Jonson	CA	3	5	27	8	4	.	.	.	.	.	2	.	17	3	1	.	.	.	.
	EMI	1	4	17[e]	1	9	.	.	1	.	13	1	.	.	.	6	2	2	.	6,
	EMO	.	16	25	22	18	.	.	.	.	14	6	12	1	6	5	2	2	3[f],	7,
	CR	.	3	11	4	10	.	.	3	.	11	7	.	.	4	7	.	4	.	13,
	Poet.	.	.	6	1	3	.	.	.	.	.	1	.	.	.	5	.	4	.	3,
	Volp.	.	5	3	2	3	.	.	.	.	.	.	.	.	.	4	1	2	.	1,
	Epic.	.	4	12	10	2	.	.	1	.	1	.	.	.	.	1	.	.	.	7,
	Alch.	.	.	11	3	4	.	.	.	.	9	1	.	.	.	5	4	1	.	21,
	BF	.	8	7	4	.	.	.	.	.	11	3	3	.	.	5	.	2	.	6,
	DA	.	.	1	.	2	.	.	.	.	4	.	.	.	.	.	1	2	.	5,1
	SN	.	.	2	.	.	.	.	.	.	1	.	.	.	.	.	.	.	.	.
	Widow	.	.	.	.	.	.	.	.	.	.	.	.	.	.	1	.	.	,7	1,
Fletcher	W.Pr.	.	1	1	1	2	.	.	1	.	.	.	.	.	.	.	.	.	.	.
	Bon.	.	.	.	.	6	.	.	.	.	.	.	.	.	.	.	2	.	.	.
	Valen.	.	.	.	.	11	.	.	.	.	.	.	.	.	.	.	.	.	.	.
	M.Thom.	.	1	3[g]	1	10	.	.	.	.	.	.	.	.	.	.	.	.	.	.
	ML	.	1	1	.	12	.	.	.	.	.	.	.	.	.	.	.	4	.	.
>1618	Chan.	.	.	.	.	13	.	.	.	.	.	.	1	.	.	.	1	.	.	.
	L.Sub.	.	4	.	.	7	.	.	.	.	.	.	.	.	.	.	.	.	.	.
1619<	HL	.	6	.	1	9	.	.	.	.	.	.	.	.	.	.	.	3	,1	.
	IP	.	2	1	.	1	.	.	.	.	.	.	.	.	.	.	.	1	.	.
	Pilg.	.	3	.	2	1	.	.	.	.	.	.	.	.	.	.	.	.	.	.
	WGC	.	2	.	.	.	.	.	1	.	.	.	.	.	.	.	.	1	.	.
	W.Pl.	.	1	1	.	9	.	.	.	.	.	.	.	.	.	.	.	.	.	.
	RW	.	.	.	.	1	.	.	.	.	.	.	.	.	.	.	.	.	.	.
	WM	.	2	.	.	3	.	.	.	.	.	.	.	.	.	.	.	.	.	.

Occurrences: [a] Once as gosh hat. [b] As S'neaks. [c] Once as gunds fut. [d] 7 times as vds fut. [e] Once as by gads lid. [f] Once as 'ds life. [g] Once as Gogs bores.

	'(s)nails	'(s)precious	'Od's	('Ud)'s, other	f($\frac{a}{e}$)ck(s)	faith	troth	marry	mass	byrlady	my reputation	hold my life
HDM	.	.	.	.	.	31	5	13	2	3	.	.
GU	.	.	.	.	.	32	1	3	1	.	.	.
AF	.	.	.	.	.	16	1	7	5	5	.	.
MD	.	.	.	.	.	47	5	15	4	5	.	1
Mons.	.	.	.	2	.	29	1	10	.	.	.	.
WT	.	.	.	.	.	14	.	2	.	2	.	.
AM	.	3	.	1	.	47	14	3	.	1	.	.
AR	.	.	.	.	.	14	1	4	.	.	.	.
JD	.	.	.	.	.	39	16	3	.	1	.	.
WYW	.	1	.	4	.	31	14	9	2	2	.	.
Malc.	.	.	.	.	.	22	8	13	1	2	.	.
DC	.	.	.	.	.	43	13	9	2	1	.	.
Fawn	.	.	.	.	.	20	5	5	.	.	.	.
Soph.	.	.	.	.	.	.	.	.	.	.	.	.
Pur.	.	.	.	.	.	39	24	7	10	1	.	.
CA	.	.	.	1	.	37	5	16	6	1	.	.
EMI	.	.	1	6	1[a]	47	9	29	7[b]	.	5	.
EMO	.	.	4	2	.	90	22	48	10	1	.	.
CR	.	.	.	.	.	30	16	21	.	.	.	1
Poet.	.	1	.	1	.	26	14	11	.	.	.	1
Volp.	.	.	.	.	.	24	6	9	.	.	.	.
Epic	.	.	.	.	.	52	7	8	1	.	.	1
Alch.	.	.	3	.	1	32	12	4	.	.	.	.
BF	.	1	1	.	.	61	9	7	.	.	.	.
DA	.	.	.	.	.	16	4	3	.	.	.	.
SN	.	.	.	.	.	11	6	2	.	1	.	.
Widow	.	.	1[c]	.	.	41	14	11	4	6	.	1
W.Pr.	.	.	.	.	.	2	2	6	.	4	.	.
Bon.	.	.	.	.	.	2	.	1	.	.	.	.
Valen.	.	.	.	.	.	2	2	.	1	.	.	.
M.Thom.	.	1	.	.	.	9	3	4	5	2	.	.
ML	.	.	.	.	.	3	2	2	1	.	.	.
Chan.	.	.	1	.	.	1	1	3	2	.	.	.
L.Sub.	.	.	.	.	.	6	3	2	2	1	.	.
HL	.	.	1	.	.	8	2	2	.	1	.	.
IP	.	.	.	.	.	5	2	6	1	1	.	.
Pilg.	.	.	.	.	.	2	1	.	.	.	.	.
WGC	.	.	2	.	.	17	7	2	.	1	.	.
W.Pl.	.	1	1	.	.	5	1	3	2	.	.	.
RW	.	.	.	.	.	2	1	1	.	.	.	.
WM	.	.	.	.	.	3	.	2	.	.	.	.

Occurrences: [a]As by my fackins. [b]Once as mack. [c]As 'odds' light (which is not found elsewhere in the plays here tabulated).

Table I.1

Band 3   Segment 2

		Length (words)	ay	yes	among	amongst	beside adv./prep.	besides adv./prep.	between	betwixt	toward	towards	while	whil(e)st	whiles
			/Affirm-atives/						Connectives						/
Chapman	HDM	17210	.	.	.	3	.	3,	4	2	.	.	4	.	.
	GU	21995	22	10	1	2	2,	3,1	.	12	2	1	4	.	.
	AF	19108	16	4	.	10	.	4,4	.	11	.	1	5	.	.
	MD	23568*	8	6	1	7	.	3,3	.	8	.	.	16	1	.
	Mons.	16636	9	5	.	7	.	3,4	.	6	1	.	4	.	1
	WT	23179	19	8	.	7	.	6,1	.	7	.	1	8	.	.
Marston	AM	14330	15	6	1	.	.	.	.	1	.	1	1	13	.
	AR	16369	14	11	3	.	.	.	.	6	.	.	1	14	.
	JD	17414	33	6	2	.	.	.	.	1	.	.	.	7	.
	WYW	17145	28	6	4	.	.	.	.	6	.	1	.	9	.
	Malc.	18571	29	17	3	5	,1	2,	.	3	.	.	1	16	.
	DC	19049	22	15	.	.	.	1,	.	5	.	.	1	6	.
	Fawn	22717	15	21	2	.	,1	1,	.	2	.	.	.	6	1
	Soph.	16653	7	4	4	1	.	.	.	2	3	.	1	16	.
X Play	Pur.	19922*	58	9	6	3	3,2	3,	8	1	2	.	1	1	.
Jonson	CA	20058	49	2	1	1	.	.	3	4	1	.	3	2	.
	EMI	25664	50	31	1	3	2,1	,2	4	3	2	1	13	1	.
	EMO	38248	92	21	7	11	.	8,2	14	3	3	1	8	3	.
	CR	33145	48	36	6	5	1,1	9,4	6	5	.	1	4	1	.
	Poet.	28727	56	33	3	3	.	,1 7,	4	3	1	1	9	11	.
	Volp.	28790	32	39	2	5	3,1	6,2	.	3	5	.	4	8	.
	Epic.	29066	55	58	6	.	4,2	6,2	10	2	3	1	11	.	.
	Alch.	28537	50	95	1	1	7,6	1,	2	1	5	1	4	.	.
	BF	36411	42	62	4	4	4,	,1	16	1	7	.	6	1	.
	DA	28584	12	63	.	2	.	1,	3	2	5	.	8	.	.
	SN	26688	25	27	3	3	1,1	4,	3	3	.	.	9	.	.
	Widow	20315*	37	7	3	3	.	.	7	4	.	.	7	.	.
Fletcher	W.Pr.	24472*	5	60	3	3	,3	,1	2	1	.	.	5	.	.
	Bon.	21049	3	13	2	3	,2	2,3	1	2	1	.	1	2	.
	Valen.	25783	3	29	1	.	1,1	5,3	.	2	.	.	4	5	.
	M.Thom.	18754	6	14	6	.	,2	2,2	1	.	.	.	1	1	.
	ML	18964	4	27	4	3	1,1	2,1	3	.	1	.	2	1	.
>1618	Chan.	19060	10	22	3	7	,2	,1	2	1	.	1	1	6	.
	L.Sub.	21392	9	24	1	3	,1	1,	3	.	1	1	1	9	.
1619<	HL	21789	14	23	2	1	1,	1,1	1	.	1	.	2	6	.
	IP	20746	6	20	2	5	.	.	2	2	1	.	1	1	.
	Pilg.	20937	11	22	3	1	1,	2,	.	1	.	.	5	.	.
	WGC	22851	5	49	.	4	,1	4,1	1	.	.	.	.	2	.
	W.Pl.	20421	3	17	3	1	,2	1,2	2	.	.	.	.	4	.
	RW	17641	3	25	1	7	.	3,	1	1	1	1	1	.	.
	WM	20227	6	15	3	3	1,	4,	3	2	1	1	1	5	.

	/Pronouns						/Verbs					/Pronoun + verb contractions							
	ye	'ee	'a = [he]	's = [his]	'em	them	has	hath	does	doth	ha'	I'd	I'm	I am	I've	thou'rt / th'art	sh'as, sh'ad	'tas, 'tad	'thas, 'thad
HDM	1	.	.	.	.	44	.	52	.	22	.	.	.	45	.	.	.	.	.
GU	3	15	1	.	4	30	15	17	16	1	.	3	.	32	.	.	1,	.	.
AF	13	.	.	2	19	46	23	32	6	8	.	2	.	35	.	.	,2	.	1
MD	8	15	1	5	47	19	30	15	20	1	3	4	1	38	.	.	,11	1	.
Mons.	3	1	.	7	20	39	15	25	11	8	.	2	.	30	.	.	,1	.	1
WT	18	.	.	14	1	43	27	51	13	7	.	1	.	31	.	.	,2	.	1
AM	7	.	1	.	.	24	.	30	1	9	8	.	.	30	.	.	,1	,1	1
AR	9	.	1	2	.	15	3	26	2	15	6	.	.	29	.	.	.	.	.
JD	6	.	1	1	.	15	.	34	.	12	7	.	.	29	.	.	.	.	.
WYW	7	.	.	.	.	29	12	24	5	10	20	.	.	44	.	.	.	.	1
Malc.	63	.	2	.	7	25	16	23	10	17	23	.	.	43	.	.	.	.	.
DC	19	.	.	2	1	23	34	19	17	9	27	.	.	51	.	.	.	.	.
Fawn	16	.	1	2	1	45	44	38	21	8	45	.	.	53	.	.	,3	.	.
Soph.	12	.	.	2	.	13	2	38	2	6	1	.	.	13	.	.	,3	.	.
Pur.	1	.	.	1	41	12	47	2	8	.	18	10	11	28	.	2,1	2[a],	5	.
CA	2	.	.	1	7	48	17	24	8	17	7	1	.	52	.	.	.	.	.
EMI	1	.	1	2	60	48	35	15	10	9	48	8	.	81	.	.	.	.	.
EMO	1	.	.	.	67	48	75	31	36	20	43	10	.	90	.	.	.	.	.
CR	1	.	.	.	42	66	39	53	23	24	8	4	.	64	.	.	.	.	.
Poet.	3	.	2	.	50	69	21	33	14	23	24	1	3	59	.	1,2	.	.	.
Volp.	.	.	.	1	53	33	47	36	18	17	32	6	2	55	.	.	.	.	.
Epic.	2	.	.	1	110	27	85	13	19	7	36	1	.	41	.	.	.	.	.
Alch.	3	.	.	7	50	19	59	19	28	13	89	4	.	44	.	.	,2	1[b]	.
BF	6	.	.	2	[111]	[19]	69	19	38	16	[137]	5	.	111	.	.	,1	.	.
DA	.	.	.	4	[85]	[15]	60	21	20	7	[100]	4	2	63	.	.	,1	.	1
SN	.	.	.	.	[53]	[46]	67	24	15	15	[65]	4	3	49	.	.	.	.	2
Widow	3	.	.	10	63	6	54	.	8	.	26	12	62	24	23	7,	4,	3	5
W.Pr.	84	.	.	6	66	6	42	4	16	1	.	1	.	99	.	.	.	.	1
Bon.	[352]	.	4	6	95	6	38	1	13	.	.	1	1	49	.	.	.	.	.
Valen.	[412]	.	2	2	71	15	48	4	7	.	.	.	.	93	.	,1	.	.	1
M.Thom.	[343]	.	.	4	27	2	43	6	26	.	1	.	1	67	.	.	.	.	1
ML	[308]	.	15	3	25	4	26	6	30	.	2	.	.	51	.	.	.	.	.
Chan.	[290]	.	4	2	44	6	45	2	5	.	.	.	6	60	.	.	.	.	4
L.Sub.	[424]	.	.	3	133	13	66	3	10	.	2	.	2	64	.	.	.	.	1
HL	[367]	.	2	7	80	5	65	5	14	.	.	.	.	89	.	.	.	.	1
IP	[258]	.	1	[1]	[64]	x	x	[.]	x	[.]	.	1	4	88	.	.	.	.	.
Pilg.	[400]	.	.	[7]	[62]	x	x	[3]	x	[.]	.	.	.	71	.	.	.	.	1
WGC	[543]	.	.	[1]	[61]	x	x	[1]	x	[.]	.	1	1	111	.	.	.	.	2
W.Pl	[288]	.	.	[6]	[23]	x	x	[3]	x	[.]	.	.	.	82	.	.	.	.	2
RW	[213]	.	.	[4]	35	x	x	[2]	x	[.]	.	.	2	106	.	.	.	2	.
WM	[176]	.	.	[6]	[41]	x	x	[.]	x	[.]	.	1	.	77	.	.	.	.	3

Occurrences: [a] Once as she'as. [b] As sh'has.

Band 3(f)

/ Other contractions

		it's	'tis	we're, w'are	you're, y'are	y'(h)ave	they're, th'are	le'me	gi'n't	i'	i'th'	i'the	a'th'	a'the	o'th'	o'the	vpo'th'	on't	of't	ex'lent
Chapman	HDM	.	34	.	.	.	.	.	.	.	.	.	.	.	.	.	.	.	.	.
	GU	.	58	.	,11	2	.	.	.	.	1	.	1	.	.	.	.	.	5	.	.
	AF	2	31	.	,15	1	.	.	.	.	1	.	2	1	.	.	.	.	2	.	.
	MD	2	42	.	,18	2	.	.	.	.	7	.	5	1	1	.	.	.	9[a]	.	.
	Mons.	5	37	.	,3	1	.	.	.	.	10	.	7	1	.	.	.	.	3[b]	.	.
	WT	5	45	.	,16	1	.	.	.	.	4	.	8	1	1	.	.	.	10[c]	.	.
Marston	AM	.	41	.	.	.	.	.	.	.	.	.	.	.	.	.	.	.	3	.	.
	AR	.	40	.	.	.	.	.	.	.	.	.	.	.	.	.	.	.	4	.	.
	JD	.	40	.	.	.	.	.	.	.	.	.	.	.	.	.	.	.	2	.	.
	WYW	.	52	.	.	.	.	.	.	.	.	.	.	.	.	.	.	.	3	.	.
	Malc.	.	52	.	.	.	.	.	.	.	4	2	.	.	.	.	.	.	2	.	.
	DC	1	65	.	2,3	.	.	.	.	.	1	1	.	7	.	.	.	.	6	1	.
	Fawn	.	62	.	.	.	.	.	.	.	.	.	.	.	.	.	.	.	6[a]	.	.
	Soph.	.	25	.	.	.	,1	.	.	.	.	.	.	.	.	.	.	.	.	.	.
X Play	Pur.	.	50	1,	5,10	.	6,	.	.	.	15	1	9	2	.	.	2	27	.	5
Jonson	CA	6	47	.	2,3	.	.	.	.	.	.	.	.	.	.	.	.	.	4	.	.
	EMI	25	29	.	.	.	.	.	.	7	.	33	.	.	.	25	.	15	.	.
	EMO	25	72	.	3,3	.	2,1	1	.	11	.	37	.	.	.	8	.	14	.	.
	CR	.	66	.	.	.	.	.	.	1	.	19	.	.	.	3	.	10	.	.
	Poet.	8	65	.	1,1	.	.	.	.	7	.	12	.	.	.	2	.	3	.	.
	Volp.	3	69	.	.	.	.	.	.	7	3	6	.	.	4	6	.	4	.	.
	Epic.	2	46	.	.	.	.	1	.	12	1	39	.	.	.	33	.[d]	6	.	.
	Alch.	3	39	.	,2	.	.	2	.	10	.	38	.	.	.	48	1[d]	13	.	.
	BF	13	47	.	.	.	.	2	.	58	2	[110]	.	.	2	[93]	1[d]	37	.	.
	DA	1	45	.	,1	1	,2	.	.	30	.	[27]	.	.	.	[39]	3[e]	18	.	.
	SN	2	31	,1	.	1	1,	.	.	10	2	[44]	.	.	1	[57]	2[f]	7	.	.
	Widow	5	77	2,1	9,23	12	25,	4	.	7	18	1	.	.	10	.	.	26	.	.
Fletcher	W.Pr.	1	54	.	1,7	.	.	.	.	.	20	.	.	.	19	1	.	14	.	.
	Bon.	.	69	1,	,2	1	2,	.	.	.	14	.	.	.	10	.	.	6	.	.
	Valen.	.	63	.	,3	.	.	.	.	.	12	.	.	.	8	.	.	11	.	.
	M.Thom.	.	65	.	1,2	.	.	.	.	1	9	.	.	.	6	.	.	8	.	.
	ML	.	80	.	1,4	.	.	.	.	.	14	1	2	.	5	.	.	8	.	.
>1618	Chan.	.	88	.	,1	1	1,	.	.	.	12	.	.	.	4	1	.	10	.	.
	L.Sub.	.	86	.	,1	.	2,	.	.	.	13	.	.	.	10	.	.	11	.	.
1619<	HL	.	75	.	.	.	1,	.	.	.	28	.	.	.	11	.	.	16	.	.
	IP	.	x	.	1,5	.	.	.	.	.	[7]	[.]	[1]	[.]	[8]	[.]	.	7	.	.
	Pilg.	.	x	.	,2	.	.	.	.	.	[15]	[.]	[.]	[.]	[9]	[.]	.	1	.	.
	WGC	.	x	.	,4	.	.	.	.	.	[8]	[.]	[.]	[.]	[6]	[.]	.	10	.	.
	W.Pl	.	x	.	.	.	.	.	.	.	[15]	[.]	[.]	[.]	[16]	[.]	.	10	.	.
	RW	.	x	.	,2	.	.	.	.	.	[20]	[.]	[.]	[.]	[12]	[.]	.	7	.	.
	WM	.	x	.	.	.	.	.	.	.	[4]	[.]	[.]	[.]	[1]	[.]	.	5[a]	.	.

Occurrences: [a] Once as an't. [b] Twice as an't. [c] 8 times as an't.
[d] As vpo'the. [e] 3 times as vpo'the. [f] Twice as vpo'the.

	woult	wou't	wou'd	Spellings: -cst	[of 'em: (')hem	(')am	(')um	em, m	'em,'m	e'm]	[of has: (')has	h'as	ha's]	[of does: doe(')s	do(')s]	otherwise	Prefixes: Total, group sp.	All:	Omnes:	1.Gent.[etc.]:	Gent.1.[etc]:
HDM	.	.	.	.	.	.	.	.	.	.	.	.	.	.	.	.	3	3	.	.	.
GU	.	.	.	.	.	.	4	.	.	.	15[a]	.	.	16	.	.	3	.	1	.	.
AF	.	.	.	1	.	9	10	.	.	.	22	1	.	6	.	.	6	.	6	.	.
MD	.	.	1	.	2	2	.	1	42	.	30	.	.	20	.	.	4	.	.	.	.
Mons.	.	.	.	.	.	20	.	.	.	.	15	.	.	11	.	.	10	.	1	+	.
WT	.	.	.	.	.	1	.	.	.	.	26	1	.	13	.	.	1	.	1	.	.
AM	.	.	.	.	.	.	.	.	.	.	.	.	.	1	.	.	.	.	.	.	.
AR	.	.	.	.	.	.	.	.	.	.	3	.	.	2	.	.	.	.	.	+	.
JD	.	.	1	.	.	.	.	.	.	.	.	.	.	.	.	.	1	.	.	.	+[b]
WYW	1	.	1	.	.	.	.	.	.	.	12	.	.	2	3	.	2	2	.	.	.
Malc.	.	.	.	.	.	.	7	.	.	.	16[a]	.	.	.	5	5	5	4	1	.	.
DC	.	.	.	.	.	.	.	.	1	.	34	.	.	10	6	1	1	.	.	.	.
Fawn	.	.	.	.	.	.	.	1	.	.	43[c]	.	1	2	19	.	1	.	.	.	.
Soph.	.	.	.	.	.	.	.	.	.	.	2	.	.	.	2	.	.	.	.	.	.
Pur.	4	.	.	2	.	.	.	7	32	2	36	2	9	2	5	1	10	1	.	.	.
CA	.	.	.	.	7	.	.	.	.	.	17	.	.	4	1	3	3	.	2	.	.
EMI	.	.	.	.	60	.	.			.	14	.	21	.	10	.	1	1	.	.	.
EMO	.	.	.	.	67	.	.			.	67	.	8	24	12	.	.	.	.	+	+
CR	.	.	.	.	42	.	.			.	36	.	3	4	16	3	6	6	.	.	.
Poet.	.	.	.	.	50	.	.			.	8	.	13	9	5	.	12	1	.	+	+
Volp.	.	.	.	.	52	.	.			.	41	.	6	.	18	.	11	2	.	.	+
Epic.	.	.	.	.	110	.	.			.	85	.	.	.	19	.	1	1	.	.	.
Alch.	.	.	.	.	50	.	.	.	.	.	57	.	2	1	27	.	3	.	.	.	+
BF	.	.	1	.	[111]	.	.	.	.	.	67	.	2	4	34	.	6	1	.	.	.
DA	.	.	.	.	[85]	.	.		.	.	52	.	8	.	20	.	.	.	.	.	+
SN	.	.	.	.	[53]	.	.	.	.	.	64	.	3	2	13	.	3	1	.	.	+
Widow	.	.	.	.	.	.	.	.	62	.	45	9[d]	.	.	8	.	2	.	.	+	.
W.Pr.	.	.	.	.	.	.	.	.	66	.	37	4	1	3	13	.	.	.	.	+	.
Bon.	.	.	.	.	.	.	.	.	95	.	29	9	.	13	.	.	3	.	.	+	.
Valen.	.	.	.	.	.	.	.	.	71	.	37	5	6	2	5	.	3	1	.	+	.
M.Thom.	.	.	.	.	.	.	.	.	27	.	41	1	1	1	25	.	7	.	.	+	.
ML	.	1	17	.	.	.	.	.	25	.	24	2	.	27	3	.	1	.	.	+	.
Chan.	.	.	.	.	.	.	.	.	43	1	41	3	1	3	2	.	1	.	.	+	.
L.Sub.	.	.	1	.	.	.	.	.	133	.	63	3	.	6	4	.	4	2	.	+	.
HL	.	.	3	.	.	.	.	.	80	.	62	3	.	12	2	.	6	2	.	+	.
IP	.	.	44	.	x	x	x	x	x	x	x	x	x	x	x	x	6	.	5	+	.
Pilg.	.	.	.	.	x	x	x	x	x	x	x	x	x	x	x	x	3	3	.	+	.
WGC	.	.	.	.	x	x	x	x	x	x	x	x	x	x	x	x	2	1	.	+	.
W.Pl.	.	.	.	.	x	x	x	x	x	x	x	x	x	x	x	x	.	.	.	+	.
RW	.	.	3	.	.	.	32	3	.	.	x	x	x	x	x	x	3	1	2	+	.
WM	.	.	.	.	x	x	x	x	x	x	x	x	x	x	x	x	4	2	1	+	.

[Band 3 continues]

Occurrences: [a] As haz (all instances). [b] One instance only. [c] 6 times as haz.

[d] Once as 'as.

Band 3(h)

Table I.1

Band 3   Segment 3   /Middletonisms

Selected words and collocations

		Length (words)	by..copy	can possible	Chaucer	comfort	fetch..again	give..due	'Has = he has	Inn a Court [+ noun]	Inns a Court [+ noun]	"Italian" joke	la(w) you	la(w) you now	lin	love alife
Chapman	HDM	17210	.	.	.	4	.	.	.	.	.	.	.	.	.	.
	GU	21995	.	.	.	1	.	.	2	.	.	.	.	.	.	.
	AF	19108	.	.	.	2	.	.	1	.	.	.	.	.	.	.
	MD	23568*	.	.	.	3	1	.	1	.	.	.	.	.	.	.
	Mons.	16636	1	.	.	6	.	1	.	.	.	.	.	.	.	.
	WT	23179	.	.	.	8	.	.	1	.	.	.	1	.	.	.
Marston	AM	14330	.	.	.	4	.	.	.	.	.	.	.	.	.	.
	AR	16369	.	.	.	10	.	.	.	.	.	.	.	.	.	.
	JD	17414	.	.	.	2	.	.	.	.	.	.	.	.	.	.
	WYW	17145	.	.	.	1	.	.	.	.	.	.	.	.	.	.
	Malc.	18571	.	.	.	5	.	.	.	.	.	.	.	.	.	.
	DC	19049	.	.	.	5	.	.	.	.	1	.	.	.	.	.
	Fawn	22717	.	.	.	4	.	.	.	.	.	.	.	.	.	.
	Soph.	16653	.	.	.	1	.	.	.	.	.	.	.	.	.	.
X Play	Pur.	19922*	1	1	.	11	2	1	7.	.	.	.	1	1	1	.
Jonson	CA	20058	.	.	.	10	.	.	.	.	.	.	.	.	.	.
	EMI	25664	.	.	.	4	.	.	.	.	.	.	.	.	.	.
	EMO	38248	.	.	.	7	.	.	.	.	.	.	.	.	.	.
	CR	33145	.	.	.	2	.	.	.	.	.	.	.	.	.	.
	Poet.	28727	.	.	.	4	.	.	.	.	.	.	.	.	.	.
	Volp.	28790	.	.	.	2	.	.	.	.	.	.	.	.	.	.
	Epic.	29066	.	.	.	10	.	.	.	.	.	.	.	.	.	.
	Alch.	28517	.	.	.	1	.	.	2	.	1	.	.	.	.	.
	BF	36411	.	.	.	6	.	.	.	.	.	.	.	.	.	.
	DA	28584	.	.	.	1	.	.	5	.	.	.	.	.	.	.
	SN	26688	.	.	.	.	.	.	10	.	.	.	.	.	1	.
	Widow	20315*	.	.	.	17	1	.	9	.	1	.	1	.	1	2
Fletcher	W.Pr.	24472*	.	.	.	12	.	.	5	.	.	.	.	.	.	.
	Bon.	21049	.	.	.	7	.	.	11	.	.	.	.	.	.	.
	Valen.	25783	.	.	.	5	.	.	4	.	.	.	.	.	.	.
	M.Thom.	18754	.	.	.	8	.	.	2	.	.	.	.	.	.	1
	ML	18964	.	.	.	.	.	.	7	.	.	.	.	.	.	.
>1618	Chan.	19060	.	.	.	6	.	.	9	.	.	.	.	.	.	.
	L.Sub.	21392	.	.	.	8	.	.	2	.	.	.	.	.	.	.
1619<	HL	21789	.	.	.	17	.	.	11	.	.	.	.	.	.	.
	IP	20746	.	1	.	5	.	.	4	.	.	.	.	.	.	.
	Pilg.	20937	.	.	.	8	.	.	8	.	.	.	.	.	.	.
	WGC	22851	.	.	.	2	.	.	3	.	.	.	.	.	.	.
	W.Pl.	20421	.	.	.	9	.	.	6	.	.	.	.	.	.	.
	RW	17641	.	.	.	7	.	.	8	.	.	.	.	.	.	.
	WM	20227	.	.	.	11	.	.	1	.	.	.	.	.	.	.

/Dekkerisms

Band 3(i)

	[adv.]-ly welcome	mass, here	I (do) protest	sasarara	save ..harmless	son and heir	spoke like	subaudi	suspectle's	third part of	troth. say true	tut, man	Adam/Eve	garlic/strong	godamercy	hair..an end	lily.hands	make buttons	marry muff
HDM	.	1	2	.	.	.	.	.	.	.	.	.	.	.	.	.	.	.	.
GU	.	.	6	.	1	.	.	.	.	.	.	.	.	.	.	.	.	.	.
AF	2	.	4	.	.	.	.	.	.	.	.	.	.	.	.	.	.	.	.
MD	.	.	9	.	.	2	.	.	.	.	.	.	.	.	1	.	.	.	.
Mons.	.	.	3	.	.	.	.	.	.	.	.	.	.	1	.	.	.	.	.
WT	1	.	6	.	.	.	.	.	.	.	.	.	.	.	.	.	.	.	.
AM	.	.	.	.	.	.	.	.	.	.	.	.	.	.	.	.	.	.	.
AR	.	.	.	.	.	.	.	.	.	.	.	.	.	.	.	.	.	.	1
JD	.	.	4	.	.	.	.	.	.	.	.	.	.	.	.	.	.	.	.
WYW	.	.	10	.	.	.	.	.	.	.	.	.	.	.	1	.	.	.	.
Malc.	.	.	.	.	.	.	.	.	.	.	.	.	.	.	.	.	.	.	.
DC	4	.	2	.	.	.	.	.	.	.	.	.	.	.	.	.	.	.	.
Fawn	.	.	7	.	.	.	.	.	.	.	.	.	.	.	1	.	.	.	.
Soph.	.	.	.	.	.	.	.	.	.	.	.	.	.	.	.	.	.	.	.
Pur.	2	1	8	1	1	5	.	.	.	.	1	.	.	.	.	.	.	.	.
CA	.	.	.	.	.	.	.	.	.	.	.	.	.	.	3	.	.	.	.
EMI	.	.	12	.	.	.	.	.	.	.	.	.	1[a]	.	.	.	.	.	.
EMO	.	1	9	.	.	.	.	.	.	.	.	.	.	.	.	.	.	.	.
CR	.	.	11	.	.	.	.	.	.	.	.	.	.	.	.	.	.	.	.
Poet.	.	.	7	.	.	.	.	.	.	.	.	.	.	.	.	.	.	.	.
Volp.	1	.	4	.	.	.	.	.	.	.	.	.	.	.	.	.	.	.	.
Epic.	.	.	8	.	.	.	.	.	.	.	.	.	.	.	.	.	.	.	.
Alch.	.	.	1	.	.	.	.	.	.	.	.	.	.	.	.	.	.	.	.
BF	.	.	1	.	.	.	.	.	.	.	.	.	.	.	2	.	.	.	.
DA	.	.	6	.	.	.	.	.	.	.	.	.	.	.	.	.	.	.	.
SN	.	.	1	.	.	.	.	.	.	.	.	.	.	.	1	.	.	.	.
Widow	.	2	5	.	.	.	.	.	.	.	.	.	.	.	.	.	.	.	.
W.Pr.	.	.	1	.	.	.	.	.	.	.	.	.	.	.	.	.	.	.	.
Bon.	.	.	.	.	.	.	.	.	.	.	.	.	.	.	.	.	.	1	.
Valen.	1	.	.	.	.	.	.	.	.	.	.	.	.	.	.	.	.	.	.
1.Thom.	1	.	1	.	.	.	.	.	.	.	.	.	.	.	.	.	.	.	.
ML	.	.	.	.	.	.	.	.	.	.	.	.	.	.	3	.	.	.	.
Chan.	.	.	.	.	.	.	.	.	.	.	.	.	.	.	2	.	.	.	.
L.Sub.	2	.	.	.	.	.	.	.	.	.	.	.	.	.	2	.	.	.	.
HL	.	.	1	.	.	.	.	.	.	.	.	.	.	.	5	.	.	.	.
IP	.	.	1	.	.	.	.	.	.	.	.	.	.	.	.	.	.	.	.
Pilg.	1	.	.	.	.	.	.	.	.	.	.	.	.	.	.	.	.	.	.
WGC	.	.	1	.	.	.	.	.	.	.	.	.	.	.	.	.	.	.	.
W.Pl.	2	.	.	.	.	.	.	.	.	.	.	.	.	.	.	.	.	.	.
RW	1	.	.	.	.	.	.	.	.	.	.	.	.	.	.	.	.	.	.
WM	.	.	.	.	.	.	.	.	.	.	.	.	.	.	.	.	.	.	.

Occurrences: [a]As ADAM, and EVE's kitchin.

Band 3(j)

		moon/horn(s)	mumble-crust	no point	oyster/open	parrot = [woman]	puss-cat	rowly-powly	Signior no	snick up	snip snap	stile/style pun	Tamburlaine	wink at small faults	/Other items deed la	float of	forfeit of	'tis Oracle	undertake a voluntary exile
Chapman	HDM	.	.	.	.	.	.	.	.	.	.	.	.	.	.	.	.	.	.
	GU	.	.	.	.	.	.	.	.	.	.	.	.	.	.	.	.	.	.
	AF	1	.	.	.	.	.	.	.	.	.	.	.	.	.	.	.	.	.
	MD	.	.	.	.	.	.	.	.	1	.	1	.	.	.	.	.	.	.
	Mons.	.	.	.	.	.	.	.	.	.	.	.	.	.	.	.	.	.	.
	WT	.	.	.	.	.	.	.	.	.	.	1	.	.	.	.	.	.	.
Marston	AM	.	.	.	.	.	.	.	.	.	.	.	.	.	.	.	.	.	.
	AR	.	.	.	.	.	.	.	.	.	.	.	.	.	.	.	.	.	.
	JD	.	.	1	.	.	.	.	.	.	.	.	.	.	.	.	.	.	.
	WYW	1	.	.	.	.	.	.	.	.	.	.	.	.	.	.	.	.	.
	Malc.	.	.	.	.	.	.	.	.	.	.	.	.	.	.	.	.	.	.
	DC	.	.	1	.	.	.	.	.	.	.	.	.	.	.	.	.	.	.
	Fawn	1	.	.	.	.	.	.	.	.	.	.	.	.	.	.	.	.	.
	Soph.	.	.	.	.	.	.	.	.	.	.	.	.	.	.	.	.	.	.
X Play	Pur.	.	.	.	.	.	.	.	.	.	.	.	.	.	.	.	.	.	.
Jonson	CA	.	.	1	.	.	.	.	1	.	.	.	.	.	.	.	.	.	.
	EMI	.	.	.	.	.	.	.	.	.	.	.	.	.	.	.	.	.	.
	EMO	.	.	.	.	.	.	.	.	.	.	.	.	.	.	.	.	.	.
	CR	.	.	.	.	.	.	.	.	.	.	.	.	.	.	.	.	.	.
	Poet.	.	.	.	.	.	.	1	.	.	.	.	.	.	.	.	.	.	.
	Volp.	.	.	.	.	.	.	.	.	.	.	.	.	.	.	.	.	.	.
	Epic.	.	.	.	.	.	.	.	.	.	.	.	.	.	.	.	.	.	.
	Alch.	.	.	.	.	.	.	.	.	.	.	.	.	.	.	.	.	.	.
	BF	.	.	.	1	.	.	.	.	.	.	.	.	.	.	.	.	.	.
	DA	.	.	.	.	.	.	.	.	.	.	.	.	.	.	.	.	.	.
	SN	.	.	.	.	.	.	.	.	.	.	.	.	.	.	.	.	.	.
	Widow	.	.	.	.	.	.	.	.	.	.	.	.	.	.	.	.	.	.
Fletcher	W.Pr.	.	.	.	.	.	.	.	.	.	.	.	.	1	.	.	.	.	.
	Bon.	.	.	.	.	.	.	.	.	.	.	.	.	.	.	.	.	.	.
	Valen.	.	.	.	.	.	.	.	.	.	.	.	.	.	.	.	1	.	.
	M.Thom.	.	.	2	.	.	.	.	.	.	.	.	.	.	.	.	.	.	.
	ML	.	.	.	.	.	.	.	.	.	.	.	.	.	.	.	.	.	.
	Chan.	.	.	.	1	.	.	.	.	.	.	.	.	.	.	.	.	.	.
	L.Sub.	.	.	.	.	.	.	.	.	.	.	.	.	.	.	.	.	.	.
	HL	.	.	.	.	.	.	.	.	.	.	.	.	.	.	.	.	.	.
	IP	.	.	.	.	.	.	.	.	.	.	.	.	.	.	.	.	.	.
	Pilg.	.	.	.	.	.	.	.	.	.	.	.	.	.	.	.	.	.	.
	WGC	.	.	.	.	1	.	.	.	.	.	.	.	.	.	.	.	.	.
	W.Pl.	.	.	.	.	.	.	.	.	.	.	.	.	.	.	.	.	.	.
	RW	.	.	.	1	.	.	.	.	.	.	.	.	.	.	.	.	.	.
	WM	.	.	.	.	.	.	.	.	.	.	.	.	.	.	.	.	.	.

>1618
_____

1619<

Table I.1

Band 4(a)

Band 4   Segment 1   /Exclamations

		Length (words)	push	pish	puh	pah	pew	p-, other	phew	tut	tush	t-, other	hum(h)	um(h)	h(e/o)! yda(y)	why
Chettle	Hoff.	20491	.	.	.	.	.	.	.	1	1	.	.	.	.	15
Haughton	Eng.	22364	1	.	.	.	.	.	.	5	2	.	.	.	8	67
X Plays	Blurt	18037*	.	.	.	.	.	1b	.	.	2	.	.	2	.	17
	Pur.	19922*	3	1	9	2	.	1	.	3	.	1	2	.	.	66
Smith	HG	16666	.	.	.	.	1	.	.	.	.	.	.	.	.	1
Daven-port	CN	19943	.	3	.	.	.	3	.	.	.	.	.	.	.	27
	KJM	17883	.	.	.	.	.	.	.	4	.	.	.	.	.	4
	NTCD	21191	.	.	.	.	.	.	.	.	5	.	.	.	.	22
Anon.	DD	21652	.	1	.	.	.	.	1	.	2	.	2	.	1	16
X Play	BB	15618	.	1	1	.	.	.	.	.	.	.	2	.	.	37
Drue	D.Suff.	17674	.	.	.	.	.	.	.	6	2	.	.	.	.	7
Heywood	Capt.	23770	.	.	.	.	.	.	.	.	5	.	.	.	1	16
	ET	22771	.	.	.	.	.	.	.	.	4	.	.	.	.	9
	2FMW	20709	.	.	.	.	.	.	.	.	2	.	.	.	.	15
X Play	Span.	17460	.	1	.	.	.	.	1	.	.	.	.	1	2	8
Armin	TMM	18972	.	.	2a	.	.	.	.	3	.	.	.	.	.	7
Barnes	D.Ch.	25183	.	.	.	.	.	.	.	1	.	.	.	.	.	14
Brewer	LK	18015	.	.	.	.	.	.	.	.	11	.	.	.	.	13
Brome	NL	26429	.	.	.	.	.	.	.	.	.	.	.	4	1	3
Cook	GTQ	25304	1	.	1	.	.	.	.	.	.	.	.	6	1	100
Daborne	CTT	20016	.	.	.	.	.	.	.	.	4	.	.	.	1	6
	PMC	19751	.	.	.	.	.	.	.	.	1	.	.	.	.	4
Day	IG	21351	.	.	.	.	.	.	.	.	5	.	.	.	.	32
	Law Tr.	16652	.	2	.	.	.	.	.	1	1	.	1	.	.	19
	HOB	15149	.	.	.	.	.	.	.	.	2	.	.	.	.	23
Field	WW	17772	.	8	.	.	.	.	.	.	.	.	3	1	1	23
	AL	19006	1	8	.	.	.	1	.	.	.	.	6	12	3	42
Mason	Turk	18519	.	.	.	.	.	.	.	1	.	.	.	.	.	6
Munday	JK	13641	.	.	.	.	.	.	.	.	2	.	.	.	.	27
	STM(S)	16410	.	.	.	.	.	.	.	.	1	.	.	.	.	12
Sampson	VB	18375	.	.	.	.	.	.	.	.	.	.	.	1	2	9
Sharpham	Fl.	16832	.	.	.	.	.	.	.	.	1	.	.	.	1	52
	CW	24854	1	.	.	.	.	.	.	.	2	.	13	.	1	78
Tomkis	Ling.	26179	.	10	.	.	.	.	.	8	.	.	5	.	.	33
	Alb.	22767	.	.	.	.	.	.	.	.	.	.	1	.	.	19
Wilkins	Mis.	25068*	.	1	.	.	.	2	.	7	.	.	.	.	.	31

* Fully counted. Occurrences: a Twice as pughe. b As ptrooh (which does not occur elsewhere in the plays of Band 4).

Band 4(b)

Author	Play	Jesu(s)	Lord('s)	God's	God	Heaven(')(s)	'Cud(')s, 'Coad(')s	'snigs	'sfoot	foot	'slid	'slud	'sblood	'swounds, 'z-	'sheart	heart	'sdeath	death	'slife, life	'slight, light
Chettle	Hoff.	.	3	2	3	11	.	.	.	.	.	.	.	1	.	1	2	.	.	.
Haughton	Eng.	1	5	10	9	.	.	.	.	.	.	.	5	5	.	.	.	.	.	.
X Plays	Blurt	1	3	5	5	2	.	.	6a	.	2	.	.	1	.	.	.	.	.	2,
	Pur.	.	.	.	1	.	,1	.	15	.	4	.	1	1	.	.	.	.	.	.
Smith	HG	.	.	.	.	2	.	.	.	.	.	.	.	.	.	.	.	1	.	.
Daven‑port	CN	.	.	.	.	6	.	.	6	.	.	.	.	.	.	.	.	.	.	.
	KJM	.	.	.	.	10	.	.	4	.	.	.	.	.	.	.	.	.	.	.
	NTCD	.	3	.	.	2	.	.	2	.	.	.	.	.	.	.	.	.	.	.
Anon.	DD	.	.	.	.	4	.	.	.	.	.	.	.	.	.	.	.	.	.	.
X Play	BB	.	.	.	.	4	.	.	2	.	.	.	.	.	.	1	.	2	.	2,
Drue	D.Suff.	.	1	.	.	8	.	.	.	.	.	.	.	.	.	.	.	.	.	.
Heywood	Capt.	.	.	1	.	1	.	.	.	.	.	.	.	.	.	.	.	.	.	.
	ET	.	1	.	.	4	.	.	1	.	.	.	.	.	.	.	.	.	.	.
	2FMW	.	.	.	.	2	.	.	5	.	.	.	.	.	.	.	.	.	.	.
X Play	Span.	.	.	.	.	3	.	.	.	1	.	.	.	.	.	.	.	1	.	.
Armin	TMM	.	1	2	8	.	1b	.	1	.	.	.	.	.	.	.	.	1	.	.
Barnes	D.Ch.	.	1	4	6	1	.	.	.	.	.	.	.	1c	.	.	.	.	.	.
Brewer	LK	.	1	.	.	1	.	.	1	.	2	.	.	.	.	.	1	1	.	.
Brome	NL	.	2	.	.	3	.	.	1	.	2	.	.	.	.	.	.	.	.	1,
Cook	GTQ	.	5	4	3	.	.	.	17d	.	2e	.	1	13	.	.	.	.	1f,	.
Daborne	CTT	.	.	.	.	1	.	.	6	.	.	.	.	8	11	.	1	.	.	.
	PMC	.	.	.	.	.	.	.	.	1	.	.	.	.	1	.	.	1	.	.
Day	IG	2	4	5	6	1	.	.	1	.	.	.	.	.	.	.	.	.	.	.
	Law Tr.	.	2	2	12	1	.	.	4	.	.	.	.	3	6	.	4	1	.	.
	HOB	.	3	.	2	3	.	.	11g	1	1	.	.	.	.	.	.	.	.	1,
Field	WW	.	4	8	7	10	.	.	3	.	.	.	.	7	.	9	.	.	2,	.
	AL	1	1	1	5	7	.	.	4	.	1	.	2	14	11	2	.	.	.	4h,
Mason	Turk	.	.	.	.	3	.	.	6	.	.	.	.	.	.	.	1	.	.	.
Munday	JK	.	2	3	.	.	.	.	.	.	.	.	.	.	.	.	.	.	.	.
	STM(S)	.	6	7	16	.	.	.	.	.	.	.	.	.	.	.	.	.	.	.
Sampson	VB	.	5	.	.	2	.	.	.	.	.	.	.	.	.	.	.	.	.	.
Sharpham	Fl.	.	1	4	2	1	.	.	.	.	.	.	.	.	1	.	.	.	.	.
	CW	.	1	6	.	2	1j	.	.	.	.	.	.	2	1	.	.	.	1,1	6,
Tomkis	Ling.	.	1	.	.	5	.	.	.	.	1	1	.	.	.	.	.	.	.	.
	Alb.	.	.	.	.	1	.	.	.	.	.	.	.	.	.	.	.	.	.	.
Wilkins	Mis.	1	1	6	9	3	.	.	12	.	.	.	1	.	.	6	.	.	.	.

Occurrences: a Once as vds foote. b As cods me. c As Coxwounds. d 13 times as Vds foot. e Twice as Vds lid. f As Vds life. g 7 times as Vds foot, once as vesfoot. h Twice as Vds light. j As Cods my life.

	'(s)nails	'(s)precious	'Od's	'(Ud)s, other	f(a/e)ck(s)	faith	troth	marry	mass	byrlady	my reputation	hold my life
Hoff.	3	.	.	.	.	2	5	3	1	.	.	.
Eng.	.	.	.	.	.	28	3	26	4	6[a]	.	.
Blurt	.	.	.	.	.	6	10	11	2	.	.	.
Pur.	.	.	.	.	.	39	24	7	10	1	.	.
HG	.	.	.	.	.	.	.	1	.	.	.	.
CN	1	.	.	.	.	8	1	5	.	.	.	.
KJM	.	.	.	.	.	4	5	2	1	.	.	.
NTCD	.	.	.	.	.	15	8	4	.	.	.	.
DD	.	.	.	.	.	2	1	1	.	.	.	.
BB	1	.	.	.	.	14	6	2	5	.	.	.
D. Suff.	.	.	.	.	.	1	.	3	.	.	.	1
Capt.	.	.	.	.	.	1	2	8	.	1	.	.
ET	.	.	.	.	.	1	7	1	.	.	.	.
2FMW	.	.	.	.	.	2	3	.	.	.	.	.
Span.	.	.	.	.	.	.	3	.	.	.	.	.
TMM	.	.	.	.	.	19	4	.	.	.	.	.
-D. Ch.	.	.	.	.	.	7	.	5	.	.	.	.
LK	.	.	.	.	.	18	.	7	.	1	.	.
NL	.	.	3	.	.	22	7	6	.	1	.	.
GTQ	.	.	.	1	.	41	8	21	.	.	.	1
CTT	.	.	.	.	.	.	.	5	.	.	.	.
PMC	.	.	.	.	.	1	1	4	.	.	.	1
IG	.	.	.	.	.	16	2	12	1	.	.	2
Law Tr.	.	.	.	1[b]	.	12	1	8	1	1	.	.
HOB	.	.	.	.	.	22	1	7	.	.	.	.
WW	.	.	.	3	.	18	14	5	.	2	.	1
AL	.	.	.	.	.	17	14	7	.	.	.	.
Turk	.	.	.	.	.	2	.	.	.	.	.	.
JK	.	.	.	.	.	6	4	3	.	1	.	.
STM(S)	.	.	.	.	.	12	6	3	.	2	.	1
VB	.	.	.	.	.	4	2	3	1	.	.	.
Fl.	.	.	.	.	.	60	6	5	1	1	.	2
CW	.	3	.	.	.	43	7	8	8	.	.	2
Ling.	.	2	.	.	.	19	1	2	.	.	.	.
Alb.	.	.	.	.	.	6	.	.	.	.	.	.
Mis.	.	.	.	.	.	23	11	2	2	1	.	.

Occurrences: [a]Once as Birlaken.

[b]As Vds Hartlings.

Band 4(d)

Table I.1

Band 4　Segment 2

		Length (words)	ay	yes	among	amongst	beside adv./prep.	besides adv./prep.	between	betwixt	toward	towards	while	whil(e)st	whiles
Chettle	Hoff.	20491	36	7	2	2	.	5,2	3	.	2	.	17	2	.
Haughton	Eng.	22364	18	17	1	2	.	,1	2	5	.	2	1	6	1
X Plays	Blurt	18037*	8	7	3	.	.	7,1	4	.	.	.	1	3	.
	Pur.	19922*	58	9	6	3	3,2	3,	8	1	2	.	1	1	.
Smith	HG	16666	2	1	.	4	.	1,	2	2	.	.	3	7	1
Daven-port	CN	19943	7	19	.	2	1,	1,2	3	6	.	1	1	5	.
	KJM	17883	6	14	.	4	.	2,1	1	4	.	6	2	12	.
	NTCD	21191	6	28	11	3	.	2,1	1	4	.	1	6	2	.
Anon.	DD	21652	3	30	5	1	.	,1	1	5	.	4	8	2	.
X Play	BB	15618	17	7	2	.	,1	1,5	.	6	1	1	1	.	.
Drue	D.Suff.	17674	6	5	.	12	.	4,	.	3	2	5	2	7	.
Heywood	Capt.	23770	14	24	.	19	.	5,3	.	15	.	4	2	7	.
	ET	22771	3	20	.	9	.	3,3	2	10	.	2	.	10	1
	2FMW	20709	4	3	2	5	.	5,	1	2	.	4	2	5	.
X Play	Span	17460	6	21	.	8	.	,4	1	1	.	.	.	4	2
Armin	TMM	18972	18	22	.	3	.	3,	.	4	.	.	14	.	.
Barnes	D.Ch.	25183	7	1	.	2	1,1	4,	.	13	.	2	.	7	.
Brewer	LK	18015	16	10	.	6	.	,2	2	2	.	3	4	3	.
Brome	NL	26429	19	20	8	4	1,	7,3	9	7	.	3	12	.	.
Cook	GTQ	25304	16	56	.	6	.	1,1	.	3	2	4	3	9	1
Daborne	CTT	20016	6	8	.	2	.	5,1	1	5	.	3	.	5	.
	PMC	19751	2	4	.	4	.	4,4	2	2	.	1	1	4	.
Day	IG	21351	13	15	1	7	.	.	.	11	.	.	1	11	.
	Law Tr.	16652	10	14	.	6	,1	1,	1	3	.	.	.	5	.
	HOB	15149	20	17	.	8	.	2,	.	5	.	1	.	5	.
Field	WW	17772	18	21	4	1	,2	5,	.	5	4	.	2	6	.
	AL	19006	12	7	2	3	.	7,	.	11	2	2	1	4	.
Mason	Turk	18519	7	3	.	6	.	.	3	5	1	1	1	2	.
Munday	JK	13641	.	.	1	3	6,2	1,	2	.	5	.	12	.	.
	STM(S)	16410	11	3	4	.	1,	.	.	4	1	.	2	6	.
Sampson	VB	18375	14	3	3	3	.	1,2	6	8	.	.	3	2	.
Sharpham	Fl.	16832	38	22	1	3	.	2,	4	1	.	1	3	1	.
	CW	24854	44	22	.	7	.	11,1	.	1	.	.	3	1	1
Tomkis	Ling.	26179	20	15	4	10	.	4,2	2	16	.	.	5	.	.
	Alb.	22767	1	13	.	5	,3	,1	.	9	.	1	14	1	.
Wilkins	Mis.	25068*	31	4	2	3	.	6,	2	14	2	.	2	6	.

	ye	'ee	'a=[he]	's=[his]	'em	them	has	hath	does	doth	ha'	I'd	I'm	I am	I've	thou'rt / th'art	sh'as / sh'ad	'tas / 'tad	'thas / 'thad
Hoff.	23	1	.	2	2	34	15	33	2	13	1	2	1	60	2	,1	.	.	.
Eng.	21	.	.	.	.	77	.	40	10	19	.	4	.	47	.	2,	.	.	.
Blurt	1	.	.	2	.	35	21	11	19	2	3	6	.	70	.	,1	.	.	.
Pur.	1	.	.	1	41	12	47	2	8	.	18	10	11	28	.	2,1	2[a],	5	.
HG	3	.	.	.	.	58	47	6	8	1	.	2	4	34	.	,1	.	.	.
CN	96	.	.	12	5	36	37	29	4	8	.	3	2	33	.	1,3	3,	.	1
KJM	35	3	1	2	4	37	16	24	3	2	.	2	1	36	.	,1	.	.	.
NTCD	.	.	.	5	1	43	1	76	1	16	.	4	9	87	2	,5	.	.	.
DD	1	.	.	4	19	49	8	24	9	4	1	7	8	38	.	,1	1[b]	.	.
BB	.	.	1	2	3	36	7	23	9	6	.	2	13	25	.	,2	1[c]	.	1
D. Suff.	4	.	.	2	2	74	18	35	1	10	1	.	.	36	.	.	.	.	.
Capt.	5	.	.	.	2	76	.	45	.	7	.	1	.	52	.	,1	.	.	.
ET	2	.	.	1	.	50	4	69	1	15	.	1	.	46	.	,1	.	.	.
2FMW	1	.	.	.	1	35	7	29	4	4	.	12	2	56	2	,3	.	1	1
Span.	8	6	5	.	29	13	28	16	11	.	12	4	2	70	.	,4	.	.	3
TMM	92	.	5	3	2	41	9	16	25	7	18	.	5	85	.	.	.	.	.
D. Ch.	8	.	.	.	.	78	.	43	.	22	.	.	.	16	.	,1	.	.	.
LK	12	.	.	.	28	19	35	10	7	4	3	5	4	34	.	,4	.	.	1
NL	21	19	.	2	24	26	56	20	18	.	17	1	1	84	.	.	.	.	1
GTQ	5	.	1	1	4	40	58	14	18	9	14	4	2	70	.	,1	.	1	1
CTT	4	.	.	3	31	59	1	52	.	25	.	1	.	65	.	1,1	.	.	.
PMC	2	.	.	.	6	41	40	8	4	25	10	2	1	66	.	,1	.	.	.
IG	7	.	3	2	56	39	10	48	.	15	40	1	2	48	.	1,1	.	.	.
Law Tr.	2	.	47	.	3	19	6	29	2	13	.	2	4	19	.	.	.	.	.
HOB	6	.	8	1	.	51	23	11	2	12	6	6	1	36	.	,1	.	.	.
WW	22	17	.	1	26	17	25	11	14	18	9	2	3	49	.	1,2	.	.	.
AL	15	14	.	2	23	26	29	30	12	11	.	2	2	36	.	1,	.	.	1
Turk	19	.	.	.	.	30	.	28	.	15	.	3	.	53	.	,2	.	.	.
JK	165	.	.	.	.	63	3	39	.	13	.	.	.	17	.	.	.	.	.
STM(S)	122	.	2	.	1	48	7	35	6	15	.	2	.	34	.	,1	.	.	.
VB	3	.	2	9	13	20	39	5	6	1	2	8	13	24	4	,1	.	.	.
Fl.	27	.	67	2	28	53	37	40	8	16	2	3	4	44	.	,3	.	1	1
CW	157	1	61	.	.	47	4	66	2	55	22	.	.	55	.	.	.	1	.
Ling.	4	.	.	1	.	118	1	55	1	17	1	1	.	52	.	,5	.	.	.
Alb.	1	.	.	9	.	24	9	34	4	6	4	11	.	56	.	1,7	.	.	1
Mis.	11	.	3	.	19	104	26	39	14	20	81	2	.	79	.	.	.	.	.

Occurrences: [a] Once as she'as. [b] As sh'has. [c] As sh'had

Other contractions →

		it's	'tis	we're / w'are	you're, / y'are	y'(h)ave	they're, / th'are	le'me	gi'n't	i'	i'th'	i'the	a'th'	a'the	o'th'	o'the	upo'th'	on't	of't	ex'lent
Chettle	Hoff.	6	32		,3													1		
Haughton	Eng.	4	42	,1	5,		1,											4		
X Plays	Blurt	7	27		,4		1,			7		2	2							
	Pur.		50	1,	5,10		6,			15	1	9	2				2	27		5
Smith	HG		40							4	1							2		
Davenport	CN		70		7,3					20	1			3				12		
	KJM		30		,6					14				4				5		
	NTCD		58	,3	1,5	1	,2			2				2				1	11	
Anon.	DD		39		,10	2	,2			2								1	6	
X Play	BB		57		,6		,2			2									7	
Drue	D.Suff.	1	26		3,4					6		3						2		
Heywood	Capt.		42		,4	2				9				5				3		
	ET	1	48	,1	,8	4				10		1		4				8		
	2FMW		59	,4		1				10				2				3		
X Play	Span.	3	62		,10	1	,1	1		1	1			1				2		
Armin	TMM	1	80	1,	5,					11								2		
Barnes	D.Ch.		25				1,							1						
Brewer	LK	1	49		,1	3	,1			4				1				16		
Brome	NL		52						3	5	5					9		17		
Cook	GTQ		61		8,8		2,			12				3				6		
Daborne	CTT	12	19		4,					1								6	3	
	PMC	2	35		2,1					2								8		
Day	IG		51							2		4	2					11		
	Law Tr.		34		,5					8	2		4			1		7		
	HOB		44		,4	1	,2			2	1			2				4		
Field	WW	1	44		,1		1,			7		2						8		
	AL	3	53		2,	1				4				5				2		
Mason	Turk		13	1,	,5		,1													
Munday	JK	1	11				1,													
	STM(S)	1	15		1,1		,3							1				3		
Sampson	VB	2	52		,4		1,2			6				9				3		
Sharpham	Fl.	2	54		,6					5	3			1				13		
	CW	5	74		1,													9		
Tomkis	Ling.	9	77				,2				1					1		1		
	Alb.		101		,14	4	1,3			9						8		8		
Wilkins	Mis.	3	53		3,1		,1			6	1							4		

Table of spelling variants (Band 4(g))

	woult	wou't	wou'd	-cst	(')hem	(')am	(')um	em,m	'em,'m	e'm	(')has	h'as	ha's	doe(')s	do(')s	otherwise	Total, group sp	All:	Omnes:	l.Gent. (etc.):	Gent.l. (etc.):
					Spellings [of 'em]						[of has]			[of does]						Prefixes	Band 4(g)
Hoff.	.	.	3	1	.	.	2	.	.	.	9	1	5	2	.	.	6	.	5	.	.
Eng.	.	.	2	1	.	.	.	.	.	.	10	.	.	.	.	.	5	2	.	.	.
Blurt	.	1	3	.	.	.	.	.	.	.	21	.	.	19	.	.	20	.	17	+	.
Pur.	4	.	.	2	.	.	.	7	32	2	36	2	9	2	5	1	10	1	.	.	.
HG	.	.	.	.	.	.	.	.	.	.	47	.	.	8	.	.	1	.	.	.	.
CN	.	.	.	.	.	.	.	.	5	.	37	.	.	4	.	.	14	.	13	18	.
KJM	.	.	.	.	.	.	.	.	4	.	15	.	1	3	.	.	8	.	7	.	.
NTCD	.	.	.	.	.	.	.	.	1	.	1	.	.	1	.	.	2	1	.	.	35
DD	.	.	.	.	.	.	.	.	19	.	8	.	.	9	.	.	20	18	.	.	4
BB	.	.	.	.	.	.	.	.	3	.	7[a]	.	.	9	.	.	5	.	2	.	22
D. Suff.	.	.	.	.	.	1	.	.	1	.	18	.	.	1	.	.	3	1	.	20	.
Capt.	.	.	.	6	1	.	.	1	.	.	.	.	.	.	.	.	3	1	.	+	.
ET	.	.	.	.	.	.	.	.	.	.	4	.	.	1	.	.	3	.	3	+	.
2FMW	.	.	.	.	.	.	.	1	.	.	6	1	.	3	1	.	4	3	.	.	.
Span.	.	1	7	.	.	.	.	.	29	.	28	.	.	11	.	.	21	.	18	.	.
TMM	.	.	.	.	1	.	.	.	.	1	9	.	.	4	17	4	2	1	.	+	.
D. Ch.	.	.	.	.	.	.	.	.	.	.	.	.	.	.	.	.	1	.	.	+	.
LK	.	1	20	.	.	.	1	.	27	.	35	.	.	7	.	.	9	2	4	7	1
NL	.	.	1	.	24	.	.	.	.	.	56	.	.	3	15	.	9	1	3	.	.
GTQ	.	.	.	.	.	4	.	.	.	.	58	.	.	18	.	.	4	1	1	+	.
CTT	.	.	.	.	.	.	.	.	31	.	1	.	.	.	.	.	13	.	10	+	.
PMC	.	3	1	.	.	.	1	5	.	.	40	.	.	4	.	.	11	.	1	+	.
IG	.	2	.	.	.	1[b]	.	.	43	12	10	.	.	.	.	.	.	.	.	+	.
Law Tr.	.	5	.	.	.	3	.	.	.	.	5	.	.	1	.	1	1	.	.	+	.
HOB	.	3	.	.	.	.	.	.	.	.	23	.	.	2	.	.	5	.	.	.	.
WW	.	.	.	2	.	.	.	.	26	.	25	.	.	14	.	.	22	.	17	+	.
AL	.	.	.	.	.	.	.	.	22	1	23	.	6	9	3	.	17	.	13	+	.
Turk	.	1	.	.	.	.	.	.	.	.	.	.	.	.	.	.	.	.	.	.	.
JK	.	.	.	2	.	.	.	.	.	.	3	.	.	.	.	.	5	.	5	+	.
STM(S)	.	.	.	.	1	.	.	.	.	.	7	.	.	5	.	1	15	8	.	+	.
VB	.	.	6	.	.	.	.	.	13	.	39	.	.	6	.	.	8	.	5	.	.
Fl.	.	6	.	.	28[c]	.	.	.	.	.	37	.	.	8	.	.	12	.	.	.	.
CW	.	1	.	.	.	.	.	.	.	.	1	.	3	1	1	.	1	.	1	.	.
Ling.	.	.	.	.	.	.	.	.	.	.	1	.	.	1	.	.	.	.	.	+	.
Alb.	.	.	.	.	.	.	.	.	.	.	8	1	.	.	4	.	.	.	.	.	.
Mis.	.	.	.	8[d]	.	.	.	.	19	.	26	.	.	.	.	14	11	5	.	.	.

Occurrences: [a] Once as h'has. [b] Once as a'm. [c] 4 times as a'm.
[d] Exclusive of 30 instances in the running titles.

Band 4(h)

Table I.1

Band 4   Segment 3

/Middletonisms

		Length (words)	by..copy	can possible	Chaucer	comfort	fetch..again	give..due	'Has = he has	Inn a Court [+ noun]	Inns a Court [+ noun]	"Italian" joke	la(w) you	la(w) you now	lin	love alife
Chettle	Hoff.	20491	.	.	.	10	.	.	1	.	.	.	.	.	.	.
Haughton	Eng.	22364	.	.	.	3	.	.	.	.	.	.	.	.	.	.
X Plays	Blurt	18037*	.	.	.	1	.	.	1	.	.	.	.	.	.	1
	Pur.	19922*	1	1	.	11	2	1	7	.	.	.	1	1	1	.
Smith	HG	16666	.	.	.	1	.	.	2	.	.	.	.	.	.	.
Daven-port	CN	19943	.	.	.	5	.	.	4	.	.	.	.	.	.	.
	KJM	17883	.	.	.	5	.	.	1	.	.	.	.	.	.	.
	NTCD	21191	.	.	.	11	.	.	.	.	.	.	.	.	.	.
Anon.	DD	21652	.	.	.	5	.	1	.	.	.	.	2	.	.	.
X Play	BB	15618	.	.	.	4	.	.	1	.	.	.	1	1	.	.
Drue	D.Suff.	17674	.	.	.	10	.	.	.	.	.	.	.	.	.	.
Heywood	Capt.	23770	.	.	.	15	.	.	.	.	.	.	.	.	.	.
	ET	22771	.	.	.	5	.	.	.	.	.	.	.	.	.	.
	2FMW	20709	.	.	.	9	.	.	.	.	.	.	.	.	.	.
X Play	Span.	17460	.	.	.	7	.	.	1	.	.	.	.	.	.	.
Armin	TMM	18972	.	.	.	4	.	.	2	.	.	.	.	.	.	.
Barnes	D.Ch.	25183	.	.	.	6	.	.	.	.	.	.	.	.	.	.
Brewer	LK	18015	.	.	.	8	.	.	1	.	.	.	1	.	.	.
Brome	NL	26429	.	.	.	4	.	.	.	.	.	.	2^b	.	.	.
Cook	GTO	25304	.	.	.	6	2	.	2	.	.	.	.	.	.	.
Daborne	CTT	20016	.	.	.	9	.	.	.	.	1	.	.	.	1	.
	PMC	19751	.	.	.	9	.	.	2	.	.	.	.	.	.	.
Day	IG	21351	.	.	.	2	.	.	.	.	.	.	.	.	.	1
	Law Tr.	16652	.	.	.	4	.	.	1	.	.	.	.	.	.	1
	HOB	15149	.	.	.	4	.	.	.	.	.	.	.	.	.	.
Field	WW	17772	.	.	.	3	.	.	.	.	.	.	1^c	.	.	.
	AL	19006	.	.	.	3	.	.	.	.	.	.	1^c	.	.	.
Mason	Turk	18519	.	.	.	3	.	.	.	.	1	.	.	.	1	.
Munday	JK	13641	.	.	.	5	.	.	.	.	.	.	.	.	.	.
	STM(S)	16410	.	.	.	8	.	.	.	.	.	.	.	.	.	.
Sampson	VB	18375	.	.	.	6	.	.	.	.	.	.	.	.	.	.
Sharpham	Fl.	16832	.	.	.	4	.	1	.	.	2^a	.	.	.	.	.
	CW	24854	.	.	.	7	.	.	.	.	2	.	.	.	.	.
Tomkis	Ling.	26179	.	.	.	1	.	.	.	.	.	.	.	.	.	.
	Alb.	22767	.	.	.	2	.	.	3	.	.	.	.	.	.	.
Wilkins	Mis.	25068*	.	.	.	16	.	.	1	.	.	.	.	.	.	.

Occurrences: a Once as Inns of Court man

b Twice as Lo yee.   c As Law ye.

	[adv.] -ly welcome	mass, here	I (do) protest	sasarara	save..harmless	son and heir	spoke like	subaudi	suspectless	third part of	troth..say true	tut, man	Adam/Eve	garlick/strong	godamercy	hair..an end	lily..hands	make buttons	marry muff
Hoff.	.	.	1	.	.	.	.	.	.	.	.	.	.	.	1	.	.	.	.
Eng.	1	.	.	.	.	.	.	.	.	.	.	1	.	.	.	.	.	.	.
Blurt	.	.	.	.	.	.	.	.	.	.	.	.	1	1	1	2	2	.	2
Pur.	2	1	8	1	1	5	.	.	.	.	1	.	.	.	.	.	.	.	.
HG	.	.	1	.	.	.	.	.	.	.	.	.	.	.	1	.	.	.	.
CN	1	.	2	.	.	.	.	.	.	.	.	.	.	.	.	.	.	.	.
KJM	1	.	1	.	.	.	.	.	.	.	.	.	.	.	.	.	.	.	.
NTCD	.	.	1	.	.	.	.	.	.	.	.	.	.	.	.	2	.	.	.
DD	.	.	.	.	.	.	.	.	.	.	.	.	.	.	.	1	1[a]	.	.
BB	.	2	1	.	.	1	.	.	.	.	.	.	.	.	.	.	.	.	.
D. Suff.	.	.	1	.	.	.	.	.	.	.	.	.	.	.	.	.	.	.	.
Capt.	.	.	3	.	.	.	.	.	.	.	.	.	.	.	.	.	.	.	.
ET	2	.	4	.	.	.	.	.	.	.	.	.	.	.	.	.	.	.	.
2FMW	.	.	.	.	.	.	.	.	.	.	.	.	.	.	.	.	.	.	.
Span.	1	.	2	.	.	.	.	.	.	.	.	.	.	.	.	.	.	1	.
TMM	.	.	1	.	.	.	.	.	.	.	1	.	.	.	.	.	.	.	.
D. Ch.	1	.	.	.	.	.	.	.	.	.	.	.	.	.	.	.	.	.	.
LK	.	.	1	.	.	.	2	.	.	.	.	.	.	.	.	.	.	.	.
NL	.	.	9	.	.	1	.	.	.	.	.	.	.	.	2	.	.	.	.
GTQ2	1	.	5	.	.	.	.	.	.	.	.	.	.	.	1	.	.	.	.
CTT	.	.	.	.	.	.	.	.	.	.	.	.	.	.	.	.	.	.	.
PMC	.	.	.	.	.	.	.	.	.	.	.	.	.	.	.	.	.	.	.
IG	.	.	4	.	.	.	.	.	.	.	.	.	.	1	.	3	.	.	.
Law. Tr.	.	.	.	.	.	.	.	.	.	.	.	.	1	.	.	1	.	.	.
HOB	.	.	2	.	.	.	.	.	.	.	.	.	.	.	.	1	.	.	.
WW	.	.	.	.	.	.	.	.	.	.	.	.	.	.	.	3	.	.	.
AL	.	.	4	.	.	.	.	.	.	.	.	.	.	.	.	1	.	.	.
Turk	1	.	.	.	.	.	.	.	.	.	.	.	.	.	.	.	.	.	.
JK	.	.	.	.	.	.	.	.	.	.	.	.	.	.	.	.	1	.	.
STM(S)	.	.	1	.	.	.	.	.	.	.	.	.	.	.	.	.	.	.	.
VB	.	.	1	.	.	.	.	.	.	.	.	.	.	.	.	.	.	.	.
Fl.	.	.	4	.	.	1	.	.	.	.	.	.	.	.	.	.	.	.	1
CW	.	2	4	.	.	.	.	.	.	.	.	.	.	1	.	1	.	.	.
Ling.	.	.	7	.	.	.	.	.	.	.	.	.	.	.	.	.	.	.	.
Alb.	1	.	.	.	.	.	.	.	.	.	.	.	.	.	.	.	.	.	.
Mis.	2	.	2	.	.	1	.	.	.	.	.	.	.	.	1	.	.	.	.

Occurrences: [a]As haire stiffe & on end.

Band 4(j)

/Other items

Author	Play	moon/horn(s)	mumble-crust	no point	oyster/open	parrot = [woman]	puss-cat	rowly-powly	Signior no	snick up	snip snap	stile/style pun	Tamburlaine	wink at small faults	deed la	float of	forfeit of	'tis Oracle	undertake a voluntary exile
Chettle	Hoff.																		
Haughton	Eng.																		
X Plays	Blurt			1			2	1	6	1	1		1						
	Pur.																		
Smith	HG																		
Davenport	CN																		
	KJM																		
	NTCD																		
Anon.	DD																		
X Play	BB																		
Drue	D.Suff.																		
Heywood	Capt.																		
	ET																		
	2FMW																		
X Play	Span.		1		1	1						1			1	1	3		1
Armin	TMM							1	1										
Barnes	D.Ch.																		
Brewer	LK																		
Brome	NL																		
Cook	GTQ												2						
Daborne	CTT													1[a]					
	PMC																		
Day	IG								1			1							
	Law Tr.																		
	HOB																		
Field	WW																		
	AL																		
Mason	Turk																		
Munday	JK																		
	STM(S)																		
Sampson	VB						1												
Sharpham	Fl.									1									
	CW																		
Tomkis	Ling.																		
	Alb.																		
Wilkins	Mis.	1																	

Occurrences: [a] As wink at all faults.

I.2. Table I.2. Some Unique Parallels

The parallels listed here do not occur elsewhere in the corpus. The elements listed under "Collocation" are the minima which have been checked through the corpus; the actual agreement between the passage in the "X" play and the "other occurrence" is in many cases very much more striking than appears here. An oblique stroke (/) signifies that the collocation appears in the "other occurrence" with order-variation of the parts separated by the stroke. Spellings in collocations are modernised.

Abbreviations of authors' names: B = Barry; D = Dekker; F = Ford; M = Middleton; W = Webster. The sign ++ indicates that the parallel was first noted in this study.

X Play	Reference	Collocation	Author	Play Reference	
Blurt	I.i.213	because .. not start	D	OF V.ii.35	++
"	III.i.123-36	Song with pity, pity	D	OF I.ii.20-35	++
"	III.iii.171	a rubbers	D	Sat.V.ii.351	++
"	III.iii.107	sweating hands	D	OF III.i.355	++
"	V.iii.186	tragic/comic(al) event	D	Sat.V.ii.113	++
FL	V.iii.278,79	distressed Geneva	B	RA V.i (I4)	++
"	II.i.20	dog-cheap	D	ITBN II.ii.85	++
Pur.	I.i (A4)	the properer phrase	M	YFG IV.v.21	++
RT	II.i.19	cut..dirty way	M	MWM I.i.75	
"	IV.ii.255	in grain..hold colour	M	MWM III.iii.81-82	
"	II.i.228	nine coaches	M	NWNH V.i.355	++
"	II.i.129-30	Rhyme: no man--common	M	MWM I.ii.87-88	++
"	I.i.18	study's ornament(s)	M	MDBW I.ii.4	
"	IV.ii.228	thanks..spirit..investions	M	MWM III.iii.70-71	
NV	I.i (151a)	t'as almost..my heart	M	YFG II.i.163	++
AQL	II.i.68-69	I..heard/one/in England	W	DLC III.ii (Flv)	
"	IV.i.82	ingeniously perceive	W	DLC I.i (Blv)	
"	V.i.133	singular fine churchman	W	DLC III.iii (F2v)	
"	II.i.50	sweet breath'd monkey	W	DLC I.ii (Clv)	
Span.	III.ii.1-2	circled..friends	F	LM V.i (L2)	
"	IV.i.6	('t)is music to	D	MML IV.iii.14	++
"	III.i.139	Peter-see-me	D	2HW IV.iii.49-50	++
"	III.i.115	pindy-pandy	D	Sh.H.IV.iv.133	++

---

[1] Occurs as Peter sa meene

I.3. Table I.3.

Corpus plays of 1606-15 containing undisguised divine names in oaths

The purpose of this table is to refute two propositions:

(1) that plays containing undisguised divine names in oaths must date from before May 1606; (2) that the lack of such oaths in Middleton must be due the date of publication or performance of his plays.

The table contains only plays of undoubted authorship, and excludes known collaborations. Dates of first performance are taken from Chambers' The Elizabethan Stage.(I have also consulted Bentley, and Harbage's Annals of English Drama, revised by Schoenbaum, but have found no certain chronological improvements.)

Numbers in parentheses give the number of instances; no number after an oath means that it occurs once. Spellings of oaths are modernized.

Abbreviations: J = Jesu(s); L = Lord; G = God. "Fore" includes before and afore.

Part I

10 plays probably first performed before, but published after, May 1606

First perf.	First edn.	Title	Oaths
1597-98	1609	The Case is Altered	J; by J (2). L; O L; fore the L (2); good L. G's foot; G's lid (2); G's light (2); G's my life; G's my witness; G's pity (2); G's precious; G's so (8); for G's love; for G's sake (5); (a, in) G's name (2); by G's bid. G; O G (4); fore G (3).
1598	1616	Englishmen for my Money	O J. L (5). G s me (5); G's sacaren; G's sekerkin (2); a G's name (2). O G (4); fore G (4) ; good G.
1601	1607	What You Will	J (4); O J (3). O L (3); by the L (2). G's foot; G's me (3); G's my life; for G's sake (2). O G (6).
1602-07	1607	Lingua	O L.
1602	1631	Hoffman	O L (2); good L. G's Lady; G's my witness. G for thy mercy; O G (2).
1604-07	1608	Law Tricks	L; O L. G's me; for G's sake. G for me; as G mend me; fore G (9); my G.
1605-06	1607	Volpone	L (5). G's precious; G's so (2). O G; fore G.
1606	1607	The Fleer	O L. G's light; G's me; G's my life; a G's name. O G (2).

First perf.	First edn.	Title	Oaths
1604– c.1605[1]	1630	2 Honest Whore	L; byth' L (2). G's so (2). G is my judge.
1604– c.1617	1647	The Woman's Prize	L. A G's name. O G.

Part II

22 plays probably first performed June 1606--December 1615

First perf.	First edn.	Title	Oaths
1606(?)	1623	Coriolanus	O G.
1607	1607	Cupid's Whirligig	L. G's light (3); G's my passion; G's precious (2).
1607	1607	The Devil's Charter	O L of heavens. For G's sake; in G's name (3). Fore G (2); O G (3);'O G of Heavens.
1607	1607	The Miseries of Enforced Marriage	By J. O L. G's precious (3); a G s name; for G's sake (2). G is my record; G of his goodness; as G save me; fore G; O G (5).
1607	1613	The Knight of the Burning Pestle	L. A G's name (2); by G's body; for G's sake; in G's name.
1607–08	1608	Humour out of Breath	L (2); O L. O G (2).
1607–08	1611	Ram Alley	L (4). For G's love. Fore G; O G (2).
c.1607	1655	The Lovesick King	O L.
1607–08	1609	Two Maids of Moreclacke	L. G's me; a G's name. G a men; G dudge me; by G; grace a G (2); O G (3).
c.1608	1638	A Shoemaker a Gentleman	G's me (2); G's my passion.
1603–09	1612	The Widow's Tears	G's me; G's my fortune; G's my patience.
1609	1611	May Day	L (7); L of heaven; good L. G's me (4); G's my judge; G's my life (3); G's pity (2); G's precious; a G's name (2); by G's Lord; for G's sake (5). O G; fore G; name of G; as G help.
1607–11	1611	The Atheist's Tragedy	L. A G's name; for G's sake. Fore G (2); O G (2).
1609	1610	Epicene	L; good L; O L (2). G's so (4); G's will; for G's love; for G's sake (6). Fore G (4); O G (4); as G help me (2).

---

[1] So Chambers. I have given reasons for dating this play c.1607 (see above, 1.2.5.1, 2.1.1).

First perf.	First edn.	Title	Oaths
1610	1612	The Alchemist	G's lid (3); G's light; G's precious; G's so; G's will (2); a G's name; for G's sake (2). Fore G (3).
c.1612	1614	Greene's Tu Quoque	L (4); O L. G's my judge; G's precious; G's will; for G's sake. As G save me; O G; so G ha me.
1609?	1612	A Woman is a Weathercock	L (4). G's lid; G's precious; G's will (2); a G's name; for G's sake (3). As G help me; by G; fore G (3); O G (2).
>1611	1618	Amends for Ladies	O J. L. G's precious. As G help me (2); O G (3).
1611	1623	The Tempest	L.
1609-12	1612	The White Devil	L (3). G's precious; for G's sake (5). G refuse me; good G; O G.
1610-16	1639	Monsieur Thomas	Good L. For G's sake (2). O G.
1614	1631	Bartholomew Fair	L; good L (3); O L (4). G's lid (2); G's my life; G's so (2); a G's name; for G's sake. Fore G (2); O G (2).

None of the above expressions occurs in any undoubted play of Middleton.

Appendix II

Grades of run-on lines: a verse test for The Revenger's Tragedy

Oliphant, in his historic article on the authorship of The Revenger's Tragedy, gave utterance to an obiter dictum which must express the feelings of many canonical investigators. "Personally," he said, "I attach more importance to the impression the verse makes upon me than I do to any other single factor ... . but I do not attempt the hopeless task of proving my case that way."[1] Since the beginning of the Revenger's Tragedy authorship controversy, to the best of my knowledge only two disputants have offered statistics of versification--Barker[2] and Fred L. Jones.[3] Barker showed that as regards feminine endings The Revenger's Tragedy agrees with Middleton's early comedies, not with The Atheist's Tragedy; Jones discovered a similar agreement with Middleton and disagreement with Tourneur as regards the occurrence of to and of at line endings. The reluctance of other scholars to venture on to this ground is probably due to two factors--textual difficulties, and weaknesses in the available theory of versification. But both of these obstacles can be surmounted.

The textual difficulties are various aspects of unreliable lineation in the first quartos of The Revenger's Tragedy and The Atheist's Tragedy. In The Revenger's Tragedy there occur some very long verse lines, which the author probably intended to be divided; also, sometimes the transition points between prose and verse are uncertain. Both of these features are easily explicable on the hypothesis of Middleton's authorship, since Middleton's habits of lineation (as revealed in his Game at Chess holograph) and of prose-verse transition produce similar textual difficulties in his early comedies. But in fact for the purposes of authorship investigation these problems are minor in The Revenger's Tragedy: they can be avoided by excluding from the argument the feature of line-length, and for other verse features considering only passages printed clearly as verse. This

---

[1] "The Authorship of The Revenger's Tragedy," p. 160.

[2] "The Authorship of The Second Maiden's Tragedy and The Revenger's Tragedy," p. 127.

[3] "Cyril Tourneur," TLS, 30 (18 June 1931), 487; and "An Experiment with Massinger's Verse," PMLA, 47 (1932), 727-40. Jones' work on "split phrases" beginning with of and to suggested to me the wider category of Preposition/Nominal line endings discussed below. Unfortunately Jones did not state what editions he used, and I cannot find in The Revenger's Tragedy (Q 1607) the split phrase introduced by of which he reports in "Experiment," p. 729.

latter is not a serious limitation, since the bulk of the verse of The
Revenger's Tragedy is not doubtful at all. The situation is somewhat
worse in The Atheist's Tragedy, for large sections of what is certainly
verse are printed as prose, especially in Acts IV and V; but the same
remedy can be applied. Moreover in those sections of The Atheist's Tragedy
which are printed as verse--over 1200 lines--the lineation is not in any way
suspect: all editors of the play have reproduced the Q1 line division, and
though this reads strangely at times, the peculiarities (which I shall
examine below) occur also in Tourneur's heroic couplet poems (1609, 1613),
where the lineation is guaranteed by rhyme. R. A. Foakes has tried to
defend Tourneur's authorship of The Revenger's Tragedy by emphasizing the
textual difficulties and suggesting that statistics may vary according to
the edition used; but the only statistics that he cites prove merely that he
does not know the difference between a feminine ending and a "light" or
"weak" ending.[1]

Foakes' mistake is, if not excusable, at least symptomatic: versification is an aspect of style which has been rather neglected in the past
fifty years. The tools of the nineteenth century were not always of the
best, but instead of being improved they have been allowed to rust. Hence,
perhaps, recent investigators of the Revenger's Tragedy problem, if they
refer to versification at all, do so merely in general terms or fall back
on quoting sample passages without much analysis of them. Schoenbaum
cites in contrast Revenger's Tragedy, III.v.75-78, 87-98 (sigs. Flv-F2;
"Do's the Silke-worme expend her yellow labours . . .") and Atheist's
Tragedy, II.i.91-106 (D2v-D3: 'He lay in's Armour; as if that had beene /
His Coffine . . ."), remarking that "in the verse of The Atheist's Tragedy
concentration has given way to discursiveness, metaphor to simile, intensity
to slackness."[2] This may be a fair critical judgment on the general
difference of impression made by these two passages; but it leaves unmention-
ed the enormous objective difference between the two verse structures.
Formal verse can always be described in terms of two independent variables,
end-rhythm and lineation. As regards end-rhythm, Schoenbaum's Revenger's

[1] "On the Authorship of 'The Revenger's Tragedy'," p.134, fn. Foakes'
error was noted by Schoenbaum in Middleton's Tragedies, pp. 424-43.

[2] Middleton's Tragedies, pp. 163-64.

Tragedy passage contains 6 feminine endings in 16 lines of verse; his
Atheist's Tragedy passage contains no feminine endings at all in 16 lines;
and the passages are typical of their plays. However, this is an aspect of
the versification of The Revenger's Tragedy which has already been covered
by Barker, and I need say no more about it. The difference in lineation
between the two passages may be described as follows: the Atheist's Tragedy
passage has more run-on lines, and above all it contains four lines of
clearly higher-grade enjambement than any in the Revenger's Tragedy passage.
Thus twice in the Atheist's Tragedy passage the line-ending splits a prepositional phrase: runnes vp/The Shoare; with/A kinde (a type of line-ending
which occurs nowhere in The Revenger's Tragedy); once, the ending divides
a part of the copula BE[1] from its complement (beene/His Coffine); and once
it divides a conjunction from the clause it introduces (if/It could). Line
endings of this kind are frequent throughout The Atheist's Tragedy; sometimes several occur close together, producing a strange effect, as in
III.iii.16-20:

> Our owne constructions are the authors of
> Our miserie. We neuer measure our
> Conditions but with Men aboue vs in
> Estate. So while our Spirits labour to
> Be higher then our fortunes th'are more base.   (G3^v)

This is more extreme, but not different in kind, from a passage in
A Funeral Poem upon the Death . . . of Sir Francis Vere:[2]

> When as the few complaints reported how
> Effectually his labours prosper'd; and
> His men grew well conform'd to his command;
> With their obedience, he did slacke the bent
> Of his severitie in punishment.
> Yet with so wise a moderation, that
> His fame to be seuere, continu'd at
> The full opinion.   (p. 163)

---

[1] I have adopted from Frank R. Palmer, A Linguistic Study of the English
Verb (London: Longman's, 1965), p. 11, the convention that a word-form
in capitals stands for the whole set of its inflections.

[2] This and the rest of Tourneur's non-dramatic works have been studied in
The Works of Cyril Tourneur, ed. Allardyce Nicoll. Page references are to
this edition.

Tourneur, it will be seen, treats the pentameter line very differently
from Middleton. Instead of loosening the line with feminine endings and
extra syllables, he keeps it rigid, cutting it off after the tenth syllable
no matter how unnatural it may be to pause in reading or delivery at the
line-end, nor how impossible it may be to stress the last syllable of the
line. Lineation of this kind has been partially covered in the past by the
terms "weak" and "light" endings;[1] but the categories of "weak" and "light"
have been used for a very miscellaneous collection of function words, and,
moreover, defined as a sub-category of masculine endings,[2] thus confusing
lineation with end-rhythm. In my studies of versification[3] I have been
forced to discard the terms "weak" and "light"; instead I divide run-on line
endings--i.e. endings where no punctuation is possible by normal present-d
rules--into four grades (one sub-divided), defined solely by the grammatica
status of the juncture with which the line-ending coincides. The English
grammar which I pre-suppose is of the "systemic" kind used by many British
linguists, but its terms can be translated equally well into those of
'traditional" English grammar, and I hope that my categories are in fact
objective and mostly non-controversial.[4] My whole scheme for the
description of line-endings can be summarized as follows:

Stopped endings

Grade A: Line-ending coinciding with end of sentence.
Grade B: Line-ending at a point where the main clause structure
                is complete, so that there is no suspension of sense.
Grade O: Line-ending before the main clause-structure is complete,
                where punctuation is possible.

---

[1]
'Weak" and "light" endings for The Revenger's Tragedy and Tourneur were
counted by E. E. Stoll, in John Webster (1905), p. 212. Stoll examined the
first acts only of Revenger's Tragedy and Atheist's Tragedy.

[2]
See Jakob Schipper, A History of English Versification (Oxford:
Clarendon Press, 1910), pp. 225-27. Nearly all the Grade 2 endings
studied for the Revenger's Tragedy problem are in fact masculine, but
feminine Grade 2 endings do occur. Separation of variables is important
if they are to be used as independent tests of authorship.

[3]
My scheme of line-endings was first devised for a study of Henry VIII
(unpublished) in 1968, and subsequently used for teaching purposes on a
wide range of English poets. Hence there is no bias effect involved
in its use for the Revenger's Tragedy problem.

[4]
I have used Barbara M. H. Strang, Modern English Structure (London:
Edward Arnold, 1962) as a reference grammar.

Run-on endings

Grade 1:   "Normal run-on." Line-ending typically between groups.[1]

This category contains all run-ons except those defined below.

Grade 2:   Extra-rapid run-on.

Grade 2- :   Line-ending dividing structures of which one element is BE

or a conjunction or a personal pronoun.

Grade 2+ :   Line-ending within groups, between words.

Grade 3:   Line-endings within words, between morphemes.

Grade 4:   Line-endings within morphemes, between phonemes.

The stopped grades do not concern us now, and run-on Grades 3 and
4 are useless for most attribution problems: in Jacobean drama I have
noticed them only occasionally, in some works of Jonson. But Grades 2-
and 2+ provide extremely good discrimination between Middleton (who avoids
them) and Tourneur (who makes frequent use of them, for example in the
passages quoted above). I shall therefore list the various cases included
in each grade.

Grades 2- and 2+:   detailed definitions   (/= line-ending)

2- :   Conjunction/; BE/ any structure, e.g. not, complement, Main Verb;
       Personal Pronoun Subject/its Verb; Verb/Personal Pronoun Object or
       Subject. (Relative and Interrogative Pronouns are not included.)

2+ :   To/Infinitive; Aux (= Auxiliary verb other than BE) / Main Verb;
       Aux/not; Aux/Aux; Preposition/Nominal (i.e. Noun-phrase or single
       noun or pronoun); within a Noun-phrase, pre-modifier/head, i.e.
       pre-modifier/pre-modifier(s)+Noun or pre-modifier/Noun; more or
       most/Adjective or Adverb.[2]

This system can be exemplified by applying it to a well-known prose passage
of Hamlet, and noticing what grade would occur at each word-division

---

[1] For the term 'group' see Strang, p. 73. A group is an immediate
constituent of clause structure.

[2] See Strang, Chapter VII, for the structure of the noun-phrase. Pre-
modifiers include determiners (articles, possessives, demonstratives,
numerals), adjectives, and noun-adjuncts. The term "adjective" is limited
to words which can be compared by means of the modifiers more, most or
the suffixes -er, -est.

if that were to coincide with the end of a verse line.[1]

 Speak (1) the (2+) speech, (B) I (2-) pray (2-) you,(B) as (2-)
I (2-) pronounced (2-) it (1) to (2+) you, (B) trippingly (1) on
(2+) the (2+) tongue, (B) but (2-) if (2-) you (2-) mouth (2-) it,
(0) as (2-) many (1) of (2+) your (2+) players (1) do, (0) I (2-)
had (1) as (2-) lief (1) the (2+) town-(2+) crier (1) spoke (1)
my (2+) lines. (A)

 I shall now compare The Revenger's Tragedy and the relevant works
of Middleton and Tourneur with respect to frequency of Grade 2 endings.
As usual, the significant statistics are those of relative frequency,
which I give as so many instances of Grade 2+ or 2- endings per 1000 lines
of compact heroic verse. By "heroic" verse I mean verse whose norm is the
pentameter, but including some longer lines and occasional half-lines. By
"compact" verse I mean (i) all verse contained in rhyme;[2] and (ii) verse
contained in speeches of more than one line, which therefore include at
least one line-ending and hence at least one possibility of a Grade 2
ending. A count of compact verse has several advantages over a count of
total verse: it gives a more realistic denominator for the relative frequency
of Grade 2, and it avoids the difficulty (sometimes impossibility) of
having to decide whether speeches of only a few words are verse or prose.
Moreover, all lines of text are counted separately: one does not have to
fit part-lines together at speech-junctions in some conjectural scheme.
I have taken as verse only that which is marked as such by shortness of
printed line, or non-sentence-initial capital at the beginning of the line,
or both. All figures for plays are based exclusively on the first edition
texts.

 Table II(1) below gives the statistics for Middleton's early plays,
The Revenger's Tragedy, The Atheist's Tragedy, and, as a specimen of
Middleton's later style, A Chaste Maid in Cheapside.

---

[1] The Hamlet text is from the Complete Works of Shakespeare, ed. Peter
Alexander (1951; rpt. London: Collins, 1964), p. 1048.

[2] Rhymed verse normally occurs in speeches of more than one line, but
there are occasional exceptions.

Table II(1). Grade 2 endings in plays

Key: P/N = Preposition/Nominal; A/N = Adjective/Nominal, i.e. Adject-
ive/Noun or Adjective/Adjective(s) + Noun. C.h.v. = compact heroic
verse.

Relative frequencies per 1000 lines are given to one decimal place.

| | Grade 2+ | | | Grade | Total | c.h.v. | r.f. per 1000 lines | |
	P/N	A/N	Other	2-	Gr.2	lines	P/N	Total, Gr.2
Phoen.	.	.	1	.	1	582	.	1.7
MT	.	.	1	.	1	444	.	2.3
MWM	.	.	2	2	4	407	.	9.8
Trick	.	.	.	.	.	232	.	.
YFG	.	.	.	2	2	445	.	4.5
Total, early Middleton	.	.	4	4	8	2110	.	3.8
CMC	.	.	1	2	3	1259	.	2.4
RT	.	.	2	3	5	1962	.	2.5
AT	32	6	20	53	111	1227	26.7	90.5

One sees that the rate of Grade 2 endings in The Revenger's Tragedy is just a little lower than the average for early Middleton (very
close to the rates of Michaelmas Term and Chaste Maid), but less than
one thirtieth of the rate of The Atheist's Tragedy. Middleton's very
low rate of Grade 2 endings is a constant feature of his style at all
periods; the close agreement with The Revenger's Tragedy is very striking, though the remarkable goodness of the match may be something of a
coincidence: all we can be sure of is that both Middleton and The
Revenger's Tragedy have very low rates. For I am not confident that all
examples of Grade 2 recorded for The Revenger's Tragedy and the Middleton plays are genuine instances intended by the author; I have simply
counted them wherever they occurred, according to the rules announced
above.   Probably some instances are due to a compositor's misinterpret-
ation of his copy; but since the same could be true of some instances in
The Atheist's Tragedy, I have preferred not to exercise editorial
judgment.[1]   A list of all instances counted is given at the end of this
appendix.

It is highly interesting that, few as they are, the Grade 2 endings
in Middleton and in The Revenger's Tragedy agree closely in type. There
are none of the Preposition/Nominal or Adjective/Nominal endings found
frequently in The Atheist's Tragedy; instead, the reliable instances
are all endings within verbal phrases, or between BE and its complement,

[1] In the only case where a line-ending may or may not be indicated by a
quarto, ath'/Diuill in Revenger's Tragedy, D1v, I have counted a Grade
2+ ending.

or after a conjunction. The single certain Grade 2+ ending in The Revenger's Tragedy, can/[Main Verb](B3), matches the single instance in Michaelmas Term: can/ [Main Verb](Flv).

There is some evidence that Tourneur's rate of Grade 2 endings was relatively constant throughout his literary career, or at least that it was always much higher than the rate of The Revenger's Tragedy. Tourneur's earliest extant work is the obscurely allegorical poem in rhyme royal, The Transformed Metamorphosis, printed by Valentine Simmes in 1600. It so happens that young Thomas Middleton had a poem of nearly equal length in the same verse form printed in the same year by the same printer--The Ghost of Lucrece. Now Lucrece, in 637 lines, has no Grade 2 endings at all but Metamorphosis in its 743 lines has three instances of Grade 2+ and one of Grade 2-, yielding an overall rate for Grade 2 endings more than twice as high as that of The Revenger's Tragedy, even though it is in a form and a tradition (the Spenserian, more or less) which might be expected to inhibit such endings. Tourneur's later poems in heroic couplets, A Funeral Poem upon the Death of . . .Sir Francis Vere (1609; hereinafter cited as Vere) and A Grief on the Death of Prince Henry (1613; hereinafter cited as Henry), have very much higher rates than Revenger's Tragedy, as Table II(2) shows.

Table II(2).   Grade 2 endings in verse works

Rhymes in the plays have been counted on the principle that what is an acceptable rhyme in a poem must be counted as a rhyme wherever it occurs in a play, even though possibly "unintentional".
F.Q. I, i-vi = The Faerie Queene, Bk. I, Cantos i-vi, studied in The Poetical Works of Spenser, ed. J. C. Smith and E. De Selincourt (London, 1912; rpt. London: Oxford Univ. Press, 1950).

| | Grade 2+ | | | Grade | Total | c.h.v. | r.f. per 1000 lines | |
	P/N	A/N	Other	2-	Gr.2	lines	P/N	Total, Gr.2
F.Q. I, i-vi	.	.	1	3	4	2664	.	1.5
Lucrece	.	.	.	.	.	637	.	.
RT, rhyme	.	.	.	.	.	459	.	.
RT, all verse	.	.	2	3	5	1962	.	2.5
Tourneur								
Metamorphosis	3	.	.	1	4	743	4.0	5.4
Vere	2	2	2	14	20	604	3.3	33.1
AT, rhyme	1	.	2	3	6	151	6.6	39.7
AT, all verse	32	6	20	53	111	1227	26.7	90.5
Henry	1	3	.	7	11	140	7.1	78.6

These figures allow us to draw some interesting conclusions. First, since in The Atheist's Tragedy the Grade 2 rate for the whole play is so much higher than that for the rhymed sections, it is clear that Tourneur

was more inclined to Grade 2 endings when writing blank verse than when
writing rhyme--as might be expected a priori, since rhyme tends to induce
end-stopping and inhibit running-on. This is especially true of rhyming
in the Spenserian tradition, where so many reversals of normal word-order
permit a very highly end-stopped verse-structure. Yet even so Tourneur's
Metamorphosis contrasts clearly with The Faerie Queene; in particular,
Tourneur in his first work uses Preposition/Nominal endings, whereas Spenser,
in the verse sampled, does not. Apparently Tourneur's rate of using P/N
endings in rhyme changed very little over the period 1600-1613, rising
slightly after 1609, to nearly double his initial rate, in the short elegy
for Prince Henry. The large difference between the overall Grade 2 rates
of Metamorphosis and Tourneur's couplet rhymes is most probably due to
the differences of genre and verse-form. All this evidence supports the
expectation that if Tourneur had written The Revenger's Tragedy about 1606-
07, the rate of Grade 2 in the rhymed sections would have been not very
different from the rate in Vere--about 33 per thousand, or about 15 instances
in 459 lines--not zero, as we actually observe.[1] In the blank verse of
The Revenger's Tragedy, 1503 lines, we could expect at least as many
instances of Grade 2 as in the blank verse of The Atheist's Tragedy--over
100, instead of the actual 5.[2] And some two dozen of these might be expected
to be of the P/N type, which The Revenger's Tragedy wholly lacks. These
are just so many statistical modes of stating what should be obvious to
every unprejudiced student--that Tourneur's treatment of verse, in all his
undoubted works, is idiosyncratic and unmistakable--and that this treatment
is unmistakably not present anywhere in The Revenger's Tragedy. To defend his
authorship of the play one would have to postulate that he totally abandoned
his own verse style at some point between 1600 and 1606 in favour of a
perfect imitation of Middleton's; and then re-accentuated his earlier
tendencies in time for Vere's death in 1609. No such freakish development
and counter-development are known for any Jacobean poet.

---

[1] A chi-squared test of significance (chi-squared = 18.9, with one degree
of freedom) yields a probability of less than .00002 that the observed
distribution of Grade 2 endings among the rhymed lines of Revenger's Tragedy,
Vere, Atheist's Tragedy, and Henry can be due to chance alone; i.e. the
odds are 50,000 to 1 that Revenger's Tragedy is not in the same rhymed-
verse style as the other works.

[2] Chi-squared for the blank verse = 130.56 with one degree of freedom,
yielding a probability of less than .00001, i.e. more than 100,000 to 1
against chance.

A survey of the sections of Revenger's Tragedy and Atheist's Tragedy printed clearly as verse in the first editions shows that the difference between the plays in rate of Grade 2 endings is fairly constant through the five acts of each play. Table II(3), below, displays the distributions.

Table II(3). Revenger's Tragedy and Atheist's Tragedy: distribution of endings in clearly printed verse.

| | | Grade 2+ | | Grade | Total | c.h.v. | r.f. per 1000 lines | |
		P/N	A/N	Other	2-	Gr.2	lines	P/N	Total, Gr.2
RT	Act								
	I	.	.	1	1	2	545	.	3.7
	II	.	.	1	1	2	457	.	4.4
	III	.	.	.	1	1	364	.	2.7
	IV	.	.	.	.	.	372	.	.
	V	.	.	.	.	.	224	.	.
	Total	.	.	2	3	5	1962	.	2.5
AT	Act								
	I	5	1	5	16	27	414	12.1	65.2
	II	9	2	6	12	29	255	35.3	113.7
	III	13	2	7	17	39	262	49.6	148.9
	IV	.	1	1	4	6	86	.	69.8
	V	5	.	1	4	10	210	23.8	47.6
	Total	32	6	20	53	111	1227	26.7	90.5

It is reasonable to conclude on all the versification evidence that Tourneur did not write The Revenger's Tragedy, but Middleton could have done so.

List of Grade 2 endings tabulated

Faerie Queene, Book I

Gr. 2+ : would/Haue slaine (iii.38.2).

Gr. 2- : reare/Her (ii.45.3); hate/Her (iii.7.7); held/Her (vi.23.1)

Phoenix

Gr. 2+ : the/Captaine (A4v, I.i.158; probably a mislineation).

Michaelmas Term

Gr. 2+ : can/Be Bawde (Flv, III.i.298; lineation guaranteed by rhyme).

Mad World

Gr. 2+ : must/Liue (C2, II.ii.47; guaranteed by rhyme); to,/Take
(H3v, V.ii.123; guaranteed by rhyme--the comma is non-grammatical).

Gr. 2- : yet/There's (A4, I.i.164); I/Must (C2, II.ii.44; probably prose
set as verse).

Your Five Gallants

Gr. 2- : fatted/Me (A4, I.i.158); for/Since (B2, I.i.333).

Chaste Maid

Gr. 2+ : the/Bottome (D3v, II.ii.91; probably a mislineation).

Gr. 2- : I/wonder (B4-B4v, I.i.200; probably a mislineation);
to be/A good House (I1, V.i.9).

Revenger's Tragedy

Gr. 2+ : can/Forget (B3, I.iii.41); ath'/Diuill (D1v, II.i.31; probably not
intended by the printer to be read as a line end, since ath' touches the
right margin, and Diuill is usually capitalized wherever it occurs).

Gr. 2- : the slaue's/Already (B3, I.iii.39); was/But some (E2, II.ii.334);
because/Wee're (F4, III.vi.25).

Atheist's Tragedy (References to quarto and to pages of Nicoll's edition).

Gr. 2+ :
  Act I: P/N: aboue/His nature (B1, 175); in/Th'abundant fulnesse
  (B1, 175); of/Our mutuall .. breathes (B4, 181); to/An absent man
  (C4v, 189); of/A nature (D1, 190). A/N: fluent/Increase (B4, 181;
  a feminine ending). Other types: should/Desire (B1v, 176); haue/
  Possess'd (B4, 181); hath/Reseru'd (C4v, 189); my/Affection (D1,190);
  can/Perswade (D1,190).
  Act II: P/N: vpon/The sands (D2v, 194); vp/The Shoare (D2v, 195);
  with/A kinde (D3, 195); from/Th'induction (E3, 204); through/The eye
  (E3v, 204); vpon/Our mindes (F2v, 211); of/Some bloudy accident (F3, 211);
  of/That death (F3, 211); vpon/An idle apprehension (F3, 212). A/N:
  faire/Aduantage (D2, 193); the rais'd/Impressions (F2v, 211). Other
  types: last/Expiring gaspe (D2v, 194); will/Distaste (E1, 199);
  did/Protect (E3v, 204); would/Informe (F2v, 211); all/Fore-sight
  (F2v, 211); might/Be (F3, 211).

Act III: P/N: of/This Phenix (F4, 214); on/These .. pillars (F4, 214; in rhyme); on/The altar (F4v, 215); vpon/His blasted Spring (F4v, 215); vpon/ A sweet young blossome (F4v, 215); of/Those Elements (G1, 416); of/Desire (G1, 216); of/Thy Iustice (G3,220); of/Our miserie (G3v, 221); in/Estate (G3v, 221); of/The Sunne (G4, 222); to/No other end (G4v, 223); vpon/ A knowne Successour (G4v, 223). A/N: foule/Deedes (F4, 215); diuine/ Impression (G4, 222). Other types: the/Description (F4, 214; in rhyme); my/Dead Father (F4v, 215; in rhyme); their/Returne (G1, 216); our/Conditions (G3v, 221); to/Be (G3v, 221); has/Depriu'd (G3v, 221); did/Not mediate (G4, 222).

Act IV: A/N: dear/Lamented bloud (I3v, 238). Other types: will/Betray (I3v, 238).

Act V: P/N: among/The planets (K2, 244); of/Thy projects (K2, 244); vnder/The burthen (K2v, 245; a feminine ending); with/Instruction (K4v, 249) with/An vnexampled dignitie (L2v, 254). Other types: that/Adulterate coniunction (L2v, 253).

Gr. 2- :
Act I: is/Not full (B1, 175); t'is/His beings excellencie (B1, 175); is/Vncharitable (B1v, 176); hee/Should (B1v, 176; in rhyme); then/Would (B1v, 176); bound/Mee (B3, 178); that/I wish (B3v, 180); or/Your louing purpose (B4v, 181); were/But (C2, 185); I/Replyed (C3v, 187); are/So neare (C4, 188; in rhyme; the same rhyme occurs in Vere, pp. 162, 172); vnlesse/Our children (C4v, 189); were/Our counsellour (C4v, 189); is/The Wealth (C4v, 189); he/Did (D1, 190); I charge/Thee (D1, 190).

Act II: and/The Towne (D2v, 194); were/Oppress'd (D2v, 194); beene/ His Coffine (D2v, 194; in rhyme); as if/It could (D2v, 195); made/Them (E1, 199); is/Inflam'd (E1, 200); when/Your brother (E3, 204); if I/Had (E3, 204); I am/So heauie (F2, 210); or/The dispositions (F2v, 211); I/Should (F2v, 211); were/The owner (F3, 211).

Act III: be/So great (F4, 214); For/Beyond (F4, 214); That/My sodaine presence (F4v, 215); is/Aboue (G1, 216); are/Created (G1, 216); or/The Marriner (G1, 216); that/A Souldier (G1, 216); you/Are (G1v, 217); then/The strongest (G1v, 217); then/The measure (G3, 220); and/Were (G3v, 221); I am/Created (G3v,221); are/My Subjects (G3v, 222); I/Ha' done (G4, 222); you/Are (G4, 222); is/Your kinsman (G4v, 223); be/Your disposs-essour (G4v, 223).

Act IV: be/A bastard (H3v, 229); that/I am (I3v, 238); Yet/The more (I3v, 238);as/Sebastian is (I3v, 238).

Act V: Since/My purposes (K2, 244); yet/Since (K4, 248); can/You (L1, 250); are/As many (L1v, 251).

Doubtful instances of Grade 2 in Atheist's Tragedy (not counted):

Gr. 2+ : like/A man (D3, 195). This would be a P/N ending in present-day English, but in the Jacobean period, when "like to" was still a common construction, like may have been felt to be a predicative adjective even in the like+Nominal construction.
        as soft/Obedience (B3v, 179). At first sight, this seems to be an A/N ending, but I think a different analysis is also plausible, as soft standing in apposition to Obedience, and deriving its pre-noun position from a transformation (Obedience as soft being the underlying form).

Gr. 2- : both/My meaning and my loue (B2v, 178); both/The soule and body (F4v, 215); both/Of wealth and dignitie (L3v, 255). These will be instances of Gr. 2- if both is taken as a conjunction.

Tourneur's Poems (References to pages in Nicoll's edition)

Transformed Metamorphosis

Gr. 2+ : in/This Pluto-visag'd-world (54); within/The once-form'd world
(73); on/The twin-top'd hill (73).

Gr. 2- : how/To free me (59).

Vere

Gr. 2+ : those/Illustrious honours (157); at/The full opinion (163);
the right/Wayes (166); on/An answerable disposition (166); particular/
Dependent seruices; (167); did/Attend (168).

Gr. 2- : as/It selfe (160); when/He did (161); are/More difficult
(162); So/The reputation (162); how/Effectually (163); and/His men
(163); that/His fame (163); bee/A disposition (164); vnlesse/Approu'd
(167); hee/Did (168);than/The natiue vertue (172); And/In honour
(170); when/My selfe (170; are/Entirely possest (172).

Henry

Gr. 2+ : aboue/The causes (207); fortunate/Succession (268); Diuine/
Perswading Contemplations (270); best/Imaginations (270).

Gr. 2- : hide/It (268); then/The last (268); be/So good (269); HEE/Was
making (269); how/Or He (269); knew/HIM liuing (270); are/Succeeded (270).

Doubtful instance of Grade 2+ in Henry (not counted): such/A passion (268).
Such is probably best excluded from membership of the noun-phrase; see
Strang, p. 116.

Appendix III

Middleton's works other than plays

It cannot be said that the authorship of any of Middleton's masques or City of London entertainments is controversial, since they are all vouched for by external evidence.[1] Nevertheless, internal evidence is available to show that the author of the various occasional shows is the same Thomas Middleton who wrote A Game at Chess and the other plays. I have summarized the essential data in Table III(2), below. The best evidence is perhaps that of spelling.

For example, the earliest of the pageants, The Triumphs of Truth, has the spellings typical of A Game at Chess, /chac'st/ (sig. C2); /the're/ (B4v) and /theire/ (D2) for they're; and only /do's/ (A4, B4v), not /does/. Some of the later pageants are much richer in spelling evidence: thus, The Sun in Aries, The Triumphs of Honour and Virtue, and The Triumphs of Integrity have the preferred spelling of Game at Chess for every instance of 'em, has, and does; and so too, for nearly every instance, has Honourable Entertainments. Clearly, all these texts must have been set from autograph copy. It is significant, too, that three different printers are involved: evidently the compositors of Allde, Eld, and Okes were maintaining the tradition of faithfulness to copy into the early 1620s.

The canon of the non-dramatic works is not quite so certain, though probably no one now doubts Middleton's authorship of the juvenilia The Wisdom of Solomon Paraphrased, Micro-Cynicon, or The Ghost of Lucrece, much less the 1604 pamphlets Father Hubburd's Tales and The Black Book. Sykes[2] and John Quincy Adams[3] have established a chain of connections from one early work to another, and thence to the plays; and the evidence in Table III(2) may help to strengthen these links. Father Hubburd's Tales has four -cst spellings, /forc'st/ (B2), /ballac'st/ (Elv), /forcst/ (F2), /placst/ (F3v); /they're/ (A3); and each of Middleton's favorite early-period oaths--faith (3 times), troth (once), marry (4 times), and mass (once The Black Book has little spelling evidence, but it contains Middleton's

---

[1] The authorship of the various sections of the Middleton-Rowley theatre masque The World Tossed at Tennis is dealt with in 4.4.2.4, above.

[2] "Thomas Middleton's Early Non-Dramatic Works," N&Q 148 (20 June 1925), 435-38.

[3] Middleton's The Ghost of Lucrece, ed. Adams, p. xvi.

rather distinctive lin[="cease"] (C4), and shares the still rarer Luxur
with Father Hubburd's Tales. There are also puh (twice), faith (once),
marry (once), they're (twice), and, as in the case of Father Hubburd's
Tales, Middleton's usual preferences for amongst and beside. Another mark
of Middleton's hand is the "Italian" joke in sig. D3 (Bullen, VIII, 28):
what Italian faces they all made [i.e. showed their backsides in running
away]--with which we may compare tis such an Italian world, many men knowe
not Before from Behinde, in Michaelmas Term, E2 (III.i.19-20); and other
more or less ingenious allusions to the Italians' alleged propensity to anal
intercourse: Mad World, E4, III.iii.63-64; More Dissemblers, C3, I.iv.
85-86; Game at Chess, I.i.331-32.[1]

Two other pamphlets have been suggested as possibly by Middleton, the
first by Eccles,[2] the second (very hesitantly) by F. P. Wilson.[3]
They are the following:

(1) The True Narration of the Entertainment of His Royal Majesty,
from the time of his departure from Edinburgh (Q 1603, printed by Thomas
Creede for Thomas Millington; STC 17153; "To the Reader" signed "T. M.").

(2) The Meeting of Gallants at an Ordinary (Q 1604, printed by Thomas
Creede; STC 17781; anonymous).

The significant internal evidence for these works is given below, in
Table III(1).

Table III(1).   Two pamphlets, 1603-04

	amo- ng	ngst	beside adv,prep.	besides adv, prep.	betw- een	ixt	towar- d	ds	whil- e	st	es	-cst
Narration	2	7	,3	6,7	2	3	4	25	2	.	.	.
Meeting	.	8	1,3	.	3	.	.	.	.	1	.	3

I suggest that The True Narration is probably not by Middleton,
since the strong preferences for besides and towards are clearly

[1] My attention was drawn to Middleton's "Italian" jokes by the work of
Robert K. Turner,jnr., "Dekker's 'Back-Door'd Italian': 1 Honest Whore,
II.i.355," NQ, 205 (1960), 25-26.

[2] "Thomas Middleton, a Poett," p. 523.

[3] The Plague Pamphlets of Thomas Dekker, ed. Wilson (Oxford: Clarendon
Press, 1925), pp. xix-xx. I have used Wilson's reprint of Meeting of
Gallants as the basis of this study.

non-Middletonian, with no parallel in Table III(2) or in the early Middleton plays; nor are there any spellings in Narration which point to Middleton.[1] It is, moreover, quite likely that the "T. M." who signed the preface was not the author Thomas Middleton, but the publisher Thomas Millington.

In contrast, the statistics for Meeting are perfectly Middletonian, and the three instances of -cst (forcst, A3v, D3; embracst, C4) are particularly persuasive. There are other spellings, too, which suggest Middleton, such as the many preterite or past participle forms in -de (hayrde, B2; venturde, braude, B2v; etcetera); and there is plenty of stylistic evidence--marry (Bl, B3v), Puh (B4), Sfoote (B4), and parallels to Black Book, Father Hubburd's Tales, and the early Middleton plays.[2] In particular, the last speech of Famine in the introductory dialogue reads like a detached fragment of The Revenger's Tragedy:

> What ist to dye stampt full of drunken wounds,
> Which makes a man reele quickly to his Graue,
> Without the sting of Torments, or the sense
> Of chawing Death by peecemeale? vndone and done,
> In the forth part of a poore short Minute?   (A4)

The Middleton parallels here include the following: reele to hell, in Ghost of Lucrece, C4 (line 450); A Drunckard now to Reele to the Devill, in The Witch, lines 442-43 (compare also Revenger's Tragedy, H4v, V.i. 51); and, as noted by Wilson (Plague Pamphlets, p. 239), "He was now passing awa in the fourth part of a minute," in Father Hubburd's Tales, C4 (Bullen, VIII, 74). Taken all together, the evidence does not amount to a proof, but if Meeting of Gallants is not by Middleton, then it is remarkably similar to his style, while the spelling evidence suggests that his autograph may have been the source of the printed text.

---

[1] The only feature in Narration which may suggest Middleton's hand is the frequent use of comfort (11 instances in 44 pages), but this is not very distinctive, and the repetitions of the word are due to the repeated context of England being "comforted' by the arrival of James.

[2] Some of these are noted by Wilson, who also, however, notes parallels to Dekker pamphlets. Possibly Meeting is a Dekker-Middleton collaboration; if so, I think Middleton wrote the final draft.

Table III(2). Middleton's works other than plays: selected features

	Printer	among: amongst	adv. beside prep.	adv. besides prep.	between betwixt	toward: towards	while	whilst	whiles	-cst	e'm/	ha's/	do(')s/
Masque													
ITM	Stansby	:1	1,	.	1:	1:	1	.	.	1	1/7	4/7	1/1
Pageants													
TT	Okes	.	,1	,2	1:2	3:	.	1	.	1	/3	.	2/2
C.A.	Okes	:2	.	.	.	1:1	.	.	.	.	.	3/5	1/1
THI	Okes	:1	.	.	1:	:1	.	.	.	.	/1	1/1	.
TLA	Okes	:1	.	.	.	2:	.	.	.	2	/5	.	1/1
Hon.	Eld	.	.	,1	1:1	2:	.	1	.	1	5/5	8/10	4/5
SA	Allde	.	.	.	.	1:	.	.	.	.	2/2	7/7	4/4
THV	Okes	.	.	.	1:	1:	.	.	.	.	1/1	4/4	4/4
TI	Okes	:4	.	.	.	2:	.	.	.	5	2/2	.	2/2
THP	Okes	:2	.	.	2:	3:	.	.	.	1	.	/2	1/1
Non-Dramatic													
WS	Simmes	3:4	.	.	9:	.	5	1	.	.	.	.	.
MC	Creede	:2	.	.	:1	.	.	1	.	.	.	.	.
GL	Simmes	.	.	.	:1	.	1	.	.	.	.	.	.
FHT	Creede	1:7	2,2	1,	7:1	.	2	5	.	4	.	.	.
B.Bk.	Creede	:6	2,5	2,	11:1	1:	.	5	.	.	.	.	.
SRS	Windet	:4	.	1,	.	1:	.	1	.	.	.	.	.
PM	Purfoot	1:3	.	.	1:5	3:	1	1	.	.	.	/5	/9
Totals:		5:37	5,8	4,3	35:12	21:2	10	16	0	15	11/26	27/41	20/30

Note: In the last three columns, the numerators represent the numbers of instances of the spellings /e'm, ha's, do(')s/, the denominators the numbers of instances of 'em, has, does in any spelling. (A blank before the oblique signifies a zero numerator; a period signifies zero numerator and zero denominator.)

Key to texts: B.Bk. = The Black Book (Q 1604); C.A. = Civitatis Amor (Q 1616, sigs. A3 through B2 only); FHT = Father Hubburd's Tales (Q 1604 for William Cotton); GL = The Ghost of Lucrece (O 1600); Hon. = Honourable Entertainments (O 1621); ITM = The Inner Temple Masque (Q 1619); MC = Micro-Cynicon (O 1599); PM = The Peacemaker (Q 1618); SA = The Sun in Aries (Q 1621); SRS = Sir Robert Sherley (Q 1609); THI = The Triumphs of Honour and Industry (Q 1617); THP = The Triumphs of Health and Prosperity (Q 1626); THV = The Triumphs of Honour and Virtue (Q 1622); TI = The Triumphs of Integrity (Q 1623); TLA = The Triumphs of Love and Antiquity (Q 1619); TT = The Triumphs of Truth (with The Running Stream Entertainment; Q 1613); WS = The Wisdom of Solomon Paraphrased (Q 1597).

Additional significant features

ITM: gin't (B3v); they're (C1v, C2); ath' (A3); t'ad (A3v); i'these (A3v),
TT: they're (B4v, D2). TLA: they're (B1); a'th' (B3). i'me (B2).
Hon.: Puh (D5v); I'ue (C6v); sh'as (D6v, E1v); t'as (E2v); a'th (B6v).
THV: you're (B2v). TI: sh'as (A4).
MC: push (B1v; rhymes with bramble-bush); Tut (C3).
FHT: Luxur (D4); You speak oracle (F1); they're (A3).
B.Bk.: Luxurs (D3); lin (C4); Puh (C1, E1); they're (B1v, twice).

Appendix IV

Dekker, Chapman, Marston: works other than plays

I have examined the poems, prose, and entertainments of several Jacobean dramatists chiefly to confirm the reality and reliability of preferences for certain connectives--preferences which are clearly manifested in their plays.

IV.1. Dekker

Table IV.1 (below) is useful in three ways: it establishes the reliability of Dekker's strong preferences for besides and whilst (also sithence, which, however, rarely occurs in plays); it proves the faithfulness to copy of the Jacobean compositors of at least eight different printers, who did not turn any of 66 instances of besides into beside; and it enables us to decide against Dekker's authorship of two non-dramatic works which were ascribed to him in the past on very inadequate grounds, and have since been used by unwary scholars as sources of "Dekker" parallels to Blurt and The Family of Love--the poem Canaan's Calamity, which is almost certainly by Thomas Deloney,[1] and the prose pamphlet The Batchelars Banquet (anonymous).[2]

Canaan's Calamity (first edition, 1618) contrasts with Dekker's usage in no less than four out of the seven synonym-groups of Table IV.1, with preferences for among, beside, while, and tut. The last of these may be untypical of its author, since Deloney's preference would seem to be for tush; otherwise the preferences of Calamity match well with those of a sample of Deloney's prose and verse, comprising the following: The Gentle Craft, Part I (Works, ed. Mann, pp. 71-136); The Garland of Good Will, Part I (ibid., pp. 297-343); and Strange Histories (ibid., pp. 383-416).

---

[1] See F. O. Mann, in his edition of Thomas Deloney's Works (Oxford: Clarendon Press, 1912), pp. 593-94. I have used Mann's text of Canaan's Calamity and of Deloney's prose and verse for this study.
  Dodson draws on Calamity for Dekker parallels (pp. 29, 88), and Eberle assumes Dekker's authorship of the poem (p. 724).

[2] For my study of The Batchelars Banquet I have used the edition of F. P. Wilson. For the authorship, see above, 1.1.2, and Wilson's introduction, pp. xxiii-xxvii. It is disconcerting that so great a scholar as Bentley should have ignored (III, 243) Wilson's demolition of the Dekker claim.
  Dodson draws on Banquet for a Dekker parallel (p. 30), and Eberle uses such parallels passim for his argument on Family of Love.

The Batchelars Banquet (first edition, 1603) is unlike Dekker in its literary style: it is robust rather than verbally witty, and it uses a number of mouth-filling oaths which are never found in Dekker: birlady, by Christ, good Christ, Jesus God, God's body, and by Cock's body. Since the pamphlet is a translation from the French Quinze joies de mariage, some of these differences might be due to the original; but in fact the translation is a very free one, the oaths in particular not corresponding at all closely to the French ones. But above all, Dekker's authorship is ruled out by the Banquet's invariable preferences for while and sith; with which we may contrast in particular the whilst and sithence in Dekker's Wonderful Year, a pamphlet printed in the same year as Banquet by the same printer, Thomas Creede. The 9 instances in Banquet of beside are also impossible for Dekker: he apparently never uses the form in non-dramatic works, and 9 instances are far too many to be produced by textual corruption.

Marilyn L. Williamson has claimed parallels between The Batchelars Banquet and Blurt, III.iii, and has suggested that these may have some bearing on the authorship problems of both Blurt and Banquet.[1] However, her parallels are not very impressive, and she herself admits that the best of them, a collocation of "peascods" and "cherries", may have been proverbial at the time. I do not think that the author of Blurt must have seen the text of Banquet, nor, therefore, that the two authorship problems are necessarily connected.

Incidentally, Table IV.1 suggests that Dekker's pamphlet The Raven's Almanac incorporates some non-authentic material, a possibility which is already quite likely on literary grounds. It can hardly be an accident that the un-Dekker-like forms sith and while occur exclusively in the appended Jew's and Ropemaker's Tales (sigs. F2-H3), whereas both instances of sithence and four out of five instances of whilst occur in the main body of the Almanac (Cl-Dlv; the last whilst occurs on Flv).

---

[1] 'Blurt, Master Constable III,iii and The Batchelars Banquet,' NQ, 202 (1957), 519-21.

Table IV.1. Dekker's works other than plays: selected features

Page-ants	amo-		bes-		betw-		towar-		whil-						sit
	ng	ngst	ide a,p	ides a,p	een	ixt	d	ds	e	st	es	tut	tush	sith	enc
Mag.E.	2	5	.	2,4	12	.	1	1	.	10	.	.	.	.	1
TNT	.	1	.	,1	.	.	1	.	.	6	1	.	.	.	.
B.Hon.	1	.	.	,2	1	.	.	.	.	4	.	.	.	.	.
L.Tem.	.	.	.	.	1	.	.	.	.	4	.	.	.	.	1
Non-Dram.															
WY	5	6	.	2,1	4	.	.	.	.	13	.	.	.	.	2
DPP	.	1	.	.	2	2	.	.	1	3	.	.	.	.	.
NFH	4	8	.	1,2	11	.	.	.	.	10	.	.	2	.	4
SDS	1	16	.	2,1	8	.	1	3	.	8	.	.	1	.	.
BL	7	19	.	1,1	8	1	1	2	.	20	.	.	.	.	2
DT	2	12	.	3,5	2	.	.	2	.	14	.	.	.	.	4
LC	.	18	.	6,4	12	.	2	.	.	15	.	.	.	.	9
FBNA	.	19	.	,1	8	.	1	6	.	3	.	.	.	.	20
GHB	2	10	.	5,2	7	.	.	1	.	4	.	.	3	.	1
Ra.Al.	1	26	.	3,3	11	.	.	2	6	5	.	.	.	2	2
W.Arm.	1	14	.	1,2	5	.	.	2	.	4	.	.	.	.	5
SHR	.	3	.	2,5	4	2	1	1	.	4	.	.	.	.	.
D.D.	1	5	.	2,	.	1	.	1	.	9	.	.	.	.	1
RR	.	13	.	.	.	.	.	3	.	5	.	.	.	.	.
Wars	.	4	.	.	.	1	.	.	.	8	.	.	.	.	.
PWPF	.	7	.	,2	4	1	.	1	.	1	.	.	.	.	2
Totals:	27	187	0	30,36	100	8	8	25	6	150	1	0	6	2	54
Batch.	.	5	5,4	6,7	8	3	3	9	19	.	1	.	7	10	.
Canaan	6	2	,1	.	2	2	.	.	11	1	.	1	.	.	.
Deloney	17	7	1,3	1,5	7	11	3	11	46	6	1	.	8	3	.

Printers (from imprints). Edward Allde: SDS, Ra.Al. Henry Ballard: FBNA. Richard Braddock: NFH. Thomas Creede: Mag.E., Wy, DPP. John Hodges: DT. Augustine Matthews: PWPF. Nicholas Okes: TNT, D.D. Nicholas Okes and John Norton: B. Hon.

Key to texts: Batch. = The Batchelars Banquet, ed. Wilson; B. Hon. = Britannia's Honour, ed. Bowers, in Dekker's Dram. Works; BL = The Belman of London (Q 1608); Canaan = Canaan's Calamity, ed. Mann, in Deloney's Works; D.D. = Dekker his Dream (Q 1620); Deloney = sample of Deloney's works, defined above (IV.1); DPP = The Double P. P. (Q 1606); DT = The Dead Term (Q 1608); FBNA = Four Birds of Noah's Ark, ed. F. P. Wilson (Oxford: Blackwell, 1924); GHB = The Gull's Hornbook (Q 1609); LC = Lanthorn and Candlelight (Q 1608); L.Tem. = London's Tempe, ed. Bowers, in Dram. Works; Mag.E. = The Magnificent Entertainment, ed. Bowers, in Dram. Works; NFH = News from Hell (Q 1606); PWPF = Penny-wise, Pound-foolish, ed. W. Bang, in Materialien, 23 (1908); Ra.Al. = The Raven's Almanac (Q 1609); RR = A Rod for Runaways (Q 1625, 1st edn.); SHR = A Strange Horse-Race (Q 1613); SDS = The Seven Deadly Sins of London, ed. H. F. B. Brett-Smith (Oxford: Blackwell, 1922); TNT = Troia-Nova Triumphans, ed. Bowers, in Dram. Works; W. Arm. = Work for Armorers (Q 1609); Wars = Wars, Wars, Wars (O 1628); WY = The Wonderful Year, Ed. Wilson, in The Plague Pamphlets of Thomas Dekker.

IV.2. Chapman

Table IV.2 covers a sample of Chapman's works other than plays: The Memorable Masque (first edition, 1613; text from Holaday's edition of Chapman's Comedies), and the Chapman prose and verse in Chapman's Poems, ed. Phyllis P. Bartlett (1941; reprint, New York: Russell and Russell, 1962).

Table IV.2. A Chapman sample

	amo-ng	ngst	bes-ide	besides adv	pr	betw-een	ixt	towar-d	ds	while e	st	es
Mem. Masque	.	3	.	4,	1	1	4	.	1	.	.	.
Poems > 1598												
Shadow of Night	.	3	.	1,		.	2	.	.	1	.	.
O.B.S.	1	1	.	3,		.	5	.	1	3	.	.
H&L, III-VI	.	2	.	.		.	6	.	.	3	.	2
Poems, 1609-29												
Eu.R.	.	.	.	1,		.	14	.	2	7	.	.
P.S.P.Ps.	.	1	.	1,		.	7	.	.	9	.	.
An Epicede	.	.	.	.		.	4	.	.	.	.	.
Eugenia	.	2	.		,1	.	7	.	.	2	.	.
And.Lib.	.	2	.	2,		.	2	.	.	1	.	.
J.A.L.	.	1	.	.		.	3	.	.	1	.	1
Pro Vere	.	.	.	.		.	2	.	.	.	.	.
J.S.A.N.	.	.	.		,1	.	.	.	.	.	.	.
Commendatory & Occasional												
Verses	.	6	.	2,	1	.	4	.	.	4	.	.
Totals:	1	21	0	14,	4	1	60	0	4	31	0	3

Key to titles: And.Lib. = Andromeda Liberata; Eu.R. = Euthymiae Raptus; H&L = Hero and Leander; J.A.L.=Justification of Andromeda Liberata; J.S.A.N.=Justification of a Strange Action of Nero; O.B.S.= Ovid's Banquet of Sense; P.S.P.Ps. = Petrarch's Seven Penitential Psalms.

Other significant features
No instance of a -cst preterite/past participle occurs in the sample; has occurs once, does 11 times, spelt invariably /has, does/.

Evidently, Chapman's preferences for amongst, besides, betwixt, and while are consistent, and agree with those found in his plays.

IV.3. <u>Marston</u>

Table IV.3 covers Marston's works other than plays, contained in Marston's <u>Poems</u>, ed. Arnold Davenport (Liverpool: Liverpool Univ. Press, 1961).

Table IV.3. Marston's works other than plays

	amo- ng ngst		beside, besides	betw- een ixt		toward, towards	whil- e st es			<u>tut</u>	<u>tush</u>
Pageant											
Arg. Spect.	.	.	.	.		.	.	1	.	.	.
Masque											
Ashby Ent.	.	.	.	.		.	.	11	.	.	.
Poems											
Pygmalion	.	.	.	.		.	.	.	.	1	.
Cer.Satires	3	.	.	.	3	.	.	4	.	2	.
Scourge	7	.	.	1	1	.	.	18	.	11	2
Love's M.	.	.	.	.		.	.	1	.	.	.
Totals:	10	0	0	1	4	0	0	35	0	14	2

<u>Key to titles</u>: Arg. Spect. = The Argument of the Spectacle presented to the Sacred Majesties of Great Britain and Denmark; Ashby Ent. = The Ashby Entertainment; Cer. Satires = Certain Satires; Love's M. = Love's Martyr; Pygmalion = The Metamorphosis of Pygmalion's Image; Scourge = The Scourge of Villainy.

Other significant features

Authorial oaths: <u>Iesu Maria</u> (p. 77); <u>Iesu</u> (p. 160); <u>Lord</u> (p. 174). No instance of a -<u>cst</u> preterite/past participle occurs; <u>has</u>, <u>does</u>, and <u>'em</u> do not occur.

As in the cases of Dekker and Chapman, Marston's clear preferences for certain connectives, obvious in his plays, are equally manifest in his other works. Moreover, his avoidance of both <u>beside</u> and <u>besides</u>, and his high frequency of <u>whilst</u>, are confirmed by the table above.

Appendix V

Middleton in Shakespeare: Timon of Athens

Two substantial cases have been made out in the past for Middleton's hand in plays of Shakespeare. I shall not consider the question of Macbeth, since I have nothing to add to the excellent treatment by David L. Frost,[1] and indeed the interpolated passages do not contain any usable evidence of authorship. Quite a different situation obtains in Timon of Athens.

Scholarly opinion on the problem of Timon has shifted from a nineteenth century consensus on plural authorship to a present consensus that the play is merely a rough draft by Shakespeare, the apparently un-Shakespearean sections of text representing a very early stage of composition. This theory was forcefully stated by Chambers,[2] and developed by Una Ellis-Fermor with an appeal to the experience of modern practitioners of blank verse.[3] Ellis-Fermor, by way of commentary mainly on the un-Shakespearean verse of I.ii, quoted twenty lines of III.v (lines 38-57[4]) containing four rhymed couplets, which she would have us believe might be a typical stage on the way to good blank verse of the mature Shakespearean type:

> Who that has ever written blank verse in any conditions
> below that of complete collection and concentration, has not
> experienced this preliminary rush of isolated fragments of
> music and thought? We may agree that Shakespeare's artistic
> experience cannot without irreverence be interpreted in terms
> of any but a very few of those upon record. Nevertheless,
> some likeness of process may perhaps be presumed.
> Taking together, then, these various indications from the
> first act of Timon . . .   (op. cit., p. 275)

I must say that I find this theory fantastic. In my own experience as a practitioner of verse (and I have written hundreds of lines of couplets and unrhymed verse), couplets are not a prelude to any tolerable kind of blank verse--indeed, they block the development of run-on blank verse of the kind used by Shakespeare about the presumed date of Timon (c. 1607) and in Timon in the clearly Shakespearean sections such as

---

[1] The School of Shakespeare, pp. 262-67.

[2] William Shakespeare, I, 480-84.

[3] "Timon of Athens: an Unfinished Play," RES, 18 (1942), 270-90.

[4] Line references to Shakespeare are to the Complete Works, ed. Peter Alexander (1951; rpt. London: Collins, 1964).

I.i.1–176.   I agree that <u>Timon</u> must be a rough draft: it is certainly in a
theatrically unviable condition, bristling with loose ends.   But this theory
though necessary, is hardly sufficient to explain the enormous discrepancy
between the versification of I.i and that of I.ii.   In the whole of I.i I ha[ve]
counted only two rhyming lines to 202 pentameter verse lines; in I.ii the
proportion is 34 pentameter rhyming lines to 140 pentameter verse lines.
And whatever may be the explanation of the remarkably bad verse of Alcibiade[s]
in III.v quoted by Ellis-Fermor, I cannot bring myself to believe that
Apemantus' prose-blank-rhyme speeches of I.ii could be developmental pre-
cursors of normal late Shakespearean blank verse.   There would seem to be
three possible explanations of such passages.   Either they are by late
Shakespeare writing uncharacteristically; or they are the remains of a much
earlier draft by Shakespeare; or they are the work of another author.

The first two explanations seem very improbable, since we have plenty
of comparative material to show that Shakespeare was never, at any period,
given to mixing prose, blank verse, and pentameter rhyme in the same speech.
The professed cynics and satirists (Thersites, Pandarus, Lear's fool, Iago)
normally speak prose; if they pass from prose into verse within a single
speech, it is never blank verse, but always rhyme either in short lines or,
if pentameter, then a clearly announced set piece or an exit tag.   Thus
Apemantus' speech at I.ii.37–51, which passes rapidly from prose to blank
to one pentameter rhyme to prose again and then to a concluding pentameter
rhyme, all without ceremony or preamble, violates all the rules of Shakespearean form.   And the presence of the couplets in this mélange renders the
"rough draft" theory inadmissable.

There remains the third possibility, which has been defended with
detailed evidence in the past.   The prose-verse mixture of I.ii is unlike
Shakespeare, but very like early Middleton, whose authorship of I.ii (and
much else in <u>Timon</u>) was first suggested by William Wells[1] and promptly
supported by Dugdale Sykes.[2]   Sykes, it is true, also claimed the presence
of John Day in a few sections of the play, on rather slender evidence; but
it will not affect the argument here if this claim is ignored.   What is
common to Wells and Sykes is that they are fairly sure of Middleton's presen[ce]

[1] "Timon of Athens," <u>NQ</u>, 12th ser., 6 (1920), 266–69.

[2] <u>Sidelights on Elizabethan Drama</u>, pp. 1–48.

as the main author of I.ii, III.i-vi, IV.ii.30-50, and IV.iii.458-536;
that they believe him to have been the original author, revised by Shakespeare; and that they base their case on versification and parallels of
word and phrase to Middleton's plays, especially to the early comedies.
The features found in Middleton but not elsewhere in Shakespeare include push
(once), t'as (twice), give thee thy due (once), respectively welcome (once),
and single words such as apperil and rioter. As in the matter of the
Webster phrases in Anything for a Quiet Life, these and other parallels are
remarkable enough to show that the case for disintegration is prima facie
strong enough to warrant a careful check by means of fresh evidence. The
obvious step is to examine the data on Shakespeare's colloquialisms and
contractions, now easily available in the play totals of the new concordance.[1]
Table V(1) summarizes the useful evidence for Timon and the later work of
Shakespeare.

Table V(1) Timon and late Shakespeare

	'em	them	has	hath	does	doth	I'm	'Has
All's Well	5	50	28	52	24	6	1	3
Measure for Meas.	.	40	7	71	9	24	.	1
Othello	.	45	8	67	16	17	.	1
Macbeth	5	50	19	52	24	6	.	.
Lear	9	45	13	49	17	13	1	.
Timon	20	66	31	29	24	9	3	5
Antony and Cleo.	3	52	22	43	29	5	.	.
Coriolanus	15	128	35	51	19	9	.	3
Cymbeline	2	71	7	79	8	20	1	.
Winter's Tale	6	61	31	42	23	7	.	.
Tempest	17	42	7	26	15	13	.	.

Through all his work Shakespeare prefers them to 'em and hath to has;[2]
he makes very little use of I'm (only 5 authentic instances outside Timon)
or of 'Has for he has (14 authentic instances outside Timon). Middleton,
of course, shows the opposite preferences and makes considerable use of I'm
and 'Has.[3]   Therefore, if there is any truth in the theory of a

[1]
  A Complete and Systematic Concordance to the Works of Shakespeare,
ed. Martin Spevack (Hildesheim: Georg Olms, 1969). All play totals
for Shakespeare in this appendix are derived from the concordance; those
for has include 'Has (listed by the concordance as h'as), and those for
does include does't.

[2]
 Statements about all of Shakespeare exclude the unreliable text Pericles
and the Fletcher collaborations Henry VIII and Two Noble Kinsmen.

[3]
 The use of 'Has in Timon and by Middleton was noted by Sykes.

considerable Middleton share in Timon, this should be manifested in a disturbance of the expected ratios of 'em to them and has to hath, and of the relative frequencies of I'm and 'Has; and this is just what we do find. The 'em:them ratio of Timon is higher than that of any unassisted Shakespeare play except The Tempest; the has:hath ratio is higher than any (has being uniquely more frequent than hath), and so are the relative frequencies of I'm and 'Has.

More significant still is the distribution of these features through the text of Timon. If the high rates of 'em, has, and I'm were mere coincidences, we should expect their peaks of relative frequency to occur independently of one another at random through the text. The independence of occurrence of 'em and has in Shakespeare can be seen from the totals for The Tempest in Table V(1). In that play, though 'em is frequent, has is not: and 'em and hath occur in the same scenes and in the mouths of the same characters, for example Stephano in III.ii. But in Timon the highest ratios, for whole scenes, of 'em to them and has to hath, as well as all three instances of I'm, occur together in the continuous stretch of text III.ii-v. Table V(2), below, gives the details of occurrences by sections.

Table V(2) Timon of Athens: distribution of selected features[1]

Section	Length (lines)	Claim	'em	them	has	hath	does	doth	I'm	I am	'Has	'tas	moe
1.1	285		.	7	.	3	2	1	.	5	.	.	1
1.2	252	M	9	9	3	2	4	.	.	4	.	2	.
2.1	35		.	.	.	.	.	.	.	.	.	.	1
2.2	234		4	8	1	4	1	.	.	7	.	.	1
3.1	62	M	.	.	3	1	1	.	.	1	.	.	.
3.2	86	M	.	.	5	1	1	.	.	3	1	.	.
3.3	41	M	.	.	2	.	2	.	1	.	1	.	.
3.4	120	M	3	1	2	1	4	.	1	1	.	.	.
3.5	117	M	2	2	5	1	.	.	1	1	1	.	.
3.6	119	M	.	4	1	2	2	.	.	3	.	.	.
4.1	40		.	.	.	.	.	.	.	.	.	.	.
4.2.a	29		.	.	.	.	.	.	.	1	.	.	.
4.2.b	21	M	.	.	1	.	1	.	.	.	.	.	.
4.3.a	457		.	15	4	7	3	3	.	10	1	.	1
4.3.b	79	M	2	.	3	.	1	.	.	.	1	.	.
5.1	226		.	19	1	4	1	4	.	4	.	.	.
5.2	17		.	.	.	.	.	1	.	.	.	.	.
5.3	10		.	.	.	2	1	.	.	.	.	.	.
5.4	85		.	1	.	1	.	.	.	.	.	.	.
Totals M:	897		16	16	25	8	16	0	3	13	4	2	0
Rest:	1418		4	50	6	21	8	9	0	27	1	0	4
Timon:	2315		20	66	31	29	24	9	3	40	5	2	4

Of the features here tabulated, only 'Has and 'tas were used by
Sykes to establish Middleton's claim to parts of Timon; hence the distributions of the others provide independent corroboration of the Wells-Sykes
theory. It is a slight point in favour of the theory that "M" sections
are not invaded by the Shakespeare markers doth and moe. Moe (for "more")
is the more certain of the two: it is fairly frequent in Shakespeare's work
of all periods, but rare elsewhere in Jacobean drama, and never used by
Middleton; instances occur in Timon at I.i.14, II.i.7, II.ii.111, and
IV.iii.395. Late Shakespeare and early Middleton both make abundant use
of does, but while doth remains frequent in Shakespeare's late work, it
occurs only once in each of Middleton's early comedies, twice in The
Revenger's Tragedy, and not at all in The Second Maiden's Tragedy (see

---

[1] IV.ii and IV.iii are divided in accordance with Wells' authorship
divisions, at the exits of the Servants (IV.ii.29) and of the Banditti
(IV.iii.457) respectively. "M" indicates a claim by Wells and Sykes that
the section in question is mainly by Middleton. Line counts are from
Alexander's edition, but all features have been studied from the photo-
graphic facsimile of the First Folio ed. Helge Kokeritz (New Haven:
Yale Univ. Press, 1954).

Table I.1). Much more striking is the fact that the ratios of 'em to them and has to hath are about normal for Shakespeare in the total of the unclaimed sections, comparing especially well with the figures for Lear and Antony and Cleopatra in Table V(1). In the "M" sections overall, the ratios 'em:them, has:hath, and I'm:I am are all within Middleton's range if we include A Chaste Maid and The Witch in our comparative material, though each ratio is rather low for Middleton before 1608 -- a fact which is not, of course, unfavorable to the Wells-Sykes theory of a minor Shakespearean presence in the 'M' sections.

It is important to notice that the interesting distribution of these features cannot possibly be due to varying compositorial preferences, since only Compositor "B" set the text of Timon.[1] Nor is a scribe likely to have turned Shakespearean them and hath into 'em and has. Harold J. Oliver, in his Arden edition of Timon, has tentatively suggested that "'em for them" may be due to a Crane transcript of the anomalous portions of the play;[2] but this theory is almost certainly wrong. Strong evidence against it-- the infrequency and distribution of parentheses in Timon--has been brought by Trevor H. Howard-Hill.[3] In any case, Crane does not turn them into 'em: the 'em and them in his transcript of Fletcher's Demetrius and Enanthe correspond exactly with the 'em and them in the Beaumont and Fletcher 1647 Folio text of the same play (there entitled The Humorous Lieutenant); and he was equally meticulous in Barnavelt, transmitting 42 'em, 6 them in Fletcher's portion against 3 'em, 33 them in Massinger's portion of the play As to has, Crane's tendency in 1624-25 was to replace it with hath, as we see from his Game at Chess transcripts and from Demetrius and Enanthe,[5]

---

[1] See Charlton Hinman, The Printing and Proof-reading of the First Folio of Shakespeare (Oxford: Clarendon Press, 1963), I, 394.

[2] Timon of Athens, ed. H. J. Oliver (London: Methuen, 1959), p. xix.

[3] "Ralph Crane's Parentheses," NQ, 210 (1965), 334-40.

[4] Hoy, "Shares," SB, 9 (1957), 145.

[5] See Bald's edition of Game at Chess, p. 171, for Crane's Game at Chess transcripts. My collation of Demetrius and Enanthe with The Humorous Lieutenant revealed that out of 23 hath in Demetrius, 17 represent Humorous Lieutenant's has. The totals for each text are: Demetrius, 47 has, 23 hath; Humorous Lieutenant, 65 has, 5 hath. My study of Demetrius and Enanthe is based on the edition by Margaret McLaren Cook and F. P. Wilson (Oxford: Malone Society, 1951).

so that the high rate of has in Timon is possibly further evidence against his presence. A scribe other than Crane may have copied the "M" sections of Timon, but there is no Jacobean scribe known whose tendency was to introduce colloquialisms;[1] most scribes, presumably, would either transmit them faithfully or replace them with formal literary features. Thus a scribal presence in the Timon "M" sections would, if anything, strengthen the case for Middleton by suggesting that 'em and has may have been even more frequent in the authorial source manuscript.

If, then, these features and the others in Table V(2) are authorial, the question remains as to whether the author concerned was truly Middleton or merely Shakespeare writing in an unusually Middletonian manner. It needs to be noted that the "M" sections of Timon do not display all the linguistic characteristics that one would expect to find in an early Middleton text of about 900 lines. There are only four instances of the oath faith (on the other hand, there are none at all outside the "M" sections). Some contractions are surprisingly rare. I'th' occurs only three times (only once in an "M" section, at I.ii.57, sig. gg3^r, col. a), whereas it is normally frequent in both Shakespeare and Middleton. I've does not occur at all, and they're only once (in an "M" section, at I.ii.123, sig. gg3^r, col. b); however, we find exactly these figures in Trick (see Table I.1). It is probably true to say that the rarity of some contractions in the "M" sections agrees better with Shakespeare's authorship than Middleton's, but none provides reliable negative evidence, and any such low figure is easily explicable if Shakespeare or a scribe were re-touching Middleton.

I believe that the evidence available at present is inadequate to resolve the problem of authorship. In combination with the oddities of versification and the remarkable parallels cited by Wells and Sykes, the case for disintegration is strong enough to justify a strong suspicion of Middleton's presence, but no more. On the other hand, the various arguments which have been adduced to prove the necessity of single authorship are equally indecisive. If the imagery of the "M" sections is of a piece

---

[1] Unless the transcriber of Blurt sigs. H2-H3v was a scribe copying from the quarto text; see Section 2.2.1, and 5.1.4.2.2, above.

with the rest of the play,[1] that is what one might expect if Shakespeare had read his predecessor's rough draft and adopted some useful ideas for his revision. Nor is it a valid argument against revision that so many inconsistencies have been left; the revision itself could have introduced inconsistencies where there were none before. And it is not at all strange that the revision did not proceed to the stage of producing a viable play: it is hard to see how it could have done so, since the history of Timon, once his fall from prosperity is accomplished, seems to be basically lacking in dramatic interest. Presumably Shakespeare and his fellows of the Kings' Men came to realise that no amount of patching could turn Timon of Athens into an attractive play for the Globe or Blackfriars, and hence it was never finished for production.

Though convincing proof of the authorship of Timon is lacking at present, it might be obtained in the future if we had a concordance to the works of Middleton as well as one to those of Shakespeare. It would then be easy to estimate the "Middletonism" of Timon, in terms of the number of words (and perhaps some categories of collocations) which occur in Middleton and in Timon but not elsewhere in Shakespeare; and the corresponding "Middletonism" of every other play of Shakespeare. If Middleton is actually present in Timon but not elsewhere in the Shakespeare canon, then there should be a very large discrepancy between the figures for Timon and those for every other Shakespeare play. The discrepancy might well yield a probability figure of less than .05; in which case, Middleton's hand in Timon might be regarded as proved at the customary 95 per cent confidence level.[2]

---

[1] This is argued, among others, by G. R. Hibbard in his edition of Timon (Harmondsworth: Penguin Books, 1970), p. 260.

[2] I have deliberately avoided entangling the authorship problem of Timon with the vexed question of the variant forms /Apemantus/ versus /Apermantus/ and Flavius versus Steward; but it is interesting to observe that Charlton Hinman believes that these and other variants "inevitably suggest different hands," which might be scribal but are "much more likely" to be authorial (Printing and Proof-reading of the First Folio, II, 285). /Apermantus/ and Flavius co-occur only in I.ii, the scene which gives the strongest impression of being nearly pure Middleton. To hazard a guess, I would suggest that the copy for I.ii might have been a Middleton autograph; for the rest of the play it must have been something different.

<u>Bibliography</u>

The bibliography is divided into three sections: (A) problem plays; (B) other primary sources; (C) secondary sources. Works are classified as "primary sources" when they are essentially embodiments of sixteenth or seventeenth century text, even though they may contain important secondary material such as editorial introductions and notes.

Editions pre-1700 are identified not by publisher and place of publication but by number in the two Short-Title Catalogues of (1) A. W. Pollard and G. R. Redgrave, 1475-1640 (abbreviated STC), and (2) Donald Wing, 1641-1700 (abbreviated Wg).

(A) <u>Problem Plays</u>

In this section, plays are listed under the author whose name appears on the title page of the substantive seventeenth century text.

ANON. <u>Blurt, Master Constable</u>. (Q 1602.) STC 17876.

----. <u>The Family of Love</u>. (Q 1608.) STC 17879.

----. <u>The Revenger's Tragedy</u>. (Q 1607.) STC 24149.

----. <u>The Revenger's Tragedy</u>. [Attributed to Cyril Tourneur.]
      Ed. R. A. Foakes. London: Methuen, 1966.

----. <u>The Second Maiden's Tragedy</u>. Ed. W. W. Greg. Oxford: The
      Malone Society, 1909.

BEAUMONT, Francis, and John Fletcher. <u>The Nice Valour</u>. (F 1647)
      Wg B1581.

----. <u>Wit at Several Weapons</u>. (F 1647.) Wg B1581.

D., T. <u>The Bloody Banquet</u>. (Q 1639.) STC 6181.

----. <u>The Bloody Banquet</u>. Ed. Samuel Schoenbaum. Oxford: The
      Malone Society, 1962.

DEKKER, Thomas. <u>The Honest Whore</u>, Part <u>I</u>. (Q 1604, 1st edn.)
      STC 6501.

MIDDLETON, Thomas. <u>Anything for a Quiet Life</u>. (Q 1662.) Wg M1979.

MIDDLETON, Thomas, and William Rowley. <u>The Spanish Gipsy</u>. (Q 1653.)
      Wg M1986.

S., W. <u>The Puritan</u>. (Q 1607.) STC 21531.

SHAKESPEARE, William. <u>A Yorkshire Tragedy</u>. (Q 1608.) STC 22340.

288

(B) Other Primary Sources

ANON.   Alarum for London. (Q 1602.) STC 16754.

-----.   The Batchelars Banquet. Ed. F. P. Wilson. Oxford:
         Clarendon Press, 1929.

-----.   Dick of Devonshire. Ed. James G. and Mary R. McManaway.
         Oxford: The Malone Society, 1958.

-----.   The Shakespeare Apocrypha. Ed. C. F. Tucker Brooke. 1908;
         rpt. Oxford: Clarendon Press, 1967.

-----.   Two Most Unnatural Murthers. (Q 1605.) STC 18288.

-----.   Wily Beguiled. Ed. W. W. Greg. Oxford: The Malone Society,
         1912.

ARBER, Edward. A Transcript of the Registers of the Worshipful
         Company of Stationers, 1554-1640. 5 vols. 1857-94; rpt.
         New York: Peter Smith, 1950.

ARMIN, Robert. Two Maids of Moreclacke. (Q 1609.) STC 773.

BARNES, Barnabe. The Devil's Charter. (Q 1607.) STC 1466.

BARRY, Lording. Ram Alley. (Q 1611, 1st edn.) STC 1502.

-----.   Ram Alley. Ed. Claude E. Jones. Materials for the Study of
         the Old English Drama, 23 (1952).

BEAUMONT, Francis, and John Fletcher. Comedies and Tragedies. (F 1647.)
         Wg B1581.

-----.   The Dramatic Works in the Beaumont and Fletcher Canon. General
         Editor, Fredson Bowers. Cambridge, Eng.: Cambridge Univ.
         Press, 1966. Vol.I.

-----.   The Wild Goose Chase. (F 1652.) Wg B1616.

BREWER, Anthony. The Lovesick King. (Q 1655.) Wg B4426.

BROME, Richard. A Jovial Crew. (Q 1652.) Wg B4873.

-----.   The Northern Lass. (Q 1632.) STC 3819.

CHAPMAN, George. The Comedies. General Editor, Allan Holaday.
         Urbana: Univ. of Illinois Press, 1970.

-----.   The Conspiracy and Tragedy of Charles Duke of Byron. (Q 1608.)
         STC 4968.

-----.   Poems. Ed. Phyllis P. Bartlett. 1941; rpt. New York:
         Russell and Russell, 1962.

CHETTLE, Henry. Hoffman. (Q 1631). STC 5125.

CHETTLE, Henry. Kind Heart's Dream. Ed. G. B. Harrison. New York:
     Barnes and Noble, 1966.

----. Piers Plainness. Ed. James Winny. Cambridge, Eng.:
     Cambridge Univ. Press, 1957.

COOKE, Jo[shua]. Greene's Tu Quoque. (Q 1614.) STC 5673.

DABORNE, Robert. A Christian Turned Turk. (Q 1612). STC 6184.

----. The Poor Man's Comfort. (Q 1655.) Wg D101.

DAVENANT, William. Albovine, King of the Lombards. (Q 1629.)
     STC 6307.

----. The Cruel Brother. (Q 1630.) STC 6302.

DAVENPORT, Robert. The City Nightcap. (Q 1661.) Wg D369.

----. A Dialogue between Policy and Piety. Ms, Folger Library,
     MS. 1919.3.

----. King John and Matilda. (Q 1655.) Wg D370.

----. A New Trick to Cheat the Devil. (Q 1639.) STC 6315.

DAY, John. Humour out of Breath. (Q 1608.) STC 6411.

----. The Isle of Gulls. (Q 1606.) STC 6413.

----. Law Tricks. (Q 1608.) STC 6416.

----. Works. Ed. A. H. Bullen. Introd. by Robin Jeffs.
     London: Holland Press, 1963.

DAY, John, William Rowley, and George Wilkins. The Travails of
     Three English Brothers. (Q 1607.) STC 6417.

DEKKER, Thomas. The Belman of London. (Q 1608.) STC 6480.

----. The Dead Term. (Q 1608.) STC 6496.

----. Dekker his Dream. (Q 1620.) STC 6497.

----. The Double P. P. (Q 1606.) STC 6498.

----. The Dramatic Works. Ed. Fredson Bowers. 4 vols. 1953-61;
     rpt. with corrections, Cambridge, Eng.: Cambridge Univ.
     Press, 1964-70.

----. Four Birds of Noah's Ark. Ed. F. P. Wilson. Oxford:
     Blackwell, 1924.

----. The Gull's Hornbook. (Q 1609.) STC 6500.

----. The Honest Whore, Part II. (Q 1630.) STC 6506.

----. If This Be Not a Good Play, the Devil is in it. (Q 1612.)
     STC 6507.

----. Lanthorn and Candlelight. (Q 1608.) STC 6485.

DEKKER, Thomas. Match Me in London. (Q 1631.)   STC 6529.

-----. News from Hell.   (Q 1606.)   STC 6514.

-----. The Non-Dramatic Works. Ed. Alexander B. Grosart. 4 vols.
        1884-85; rpt. New York: Russell and Russell, 1963.

-----. Old Fortunatus. (Q 1600.)   STC 6517.

-----. Penny-wise, Pound-foolish.   Ed. W. Bang.   In Materialien
        zur Kunde des älteren Englischen Dramas, 23 (1908).

-----. The Plague Pamphlets of Thomas Dekker. Ed. F. P. Wilson.
        Oxford: Clarendon Press, 1925.

-----. The Raven's Almanac. (Q 1609.)   STC 6519.

-----. A Rod for Runaways. (Q 1625, first edition.) STC 6520.

-----. Satiromastix.   (Q 1602.)   STC 6521.

-----. The Seven Deadly Sins of London.   Ed. H. F. B. Brett-Smith.
        Oxford: Blackwell, 1922.

-----. The Shoemaker's Holiday. (Q 1600.)   STC 6523.

-----. A Strange Horse-Race.   (Q 1613.)   STC 6528.

-----. Wars, Wars, Wars.   (O 1628.)   STC 6531.

-----. The Whore of Babylon. (Q 1607.)   STC 6532.

-----. Work for Armorers. (Q 1609.) STC 6536.

DELONEY, Thomas. Works. Ed. F. O. Mann. Oxford: Clarendon Press,
        1912.

DRUE, Thomas. The Duchess of Suffolk. (Q 1631.) STC 7242.

EYRE, G. E. Briscoe. A Transcript of the Registers of the Worshipful
        Company of Stationers, 1640-1708. 3 vols. 1913-14;
        rpt. New York: Peter Smith, 1950.

FIELD, Nathaniel. Amenda for Ladies. (Q 1618.) STC 10851.

-----. A Woman is a Weathercock. (Q 1612.)   STC 10854.

FLETCHER, John. Demetrius and Enanthe. Ed. Margaret McLaren Cook
        and F. P. Wilson. Oxford: The Malone Society, 1951.

-----. Monsieur Thomas. (Q 1639.)   STC 11071

-----. Rule a Wife and Have a Wife. (Q 1640.) STC 11073.

FORD, John. The Broken Heart. (Q 1633.)   STC 11156.

-----. The Fancies Chaste and Noble. (Q 1638.)   STC 11159.

-----. The Lady's Trial. (Q 1639.) STC 11161.

-----. The Lover's Melancholy. (Q 1629.)   STC 11163.

-----. Love's Sacrifice. (Q 1633.)   STC 11164.

-----. Perkin Warbeck.   (Q 1634.)   STC 11157.

FORD, John. 'Tis Pity she's a Whore. (Q 1633.) STC 11165.

GOFFE, Thomas. The Careless Shepherdess. (Q 1656.) Wg G1005.

----. The Courageous Turk. (Q 1632.) STC 11977.

----. The Raging Turk. (Q 1631.) STC 11980.

----. The Tragedy of Orestes. (Q 1633.) STC 11982.

HAUGHTON, William. Englishmen for my Money. (Q 1616.) STC 12931.

HENSLOWE, Philip. Diary. Ed. R. A. Foakes and R. T. Rickert.
Cambridge, Eng.: Cambridge Univ. Press, 1961.

HERBERT, Sir Henry. Dramatic Records. Ed. Joseph Q. Adams.
New Haven: 1917; rpt. New York: Blom, n.d. [1964?]

HEYWOOD, Thomas. The Captives. Ed. A. Brown. Oxford:
The Malone Society, 1953.

----. The English Traveller. (Q 1633.) STC 13315.

----. The Fair Maid of the West. Part II. (Q 1631.) STC 13320.

JONSON, Ben. Volpone. (Q 1607.) STC 14783.

----. Volpone. Ed. Henry De Vocht. Materials for the Study of the
Old English Drama, 13 (1937). [Type-facsimile of Q 1607.]

----. Works. Ed. C.H. Herford and Percy and Evelyn Simpson.
11 vols. Oxford: Clarendon Press, 1925-52.

LANGBAINE, Gerard (the younger). An Account of the English
Dramatick Poets. 1691; facsimile rpt. Hildesheim: Georg
Olms, 1968.

----. Momus Triumphans. 1688; facsimile rpt. New York: AMS Press,
1970.

M., T. The True Narration of the Entertainment of His Royal Majesty,
from the time of his departure from Edinburgh. (Q 1603.)
STC 17153.

MARKHAM, Gervase and Lewis Machin. The Dumb Knight. (Q 1608.)
STC 17398.

MARSTON, John. Antonio and Mellida. (Q 1602.) STC 17473.

----. Antonio's Revenge. (Q 1602.) STC 17474.

----. The Dutch Courtesan. (Q 1605.) STC 17475.

----. Jack Drum's Entertainment. (Q 1601.) STC 7243.

----. The Malcontent. (Q 1604, augmented, 3rd edn.) STC 17481.

----. Parasitaster, or the Fawn. (Q 1606, 2nd edn.) STC 17484.

----. Poems. Ed. Arnold Davenport. Liverpool: Liverpool Univ.
Press, 1961.

MARSTON, John. Sophonisba. (Q 1606.) STC 17488.

----. What You Will. (Q 1607.) STC 17487.

MASON, John. The Turk. (Q 1610.) STC 17617.

MASSINGER, Philip. Believe as you List. Ed. C. J. Sisson.
Oxford: the Malone Society, 1927.

----. The Bondman. (Q 1624.) STC 17632.

----. The City Madam. (Q 1658.) Wg M1046.

----. The Duke of Milan. (Q 1623.) STC 17634.

----. The Emperor of the East. (Q 1632.) STC 17636.

----. The Great Duke of Florence. (Q 1636.) STC 17637.

----. The Maid of Honour. (Q 1632.) STC 17638.

----. A New Way to Pay Old Debts. (Q 1633.) STC 17639.

----. The Parliament of Love. Ed. K. M. Lea. Oxford: the Malone
Society, 1928.

----. The Picture. (Q 1630.) STC 17640.

----. The Renegado. (Q 1630.) STC 17641.

----. The Roman Actor. (Q 1629.) STC 17642.

----. Three New Plays. (O 1655.) Wg M1050.

----. The Unnatural Combat. (Q 1639.) STC 17643.

MERES, Francis. Palladis Tamia. (O 1598.) STC 17834.

MIDDLETON, Thomas. The Black Book. (Q 1604.) STC 17875.

----. A Chaste Maid in Cheapside. (Q 1630.) STC 17877.

----. A Chaste Maid in Cheapside. Ed. Charles L. Barber.
Edinburgh: Oliver and Boyd, 1969.

----. Civitatis Amor. (Q 1616.) STC 17878.

----. Father Hubbard's Tales. (Q 1604.) STC 17880.

----. A Game at Chess. MS, Trinity College Library, Cambridge,
Eng., O.2.66.

----. A Game at Chesse. Ed. R.C. Bald. Cambridge, Eng.: Cambridge
Univ. Press, 1929.

----. The Ghost of Lucrece. Ed. with a facsimile reprint of O 1600
by Joseph Quincy Adams. New York: Scribner's, 1937.

----. Hengist, King of Kent. Ed. R. C. Bald. New York: Scribner's,
1938.

----. Honourable Entertainments. (O 1621.) STC 17886.

----. The Inner Temple Masque. (Q 1619.) STC 17887.

MIDDLETON, Thomas. A Mad World, My Masters. (Q 1608.) STC 17888.

----.   A Mad World, My Masters. Ed. Standish Henning. Regents
         Renaissance Series. London: Edward Arnold, 1965.

----.   Michaelmas Term. (Q 1607.) STC 17890.

----.   Michaelmas Term. Ed. Richard Levin. London: Edward Arnold, 1967.

----.   Micro-Cynicon. (O 1599.) STC 17154.

----.   No Wit, No Help Like a Woman's. (O 1657.) Wg M1985.

----.   The Peacemaker. (Q 1618.) STC 14387.

----.   The Phoenix. (Q 1607.) STC 17892.

----.   Sir Robert Sherley. (Q 1609.) STC 17894.

----.   The Sun in Aries. (Q 1621.) STC 17895.

----.   Thomas Middleton. Introd. Algernon Charles Swinburne. Ed.
         Havelock Ellis. Mermaid Series. 2 vols. London: Vizetelly,
         1887-90.

----.   A Trick to Catch the Old One. (Q 1608.) STC 17896.

----.   The Triumphs of Health and Prosperity. (Q 1626.) STC 17898.

----.   The Triumphs of Honour and Industry. (Q 1617.) STC 17899.

----.   The Triumphs of Honour and Virtue. (Q 1622.) STC 17900.

----.   The Triumphs of Integrity. (Q 1623.) STC 17901.

----.   The Triumphs of Love and Antiquity. (Q 1619.) STC 17902.

----.   The Triumphs of Truth, with The Running Stream Entertainment.
         (Q 1613.) STC 17904.

----.   Two New Plays. [Contains More Dissemblers Besides Women and
         Women Beware Women.] (O 1657.) Wg M1989.

----.   The Widow. (Q 1652.) Wg M1015.

----.   The Wisdom of Solomon Paraphrased. (Q 1597.) STC 17906.

----.   The Witch. Ed. W. W. Greg and F. P. Wilson. Oxford: The Malone
         Society, 1948.

----.   Women Beware Women. Ed. Charles Barber. Edinburgh: Oliver and
         Boyd, 1969.

----.   Works. Ed. A. H. Bullen. 8 vols. London, 1885-86;
         rpt. New York: AMS Press, 1964.

----.   Works. Ed. Alexander Dyce. 5 vols. London: E. Lumley, 1840.

----.   Your Five Gallants. (Q n.d.; [1608?] 1st edn.) STC 17907.

MIDDLETON, Thomas and William Rowley. The Changeling. (Q 1653.) Wg M1980.

----.   A Fair Quarrel. (Q 1617; first issue.) STC 17911.

----.   A Fair Quarrel. (Q 1622.) STC 17912.

MUNDAY, Anthony. John a Kent and John a Cumber. Ed. M. St.C. Byrne.
        Oxford: The Malone Society, 1923.

-----. Sir Thomas More. Ed. W. W. Greg. Oxford: The Malone Society,
        1911.

PUDSEY, Edward. Commonplace Book. MS, Bodleian Library, Eng. poet.
        d.3. Extracts printed by Juliet Gowan (see "Secondary Sources"),
        and reproduced in private communication from Bodleian Library.

RICHARDS, Nathaniel. Messalina. Ed. A. R. Skemp. Materialien zur
        Kunde des älteren Englischen Dramas, 30 (1910).

ROWLEY, William. All's Lost by Lust. (Q 1633.) STC 21425.

-----. All's Lost by Lust and A Shoemaker a Gentleman. Ed. Charles
        W. Stork. Philadelphia: Univ. Pennsylvania, 1910.

-----. A New Wonder, A Woman Never Vexed. (Q 1632.) STC 21423.

-----. A Shoemaker a Gentleman. (Q 1638.) STC 21422.

SAMPSON, William. The Vow-Breaker. Ed. Hans Wallruth. Materialien
        zur Kunde des älteren Englischen Dramas, 42 (1914).

SHAKESPEARE, William. Comedies, Histories and Tragedies. (F 1623.)
        STC 22273. Photographic facsimile ed. Helge Kokeritz.
        New Haven: Yale Univ. Press, 1954.

-----. Complete Works. Ed. Peter Alexander, 1951; rpt. London: Collins,
        1964.

-----. Timon of Athens. Ed. G. R. Hibbard. Harmondsworth: Penguin
        Books, 1970.

-----. Timon of Athens. Ed. H. J. Oliver. London: Methuen, 1959.

SHARPHAM, Edward. Cupid's Whirligig. (Q 1607.) STC 22380.

-----. The Fleer. (Q 1607.) STC 22384.

SHIRLEY, James. The Maid's Revenge. (Q 1639.) STC 22450.

-----. The School of Compliment. (Q 1631.) STC 22456.

-----. The Wedding. (Q 1629.) STC 22460.

SMITH, W. The Hector of Germany. (Q 1615.) STC 22871.

SPENSER, Edmund. The Poetical Works. Ed. J. C. Smith and E. De
        Selincourt. 1912; rpt. London: Oxford Univ. Press, 1950.

TOMKIS, Thomas. Albumazar. (Q 1615.) STC 24100.

-----. Lingua. (Q 1607.) STC 24104.

TOURNEUR, Cyril. The Atheist's Tragedy. (Q 1611.) STC 24146.

-----. Works. Ed. Allardyce Nicoll. London: Fanfrolico Press, 1929.

WEBSTER, John.   The Devil's Law Case. (Q 1623.)   STC 25173.

----.   The Duchess of Malfi.   (Q 1623.)   STC 25176.

----.   The White Devil.   (Q 1612.)   STC 25178.

----.   Works.   Ed. F. L. Lucas.   4 vols.   London: Chatto and Windus,
          1927.

WILKINS, George.   The Miseries of Enforced Marriage.   Ed. G. H. Blayney.
          Oxford: The Malone Society, 1963.

(C) Secondary Sources

BALD, R. C. "The Chronology of Middleton's Plays." Modern Language
        Review, 32 (1937), 33-43.

----. "An Early Version of Middleton's Game at Chesse." Modern
        Language Review, 38 (1943), 177-180.

----. "The Foul Papers of a Revision." The Library, 4th series, 26
        (1945), 37-50.

----. "A New Manuscript of Middleton's Game at Chesse." Modern
        Language Review, 25 (1930), 474-78.

BARBER, Charles. "A Rare Use of the Word Honour as a Criterion of
        Middleton's Authorship." English Studies, 38 (1957), 161-68.

BARKER, Richard Hindry. "The Authorship of The Second Maiden's Tragedy
        and The Revenger's Tragedy." Shakespeare Association Bulletin,
        20 (1945), 51-62, 121-33.

----. Thomas Middleton. New York: Columbia Univ. Press, 1958.

BAUGH, Albert C. "A Seventeenth Century Play List." [Anthony à Wood's.]
        Modern Language Review, 13 (1918), 401-11.

BENTLEY, Gerald Eades. The Jacobean and Caroline Stage. 7 vols.
        Oxford: Clarendon Press, 1941-68.

BERGER, Thomas L. "A Critical Old-Spelling Edition of Thomas Dekker's
        Blurt, Master Constable (1602)." Diss. Duke, 1969.

BYRNE, M. St. Clare. "Bibliographical Clues in Collaborate Plays."
        The Library, 4th ser., 13 (1932), 21-48.

CAWLEY, A. C. English Domestic Drama: A Yorkshire Tragedy. Leeds:
        Leeds Univ. Press, 1966.

CHAMBERS, Sir Edmund K. The Disintegration of Shakespeare. London:
        British Academy, 1924.

----. The Elizabethan Stage. 4 vols. Oxford, 1923; rpt. Oxford:
        Clarendon Press, 1951.

----. William Shakespeare: A Study of Facts and Problems. 2 vols.
        Oxford: Clarendon Press, 1930.

DENT, R.W. John Webster's Borrowing. Berkeley: Univ. California
        Press, 1960.

DILLON, Andrew. "Thomas Middleton, The Family of Love: a critical
        old-spelling edition." Diss. New York, 1968.

DODSON, Daniel B. "Thomas Middleton's City Comedies." Diss. Columbia,
        1954.

DUNKEL, W. D. "The Authorship of Anything for a Quiet Life." PMLA, 43 (1928), 793-99.

----. "The Authorship of The Puritan." PMLA, 45 (1930), 804-08.

----. "The Authorship of The Revenger's Tragedy." PMLA, 46 (1931), 781-85.

----. "Did Not Rowley Merely Revise Middleton?" PMLA, 48 (1933), 799-805.

EBERLE, Gerald J. "Dekker's Part in The Familie of Love." Joseph Quincy Adams Memorial Studies. Ed. James G. McManaway et al. Washington, D.C.: Folger Library, 1948, pp. 723-38.

ECCLES, Mark. "Middleton's Birth and Education." Review of English Studies, 7 (1931), 431-41.

----. "Thomas Middleton a Poett." Studies in Philology, 54 (1957), 516-36.

ELLEGARD, Alvar. A Statistical Method for Determining Authorship: the Junius Letters, 1769-1772. Goteborg, Sweden: Goteborg University, 1962.

ELLIS-FERMOR, Una M. "The Imagery of The Revenger's Tragedie and The Atheist's Tragedie." Modern Language Review, 30 (1935), 289-301.

----. "Timon of Athens: an Unfinished Play." Review of English Studies, 18 (1942), 270-90.

ERDMAN, David V. and Ephraim G. Fogel, eds. Evidence for Authorship. Ithaca, N.Y.: Cornell Univ. Press, 1966.

EWEN, C. L'Estrange. Lording Barry, Poet and Pirate. London.: printed for the author, 1938.

FLEAY, Frederick G. A Biographical Chronicle of the English Drama, 1559-1642. 2 vols. London, 1891; rpt. New York: Burt Franklin, n.d.

FOAKES, R. A. "On the Authorship of The Revenger's Tragedy." Modern Language Review, 48 (1953), 129-138.

FROST, David L. The School of Shakespeare, Cambridge, Eng.: Cambridge Univ. Press, 1968.

GOWAN, Juliet. "Edward Pudsey's Booke and the Authorship of Blurt Master Constable." Research Opportunities in Renaissance Drama, 8 (1965), 46-48.

GREG, W. W. "Authorship Attributions in the Early Play-lists." Edinburgh Bibliographical Society Transactions, 2 (1946), 305-29.

----. A Bibliography of the English Drama to the Restoration. 4 vols. London: The Bibliographical Society, 1939, 1951, 1957, 1959.

HARBAGE, Alfred. Annals of English Drama. Revised S. Schoenbaum. London: Methuen, 1964.

HINMAN, Charlton. The Printing and Proof-Reading of the First Folio of Shakespeare. 2 vols. Oxford: Clarendon Press, 1963.

HOLMES, David M. The Art of Thomas Middleton: A Critical Study. Oxford: Clarendon Press, 1970.

----. "Thomas Middleton's Blurt, Master Constable or The Spaniard's Night Walk." Modern Language Review, 64 (1969), 1-10.

HOWARD-HILL, Trevor H. "Ralph Crane's Parentheses." Notes and Queries, 210 (1965), 334-40.

HOY, Cyrus H. "The Shares of Fletcher and his Collaborators in the Beaumont and Fletcher Canon." Studies in Bibliography, 8 (1956), 129-46; 9 (1957), 143-62; 11 (1958), 85-106; 12 (1959), 91-116; 13 (1960), 77-108; 14 (1961), 45-67; 15 (1962), 71-90.

HUEBERT, Ronald M. "On Detecting John Ford's Hand: a Fallacy." The Library, 5th ser., 26 (1971), 256-59 .

JACKSON, MacDonald P. "Affirmative Particles in Henry VIII." Notes and Queries, 206 (1962), 372-74.

JOHNSON, Lowell E. "A Critical Edition of Thomas Middleton's No Wit, No Help like a Woman's". Diss. Winsconsin, 1964.

JONES, Fred L. "Cyril Tourneur." The Times Literary Supplement, 30 (18 June 1931), 487.

----. 'An Experiment with Massinger's Verse.' PMLA, 47 (1932), 727-40.

KAISER, Donald F. "The Puritan, or, the Widow of Watling Street: a critical edition." Diss. Wisconsin, 1966.

KOKERITZ, Helge. Shakespeare's Pronunciation. New Haven: Yale Univ. Press, 1953.

LAKE, David John. "Middleton's Hand in The Puritan: the Evidence of
      Vocabulary and Spelling". Notes and Queries, 217 (December,
      1972), 456-60.

----. "The Revenger's Tragedy: Internal Evidence for Tourneur's
      Authorship Negated." Notes and Queries, 216 (December 1971),
      455-56.

LAVIN, J. A. "Printers for Seven Jonson Quartos." The Library,
      5th ser., 25 (1970), 331-38.

LAWRENCE, W. J. Speeding up Shakespeare. London, 1937; rpt. New York:
      Benjamin Blom, 1968.

LLOYD, Bertram. "The Authorship of The Welsh Ambassador." Review of
      English Studies, 21 (1945), 192-201.

McKENZIE, D.F. "A List of Printers' Apprentices, 1605-1640." Studies
      in Bibliography, 13 (1960), 109-41.

McMANAWAY, James G. "Latin Title-Page Mottoes as a Clue to Dramatic
      Authorship." The Library, 4th ser., 26 (1946), 28-36.

MAXWELL, Baldwin. "Middleton's The Phoenix." Joseph Quincy Adams
      Memorial Studies. Ed. James G. McManaway et al. Washington,
      D.C.: Folger Library, 1948, pp. 743-53.

----. "A Note on the Date of Middleton's The Family of Love."
      Elizabethan Studies and Other Essays in Honour of George F.
      Reynolds. Univ. Colorado Studies, Ser. B Studies in the
      Humanities, vol. 2, no. 4. Boulder, Colorado: Univ. of Colorado,
      1945, pp. 195-200.

----. Studies in Beaumont, Fletcher and Massinger. 1939; rpt. London:
      Frank Cass, 1966.

----. Studies in the Shakespeare Apocrypha. New York: Columbia Univ.
      Press, 1956.

MILLER, C. William. "A London Ornament Stock: 1598-1683." Studies in
      Bibliography, 7 (1955), 125-51.

MOSTELLER, Frederick, and David L. Wallace. Inference and Disputed
      Authorship: The Federalist. Reading, Mass.: Addison-Wesley,
      1964.

MURRAY, Peter B. "The Collaboration of Dekker and Webster in Northward Ho
      and Westward Ho." Papers of the Bibliographical Society of
      America, 56 (1962), 482-86.

MURRAY, Peter B. A Study of Cyril Tourneur. Philadelphia:
Pennsylvania Univ. Press, 1964.

----. A Study of John Webster. The Hague: Mouton, 1969.

OLIPHANT, Ernest H. C. "The Authorship of The Revenger's Tragedy,"
Studies in Philology, 23 (1926), 157-168.

----. "The Bloodie Banquet." The Times Literary Supplement, 24
(17 December 1925), 882.

----. The Plays of Beaumont and Fletcher. 1927; rpt. New York:
AMS Press, 1970.

----. "Problems of Authorship in Elizabethan Dramatic Literature."
Modern Philology, 8 (1911), 411-59.

----. Shakespeare and His Fellow Dramatists. 2 vols. New York:
Prentice-Hall, 1929.

PALMER, Frank R. A Linguistic Study of the English Verb. London:
Longman's, 1965.

PEARSON, E.S. and H.O. Hartley. Biometrika Tables for Statisticians.
2 vols. 3rd edn. Cambridge, Eng.: Cambridge Univ. Press, 1966.

PHIALAS, P. G. "Middleton's Early Contact with the Law." Studies in
Philology, 52 (1955), 186-94.

POWER, William. "Middleton's Way with Names." Notes and Queries,
205 (1960), 26-29, 56-60, 95-98, 136-40, 175-79.

PRICE, George R. "the Authorship and Bibliography of The Revenger's
Tragedy." The Library, 5th ser., 15 (1960), 262-77.

----. "The Authorship and Manuscript of The Old Law." Huntington
Library Quarterly, 2 (1953), 117- 39.

----. "The Early Editions of A trick to catch the old one." The
Library, 5th ser., 22 (1967), 205-27.

----. "The First Editions of Your Five Gallants and of Michaelmas Term."
The Library, 5th ser., 8 (1953), 23-29.

----. "The Quartos of The Spanish Gypsy and Their Relation to The
Changeling." Papers of the Bibliographical Society of
America, 52 (1958), 111-25.

----. "Setting by Formes in the First Edition of The Phoenix." Papers
of the Bibliographical Society of America, 56 (1962), 414-27.

----. "The Shares of Middleton and Dekker in a Collaborated Play."
Papers of the Michigan Academy of Science, Arts, and Letters,
30 (1944), 601-15.

----. Thomas Dekker. New York: Twayne, 1969.

ROBB, Dewar M. "The Canon of William Rowley's Plays." Modern
  Language Review, 45 (1950), 129-41.

SARGEAUNT, M. Joan. John Ford. 1935; rpt. New York: Russell and
  Russell, 1966.

SCHIPPER, Jakob. A History of English Versification. Oxford:
  Clarendon Press, 1910.

SCHOENBAUM, Samuel. "Blurt, Master Constable: A Possible Authorship
  Clue." Renaissance News, 13 (1960), 7-9.

----. Internal Evidence and Elizabethan Dramatic Authorship.
  London: Edward Arnold, 1966.

----. "Middleton's Share in The Honest Whore, Parts I and II."
  Notes and Queries, 197 (1952), 3-4.

----. Middleton's Tragedies. New York: Columbia Univ. Press, 1955;
  rpt. New York: Gordian Press, 1970.

SMITH, Kate Parker. "The Spanish Gipsy by Thomas Middleton and
  William Rowley: a critical edition." Diss. Northwestern,
  1944.

SPEVACK, Martin, ed. A Complete and Systematic Concordance to the
  Works of Shakespeare. Hildesheim: Georg Olms, 1969.

STOLL, E.E. John Webster. Cambridge, Mass.: Harvard Co-operative
  Society, 1905.

STRANG, Barbara M. H. Modern English Structure. London: Edward
  Arnold, 1962.

SWINBURNE, Algernon Charles. Complete Works. Ed. Sir Edmund Gosse
  and T. J. Wise. 20 vols. London: Heinemann, 1925-27.

SYKES, H. Dugdale. "Cyril Tourneur: The Revenger's Tragedy: The
  Second Maiden's Tragedy." Notes and Queries, 12th ser.,
  vol. 5 (September 1919), 225-29.

----. Sidelights on Elizabethan Drama. London:
  Oxford Univ. Press, 1924.

----. Sidelights on Shakespeare. Stratford on Avon: Shakespeare
  Head Press, 1919.

----. "Thomas Middleton's Early Non-Dramatic Works." Notes and
  Queries, 148 (1925), 435-38.

TURNER, Robert K., jnr. "Dekker's 'Back-Door'd Italian': 1 Honest
  Whore, II.i.335.' Notes and Queries, 205 (1960), 25-26.

WELLS, William. "Timon of Athens". Notes and Queries, 12th ser.,
  6 (1920), 266-69.

302

WIGGIN, Pauline G.   An Inquiry into the Authorship of the Middleton-
        Rowley Plays. Radcliffe College Monographs, 9. Cambridge,
        Mass., 1897.

WILLIAMSON, Marilyn L.   "Blurt, Master Constable III, iii and The
        Batchelars Banquet". Notes and Queries, 202 (1957),
        519-21.

WILSON, F. P.   "Ralph Crane, Scrivener to the King's Players."
        The Library, 4th ser., 7 (1926), 194-215.

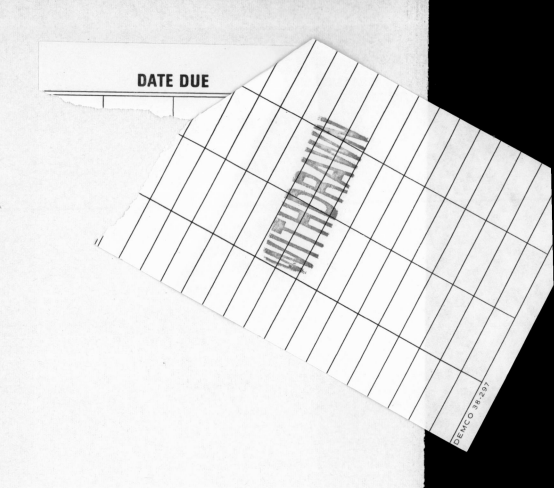